D1422509

Forgotten Bastards of the Eastern Front

SERHII PLOKHY

Forgotten Bastards of the Eastern Front

An Untold Story of World War II

ALLEN LANE
an imprint of
PENGUIN BOOKS

ALLEN LANE

UK | USA | Canada | Ireland | Australia
India | New Zealand | South Africa

Allen Lane is part of the Penguin Random House group of companies
whose addresses can be found at global.penguinrandomhouse.com.

First published in the United States of America by Oxford University Press 2019
First published in Great Britain by Allen Lane 2019
001

Copyright © Serhii Plokhy, 2019

www.greenpenguin.co.uk

MIX
Paper from
responsible sources
FSC® C018179
www.fsc.org

Penguin Random House is committed to a
sustainable future for our business, our readers
and our planet. This book is made from Forest
Stewardship Council® certified paper.

CONTENTS

PREFACE

In 1950, Winston Churchill named one of the volumes of his World War II memoirs, "Grand Alliance." He borrowed that term from the name used when England, Scotland, and European powers joined together against France in the late seventeenth and early eighteenth centuries, a partnership that diminished the power of France and led to the rise of Britain. Like its early modern predecessor, the Grand Alliance of the twentieth century turned out to be an astonishing success when it came to achieving its immediate goals. American assistance to Britain and the USSR through the Lend-Lease program, the opening of the second front in Europe in June 1944, and the Soviet declaration of war on Japan in August 1945 were the most salient features of Allied cooperation. The summits of the Big Three—as Roosevelt, Stalin, and Churchill were called by the media—first in Teheran in 1943 and then in Yalta in 1945, ensured the unity of the Allied powers throughout the war, leading to the defeat of the Axis and helping to produce a new international order and the organization that embodied it, the United Nations, the longest-lived international coordinating body in world history.

Greater than the military success of the second Grand Alliance was the expectation that it would continue into the postwar era, and greater still was the disappointment that followed its collapse a few years later. By 1948 the world was effectively divided into two camps, with the United States and Britain belonging to one and the Soviet Union and its Eastern European satellites to the other. The following year saw the formation of the North Atlantic Treaty Organization, a military alliance of the Western powers, followed in 1955 by the Warsaw Pact between the Moscow-led communist regimes of Eastern Europe. By that time the world found itself threatened not only with a new world war but also with the possibility of nuclear annihilation. The Grand Alliance ended in a Grand Failure, symbolized by Churchill's other famous coinage, the "Iron Curtain" that divided postwar Europe in half.

"What went wrong?" was the question asked throughout the world. Who was responsible for the start of the Cold War? Some pointed to Joseph Stalin and his efforts to carve up Iran and take control of the Black Sea straits, as well as his imposition of communist regimes in Eastern Europe. Others suggested that America's use of the atomic bomb in August 1945 and its subsequent refusal to share the new technology with the Soviet Union had shifted the world's power balance, leaving Stalin no choice but to consolidate his wartime geostrategic gains. This book will take a different track, revealing the roots of Cold War conflicts and nightmares in the story of the Grand Alliance itself. My main argument is quite simple: that it was doomed from within by conflict between the Soviet and American political traditions and cultures, and that it began to fall apart during rather than after World War II.

This is the story of collapse from below, focusing on the only place where the Soviets and Americans actually got the chance to live and fight side by side—the three American Air Force bases established on Soviet-controlled territory in April 1944. Taking off from airfields in Britain and Italy, American airplanes would bomb their targets and then land at these bases, which were located in the Poltava area of today's Ukraine, repeating the bombing on their way back to Britain or Italy. For the final year of the war in Europe, Americans worked intimately with Soviets. The Poltava bases were not small or merely symbolic. Thousands of pilots, airplane mechanics, and rank-and-file soldiers participated in the shuttle operations. Moreover, tens of thousands of Ukrainian citizens were able to meet US Airmen and, in some cases, establish close personal relations with them. Thus, this story is very much about people—their lives, views, and emotions.

The history of the air bases in Ukraine in 1944–1945 has a significant literature. The American side is well documented, thanks to the vast array of sources available to scholars in US archives and library collections. Four well-documented and more or less contemporaneous official histories of *Frantic*, as the American shuttle-bombing operations were called by the commanders of the US Strategic Air Forces in Europe, each covering a different period of time, have been preserved. The archives of the US Air Force Historical Agency at Maxwell Air Force Base in Alabama and the documentary collection of the US Military Mission to Moscow at the National Archives and Records Administration in Maryland, the Averell Harriman Archive at the Library of Congress, and President Roosevelt's papers at the FDR Presidential Library and Museum in Hyde Park, New York, provide rich source material for this account of the bases and those of my predecessors.[1]

What makes this account quite unique is the use of previously unavailable sources—files of the Committee for State Security (KGB) and its predecessors, documenting Soviet military counterintelligence and secret-police surveillance of Americans and their contacts in the Red Army Air Force and the local population. The files begin with the establishment of the bases and continue into the onset and mounting tension of the Cold War from the late 1940s to the early and mid-1950s. The Revolution of Dignity in Ukraine, which took place in 2013–2014, resulted among other things in an archival revolution—the unprecedented opening of former KGB archives, including World War II materials inherited from military counterintelligence. The reports of spies and the memos of their masters and handlers—comprising about two dozen thick volumes—have now become available to scholars and the public at large. As the Americans suspected, the Soviets actively spied on their allies, recording not only their actions but also their views.

With a level of clarity and precision that few sources can match, the KGB documents describe Soviet attitudes toward American servicemen, the evolution of relations between Soviets and Americans on the Poltava-area bases, and the transformation in the guests' attitudes toward their hosts. Taken together, American military records and Soviet counterintelligence reports provide a solid basis for our understanding of the role of politics, ideology, and culture in forging elations between the wartime allies. They leave little doubt that relations deteriorated not only because of the disappearance of the common enemy, or ideological incompatibility, or the change in Soviet and American geopolitical calculations as the war drew to its conclusion. No less important was the experience of these American servicemen, which turned even most of the pro-Soviet among them into committed opponents. The conflict of profoundly different worldviews and values shared by the rank-and-file participants of the Soviet-American encounter undermined the Grand Alliance even before the greater geopolitical reasons for its existence disappeared, reasons that conflict presaged and reflected.

With the winds of the new Cold War becoming chillier by the day, we need to look back at how the Grand Alliance played out in those American airbases in Ukraine in 1944–1945 and learn from the experience of those who did their best to make it work. One obvious lesson to future generations is that partnerships can be sustained for some time by the need to defeat a common enemy, but no mutual trust and enduring relationship can be established between allies with incompatible visions of the just political order and, at the end, of freedom and tyranny.

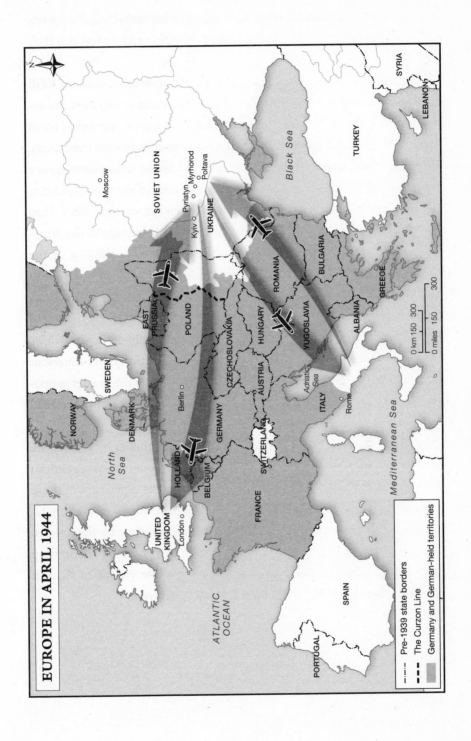

EUROPE IN APRIL 1944

Pre-1939 state borders
The Curzon Line
Germany and German-held territories

PROLOGUE

On a warm day in May 1958, a year that inaugurated the crises that led to the construction of the Berlin Wall, a KGB mobile team in Ukraine picked up a subject of surveillance they code-named "Tourist." The man was approximately 35–36 years of age, of medium height, and on the slim side. He had a slightly elongated face, a large straight nose, and was wearing glasses. The subject was dressed in a greenish shirt and dark gray pants, tight by Soviet standards, which suggested that he was a foreigner.

They began to follow Tourist at the exit from the Kyiv Highway to the city of Poltava in central Ukraine—a couple dozen miles away from the city. He was driving a Soviet-made Volga sedan. Once in Poltava, Tourist showed particular interest in the Corpus Park, the Poltava Victory monument, and the local museum and theater. As one might expect of any tourist, he took pictures of all those places. But his interest in one of the ordinary-looking houses in central Poltava aroused suspicion. Tourist arrived at Number 28 on Pushkin Street and knocked on the door. There was no answer. He then entered the courtyard, where he met a woman from a neighboring house.

He asked her something. The surveillance team managed to catch only one word, "Nina." The woman then pointed to one of the doors off the courtyard. Tourist knocked on that door; again there was no answer. He then got back into the car and drove off. His entire visit to Poltava lasted less than three hours. The KGB surveillance team filed their report. They had no idea who Tourist was, or what he was doing in the city. All they knew for certain was that he did not find whoever he was looking for.[1]

"Tourist" was thirty-nine-year-old Franklyn Holzman, a former radar mechanic in the US Air Force who has spent a good part of 1944 and almost half of 1945 at the US air bases in Soviet Ukraine. The author of a book on Soviet taxation, he was visiting Moscow and Kyiv and decided to make a stopover in Poltava, where he had spent eight months, a memorable period that helped decide his future career as a scholar of Soviet economics. The woman he had been looking for was Nina Afanasieva, whom he had met in Poltava in December 1944 and who, on the orders of the secret police, had broken contact with him in the spring of 1945. The Poltava KGB would spend the rest of 1958 and much of the following year trying to find Nina Afanasieva. They eventually located her in the city of Mykolaiv in southern Ukraine. Upon investigating, they found no proof that she had tried to make contact with Holzman. She was allowed to continue living a normal life.[2]

By the time of Holzman's visit in 1958, World War II had been over for more than a decade and the Cold War was reaching its height. The former allies had become adversaries. Holzman knew nothing of the KGB surveillance and suspicions. Until the end of his life in September 2002 he maintained positive memories of his wartime service in the Soviet Union. In his Lexington home in Massachusetts he kept photographs, letters, and embroidered Ukrainian tablecloths that reminded him of the days when Americans and Soviets had fought together. Yet when asked, Holzman, an accomplished scholar of the Soviet economy, was never able to explain some crucial aspects of his wartime experience, especially the question of why the Soviets had allowed American bases to be established on their territory in the first place.[3]

Part I

GRAND ALLIANCE

Mission to Moscow

T he welcoming party had reached the Central Airport in Moscow well ahead of the arrival of the guests. It was the late afternoon of October 18, 1943, and with the night temperatures hovering around freezing level, unusually cold even by Moscow standards. Viacheslav Molotov, the Soviet foreign minister, a stocky man with a square jaw, a Mexican-style moustache, and glasses perched on his slightly pointed nose, was getting cold. So were his numerous deputies, the officers and soldiers of the honor guard, and the musicians of the brass band. Although the airport was less than five miles from the Kremlin, a fifteen-minute drive at most for a government motorcade, Molotov had not wanted to take any risks and came early. The guests he was to receive were US Secretary of State Cordell Hull and British Foreign Secretary Anthony Eden.[1]

With time on their hands, Molotov and his party found shelter from the chilly weather in the airport building, the first terminal in the Soviet Union to become operational. The airport—popularly known as Khodynka after the Khodynka Field, where in May 1896 more than 1,300 people had been trampled to death by festive crowds celebrating the coronation of the last Russian emperor, Nicholas II—was the cradle of Soviet aviation. In 1922, five years after the revolution and only one year after the end of the subsequent civil war, the victorious Bolsheviks had launched their first international flight, to Königsberg and Berlin, from Khodynka Field. Russia and Germany, the two international outcasts at the end of World War I, were looking to the future together, and the sky was anything but the limit to their cooperation. On the contrary, it offered opportunities to enhance their relations. Seventeen years later, in August 1939, Hitler's foreign minister, Joachim von Ribbentrop, flew to Moscow by the same route to sign the pact with Molotov that provided for a German-Soviet condominium in Europe, and launched World War II.[2]

Now, at the very airport where Ribbentrop had landed only four years earlier, Molotov awaited the arrival of new allies. The Soviet Union needed Cordell Hull and Anthony Eden to help defeat its erstwhile ally, Germany. Contrary to all assurances, Hitler had invaded the Soviet Union in June 1941, and by December of that year his troops had advanced all the way to Moscow, a few dozen miles from the capital's airport. But now the situation was not so dire. The Red Army had driven the Germans back from Moscow in December 1941, and in February 1943, with the help of American supplies pouring into the USSR under Roosevelt's Lend-Lease program, defeated them at Stalingrad. The tide of war had turned in favor of the Soviets.

Yet the prospect of victory was still distant. In October 1943, the Red Army was still fighting the Germans in the middle of Ukraine and getting ready to attack Hitler's Eastern Wall—the defensive line along the Dnieper. That river, as wide as 700 meters or 2,300 feet in places, was a formidable obstacle. Nikolai Gogol's claim in his novel of Cossack life, *Taras Bulba*, "rare is the bird that flies to the middle of the Dnieper," was no idle observation. The Battle of the Dnieper, which had begun in August 1943 and would continue into early winter, would cost the Red Army up to 350,000 officers and soldiers dead, with total casualties of almost 1.5 million. With victories like that, the Red Army could soon run out of men. The Soviet leaders needed American help.

Molotov had flown to London and Washington in May 1942, pushing for a joint British-American second front in Western Europe. Roosevelt promised to help, but the British were dragging their feet. The invasion began in July 1943, not in Western but in Southern Europe, with the Allies landing on the shores of Sicily—a British-endorsed plan meant to protect their Mediterranean route to India. By early September they were fighting on the Italian mainland. Molotov's boss, Joseph Stalin, was by no means happy. The Germans could defend the Apennine Peninsula without withdrawing any divisions from the Eastern Front. As far as the Soviets were concerned, this was no second front. Only a landing in France would force Hitler to withdraw divisions from the East, and they wanted it as soon as possible. They also needed a continuing supply of Lend-Lease armaments, including the newest aircraft that only America knew how to produce and could supply. They hoped that Cordell Hull would help to deliver both.[3]

■

What Molotov and his party soon saw in the sky was a perfect embodiment of American power and technological superiority. Sometime after 4:00 p.m. three huge silver Douglas C-54 Skymasters, glistening in the last rays of the autumn sun, appeared above Khodynka Field and began to maneuver for landing.

The Soviets wanted the Skymaster as part of Lend-Lease, but the Americans were hesitant to deliver one of their newest planes—it was only in its second year of operation. Washington needed C-54s for the Pacific war and the forthcoming invasion of Europe. The four-engine Skymasters were 93 feet in length, with a wingspan of 117 feet. They could cover a distance of up to 4,000 miles at an altitude of 22,000 feet, with a cruising speed of 190 miles per hour. With a crew of four, the plane could take up to fifty soldiers on board. Originally designed as a passenger plane and later converted to military purposes, the plane could be reconverted and indeed served as flying headquarters for American leaders and military commanders. In January 1943 President Roosevelt used the presidential C-54, popularly known as the "Sacred Cow" because it was so heavily guarded, to fly to Casablanca for a meeting with Prime Minister Winston Churchill of Great Britain. To Stalin's deep satisfaction, the two Western allies decided to wage war until the complete defeat or "unconditional surrender" of Germany.[4]

Secretary Hull and his party needed all the comfort that the VIP version of the Skymaster could offer on their long trip to Moscow. Having taken off from Washington on October 7, they had first to fly to Puerto Rico and then embark on a sea voyage to Casablanca. There they boarded planes that had crossed the Atlantic without their human cargo and flew to Algiers, then to Cairo, then Teheran, and finally to Moscow. Hull, who had turned seventy-two shortly before the trip, was in visibly poor health and anything but a happy traveler. The doctors, fearing that at an altitude above 8,000 feet he would suffer a heart attack, sent a Navy doctor to administer oxygen to Hull as required. The secretary of state was determined to reach Moscow.

The second most important person on Hull's team was the newly minted US ambassador to Moscow, Averell Harriman. The tall, lanky New Yorker was about to mark his fifty-second birthday but looked much younger. His open face, with its large, manly features and broad smile, made him popular with women and helped secure his reputation as a successful dealmaker. Like many members of Roosevelt's administration during the war, Harriman had been a businessman. With the help of his friend and the president's right-hand man, Harry Hopkins, Harriman joined the Roosevelt administration in the spring of 1941. Roosevelt needed someone with business experience to administer his Lend-Lease program with Britain. Harriman traveled to London to become the president's special representative in Europe, with responsibility for running a billion-dollar program to provide American supplies to Britain and keep it afloat in the war with Germany. In September 1941 he flew from London to Moscow to negotiate with Stalin an extension of Lend-Lease to the Soviet Union, and in October 1943 Roosevelt appointed Harriman US ambassador in Moscow.

Roosevelt wanted Harriman to go to Moscow to reassure Stalin about American goodwill, establish closer military cooperation in the run-up to the second front, and, last but not least, negotiate with him on the future of Eastern Europe, especially Soviet plans for territorial acquisitions at the expense of the Baltic states, Poland, and Romania on the basis of the 1939 Molotov-Ribbentrop Pact. Roosevelt wanted the Soviets to restrain their ambitions in exchange for future cooperation with the United States and Britain. He was prepared to offer Stalin the right to negotiate as an equal with the Western powers, give assurances of Soviet access to Baltic ports through international agreements, and provide financial and technical assistance in rebuilding the war-torn Soviet Union.[5]

Before leaving Washington, first for London and then for Moscow, Harriman received Roosevelt's assurances that he would be privy to all aspects of American-Soviet relations, including military cooperation. Not only was Harriman's wish granted but also he got to choose the military mission's head. General George Marshall, the US Army chief of staff, agreed to send to Moscow one of the two people suggested by Harriman, the forty-seven-year-old secretary of the Combined Chiefs of Staff, Major General John Russell Deane, who was highly capable and respected in Washington. General Deane, known to his friends as Russ, was now on the same flight to Moscow as Harriman and Hull. "I was eager, hopeful, confident, and happy," wrote Deane later about the feelings he had on the flight. Like Harriman, Deane believed that he could get along with the Soviets. After all, getting along with the Americans was in their interest as well. He was happy to leave behind his secretarial duties in Washington and take charge of his own command. He also welcomed the opportunity to work with Harriman, whom he respected and admired.[6]

If Harriman saw it as his main task in Moscow to negotiate a postwar settlement in Europe, Deane's prime objective was the coordination of the Soviet-American effort to defeat Germany. The second front—the invasion of France—was still months away, but here was an opportunity to begin immediate cooperation with the Soviets. Before their departure for Moscow, both Harriman and Deane were approached by General Henry "Hap" Arnold, the commander of the US Air Force, then engaged with the British Royal Air Force in joint bombing raids on Germany and its European allies. American pilots would bomb Germany from British bases and then return to Britain. Arnold wanted Harriman and Deane to convince the Soviets to allow the US Air Force to establish bases on Soviet-held territory. Bombers could then fly much farther behind the German lines, taking off from Britain and landing in the Soviet Union, then flying back a few days later with a new supply of bombs, not only to destroy German industrial targets in Eastern Europe but also to soften up their defenses on the Eastern Front.

It sounded like a win-win proposal. "Harriman and I," recalled Deane, "were delighted with Arnold's attitude and went to Russia feeling certain that sheer logic would enable us to carry out his wishes." They believed that bases on the Soviet side of the Eastern Front would prepare the ground for similar bases in the Far East, where the American commanders were counting not only on Soviet participation but also on the acquisition of air bases to launch bombing raids on the Japanese mainland. Deane, who was not an airman himself but, as secretary of the Joint Chiefs of Staff, had had many dealings with Arnold and the US Air Force in Europe, was eager to make the air base proposal his top priority in Moscow. On the way from the United States to the Middle East and then to the Soviet Union, he made a stopover in London to visit the headquarters of the US Eighth Air Force, which was raiding German targets in Europe. He met with commanding officers there and collected materials on the results of the strategic bombing of Europe, as well as a list of targets in Eastern Europe that the American pilots could not reach unless they were granted landing rights in the Soviet Union. With his task cut out for him, Deane looked forward to the start of his Moscow mission.[7]

The Skymaster flight from Teheran to Moscow was nothing if not a demonstration of the desire of American and Soviet airmen to work together. In Teheran the Soviets added their own radio operator and navigator to the American crew to ensure that the plane would not get lost in Soviet airspace or be mistaken for an enemy aircraft. But if the desire to work together was there, the opportunity to do so was limited indeed. Ambassador's Harriman's daughter, Kathleen, who accompanied him on the flight, wrote to her sister, Mary: "Shortly after we got going, I got a formal note from Hull's pilot...that the pleasure of my company was requested up front." When Kathleen walked to the cockpit of the Skymaster, she noticed the American pilots arguing with their Soviet counterparts. The Soviets insisted on flying at a high altitude, while the Americans refused, as the doctors had prohibited Hull from flying above 8,000 feet. The problem, as Kathleen wrote later to Mary, was that "no one spoke any known language in common." Neither did Kathleen, but the American pilots still put her between themselves and their Soviet counterparts. The presence of a young woman calmed both sides.

Kathleen Harriman, or Kathy, as she was known to her friends and family, had joined her father in London in May 1941, working first for the International News Service and then for *Newsweek*. At twenty-six, an equestrian enthusiast, Kathy was tall and sporty. Her broad smile and outgoing personality made her popular with men. Unlike the ailing Secretary Hull, she was looking forward to her Moscow adventure. In her time in Moscow she would learn Russian and become a hostess at the American embassy, smoothing over quite a few conflicts between Soviet and American diplomats and military officers, who tended to behave with greater reserve in female company. She had already discovered that talent on the flight to Moscow. "By the time we neared Stalingrad all tension and difficulty ceased & in sign language the Battle of Stalingrad was fought out for us," wrote Kathy to her sister. "By the time we reached Moscow we were all fast friends."[8]

To the disbelief of the American pilots, the Soviet navigator was bringing the Skymaster to its destination by following rivers, railroads, and highways. They flew over the Kremlin before making their landing at the Moscow Central Airport. "From the window of my plane," wrote John Deane later, "I could see the domes of the Kremlin blackened with war paint, the sparkling waters of the Moscow River, Red Square, St. Basil's Church, and the glistening bayonets of a guard of honor waiting in the field below to salute for the Soviet Union our great Secretary of State, Cordell Hull." After circling the airport and locating the landing strip, the Skymaster made its final approach. The long trip from Washington to Moscow was finally over.[9]

Viacheslav Molotov, his deputies and entourage, whom Deane found "blue with cold that had penetrated to the marrow," greeted the American delegation, clearly happy that their freezing wait had come to an end.

Molotov and Hull inspected the guard of honor. The band played the Soviet anthem, the *Internationale*, the hymn of the European socialist movement. Its lyrics promised nothing good to the capitalist world: "We will destroy this world of violence / Down to the foundations, and then / We will build our new world," went the Russian translation of the song. The band went on to play "The Star-Spangled Banner." Its words, "In God is our trust," occasioned no diplomatic embarrassment, as neither anthem was sung. Deane found the performance of the American anthem "excellent though slightly unfamiliar."[10]

Also waiting on the tarmac to greet the Americans was the British delegation to the Moscow talks, led by Foreign Secretary Anthony Eden. It was a solemn occasion. After Molotov went to the microphone to welcome the Allies, Hull and Eden responded with brief greetings of their own. Hull said that it gave him "special satisfaction to visit Moscow, the capital of the country united with my own in common cause." Later that day Hull, Eden, and Molotov, accompanied by their respective delegations, met in Molotov's Kremlin office to define that cause and how best to attain it. They agreed to issue a short communiqué listing the names of the US and British officials who had arrived in Moscow and the Soviet officials who met them at the airport, though no purpose of the visit was announced to the media.[11]

There was good reason not only for secrecy, given wartime conditions, but also for restraint in commenting publicly on possible outcomes of the visit. The leading Allied diplomats came to Moscow to take part in the first ministerial conference on the postwar world order. The participants in the Moscow Conference, as the meeting later came to be known, had high ambitions, but there was no telling whether the visions of the future presented by the three allies would coincide. Over the course of twelve days, from October 19 to October 30, the three foreign ministers would discuss the creation of the United Nations Organization and the launch of a European Advisory Commission to deal with liberated countries and territories in Europe. They would debate the eradication of fascism in Italy, the restoration of Austrian independence, and the prosecution of those guilty of war crimes. It was the start of a long process of looking for common ground in the organization of the postwar world. Difficulties lay ahead, but the hopes were flying high.[12]

Soviet-American cooperation was entering a new era, and Harriman and Deane believed that it would be a bright one. Meeting with Molotov on October 21, Harriman told the Soviet foreign commissar that he had come "as a friend." He expressed his hope that one day the two of them would take a flight in Harriman's high-speed plane. Having become exceptionally close to Churchill during his days in London, Harriman was now trying to make friends in Moscow and in particular to establish personal relations with Molotov. Inviting friends in government to enjoy his family's fortune—Harriman's father had been a railroad tycoon and he was a millionaire many times over—by attending dinners, riding horses, and driving in fast cars and planes had worked in both business and politics in the West. Harriman was trying the same approach in Moscow, offering friendship and expecting friendship in return.[13]

Before long both Averell and Kathy Harriman were developing an emotional attachment to the country and its people. "Now I'm just beginning to realize that the good old Russian communiqués that deal in impersonal heroics and the huge number of dead, missing and wounded mean something very personal here in the way of friends and family," wrote Kathy to Mary on November 5. "When you get down to it, despite the teachings that the State comes first, the Russian still is a human being and funny enough, the government treats him as such—and so the reason for periodic fireworks when a new victory is announced and the dressing up of the bombed buildings."[14]

The American team had arrived in Moscow full of enthusiasm and determined to advance Soviet-American relations to a new stage, including not only summit meetings between the leaders of the Grand Alliance but also direct military cooperation between American and Soviet forces. General Deane, whose job was to establish such cooperation, was as eager to succeed as anyone else. He believed that he could achieve his goal by breaking through the façade of the communist state to the shared humanity behind it.

2

Stalin's Verdict

On first meeting Joseph Stalin at the closing banquet of the Moscow Conference on the evening of October 30, 1943, General Deane was surprised to see how short he was. He was also struck by the deep iron-gray color of the dictator's hair, but mostly by the "kindly expression on his deeply wrinkled, sallow face." Stalin was wearing a military uniform with the shoulder boards of a marshal of the Soviet Union, the military rank bestowed on him in March 1943 after the Red Army's victory at Stalingrad. He walked around the room greeting Soviet guests and members of the American and British delegations, of whom there were close to sixty, "always bent over, seldom looking one in the eye, and saying nothing whatever."[1]

That evening Deane not only shook hands with the marshal but also had a drink with him. At the banquet table, which the general found "beautiful beyond description," a toasting contest began with Molotov, who raised his glass to British-American-Soviet friendship. Deane knew that this was just the beginning and braced himself for a night of heavy drinking. The US embassy personnel had told him and Harriman upon their arrival in Moscow that the only way to get the Soviets' respect was to outdrink them.

"It is hard to cheat on toast drinking," Kathy Harriman, who attended quite a few banquets in Moscow, wrote Mary, "as you have to turn glass upside down at the end of it and the drops of liquor that fall out are, according to the Russian custom, drops of misfortune you wish on the person you are drinking with."

Her father made his staffers happy and proud when a few days later, at a lavish reception thrown by Molotov to mark October Revolution Day, he out-drank not only his Soviet hosts but also his British counterpart, Sir Archibald Clark Kerr. According to Kathy, Kerr "rose to his feet for a toast with some difficulty, put his hand out to steady himself on the table, missed it and fell flat on his face at Molotov's feet, bringing a goodly number of plates and glasses clattering down on top of him." Both Harrimans would have a terrible hango-ver the next day—the bottoms-up toasts were given with glasses full of vodka, not wine. But the previous evening they had made their countrymen proud. "All the Americans were very pleased," wrote Kathy to her sister.[2]

Deane, having acquainted himself with bottoms-up toasts at the first conference banquet he attended, knew that sooner or later it would be his turn to propose a toast. As he remembered later, he wracked his "brain for something cute to say." Rising to his feet, he announced that he was hon-ored to be the head of the US military mission in Moscow, which he saw as a vanguard of millions of Americans who would join their Soviet allies in the war. The Soviets, who wanted only one thing from the conference—a pledge to open the second front—were delighted to hear those words from an American general. Deane then delivered a punch line, toasting to the day when the British and American advance guards would meet their Red Army counterparts on the streets of Berlin. Ironically, the meeting in Berlin prophesied by Deane would lead to the partitioning of the German capital a few years later, but at the time no one could see anything troublesome about all three powers joining forces there.

The toast was a great success. Everyone drank bottoms-up but then, to Deane's surprise, remained standing. He realized why only when he was nudged by a neighbor and turned his head. Next to Deane stood Stalin him-self, a glass in his hand. After listening to the toast, the Soviet dictator had left his seat and walked around the table, behind the guests, his diminutive figure obscured from Deane's view. They drank bottoms-up together. Deane was drinking vodka and Stalin probably his usual red wine, which he often diluted with water. Getting his guests drunk and listening to what they had to say in a state of extreme intoxication was an old trick of Stalin's, practiced more on members of his court than on foreign visitors.[3]

For Deane, the conference was ending on a high note. His toast at the banquet "stole the show," according to Hull. He was also optimistic about making progress on the top priority of his Moscow agenda—getting permission to open American air bases on Soviet-held territory.

Serving in Washington at the Chiefs of Staff headquarters, Deane was well aware that American and British air operations in Europe were going very badly. As of the fall of 1943, the objective of grounding the Luftwaffe in preparation for the invasion of France in 1944 was as far from being achieved as ever. The Luftwaffe was alive and kicking, exacting an ever higher price on the British and American planes bombing German targets. The same applied to the German air-defense systems, which could not be suppressed.

In 1943 the Royal Air Force lost 2,700 heavy bombers, either shot down or damaged. Bombing raids on Berlin alone, which began in November 1943 and continued until March 1944, caused the loss of 1,128 British aircraft. American losses were also staggering. During the second week of October 1943, the month Deane arrived in Moscow, the Eighth Air Force, operating from Britain, lost 148 bombers. The loss rate of the bombing raid on October 14 stood at 20.7 percent, and the damage rate reached 47.4 percent. Raids deep into German territory unescorted by fighters were becoming prohibitively costly, and fighters such as the Mustang P-51 were unable to reach Eastern Europe because their gasoline tanks could not carry sufficient fuel.

Hap Arnold believed that he had a solution to the Luftwaffe problem, which was shuttle bombing. Bombers would take off from air bases in Britain and Italy, fly over German-held territory and, instead of turning back before they could reach German airplane factories and airfields in eastern Germany and Eastern Europe, would land on bases behind the Soviet lines. In addition to reaching otherwise unattainable targets, the bombers would help to disperse the Luftwaffe airplanes, which would now have to fight on two fronts. The Soviets, who had no long-range aviation to speak of and did not harass the Germans beyond the area of their ground operations, would benefit as well, since American bombers could hit targets suggested by the Soviet command. This is why Arnold had insisted on making shuttle-bombing operations one of Deane's key priorities in Moscow.[4]

Deane was happy to oblige, but as the Moscow conference began he soon realized that the only question the Soviets wanted to discuss was that of the second front. They sought confirmation of earlier Allied pledges, first made by Roosevelt to Molotov in June 1942, to land in Europe as soon as possibe. Deane and Lieutenant General Sir Hastings Ismay, Churchill's chief military adviser, did their best to convince the Soviets that the second front would indeed be opened in 1944. Deane made use of the positive response to his presentation to broach the subject he cared most about—establishing US air bases on Soviet-held territory. He was prepared to open his own "second front" right away.[5]

As Deane recalled later, the request, which he made on the very first day of the conference, "hit the Soviet representatives as a bolt from the blue." In responding, Molotov played for time. He agreed to consider the proposal, which included two additional requests from General Arnold: to establish better exchange of weather information between the US and Soviet air forces and to improve air communication between the two countries. Molotov promised to get back to Deane and his colleagues in due course. Deane recalled the exchange as his first lesson in dealing with Soviet officials: "no subordinate official in Russia may make a decision on matters in which foreigners are involved without consulting higher authority, and usually this higher authority is Stalin himself."[6]

It took the Soviet foreign commissar two days before he could tell the conference participants that he was in favor of the proposal. In reality, he feared the building of Western bases on Soviet territory. Apprehension of foreign presence could be traced back in Russian culture to the early seventeenth century, when Polish and Ukrainian Cossack detachments took Moscow and pillaged a good part of Muscovy, but there were more recent precedents as well. The Soviet leaders' thinking was rooted in the experience of the revolution and civil war, when foreign troops, including British, French, and American expeditionary forces, had landed in Murmansk on the Barents Sea, Odesa on the Black Sea, Baku in the center of the Caspian oil fields, and Vladivostok in the Far East in 1918 to support anti-Bolshevik forces. They would not withdraw until 1920. To add insult to injury, the American intervention had happened on the watch of Assistant Secretary of the Navy Franklin Delano Roosevelt (1913–1920), while the British effort had been spearheaded by none other than Winston Churchill, minister for munitions (1917–1919) and secretary of state for war (1919–1921).

"I knew them all, capitalists, but Churchill was the strongest, the smartest among them. Of course he was 100 percent imperialist," remembered Molotov, who had organized Bolsheviks in Ukraine in 1918–1920 against their numerous enemies there, including the French expeditionary corps in Odesa. Continuing his recollections of Churchill's imperial behavior, Molotov told a sympathetic interviewer in the 1970s: "He said: 'Let us establish our airfield at Murmansk, for you are in a difficult situation.' 'Yes,' we said, 'it's a hard time for us, so send these forces to the front. We'll guard Murmansk ourselves.' He backed down after that." Molotov recalled the American offer to open air bases in the Far East as nothing short of a land grab by Roosevelt: "He wanted to occupy certain parts of the Soviet Union instead of fighting. Afterwards it would not have been easy to get them out of there."[7]

Now, in October 1943, Stalin and Molotov had to decide what to do with the new American request for air bases. The Red Army was beginning to cross the Dnieper, making the Soviet position more secure than ever before. But the Soviet leaders wanted several things from the Western allies, and they presented their wish list as the conference moved along: the opening of the second front; Turkey entering the war against Germany to draw

German divisions away from the Soviet front; and Sweden allowing Soviet air bases on its territory. They decided to keep the issue of Allied air bases in play, using them as a bargaining chip to get what they really wanted from the Americans.

On October 21, 1943, two days after Dean's proposal, Molotov told the American delegation that the Soviet government "approved in principle" the request to establish US air bases in the Soviet Union, along with the proposals to improve the exchange of weather information and air traffic. Secretary Hull thanked Molotov and, considering the matter settled, left Deane to discuss the details with his counterparts in the Red Army general staff. "I, of course, was elated—less than a week in the Soviet Union and three major objectives achieved," recalled Deane. "Wouldn't the Chiefs of Staff be proud of me!"[8]

On October 26, in response to Deane's request, Washington cabled him specifics with regard to the bases. "Our requirements are estimated at approximately ten bases, so located as to provide best shuttle for heavy bombers striking appropriate targets from Uncle King [UK] and Italy, as well as being properly located to strike appropriate targets before returning to Uncle King and Italy." The chiefs of staff wanted the Soviets to supply gas, ammunition, bombs, and housing in order to keep the number of US (code-named "Uncle Sugar") personnel at the bases to a minimum. It was a long and detailed telegram. The chiefs of staff meant business and assumed that they were already in the game.[9]

Encouraged by the response from Molotov, Deane meant business too. "I scarcely left the telephone for days, and each time I did I inquired at once upon my return if any [Soviet] General Staff officers had called me to arrange the details of shuttle bombing," he recalled. No one called Deane or looked for him. It was then that Deane realized, as he later wrote, that "approval in principle" by the Soviets meant "exactly nothing." He decided to take matters into his own hands and insisted on recording his request, and Molotov's approval of it "in principle," in the final protocol of the conference. Molotov refused, stating that the proposal had not been discussed at the conference and thus did not belong in the protocol. Deane insisted on including discussion of the bases in the protocol. That did not help. The Soviets refused to cooperate.[10]

■

The breakthrough finally came on November 29, 1943 in Teheran, when Roosevelt raised the question of air bases in the meeting with Stalin and the dictator promised to look into the matter. On December 26, Molotov gave Harriman a memorandum stating, that the Soviet government did not object to the American proposal to establish US air bases, and, further, that the command of the Soviet Air Force would be instructed to start preliminary consultations with the American representatives. Harriman and Deane were cautiously optimistic. "While these agreements only scratch the surface of the projects we have before the Soviet government and while they are still in the conversation state, I feel that they are an indication of the change in the attitude and will open the door to further acts of collaboration," cabled Deane to the Chiefs of Staff on December 27.[11]

Although the door was opening, the hinges were rusty. In Washington, General Arnold was losing hope that he would ever see his bombers land on Soviet soil. On January 29, a month after Harriman's meeting with Molotov, he forwarded a telegram to John Deane from General Carl Andrew Spaatz, the commander of the Eighth Air Force and the United States Strategic Air Forces in Europe (USSTAF), who was stationed in England. The telegram, addressed to Arnold, raised the question of shuttle-bombing operations, suggesting that they begin with 120 bombers. More importantly, Spaatz wrote that shuttle bombing could start without establishing US air bases (a clear departure from the earlier American position), as US personnel could be dispatched to existing Soviet bases with the task of assisting Soviet technicians. It appeared that Arnold, who had forwarded the telegram to Deane, still wanted landing rights in the USSR but was no longer insisting on bases.[12]

The telegram spurred Harriman into action. On January 30 he requested a meeting with Stalin to consider Roosevelt's request for air bases. It was then that something clicked in the Kremlin's secretive machine, and Harriman was invited to Stalin's office to discuss the air bases that Arnold no longer hoped to obtain. The meeting took place at 6:00 p.m. on February 2 in the presence of Molotov. According to the US memorandum of conversation, Harriman started with a reference to Roosevelt's request and went on to make the case for shuttle bombing, which would allow the Allies to "penetrate more deeply into Germany." After listening to Harriman, Stalin finally gave his personal approval to the project. He told the ambassador that the Soviet government "favored" the proposal, a clear improvement on Molotov's "approved in principle" and "do not object" formulas. Stalin suggested that operations begin with 150 to 200 planes. He offered two airfields where reconnaissance planes could land and suggested that the Soviets would provide three air bases for bombers in the northern sector of the Eastern Front, and three more in the southern.[13]

Harriman and Deane could hardly believe what had happened. With Spaatz and Arnold already giving up hope of obtaining Soviet bases, Stalin unexpectedly made a U-turn and gave his full support to the operation. "I shall never forget our elation the night that Harriman, after his meeting with Stalin, dropped by to give me the good news," remembered Deane later. He cabled the chiefs of staff. "Marshal Stalin tonight informed the ambassador that he agreed to the shuttle bombing project," began his telegram, which went on to discuss details of the next step of the operation, including the acquisition of Soviet entry visas for officers to be sent immediately from London to Moscow. The news created a sensation in Washington. General Arnold forwarded congratulations to Deane from George C. Marshall—the Chief of Staff of the US Army—himself. "Very apparent it is that congratulations are in order for the equanimitous and capable manner in which you have handled negotiations," read the cable. Harriman also received congratulations from the White House.[14]

No one could say what or who had made Stalin finally concede on the issue of the bases and overcome fears of outside intervention. Was he finally convinced that the Americans were serious about opening the second front, or did he hope to ensure it by offering them what they wanted? For the Americans in Moscow, it no longer mattered. "Who said the Russians were not co-operative? Who said we couldn't work together?" wrote Deane, recalling the jubilant atmosphere of those days in the US Ambassador's residence in Moscow called Spaso House. "All that was needed was the frank approach, understanding, and persistence, so well exemplified in Averell and me." Deane's optimism seemed finally vindicated. The Americans and Soviets would work together, not just coordinating their battles on different fronts but also jointly planning and executing operations to "cause the German to feel the allied blows more," as Stalin told Harriman at their meeting. The future looked bright again.[15]

3

Going Frantic

Stalin kept his word. Three days after Harriman received his approval for US Air Force use of Soviet bases, Molotov called a meeting with the commanders of the Soviet Air Force to which he invited Harriman and Deane. The meeting took place on February 5, 1944. The Soviet commanders were represented by Chief Air Marshal Aleksandr Novikov, whom Deane called "the General Arnold of the Red Air Force" and his chief of the directorate in charge of the formation of new Air Force units, Colonel General Aleksei Nikitin.

Novikov and Nikitin, who shared the same year of birth, 1900, belonged to the new crop of Soviet aviators who were put in charge of the Red Army Air Force after its disastrous defeats by the Luftwaffe at the start of the German-Soviet war. Back then, during the first weeks of Operation Barbarossa, the Soviets lost almost half their airplanes—close to 4,000 of the available 9,500. Many were bombed on the airfields without ever having had a chance to engage in battle. Appointed in the following year to lead the embattled Air Force, Novikov, with Nikitin's help, reorganized it and, with the help of Airacobras, Douglasses, and other aircraft supplied by the United States through the Lend-Lease program, turned it into an effective fighting machine. They still did not accept or try to master the basics of strategic bombing, but their fighter and bomber pilots did exceptionally well in supporting Red Army front-line operations, where they first challenged and then, by late 1943, overcame the Luftwaffe's control of the skies.[1]

The two commanders of the Soviet Air Force, unlike their political bosses, were eager to cooperate with the Americans. In the cable he sent to Washington that night, Deane advised Generals Arnold and Spaatz: "It was agreed that your representatives should arrive as soon as possible and permission was granted for them to come on direct route from United Kingdom to Moscow." The ball was now in the American court, especially that of the fifty-three-year-old General Carl Andrew Spaatz, who was then in the process of assuming command of all American Air Forces in Europe (USSTAF), including the Eighth Air Force in Britain, which he had previously commanded, and the Fifteenth Air Force in Italy. Both would participate in the shuttle-bombing operations if air bases were in fact established on Soviet territory. Spaatz needed no reminders. On February 6, the day after Deane's meeting with the Soviet Air Force commanders, Spaatz appointed Colonel John S. Griffith commanding officer of the shuttle-bombing project, which was code-named "Baseball." The Americans were getting ready to play their favorite game, engaging in the so-called national pastime. They would try and score the runs; the Soviets would have to provide the bases.[2]

But they had to hurry if the bases were to be made ready in advance of the Allied invasion of Europe. It was a huge task that required extensive planning, the formation of brand-new Air Force units to operate the bases, and the delivery of hundreds of men and hundreds of thousands of tons of equipment, supplies, and ammunition deep in Soviet territory. Deane and the American airmen would be racing against time. The basepaths were turning into an obstacle race, with the Soviets creating the hurdles, and it was anyone's guess whether the American team would make it on time.

Major Albert Lepawsky, a city planner and former university professor from Chicago who had been assigned to the planning team of the new operation, used baseball terminology to formulate its overall goals. To his thinking, the whole point of this game was to convince the home team of how well the visiting team played, thereby issuing a kind of challenge to the home team to let them play on all their ball fields. What Lepawsky had in mind was the establishment of American bases not only in the western USSR but also in the Far East, where they would be used to help invade the Japanese islands.

That was in the future. The immediate goal of the shuttle operations was to help the US Air Force defeat the Luftwaffe in preparation for the Allied invasion of Europe. Thus, the German airfields, airplane factories, and oil refineries located in Eastern Europe that supplied the planes with scarce fuel were the prime targets of the operation. The secondary task was to distract the Luftwaffe from Western Europe by opening that second front in the East—a difficult undertaking, as the Soviet strategic air force was still in its infancy, and the Soviet command still did not believe in the benefits of strategic bombing.[3]

Colonel John Griffith, the commander of the new shuttle-bombing operation, seemed an ideal candidate to lead a project involving the Soviet Union. A native of Seattle, he became a flying ace while serving in the British expeditionary force during World War I. As part of the British Royal Flying Corps, he was dispatched to the Russian North in the middle of the Bolshevik Revolution and Civil War. Back then he was fighting against the Bolsheviks. Now he was asked to fight on their side. His own political sympathies and antipathies aside, Griffith was first and foremost a very efficient officer. Within ten days of his appointment, Griffith and his officers managed to produce a detailed plan for the start of shuttle bombing, one that envisioned four missions per month, each conducted by 200 American bombers.

By February 28, after a week-long air journey via Cairo and Teheran, Griffith was in Moscow, sitting next to Aleksei Nikitin, and discussing the details of the operation. Deane, who escorted Griffith to Nikitin's office, asked for airfields closer to the center of the front line and located as far west as possible—the less territory bombers taking off from Britain and Italy had to cover, the better. Nikitin was reluctant to offer bases close to the Soviet front line, suggesting that many of them had been destroyed. He offered instead the bases in central Ukraine, on the southern sector of the Soviet front and relatively far from the front line.[4] Deane saw no choice but to take what was offered. He proposed an inspection of the airfields as early as the next day. According to the US memorandum of conversation, Nikitin promised to "get busy about making arrangements." It was a good beginning.

Colonel Griffith and his team got ready for the flight. But the next day passed without a word from General Nikitin, then another, and another. Griffith was becoming ever more impatient. He had been given three weeks to prepare for the start of shuttle bombing. It took him a week to get to Moscow, and during his first week there all he had been able to accomplish was to hold one meeting with the Red Air Force commanders. Deane was trying to calm Griffith and his second in command, Colonel Alfred Kessler, who was equally impatient. "They had been used to dealing with the British, who were at least approachable," recalled Deane in his memoirs. "They could not get to the Russians to let off steam—but they could get to me. Much of my time was spent in smoothing their feathers."[5]

It took more than two weeks for Griffith and Kessler to see the proposed bases, as their flight was not cleared until March 31. From Moscow they flew south to central Ukraine. There, on the left bank of the Dnieper River in the lands of the former Hetmanate, the Cossack state of the seventeenth and eighteenth centuries, were three old Cossack towns: Poltava, famed for the Battle of Poltava (1709); Myrhorod, the home town of the writer Nikolai Gogol (Mykola Hohol in Ukrainian); and Pyriatyn. All three had airfields built by the Soviets before the war and used by the Germans during their occupation of the territory in 1941–1943. Those airfields were now being offered to the Americans.

At Poltava the Germans had damaged or destroyed all the buildings with the exception of one barrack. There was no "water, sewage or power system," Griffith wrote to his commanders in England. The concrete runway could not be extended because of the existing structures, but there was enough space to build a new runway using metal mats. The branch line leading to the main railway had been destroyed by the Germans, but the American visitors thought it could be rebuilt. At Myrhorod, another base fifty miles northwest of Poltava, there were no remaining buildings of any kind, which meant that the existing runway could be extended at will. Pyriatyn, fifty miles west of Myrhorod, had no buildings or concrete runways, so the inspection party could not land. None of the bases much impressed the Americans. Griffith believed that the Soviets were either unable or unwilling to offer anything else or better, and that they had to take what they could get.[6]

By the time Colonel Griffith visited the Poltava and Myrhorod airfields and made his recommendation to accept the bases, he was serving his last days as commander of the "Baseball" shuttle-bombing project, now renamed "Frantic." What the officers who gave the project its new name had in mind was the panic and distress that shuttle bombing would cause the Germans. But it accurately reflected Griffith's state of mind, given the never-ending difficulties caused by his Soviet hosts. The perpetual delays in obtaining permission to inspect airfields, shipping equipment, or getting responses to simple questions were driving him insane. Apart from that, the Soviets insisted on full control over American actions. Griffith's own Douglas C-47 Skytrain airplane could be flown to and from Teheran only by a Soviet pilot. The authorities also wanted Soviet navigators and radio operators to accompany any American plane and insisted on having their own crew fly the American hospital plane.

Deane was determined to keep peace with the Soviet commanders at almost any price. "Colonel Griffith believes that operations under the above conditions will be highly restricted and that these matters should be brought to your attention," cabled Deane to London and Washington. "However I do not feel that they should be made a major issue at this time, but rather that it will pay us in the long run to attempt to break down these restrictions gradually." Deane and Griffith clearly did not see eye to eye, and Griffith wanted to make his disagreement with the commanding officer known to his superiors. Deane, for his part, believed that Griffith, who had helped anti-Bolshevik forces fight the Red Army during the revolution, had the wrong attitude and would have to be replaced if the project was to succeed. Griffith had to go, the first victim of Deane's and the Air Force commander's desire to keep the Soviets happy and the prospects for *Frantic* alive. In early April, Deane informed the Soviets that the colonel was being transferred to the United States.[7]

Colonel Kessler replaced Griffith on April 8. Like his commander, Kessler was initially taken aback by the slow pace of negotiations with the Soviets, but he brought a different attitude to the problems. In 1943, Kessler had spent three weeks in the Soviet Union as a member of the US delegation led by Donald M. Nelson, the chairman of the US War Production Board. A graduate of West Point and the Massachusetts Institute of Technology, where he had earned a degree in aeronautical engineering, Kessler had been impressed by Soviet military production and by the Soviets in general. For that reason, Deane felt much more comfortable working with Kessler than with Griffith, and did not even mention Griffith's name in his memoirs about his tenure in Moscow.[8]

On April 15, 1944, after customary delays caused by the Soviet side, Kessler and a handful of his aides, as well as close to 3,000 pounds (1,350 kilograms) of baggage, including the equipment they needed to start work, were flown to Poltava by a Soviet plane. Deane could finally celebrate a small victory. On the day Kessler left Moscow for Poltava, Deane cabled Spaatz in London and Arnold in Washington: "Kessler and the remainder of his staff moved to Poltava today." He asked for Kessler's speedy promotion from colonel to brigadier general. Deane was, as always, in a hurry; the bases were supposed to be ready before the main part of the American contingent had reached the Ukrainian steppes. And they were already on their way—four echelons of the American servicemen, more than 1,200 airmen altogether.[9]

Colonels Griffith and Kessler, who had flown to Moscow in February 1944 with a handful of officers, constituted the first echelon of the *Frantic* task force. The second and third echelons were larger but numbered dozens rather than hundreds of officers and GIs, and thus could be flown to Poltava from Teheran. The fourth, and last—as well as largest—echelon consisted of 67 officers, four warrant officers, and 680 enlisted men—more than half the US contingent in the USSR, limited by the Soviets after long negotiations to 1,200 men. They traveled by sea, crossed deserts, mountains, and steppes, the entire journey taking almost two months.

The fourth echelon began to assemble in Camp Jefferson Hall (AAF 59) near the town of Stone in Staffordshire, between Birmingham and Manchester, in early March 1944. It consisted of the airplane technicians and ground personnel, and had been selected from units of General Spaatz's Eighth Air Force. They were chosen individually, not as members of existing units, which made for a diverse and sometimes not very agreeable group—commanders eagerly seized the opportunity to dismiss those whom they considered troublemakers and misfits. But the selection officers did their best to ensure that those who made the cut were experienced in their jobs and in reasonably good health. Those without experience or diagnosed with such things as venereal disease (common enough), hernias, or bad teeth were vetted out.[10]

Those selected for the mission had no idea where they were going and for what purpose. The destination would be kept secret until they were about to cross the Soviet border. On March 25, the echelon boarded a train and traveled to Liverpool to embark on the British HMT (Hired Military Transport) ship *Alcatrana*. The ship, with its US Air Force passengers on board, headed first from Liverpool to the Firth of Clyde in British coastal waters shielded from the Atlantic and German submarines by the Kintyre Peninsula. She waited there for other ships to arrive and form a convoy headed for Gibraltar.

On the evening of April 12, after steaming along the North African coast and, on one occasion, dropping depth charges to hit suspected German submarines, the *Alcatrana* anchored at Port Said, Egypt. The men of the fourth echelon disembarked, collected their baggage and supplies, and moved to Camp Huckstep, an Allied military base eight miles from Cairo, named after a GI killed in a plane crash in North Africa in 1943. They would spend two weeks there, making preparations for the rest of the trip, which they were told would bring them to Teheran, relaxing and partnering with the American Red Cross. The unit's diary noted that the Air Force would "take every man to see the Pyramids, the Sphinx, Masks and other ruins of ancient Egyptian Civilization."

Palmer Myhra, a twenty-two-year-old radar and radio operator from Wisconsin, recalled that climbing them was no mean feat. The pyramids were built of stone blocks four feet high, and it was easy to slip and roll down more than a hundred steps to the bottom. In fact, as the Americans learned, a British soldier had fallen to his death a few days earlier. Still, Myhra also remembered the "feeling of elation when we finally reached the peak. We could see most of the Nile delta from there."[11]

On the afternoon of April 23, the first of the two detachments of the fourth echelon boarded a train for the trip from Cairo to Haifa. It took them 36 hours to cover a distance of under 300 miles. From Haifa they traveled in trucks. If the sea leg had been dangerous and the train leg uncomfortable, the motor trip through deserts and mountains was both. They had to cover close to 550 miles of rough terrain from Haifa to Baghdad, the first long leg of their trip to Teheran. In some areas they averaged less than sixteen miles per hour, "the mountainous roads and steep climbs preventing making better time," wrote Captain Charles N. Manning, who was entrusted with keeping the trip diary. But the main problem was scarcity of water: the men "were permitted to draw water only once at each stop," reads the diary. If there was little water to drink, there was none with which to shower. They finally arrived in Baghdad on May 1 and were given two days to bathe and rest.

On the morning of May 3 they were on the road again, now headed by truck to Hamadan, southwest of Teheran, another 366 miles of difficult terrain. They arrived on the afternoon of May 5. For 47 enlisted men and 6 officers, that turned out to be the last stop on their journey. The Soviets had, as noted, insisted on a strict limit of 1,200 Americans at the Poltava-area bases, and those 53 Americans were extras. They were reassigned to the Persian Gulf command, not knowing what they would miss. The rest of the troops, some 650 men, still had no idea where they were going. The presence of Russian speakers in their ranks indicated the Soviet Union as their destination, but there were also those who spoke Chinese. Most guessed that they would be reinforcing American troops in China and building air bases to fight the Japanese.

The officers and soldiers of the fourth echelon (the latter were more and more often referred as GIs, or "Government Issue," irrespective of whether they served in the army or in the air force) learned their destination only on May 10, when they entered the Soviet-controlled area of northern Iran. Some saw the big red star with which the Soviets had marked a building on the border of their zone and assumed that it was a Texaco gas station. It took them a while to figure out that they were entering the Soviet zone. On

May 11 they reached Tabriz, the main city of Iranian Azerbaijan. A Soviet train was waiting there to pick them up. The long-suffering travelers bathed and had dinner before departing at 8:30 p.m. on May 11. Many remembered the last leg of their journey as the most pleasant. The coaches were comfortable, not overcrowded, and there was plenty of food and drink.[12]

Captain Manning, who spent pages describing the previous difficulties of the trip, relaxed as well. His log of the previous five days of travel, from Tabriz to Poltava, filled barely half a page of his records. That leg of the trip was documented by the Soviets, mostly commanding officers and interpreters, who filed detailed reports with the Red Army military counterintelligence unit.

Meeting Americans for the first time in their lives, many Soviet officers were truly impressed. They noted with some envy how well equipped and supplied the Americans were: every officer and soldier had a pack weighing up to 80 pounds and one or two suitcases of personal belongings— unheard-of luxury by Soviet standards. The Soviets were also surprised by the democratic spirit of relations between American officers and GIs. "Outward discipline is not wholly satisfactory; greetings and subordination to superiors are hardly to be seen. An American soldier talks to an officer with his hands in his pockets, a cigarette between his teeth, and so on," wrote a Red Army officer in amazement. He was accustomed to the practice inherited from the Russian imperial army, which required a soldier to salute and stand at attention when speaking to an officer. The Soviets found the American attitude toward security too lax. They were appalled that the Americans failed to post sentries while traveling through unfamiliar territory and, upon arrival in Poltava, left weapons unattended in the coaches.

Perhaps what most surprised the Soviets was how freely their American guests accessed Soviet publications and expressed their political views. "They read our newspapers, magazines, and other literature without restriction and take great interest in the bulletins of the Soviet Information Bureau," wrote the Soviet commander in charge of that leg of the trip. He was under strict orders not to read any "bourgeois propaganda" that might be offered by the Americans and to prevent his subordinates from doing so. Accustomed to the control exercised by the Soviet secret police and counterintelligence officers over relations with foreigners, the Soviet commander expected the same from the Americans and was taken aback that a US Air Force captain acting as a liaison officer "had no particular influence on [his] officers or even the enlisted men." In the Soviet commander's view, the captain had failed to fulfill his duties as political watchdog.

The Soviet officers considered themselves ideologically superior to the Americans. In their opinion, their guests from the capitalist world were failing to see the light of communist truth. "Their political outlook is limited, officers and soldiers alike," reads one of the counterintelligence reports. They picked up elements of racism in the attitude of some of the officers and enlisted men. "The southern part [of the United States] is disposed against the Negroes and speaks very badly [about them]," reads the report filed by the same Red Army officer. "In conversation, a lieutenant colonel from the southern United States spoke openly of his dissatisfaction with President Roosevelt, saying that if he were to be reelected, he would remain president for life and give complete freedom to the Negroes." The Soviets were confident that communism alone could solve all the world's problems, including ethnic and racial ones.

All the Soviets noted the positive attitude of the Americans toward them. The Americans knew the names of top Soviet commanders, such as Marshal Georgii Zhukov, and were shocked by the extent of destruction caused by the war. While the Americans were friendly toward the Soviets, their attitude toward their British allies appeared surprisingly hostile. In Tabriz, when a Red Army officer raised a toast to Stalin, Roosevelt, and Churchill, he noticed that the Americans officers drank with enthusiasm to Stalin and Roosevelt but showed indifference to Churchill. "The attitude toward England is generally unfriendly," reported one of the Soviet interpreters attached to the echelon. "When they speak of England, they place it last: Russia, China, and only then England when it comes to allies."

Major Ralph P. Dunn, the commanding officer of the second detachment of the fourth echelon, was pleased by the reception that he and his men received from Red Army officers and civilians at train stops. He compared it favorably to what the Americans had encountered in the Middle East, where, according a Soviet interpreter who spoke to Dunn, there were "cases of theft and rude behavior on the part of the inhabitants." At the end of the trip Dunn presented the Soviet military officer in charge of transporting his detachment with a bracelet of animal bone—a gift for the officer's wife—and a letter of thanks to his commanders. "All the Americans were very well disposed toward our officers, and that was expressed in a mutual exchange of gifts," reported the Soviet commander of the echelon. "After we reached Poltava, they would come into our wagon every half hour to say how sorry they were that we would have to part so soon."[13]

Major Dunn's detachment of fewer than 400 men (the entire fourth echelon on its departure counted 680 servicemen) reached Poltava on the evening of May 16, 1944. With the new arrivals there were now 922 Americans at the Poltava-area bases. Most of them—416 servicemen—stayed in Poltava, 243 were dispatched to Myrhorod, and 263 to Pyriatyn. Operation *Frantic* was about to enter its decisive stage. The Americans had managed to reach the Ukrainian bases before the Allied invasion of Western Europe, and chances were that the bases would become operational by D-Day. John Deane could celebrate his first real victory. Not only had he managed to get over all of the hurdles by the Soviets since he first broached the idea of the bases in October 1943, he had made them keep their word. The cost was high, including the dismissal of the first commander of the shuttle-bombing operation and long periods of uncertainty and confusion, but the results were plain to see and the future looked promising.[14]

Poltava

Ever since the Teheran Conference in late November 1943, Averell Harriman had wanted Colonel Elliott Roosevelt to come to Moscow to help with the negotiations on the US air bases. The forty-three-year-old son of the president was the commanding officer of the 90th Photographic Wing, the US Air Force unit that provided reconnaissance for the Twelfth and Fifteenth Air Forces, the latter stationed in Italy and conducting bombing raids over Central and Southeastern Europe. At Teheran, President Roosevelt had asked Stalin to allow his son to take a reconnaissance flight from Italy over Europe and land in the Soviet Union. Stalin had promised to discuss the issue with Harriman in Moscow.[1]

Once Stalin gave his approval for the American bases on February 2, 1944, Harriman asked General Dwight Eisenhower, the supreme Allied commander in Europe, to send Elliott Roosevelt to Moscow. With the president's son at his side, Harriman hoped to make not only Molotov but also Stalin more malleable to American requests. At Teheran, Stalin had treated Colonel Roosevelt with special respect and showered him with attention. Harriman wanted Colonel Roosevelt in Moscow, if only for a few short days, but Roosevelt was busy with other assignments. When in May 1945,

Elliott was finally cleared to go to Moscow, the US ambassador was out of town, visiting General Eisenhower and Churchill in London and FDR in Washington. The visit of the president's son to the Soviet Union would take place in the absence of the man who had initiated it.[2]

With Harriman away, John Deane did his best to exploit Elliott Roosevelt's presence in Moscow to speed up the opening of American bases in Ukraine. As predicted, Elliott's arrival helped to open Kremlin doors. On May 11, 1944, he accompanied Deane and Major General Frederick Anderson, the representative of General Spaatz, the commander of the US Strategic Air Forces in Europe (USSTAF), to a meeting with Molotov, who treated Elliott as an "old acquaintance," as Anderson wrote to Spaatz. On May 14 Anderson, Deane, and Roosevelt flew to Ukraine to visit the newly formed Eastern Command (ESCOM), which included the airbases in Poltava, Myrhorod, and Pyriatyn. They saw the airfields under construction and American tent cities to which the new commanding officer on the ground, Colonel Kessler, would refer as "small patches of America." There they met the Soviet commanders, impressing the importance of the operation upon them, and got their first glimpse of the country where American airmen would be living and fighting behind Stalin's lines. It was a sobering sight. Three years of warfare had wreaked terrible destruction.[3]

Colonel Alfred Kessler had accomplished a lot before Roosevelt's arrival. On April 18, three days after landing at Poltava, he produced plans for the reconstruction of the air bases and immediately got to work to implement them. Deane, who visited Poltava, Myrhorod, and Pyriatyn for an inspection in late April, was satisfied with what he saw there. In the cable that he sent Generals Spaatz and Arnold on April 29, Deane went out of his way to praise the efforts of his men in Ukraine. He could not "emphasize too strongly what a good job Kessler and his staff are doing. They are living under the most difficult conditions in an area that has been completely devastated by the Germans." He was extremely pleased that "the whole atmosphere of the place between the Russians and Americans on the ground is one of extreme friendliness and cooperation." Deane also did his best to reassure the Air Force bosses, who were concerned that progress at the bases was slower than expected. "Russians have very definite ideas as to how things should be done," he wrote, "things progress in the tempo that they set."[4]

The Soviet effort was led by the forty-three-year-old Aleksandr Perminov, the commander of the 169th Special-Purpose Air Base (ABON), with responsibility for all three of the airfields. A lanky man with a long face, Perminov had received his general's rank on February 4, only a few months earlier. An ethnic Russian, he had joined the Communist Party in 1920 and the Red Army in 1921. He was only twenty-two at the time. When the German-Soviet war began in June 1941, Perminov was a colonel and chief of staff of the 14th Air Division of the Red Army in the Ukrainian city of Lutsk. On June 22, 1941, the first day of the war, his division lost forty-six airplanes, destroyed by the Luftwaffe while still on the ground. Altogether it lost eighty-two airplanes within a few days. Perminov's commanding officer was court-martialed and sentenced to ten years' imprisonment. Perminov was untouched by the purge of Soviet Air Force officers. In February 1944, the month of his promotion to general, he was given the Order of Mikhail Kutuzov, one of the highest Soviet awards for senior-rank commanders, and appointed commander of the Soviet airfields provided for American use.[5]

Kessler, his American counterpart, who had previously served as commanding officer of the 13th Combat Bomb Wing of the Eighth Army Air Force in Britain under Spaatz and taken part in bombing raids on Germany and North Africa, found in Perminov a battle-scarred aviator he could work with. Major James Parton, a historian of the US Fifteenth Army Air Force who visited Poltava in 1944, characterized Perminov as a "keen, straightforward flyer" who "used his authority to the utmost to slash red tape and settle the myriad daily problems on the spot." "Kessler and Perminov took an immediate liking to each other and proved to be a good team," recalled Deane. The readiness of Soviet Air Force commanders to accommodate their American counterparts that Deane had noticed in Moscow was now apparent in Ukraine.[6]

At Poltava, the Germans had destroyed or attempted to destroy every building in the proximity of the air base. Only one six-story building had miraculously survived the German demolition squads. When Captain Robert H. Newell of the US medical service inspected the building, he discovered that there was no glass in most of the windows, electricity was available in only two rooms, and the living quarters were full of rodents and insects. He found the bathrooms "malodorous" and described the bathing facilities as "unsanitary, inadequate, and primitive." Newell suggested that the building be demolished altogether. As far as sanitation was concerned, it was easier to house not only the personnel but also the ESCOM headquarters in the tent city nearby.[7]

The Soviets, adamant that both they and the Americans should use the building, began to repair it. They were in for a nasty surprise. On April 27, Red Army soldiers who entered the building's basement discovered a charge consisting of three undetonated air bombs, each 550 pounds (250 kilograms) in weight. There were three equally powerful charges elsewhere—two in the main building and one in an adjoining structure. If detonated, the charges could demolish the buildings they were hidden in. All four charges were connected by radio cables to a radio set buried in the soil just under 1,000 feet (300 meters) from the main building. The charges could be detonated by a radio signal, and the batteries in the radio set might last up to half a year. It had been seven months since the Red Army had recaptured Poltava, but the charges were not detonated, apparently because of damage to the wires leading from the radio set to the air bombs. General Aleksei Nikitin ordered the evacuation of the building and the resettlement of the American officers. Eventually Stalin himself would be briefed on the accident as Soviet engineers tried to figure out how the apparatus worked. They had never encountered such sophisticated radio-triggered explosive devices.[8]

Despite all the difficulties, work at Poltava and the other two bases proceeded at neck-breaking speed. "Frantic" took on new meaning as the project became something of a race against time. Plans for the reconstruction of the Myrhorod and Pyriatyn bases were ready by April 22. In one place the Soviets were turning a former girls' school into living quarters; in another they were refurbishing old artillery barracks. On April 24 the first American engineers, signal officers, and medical personnel arrived by plane from

Teheran. On April 26 the first permanent personnel were dispatched to Pyriatyn, and a day later to Myrhorod. On April 28 the first equipment reached Poltava from Murmansk, where it had been shipped from the United Kingdom. The metal matting that was supposed to be unloaded first was actually the last to leave the ships, as it had been placed at the bottom of the cargo holds, but it began to arrive as well. The Americans and Soviets got busy laying down new airstrips and extending the old ones.[9]

The metal matting, technology unknown to the Soviets, made quite an impression on Stalin himself. In March 1944, when General Nikitin reported to him that the Red Air Force was largely grounded by rains that had turned airstrips into mud flats, Stalin asked the general whether the metal matting for airstrips was produced in the Soviet Union. "No," responded Nikitin, "A great deal of metal is required for the airstrips: every strip weighs about 5,000 tons." Stalin interrupted his commander: "How do you know how much metal is produced in the country? Are you a specialist?" He ordered Nikitin to prepare a memo and submit it to the State Defense Council, the main Soviet governing body during the war.[10]

The Soviets did their best to deliver to Poltava bases and install the metal matting. Produced by Pittsburgh steelworkers, the mats were shipped first to Britain, then to Murmansk and Arkhangelsk, and delivered by train to Poltava and adjacent bases—all in record time. Miraculously, the Soviets found enough trains to ship the mats from the northern Russian ports to Ukraine in the middle of preparations for a major offensive in Belarus that was to begin on June 22, 1944. The arrival of every new shipment at the Poltava-area bases was treated as a festive event. Deane and his companions saw how, at one of the railway stations, "Russian soldiers went into raptures as each piece of American equipment was unloaded from the trains."

To the surprise of the Americans, most of the work involved in placing the mats was done by Red Army women. In March the Soviets had promised two engineer battalions, each 339 soldiers strong, to help with the reconstruction of the bases. No one expected that the battalions would be largely female. "The airfields were swarming with Russian women laying down the steel mat," remembered Deane. "The girls work at everything," recalled Sergeant Joseph M. Sorenson in an interview for the US Army magazine *Yank* a few months later: "they are truck drivers, snipers, pilots, artillerymen, engineers, antiaircraft gunners, clerks—just everything." The Red Army women were eager to outdo the men, especially American men. When they were told that the norm for a GI was to lay down ten yards of mats per day, they made sure to lay twelve. "It was apparent that there would be no delays on this score," remembered Deane.[11]

■

The Soviets and Americans did their best to overcome differences of language and culture as they worked together. The language gap was not only a hurdle; it was an opportunity for the occasional prank. One of the US personnel taught a Soviet soldier guarding the entrance to headquarters to greet every American officer with the following words: "Good morning, you filthy son of a bitch." The soldier was proud when he said those words: his pronunciation was not perfect, but the message got through. Deane thought such episodes meant that the Soviets and Americans were learning to get along.[12]

Colonel Elliott Roosevelt, who arrived at the Poltava-area air bases in mid-May together with Major General Frederick Anderson, described the Poltava airfield as "little more than the shambles the Nazis had left when they retreated." Like everyone else, he was surprised by the massive employment of manual labor where the Americans would have used machines, and impressed by the work of women in uniform, whom he called "husky Amazons, who thought nothing of tossing around fifty gallon gasoline drums like toys."[13]

The program of Colonel Roosevelt's visit to the Poltava bases included both an inspection of the airfields, and a tour of the city of Poltava, sponsored by Major General Perminov. The city lay in ruins. Poltava and the surrounding area had witnessed a major battle in September 1943, when the Red Army recaptured the region from the retreating Germans. By May 1944, its streets were cleaned of rubble but the surviving structures were still missing window glass and sometimes portions of their walls and roofs. The Soviets counted the losses. Completely or partially demolished were 45 schools, 9 hospitals, and numerous theaters and museums. Also lost was 3.8 million square feet (350,000 square meters) of housing.[14]

One of the first things the Soviets did after the takeover of the city was to build a monument to Stalin, but there were a few old prewar buildings monuments standing. "The city of Poltava was terrible," recalled Soviet airplane technician Vladlen Gribov, assigned with a friend to the Myrhorod air base, as he described his impressions on first visiting the city in mid-April 1944. "We walked the city, searching for at least one building that had remained intact. No! Bare walls with holes where windows had been. Neither roofs nor ceilings. Graves in the city gardens and in the yards. On one of them, a sign: 'Here lie two fighters and a woman brutally tortured by the Germans.' A boy of eight or nine tells us: 'And there is a well into which they threw children!'"[15]

Poltava began in the mid-fifteenth century as an outpost of princely rule on the contested steppe frontier between the local Ukrainian population and the Crimean Tatars. It became famous in the seventeenth and eighteenth centuries as one of the centers of the Ukrainian Cossacks, who created their own state on the banks of the Dnieper River and fought first with the Tatars, then with the Poles, and finally with the Russians, who took control of the region in the mid-seventeenth century. In the early eighteenth century, the pro-independence aspirations of a Cossack leader, Hetman Ivan Mazepa, brought to Poltava Charles XII of Sweden, who counted on Mazepa's support in his war with Peter I of Russia. In June 1709, in what became widely known as the Battle of Poltava, Peter defeated Charles and his Ukrainian supporters. The victory helped Peter win his war with Sweden and set Russia on the path to becoming a European superpower.[16]

The nineteenth century brought a different kind of fame to Poltava. It briefly became the seat of the governor general of "Little Russia"—the name of the former Cossack lands now incorporated into the Russian Empire—and a center of cultural and literary activity. A native son, Ivan Kotliarevsky, produced the first literary works in the modern Ukrainian language. His play *Natalka from Poltava* became a classic of the Ukrainian theater and helped turn the local dialect into the basis of the modern Ukrainian language. The Poltava region was rich enough in local talent to support the development of not one but two literatures. Nikolai Gogol, born near the city of Myrhorod (where one of the US bases was located, of course) laid the foundations of modern Russian prose with *Taras Bulba*, and a collection of short stories with the Russian title *Mirgorod*. The family of another well-known Russian literary figure, Vladimir Korolenko, came from Poltava, where the writer died and was buried in 1921.

Like all American visitors to the city, General Anderson and Colonel Roosevelt were taken to downtown Poltava to tour places of interest and monuments marking the city's memorable dates and honoring its favorite sons. The main attraction was the Corpus Garden, a city park located on the former site of the imperial officers' school and used for public gatherings, concerts, and dances. The Corpus Garden's centerpiece, a monument to the Russian victory of 1709 over the Swedes, was built a century after the battle. The column, topped with the Russian imperial eagle, miraculously survived both the Soviet anti-tsarist campaigns and the German occupation. The marauders only removed the old cannons from the foot of the monument. American servicemen in Poltava included the column in many of the photographs they took.[17]

The American guests were also taken to another city park to see Korolenko's house. All that remained was a tombstone bearing an inscription with Korolenko's name and dates. The house was in ruins, destroyed either by the retreating Germans or advancing Soviets amid the chaos that engulfed the city during the Soviet retreat in 1941 and their return in 1943. All but destroyed by fire was another city landmark—the local museum, designed in the early twentieth century by one of Ukraine's best modern artists, Vasyl Krychevsky. The pseudo-baroque style of the museum was a reminder of the Cossack past of the city and region. Only the walls remained, featuring elements of traditional Ukrainian ornament.[18]

On the streets of Poltava, the Americans saw an impoverished population. War had brought more hardship to a region devastated less than a decade earlier by the 1933 man-made famine caused by the Stalin regime's collectivization of agriculture and the shattering of Ukrainian political and cultural aspirations. Among the hardest-hit regions of Ukraine were those of Poltava, Myrhorod, and Pyriatyn, where the death toll in some villages reached as high as half the population. Altogether, close to four million died in Ukraine between 1932 and 1934. The World War II losses accounted for another seven million, approximately 15 percent of the country's prewar population, making Ukraine proportionally the third most war-ravaged nation after neighboring Belarus and Poland.[19]

Poltava had had a population of almost 130,000 before the start of the German-Soviet war in June 1941. When the Germans, who took control of the city in September 1941, did their own census in May 1942, they counted only 74,000 people. Ukrainians accounted for 93 percent of the population, Russians for more than 5 percent. For the first time in centuries, the minorities did not include Jews, most of whom had been lucky enough to leave the city before the arrival of the Germans. Those who could not leave or decided to stay for family reasons were rounded up and killed—up to 2,000 in the city alone, and approximately 9,000 more in the towns and villages of the region.[20]

Most of those on the streets of Poltava in May 1944 were women, children, and the elderly. Women had accounted for more than 60 percent of the city's population in 1942. Their percentage probably grew, as the Soviets drafted most of the local men into the Red Army after retaking the city in September 1943. Young Poltava women were about to become objects of special attention on the part of American GIs, and the Corpus Garden with its monument would become a rendezvous point for most dates. At the time of Anderson's and Roosevelt's visit to the city, the men of the fourth echelon had finally arrived there after their epic two-month voyage.[21]

Deane, Anderson, and Roosevelt left Poltava for Moscow in the morning of May 15, 1944. Perminov gave a send-off dinner the previous night, with no shortage of food and drink. When the Soviets poured more liquor for dessert, Anderson turned to Deane and asked, "When will this end?" Deane, who was well aware of the tradition of drinking toasts bottoms-up, replied: "This is Mother Russia; wait a bit, it's just getting started." The partying continued.

The friendly atmosphere around the table was put to the test at the end of the dinner, when the Americans were informed that they were not cleared to fly to Teheran, as originally planned. The Soviets wanted them to return to Moscow to talk to General Nikitin and clear up a number of issues raised at the previous meeting. The official reason cited for the cancellation of the flight to Teheran was bad weather. One of the Americans present, Brigadier General Edward Peck Curtis, General Spaatz's chief of staff, was outraged. "Then why don't you forbid us to fly to Berlin when the weather turns bad?" he asked his Soviet counterparts. The Americans began demanding permission to fly directly to Cairo. The Soviets tried to smooth the situation over, claiming that the Americans were important figures, and there was no need to risk their lives.[22]

The minor incident at the dinner table notwithstanding, Deane left Poltava deeply satisfied with the results of the visit. American planes were flying largely unobstructed between the Poltava air bases and Moscow, as well as between Poltava and Teheran. Getting permission from the Soviet Air Force for flights had become routine, although—as usual—the Soviets insisted that their navigators be on board. Visa issues had finally been resolved as well, with the Soviets setting up border posts at the bases. Deane wrote later: "Toward the end of May 1944 the bases were completed and operations were about to start."[23]

Colonel Roosevelt was equally optimistic about the results of the visit. He left the place full of respect for "the vigor with which [the Red Army] overcame obstacles" and "carried away the impression that the Russians were almost childishly eager to get along with us, cooperate with us." Indeed they were.[24]

Part II

THE BATTLES OF POLTAVA

Soft Landing

Bill Lawrence's voice "choked with indignation," wrote John Deane, recalling his conversation with the *New York Times* reporter on the morning of June 1, 1944. Lawrence, a rising star in the US media—he would stay with the *Times* until joining ABC News in 1961 to become the network's evening news anchorman—had good reason to be upset.[1]

Back in March he and his colleague, Harrison Salisbury, a United Press foreign editor and future recipient of the Pulitzer Prize for his journalism, had learned that something important was afoot in military relations between the United States and the Soviet Union. American airmen were arriving in Moscow from Britain in unprecedented numbers, and rumors were circulating among foreign correspondents in Moscow about American plans to supply one hundred B-17 Flying Fortresses to the USSR. Colonel Elliott Roosevelt, who visited Moscow in mid-May, had dinner with seven American correspondents, further fueling speculation about a major new development in Soviet-American relations that involved the US Air Force. From his sources in American diplomatic and military circles, Lawrence eventually learned what was really going on: American shuttle bombing between air bases in Britain, Italy and, now, the Soviet Union was about to start. He and Salisbury began knocking on the doors of the American military mission in Moscow, asking for confirmation and getting ready to file their story.[2]

Deane had a problem. On May 11, during Colonel Roosevelt's visit with Molotov, it was agreed that publicity about the shuttle bombing would come from the Soviet media first. Alerted by Lawrence and Salisbury's inquiries that the news had already been leaked to American and British reporters, Deane offered the journalists a deal. They would be invited to the air bases to see the American airplanes, but only in exchange for silence beforehand. "I had taken them into my confidence and they had agreed to avoid any conjecture stories based on the influx of American personnel," wrote Deane later. He contacted his most powerful ally in the Soviet command, General Nikitin, and through him secured a promise from Molotov's Commissariat of Foreign Affairs to allow American and British reporters to come to Poltava for the arrival of the first Flying Fortresses. But when the time came, the press pool of about thirty reporters learned that only five of them had been cleared by Molotov's commissariat to go to Poltava.

That was what the highly agitated Lawrence was trying to explain to Deane when he called him on June 1. The general immediately got on the phone with officials in Molotov's commissariat. "After a frantic time spent on the telephone calling Foreign Office officials and answering calls from disappointed correspondents, I succeeded in having the quota raised to ten Americans and ten British correspondents," recalled Deane later. But Lawrence, Salisbury, and the rest of the reporters would not take the new deal. They told the Soviets that either all of them were going or none. "The British and American Newspaper Guild staged the first labor strike in Soviet Russia," recalled Deane. "A united front for the first time in Moscow history," wrote Salisbury. About thirty reporters went to the airport, but refused to board the plane until all their colleagues were cleared for the trip. Molotov backed off. "Their action was effective," wrote Deane, "and at noon all of them were put aboard a Soviet plane and sent to Poltava."[3]

The American journalists would soon see and report an exciting development in the history of the Grand Alliance: hundreds of American airplanes were about to land on Soviet-held territory. The war in Europe was entering a new stage. No one knew when D-Day and the opening of the second front in Western Europe would come, but they all knew the day of the opening of a new air front in Eastern Europe. It was Friday, June 2, 1944.

■

Among the Americans eager to witness the arrival of the American airplanes was Kathy Harriman, who "had been living in hopes for the day when I'd see our aircraft land on Soviet soil," as she wrote Mary in early June 1944. On the afternoon of June 1, after bidding farewell to the correspondents leaving for Poltava, Deane stayed at the Moscow airport to welcome back Kathy and her father. They were returning via Italy and Iran from a more than month-long trip to London and Washington. On the way to Spaso House, Deane told them that he was immediately leaving for the "airbase." Harriman right away responded that he was going too. "I just sat quiet and held my breath," recalled Kathy. She was afraid of being left behind, as she assumed that females (she heard a story about female reporters from the West) were not welcome at the top-secret base.

At Spaso House, Kathy, as she later wrote to her sister, "found an opportune moment and suggested perhaps it would be a good idea if I went too." Her father was not pleased and pretended to be surprised by the suggestion, but she was ready to preempt his objection by pointing out that there were female nurses at the base, so that another female presence there should not be a problem. To strengthen her case, she cited top-secret information known to very few at the time: General Ira C. Eaker, commander in chief of the Mediterranean Allied Air Force, which included the US Twelfth and Fifteenth Air Forces, and who had just hosted Harriman and Kathy in Italy, would be leading the first shuttle-bombing mission to the Soviet Union. Kathy had promised Eaker that she would be there to see him land. Harriman's resistance was broken. The two of them would be flying to Poltava.[4]

Tired but excited—they had awoken at 4:30 in the morning in Teheran and flown the whole day, first to Moscow and then to Poltava—the Harrimans reached the air base late in the afternoon of June 1 amid what Kathy described as "the cheers of the assembled air corps and press who'd heard that we'd not be back in time to make it." They were right on time for a concert organized by General Perminov to entertain the Americans and his own troops. "The concert was held in the roofless, wall-less remains of what must have been a largish building," wrote Kathy later. In fact, it was a bombed-out hangar with only two brick walls still standing. The interior was filled with long benches, many built out of the remaining bricks and covered with wooden boards. "The stage had been fixed up with a roof," wrote Kathy, but the benches were in the open. She remembered that the audience was "very enthusiastic."[5]

The cameras of the American and British reporters were already rolling to capture the whole event. Judging by the footage, the Soviets—Red Army servicemen and local participants—performed mostly folk songs and dances, both Russian and Ukrainian. Most of the applause went to the Cossack dancers and a number in which two Red Army soldiers, one standing on the shoulders of the other and both covered with a huge skirt, imitated the dance of an oversized village woman. The biggest hit of all was the Red Army band, especially the drummer. The reporters would soon learn his last name—Gvozd, meaning "nail." He placed his small drum between the legs of an upside-down stool and truly nailed the rhythm of the piece he was performing. The GIs told the reporters that he would be a true find for any jazz band in the United States.[6]

Kathy noted that while the Soviets in the audience clapped to show their appreciation, the Americans whistled. As she wrote, the "cat calling" created "one of the first difficulties we ran into down there on this American-Soviet venture." She continued: "In Russia any form of whistle is the prime way to insult an entertainer and get him off the stage!" Deane recalled a similar episode when a Soviet female dancer had been driven off the stage by whistling GIs. The Americans next to Perminov rushed to explain that in the United States whistling was a sign of utmost approval, and the general passed on that information to the distressed performer. The dancer, as Deane recalled later, "returned at once and shook more muscles than the GI's knew she had. She was thereupon rewarded with a shrill crescendo of whistles that threw her into ecstasies."[7]

Later in the evening, at the dinner hosted by General Perminov, Kathy found herself next to a Soviet general who tried to speak English to her.

When the waiters served stew, the general told Kathy that the meat in it was "cow." She responded that he probably meant "beef," but the general insisted that he meant cow, "the kind you can milk." Kathy decided not to argue with the general, whom she described as a "Siberian," referring to his place of birth and his tough look. "It tasted good anyway," wrote Kathy to her sister. As in all Soviet-American relations at the time, what mattered and overrode everything else was the reason underlying the cooperation. And in early June 1944, the two sides were about to raise that cooperation to a new level.[8]

The next morning, June 2, 1944, Kathy Harriman woke up to a cacophony of sounds. "Aside from the fact I damned near froze to death, I slept wonderfully in between wondering why Ukrainian cocks crow for hours on end and what the hell a full orchestra (brass band) was doing playing in the yard," she wrote. Apparently the drummer Gvozd and his fellow musicians were practicing their skills in preparation for the ceremony welcoming the American airplanes to Poltava. Harriman spent a good part of the morning wandering around the camp, visiting the American nurses in the hospital tent—"trim as a doll house"—and talking to the GIs. "Morale was sky high, firstly I guess because that day exciting things were to happen and secondly because our boys in Russia are sort of a pioneering group," she wrote to her sister two days later.[9]

It was "dark and overcast in Ukraine," recalled John Deane, who had accompanied the Harrimans to Poltava the previous day. He described the mood of that cloudy morning as one of "suppressed excitement—everyone pretending an outward calm to cover the anxiety seething within." Deane and others in the top leadership knew that the bombers and fighters of the Fifteenth Air Force in Italy were supposed to leave their bases early that morning and hit targets in and around the city of Debrecen in Hungary before continuing east and landing in Poltava. But they did not know whether the operation had actually been launched, whether the weather was favorable, and what, if anything, had happened above Debrecen. Radio operators were trying unsuccessfully to get any indication that the operation was under way. Then, at half past twelve, they finally got a message that the Flying Fortresses and the fighters accompanying them had taken off from the Italian bases on time. That meant they might appear above Poltava at any minute.

Deane got into a car and rushed to the concrete-and-metal airstrip—the joint project of the American engineers and the Red Army female soldiers. He arrived just as the Flying Fortresses of the Fifteenth Air Force had begun to appear in the Ukrainian sky. "The sky was filled with them," wrote Deane later, "and huge as they were, they seemed much bigger with their silver wings silhouetted against the black sky above." For Deane, it was a dream come true—after months of hard work punctuated by days and sometimes weeks of frustration. "For an American standing on the field below it was a thrill beyond description," he wrote in recollection. "There in the sky was America at war—these few planes epitomized American power, the skill of American industry and labor, the efficiency of American operations, and the courage of American youth."[10]

Approaching the Poltava base was an armada of B-17 heavy bombers, popularly known as "Flying Fortresses." The four-engine Boeing-made airplane had a crew of ten, a length of more than 74 feet, a wingspan of more than 103 feet, a flying range of 2,000 miles, and could develop a cruising speed of 182 miles per hour. Each plane was armed with thirteen .50-inch M2 Browning machine guns, and on a long-range mission such as the flight to Poltava it could deliver up to 4,500 pounds of bombs. They cost under a quarter million dollars to produce and were worth every penny, as far as the American public was concerned. The Flying Fortress had become the most recognizable American airplane of the war and a symbol of American air power.[11]

The B-17s put on the most impressive air show that the Soviets had ever seen. "They came on, their motors roaring over the field, filling the space of this luscious land, roars rebounding from the ruins of a nearby city, squadron after squadron, until their shapes created castle-like designs in the sky," wrote the Canadian reporter Raymond Arthur Davies. "One received the impression of great power. Then gracefully peeling off from formations, they came down one after another." It took the planes up to two hours to land. The touch-downs were met with a sigh of relief by the Red Army women who had built the runway. "Would it buckle? Had they been careless?" wrote Deane, describing their feelings. He added: "Their relief was audible as the first Fortresses rolled down its entire length."[12]

Kathy Harriman arrived at the airfield in the company of her father and General Perminov. They drove in a Buick, which had some trouble negotiating the rough terrain around the airfield, and made it just in time. "We were driving out to the field when the first bombers appeared as specks off in the horizon," she recalled, "it looked like thousands, then suddenly the first squadron was overheard with its welcome roar." "Jesus—but it was exciting," she wrote Mary, "more so than anything I ever saw in England." Averell Harriman was equally elated, telling his daughter that "he didn't think he'd ever before been so thrilled by anything."

The Harrimans' excitement was shared by Perminov, who was sitting in the back of the Buick next to the ambassador. For Perminov, as for Deane, the arrival of the planes meant the fulfillment of long days and nights of planning, coordination, conflicts, compromises, and occasional small victories. "He bubbled over with joy," wrote Kathy, and went to give her father a kiss. Harriman restrained him, but Perminov "let out a few more Russian equivalents of cowboy hoots." More than anything else, the Soviets were impressed by the strength and order that the American armada displayed to anyone who raised his eyes to the sky, and with the roar of airplane engines, it was difficult not to look up.[13]

The young Soviet airplane technician Vladlen Gribov, who witnessed the arrival of the Flying Fortresses at the Myrhorod air base, where there were no clouds or rain to obscure the airplanes in all their splendor, was particularly impressed by the way in which they approached the base. "I had seen large groups of planes earlier," wrote Gribov years later, "but at a great height and, if they were bombers, then usually in long files. But here the planes flew low, in close formation, with six in each group and more than ten files. The space they occupied seemed to be a kilometer wide and two kilometers long, literally blocking out the sunny sky." The Soviet reporters were no less impressed. To them, the way in which the planes approached the air bases after completing a long raid was proof of the mastery of the American airmen. "Having flown a long distance over the countries of Europe, the bombers proceeded in strict formation, which attests to the great expertise of the pilots, their teamwork and first-rate organization," wrote *Pravda* (Truth), the main mouthpiece of the Stalin regime, a few days later.[14]

■

That was exactly the impression that General Eaker, commander of the Mediterranean Allied Air Force, wanted to make on his Soviet allies. As planned, he led the bombers of the Fifteenth Air Force in person on their mission to Ukraine.

Altogether 200 planes and more than 1,400 men took off from the Italian airfields early in the morning of June 2, 1944 with the goal of bombing targets in Hungary. The real goal of the Eaker task force was not so much to bomb Debrecen as to impress Poltava. "It is imperative that we gain the full confidence and respect of the Russians by starting our collaboration with an efficiently executed operation of immediate significance to them," wrote Eaker in his planning report on the mission. As it was assumed that the Poltava bases did not yet have adequate facilities for serious repairs to damaged airplanes, it was suggested that the task force avoid unnecessary confrontation with the Luftwaffe. In fact, the rest of the Fifteenth Air Force that was employed over the Balkans that day had the task of distracting German attention from the Poltava force, allowing it to achieve its bombing objective with minimal losses. The air route to Ukraine was chosen expressly to avoid German flak batteries as much as possible.[15]

From the start, the first shuttle mission, dubbed *Frantic Joe*, was meant to be more symbolic than substantial. With Stalin and Molotov having dragged their feet all the way to May 1944, many of the original goals of the *Baseball* and *Frantic* operations had been rendered all but obsolete. By then the Allied air forces had all but annihilated whatever threat the invasion might face from the Luftwaffe. In early June the Allied command had at its disposal up to 12,000 planes that could be sent into battle over Europe, to be countered by 300 German planes—a ratio of more than 40:1. The outcome of the air war was clear even before it began.[16]

Unexpectedly, choosing the targets to be bombed during the first mission had become anything but an easy task. Negotiations had begun in early May, with the Americans suggesting the bombing of the Heinkel airplane plants near Riga in Latvia and Mielec in Poland. The US Air Force wanted to use shuttle bombing mainly to achieve its original goal—that of crippling the Luftwaffe and the German air industry. The Soviets, more concerned with the German mechanized divisions on the Eastern Front, wanted to leave them without gasoline and suggested that the Americans bomb the Ploesti oil fields in Romania. In England, USSTAF Commander Spaatz was glad to oblige and added the oil refineries to the bombing list, suggesting also the marshaling yards in Lviv, Brest, Vilnius, and Kaunas, all in close proximity to the German battle lines on the Eastern Front. To Spaatz and Deane's surprise the Soviets refused to approve the target list or to supply one of their own, and negotiations stalled.

The Red Army commanders were getting ready to launch a major offensive code-named *Bagration* in Belarus. It would result in the Red Army's advance all the way to the borders of East Prussia, and Deane suggested to Spaatz that the Soviets did not want to attribute any part of their expected achievement to the results of American bombing. He also believed that the Soviets did not trust the Americans and did not want them to know where the main thrust of their attack would take place. "The three targets originally selected by Spaatz," wrote Deane later, "were distributed at equal distances across the Russian front. The Russian attack when finally launched had its main effort in the north, and for this reason they did not want an American attack on Riga which would attract German fighter aircraft to that area. They could not tell us this without revealing the plans for their offensive."

Deane suggested that Spaatz select the first targets on his own and, instead of asking the Soviets for approval, simply inform them what they would be. That would not oblige the Soviets to show their hand in any way. Deane turned out to be right: when Spaatz named the marshaling yards at Debrecen as the first target for *Frantic Joe*, the Soviets did not protest. Hitting targets in Hungary would distract the Germans from the main offensive in the north. The operation was in their interest, but for reasons of secrecy the Soviets were not object to say either yes or no.[17]

General Eaker, who of course had decided to lead the mission in person to ensure that everything went according to plan, selected some of the best units of the Fifteenth Air Force to take part. It was scheduled for the first day in June with favorable weather. Four bomber groups—the 2nd, 97th, 99th, and 483rd, for a total of 130 B-17 aircraft—were allocated for the mission. The famed Flying Fortresses, which had been a standard part of the air arsenal since 1938, were protected on the flight to Ukraine by a much more recent acquisition of the US Air Force, the P-51 long-range Mustang fighters, which had gone into service in January 1942.

The Mustangs were operated by one pilot, and had a length of 32 feet, a cruising speed of 362 miles per hour, and a flying range of 1,650 miles. Their production cost was less than a quarter of that required for a B-17— about $50,000—and their main task was to protect the Flying Fortresses on their strategic bombing missions with their six 0.50 caliber machine guns. As of March 1944, the Mustangs carried drop gas tanks that increased their range of operations, making it possible to undertake a lengthy mission, like the one to Poltava. There were seventy P-51 Mustang fighters in the 325th Fighter Group.[18]

The ultimate destination of the task force had been kept secret from the pilots and crews, leading them to speculate that they might be going anywhere in German-controlled Europe. When the destination was finally revealed to them immediately before takeoff, the pilots had welcomed the news with happy whistles. They were told to be on their best behavior at the Soviet bases. "Impressions created will color the thinking of the entire Russian military establishment and set the stage for future relations," read the instructions. "Our performance will be the yardstick by which the Russians will judge the fighting capabilities, the discipline, the morale and the energy of the whole of the American forces, Ground, Naval, and Air."[19]

General Eaker flew to Poltava in a B-17 known as "Yankee Doodle II," decorated with an image of the beloved American figure and the musical score of the song. The aircraft was part of the 97th Bomber Group, in which Eaker had flown his first bombing mission from Britain to Germany in August 1942. The bombers had taken off before 7:00 a.m. from bases near Foggia in Italy, grouped into formation over the Adriatic and crossed Yugoslavia, encountering neither enemy fighters nor flak. Unobstructed, they dropped their bomb load on the locomotive depot and marshaling yards of Debrecen, hitting their targets. At that point they were joined by the P-51 fighters and set their course over the Carpathian Mountains toward the Dnieper River.

The only flak that the task force had encountered was near the city of Chernivtsi in the Bukovyna region of Ukraine. The fire was highly inaccurate but there were still losses: an engine on one of the Flying Fortresses caught fire, causing the plane to explode. It was gone in a split second—the pilots of B-17s nearby saw no parachutes after the explosion. The casualties, apart from the ten-man crew, included a P-51 pilot who was flying to Poltava as a passenger. A number of planes returned to Italy after experiencing mechanical problems. For the American doctors and nurses at Poltava, the day was uneventful when it came to their direct duties. The only patient they got to treat was a pilot who suffered an attack of appendicitis.[20]

The first plane to touch down on the Poltava runway was General Eaker's Yankee Doodle. It stopped in front of the receiving party of American and Soviet generals led by Averell Harriman. Eaker emerged from the plane and walked toward the welcoming party, paying no attention to the drizzling rain, to receive their greetings and smiles. Eaker's name was supposed to be kept secret from the general public until he was safely back in Italy. Had a commander of his stature suffered an accident, neither the Americans nor the Soviets wanted it to be associated with the shuttle bombing and cast a shadow over their first joint air operation. Thus, when writing to her sister, Kathy Harriman referred to Eaker as "our ex-host from Naples" and "our big boy." The Canadian reporter Raymond Arthur Davies called him a "high-ranking U.S. officer" in his news story.

Immediately on approaching the welcoming party, General Eaker presented General Perminov with the medal of the Legion of Merit and read the citation. Clearly moved, Perminov responded, as Deane later recalled, by giving all credit for the preparation of the bases to his American counterpart, Colonel Alfred Kessler. He also praised the pilots, stating, according to one news report, that "today's operation was most brilliantly carried out." Perminov's staff presented Eaker with a bouquet of flowers, "a usual Russian custom when a general enters a town victorious," wrote Kathy, who also received a bouquet. The photos taken at the ceremony show a reserved but happy Eaker and a broadly smiling Kathy. Deane made a brief speech, hailing *Frantic Joe* as a landmark event in Soviet-American cooperation. "Then we stood around for a while everyone was swapping short snorters [signatures of fellow travelers], pictures were taken... and the bombers continued to land," wrote Kathy.[21]

The happy occasion did not pass without an accident of sorts. General Slavin—a Soviet military intelligence officer and Deane's liaison with the General Staff, who had flown to Poltava on the same plane as Deane and the Harrimans the previous day—not only did not make it into the pictures but missed the ceremony altogether. As there had been no news about the American shuttle mission and General Slavin had nothing to do around the base, he took an afternoon nap, awakened only by the sound of the arriving bombers. By the time he realized what was going on, everyone had already left the tent camp for the airfield, and the general had to run to make it in time for the ceremony. He did not get farther than an American sentry guarding the approaches to the field. "The red trimmings of the General Staff inspired none of the fear in our sentries' hearts that it did in those of Red Army soldiers," remembered Deane. When Slavin finally arrived at the airstrip, he "attacked Perminov with such a heat that I thought he would have apoplexy," recalled Deane. His Legion of Merit medal aside, Perminov was clearly worried about the consequences of the incident, and Deane did his best to assume American responsibility for the misunderstanding.[22]

If Slavin's outburst spoiled Perminov's day, other Americans and Soviets were in a celebratory mood. Raymond Arthur Davies and other reporters in the crowd interviewed Americans on the base and the arriving pilots, who were being debriefed in a tent next to the one assigned to the correspondents. They were jubilant. "I have never seen a more friendly attitude," commented Lieutenant Albert M. Jaroff from Portland, Oregon. "Russian warmth towards Americans," he said, "is unequaled anywhere in the world." He added: "We aren't just here to fight Germans [but to] represent America like diplomats." Jaroff was an Air Force intelligence officer who had arrived in Poltava a few weeks earlier with the fourth echelon and was assigned to the Myrhorod air base. His family originally came from Odesa in southern Ukraine, and he was clearly happy to be back in his ancestral homeland, fighting the common enemy.

Davies also described the meeting of two brothers, Igor and George McCartney, who had not seen each other for more than a year. "The door opened," wrote Davies. "A young private stepped out. Just as his leg left the upper rung of the short aluminum ladder, he looked at a bunch of fellows standing nearby. His eyes widened. 'George!' he shouted. George was in the crowd, but he thought someone else was wanted. He turned around and was about to walk away when the lad from the plane jumped to the ground and ran towards him. 'George! George!' he kept on shouting. 'George, don't you know me?' George stopped, looked, then rushed to the newcomer. 'Igor! Igor!' he cried. They embraced. A little later the two boys, surrounded by correspondents, were telling their story." They had been born in Harbin to a Russo-Ukrainian family fleeing the Russian Revolution, got their Irish last name from their stepfather, and enlisted in the US Army, one in December 1942, the other in February 1943. They had not seen each other since then. "How do you like the Soviet Union?" asked Davies. "It's just like home to us," both replied at once.[23]

Happiness and excitement were the order of the day. "Every one of us is glad to be here," said the twenty-two-year-old Charles Williamson of Norfolk, Virginia, who, according to Davies, had already participated in 47 combat missions, 12 more than required at the time for a bomber pilot to complete the tour of duty and be reassigned to a training base. "It certainly was a wonderful day and I do not imagine I will forget it for a long time," wrote Kathy to Mary a few days later. She left Poltava for Moscow together with her father and Generals Eaker and Deane late in the afternoon of June 2.[24]

The photos and footage taken on that memorable day by the American photographers and film crews show the rest of the American senior officers being led on a tour of Poltava by General Perminov, all dressed in trench coats, supporting the recollections of participants that June 2 was an unusually cold day by Ukrainian standards, although there is no sign of rain in the photos. The weather did not seem to matter. "The day our first landings were made marked the high tide of our military relations with the Soviet Union," wrote Deane a few years later. The drizzling rain notwithstanding, in their minds the sun was shining brightly on the future of Soviet-American cooperation.[25]

6

Comrades in Arms

In late May 1944, soon after returning to London from his trip to Moscow and Poltava, Colonel Elliott Roosevelt and a member of his traveling party, Brigadier General Edward Peck Curtis, were invited to an evening of bridge with the supreme Allied commander in Europe, General Dwight Eisenhower. As the president's son later recalled, he and Curtis went down "in ignominious defeat before the deadly efficiency of Ike Eisenhower." Eisenhower and his aide Harry Butcher, however, were interested in more than a game of bridge. As Roosevelt recalled, they were "pumped dry" with questions about their Soviet trip.

"What was it like? What was their army like? How were their fliers? How was their discipline? What did they think of us?" Those were the questions that interested the supreme Allied commander. He wanted to know not only what the political leaders and military commanders in Moscow were saying and thinking about the Americans but the prevailing attitudes among the officers and soldiers of the Red Army. "The big thing for all of them," answered Roosevelt, "is still the second front. That's the one big test of what they think of us. If it comes off, okay. If not…." "If, what is this if?" interrupted Eisenhower. When the president's son explained that he had in mind the promises given to Stalin by his father and Churchill at Teheran, Eisenhower told him that he knew nothing about those promises. He then added: "But I know about the invasion of France. The Russians needn't worry about that one."[1]

The Allied cross-channel invasion of Europe began in the early morning of June 6, 1944, four days after Eaker's Fifteenth Air Force bombers and fighters had safely arrived at the Poltava airfield. Around midnight British summer time, the Royal Air Force started dropping dummies behind the Wehrmacht's defensive lines to distract and confuse German anti-paratrooper detachments. One hour later real paratroopers began their descent on German-held territory. An hour after that, around 2:00 a.m., General Spaatz's Strategic Air Forces in Europe joined the British assault and began their bombing raids across the Channel. Altogether 2,200 American, British, and Canadian bombers took part in the invasion.

Around 3:00 a.m., under cover of darkness, the first US ships began dropping anchor near Omaha Beach. At 5:30 a.m. the Allied battleships started the bombardment of German coastal defenses. General Eisenhower's grand armada of ships and landing craft, numbering more than 5,500 vessels with more than 150,000 troops on board, began the invasion of France. Despite heavy casualties—4,000 men killed and more than 6,000 wounded—the invasion was a great success. The bridgeheads established on the first day and extended afterward made it possible to deploy 875,000 men to the new European front by the end of June 1944. The second front everyone had been talking about for so long was finally there. The airmen on the Poltava-area bases were prepared to help move it eastward. But before that could happen, the new comrades in arms would have to learn how to live and fight together.[2]

When John Deane, now in Moscow, first heard about the Allied landing in Normandy, he reacted to the news with the same sense of jubilation and relief felt by so many others. He had more than one reason to feel happy.

In the previous months he had been under constant pressure to convince his Soviet contacts that the Americans actually meant what they had said at Teheran, where Roosevelt had promised Stalin an invasion of Europe in May. In February 1944, in the middle of crucial negotiations on the Poltava bases, Deane had sought to overcome Soviet skepticism by betting General Slavin twelve bottles of vodka that the invasion would take place in May. "I think this did more to convince the General Staff of the firmness of our plans than did the promise of Churchill and Roosevelt." As D-Day was postponed to June, Deane had to pay his debt to Slavin. That alleviated the tension, but not by much. With the invasion now a reality, Deane could finally feel rehabilitated. He put on his uniform and walked to the US embassy, expecting to be cheered by the Muscovites. To his disappointment, no one paid any attention to the American general in the streets; most Russians would probably have been unable to recognize a US uniform.[3]

In Poltava and other US bases in Ukraine the US pilots got news of the invasion around 9:00 a.m. local time. Raymond Davies, who had stayed at the base after the arrival of the American Flying Fortresses four days earlier, recounted the moment in one of his reports: "A transport plane roared onto the field at the American base and an excited pilot rushed out shouting 'Hey, fellows, it's here. We've invaded Europe.'" As it turned out, the news came not from the Allied command or the American or British media, which were silent, but from the Germans. Berlin radio announced at 6:48 a.m. London time that Allied paratroopers were landing in France. Hitler was still asleep at his Berghof retreat in the Bavarian Alps, and his generals were reluctant to use reserves without the Führer's command. But the news had already broken for the rest of the world to evaluate and draw its own conclusions.

At Poltava, the radio operators turned on their equipment and heard the bulletin from Berlin, followed by confirmation from the headquarters of the Fifteenth Air Force in Italy. Then the British broadcast Winston Churchill's speech to Parliament in London delivered that afternoon. He declared that 4,000 ships had taken part in the invasion and that the Allies had 11,000 aircraft at their disposal to support the landing. "The battle that has now begun will grow constantly in scale and in intensity for many weeks to come, and I shall not attempt to speculate upon its course," declared Churchill. "This I may say, however. Complete unity prevails throughout the Allied Armies. There is a brotherhood in arms between us and our friends of the United States."[4]

The news was widely discussed at the base. Some doubted that the numbers cited by Churchill were accurate, and with reason. The number of aircraft cited was part of a propaganda effort to intimidate the Germans and lift spirits at home. In reality, the Allies had roughly 4,000 aircraft in the air. Still, the mood was on the whole upbeat. Lieutenant Colonel Slusar, who heard the news on his return from a bombing run, told his Soviet interlocutors that he had returned to the base in an excellent mood because he had shot down a German fighter but was even happier to learn about the opening of the second front. He was ready to go back into battle immediately, despite being tired from his previous flight. First Lieutenant John L. Fredericks thought that the opening of the second front was long overdue and expected the war to be over by late 1944, or early 1945 at the latest—a view that was widely shared for a time. "Guess we will be going home soon," overheard Davies, a young navigator who had flown to Poltava from Italy a few days earlier.[5]

Soviet reaction to the news was not as exuberant as American, but overall very positive as well. Palmer Myhra, a young radar operator who doubled as a gunner on one of the bombing raids and got the news while in the air, remembered later: "All was in celebratory mood that day, but it did not seem to impress the Soviets very much.... To the Soviets it was probably another day in the war." Davies had a more positive assessment of the Soviet reaction. He wrote that the young Ukrainian women working at the base's kitchen greeted the news with skepticism. Only when they realized that Davies and other reporters spreading the news were serious did they exclaim: "How good, how wonderful!" Their enthusiasm was shared by most of the Red Army soldiers and officers. "Now, together, we will give the Germans hell," enthused a Red Army private. A young lieutenant echoed him: "Nothing can stop us anymore!" Everyone was excited and wanted details. Information was scarce, but it was clear that the invasion had begun and was progressing. Allied victory was now in sight.[6]

That night Raymond Davies flew back to Moscow to report on the reaction to D-Day there. He was told by fellow reporters that in Moscow the news had been announced from loudspeakers. "At a corner near the Hotel Metropole, where the correspondents reside, about twenty people stopped to listen," wrote Davies. "Then as the first words of the announcer began to come over, people dropped everything and hundreds rushed across the street, counter to traffic regulations and formed a solid group listening in silence. They shook hands, some embraced, and all raced to their offices or homes to spread the news."[7]

Kathy Harriman, also back to Moscow, met that day with Soviet cultural officials to plan an exhibition of American photographs. The meeting turned into a celebration of the news from France. US embassy officials were toasted in the restaurants that evening. The American diplomats noticed a profound change in the tone of the Soviet press around the time of the Normandy landing. The "chary praise and criticism" of the Allies, who were allegedly dragging their feet on the second front, was now replaced with expressions of "admiration and appreciation," wrote Maxwell M. Hamilton, a member of the US embassy staff, in a report to Washington. Stalin himself could not have been more cheerful when he welcomed Averell Harriman to his office on June 19. "We are going along a good road," he told the American ambassador.[8]

■

On June 6, the day of the Normandy invasion, 104 B-17 Flying Fortresses and 45 P-51 Mustangs took off from the Poltava-area bases for Galați in Romania, their target being the German airfield nearby. It was the first American bombing mission to be launched from Soviet territory.

A few days earlier, General Eaker had convinced the Soviet air command to allow his planes to bomb the target they had wanted to hit all along—the German airplane factory in the Polish city of Mielec, halfway between Lviv and Krakow. Eaker was happy to mention that agreement to Molotov when he and Harriman met with the Soviet foreign commissar on June 5; Molotov gave his tacit approval. But bad weather stood in the way—Central Europe was overcast, so the bombers instead flew south to Galați, still going after Luftwaffe targets. With more than 200 tons of bombs dropped on the target, the mission was declared a success. The Flying Fortresses returned to the Ukrainian bases with no losses at all. Two Mustang fighters did not make it back, although the American pilots shot down six German fighters.[9]

That the first air raid from Soviet territory was undertaken on the same day as the Normandy landing gave an additional boost to American morale. There were strategic advantages as well. "Presence of your force in Russia more important at this point than returning to Italy," cabled General Spaatz in London to Eaker at Poltava on June 7. He wanted the American bombers to stay, wait for better weather, and try to bomb Mielec. At stake was more than an attack on a Luftwaffe airplane factory: Spaatz wanted to keep Eaker in the Soviet Union, threatening from the east at a time when the Germans needed every available aircraft in France to fight off the Allied invasion. The Soviets did not object. The American bombers and fighters would stay, with Operation *Frantic Joe* lasting until June 11, 1944, nearly nine full days[10]

Eaker took the opportunity to make one more trip to Moscow. At a reception hosted by Ambassador Harriman in honor of Air Force officers who had participated in the planning and execution of the shuttle-bombing operations, he bestowed the Order of the Legion of Merit on the two highest-ranking Red Air Force officers involved in *Frantic*, the commander of the Soviet military Air Force, Marshal Novikov, and his deputy, General Nikitin, who had contributed most to the success of the operation. With the second front opened and the first shuttle-bombing operation a success, the mood was sky-high in Moscow and Washington alike. "We were sure that the accord thus attained would spread to other fields of military collaboration," wrote John Deane later.[11]

With the excitement of the arrival receding into the past and bad weather still preventing any further missions, American life at the bases began settling into a routine. The Soviets did their best to entertain the American guests by holding concerts that featured Red Army performers and local folk ensembles, as well as dances. The official historian of the 15th Air Force, Major James Parton, who came to the Poltava air base on June 2 and, like everyone else, was stranded there for the next nine days, wrote that with little to do, the crews "lolled in the warm sun, played softball in the thick clover, ambled curiously through the ruined towns, flirted with the few American nurses, made a few tentative approaches to the somewhat meaty Russian girls, griped about the plain food and went to bed early."

Those Americans who manned the ground crews at the three airfields had more time and opportunity to get acquainted with the life around them than did the pilots. Those who came from farms, like Palmer Myhra, found it interesting to compare living and working conditions in Ukraine with those back home. "The houses in most cases were small, consisting of maybe two rooms with sleeping room up above," wrote Myhra decades later. "The walls were often decorated with pictures or religious icons." Myhra found that houses also had a picture of Lenin, Stalin, Engels, or Marx and assumed that it was something mandated by the state.[12]

A big surprise to the Americans was the depth of the Ukrainian black soil. Myhra's friend Donald Barber, who had grown up in South Dakota, told him with astonishment that he had seen "some men digging a hole four or five feet deep, all black dirt." He now understood why Ukraine was called the "breadbasket of Europe." However, neither Myhra nor Barber was impressed by the attitude of the locals toward working that rich land. "Under their collective farm system farmers didn't put in as much interest or effort as they would have if they owned the land," wrote Myhra. Another surprise was the lack of mechanization. While watching local women marching to the fields every morning with hoes on their shoulders, Myhra could not help but recall his own farm. "I would think of my father back home in Wisconsin with his little Ford tractor producing more than all those who used a hoe," wrote Myhra. Once he saw the locals using a repaired German tank to do the plowing.[13]

Then there were cultural pecularities. "American flyers," wrote Parton, "registered mild surprise at seeing Russian soldiers dancing together; Russians showed equal surprise at US jitter-bugging." Through daily interaction, the two sides were discovering similarities and differences. The Soviets found the Americans open, eager to make friends, and ready to exchange almost anything they had for a souvenir: a red star from a soldier's uniform, metal buttons with Soviet symbols, cigarette lighters and cigarette cases. Some Americans were surprised by Soviet drinking habits. "It seemed that the more you could drink and still stand on your feet to the Russians especially, the more you were a 'real man,'" wrote Myhra. That was just the beginning of their gradual acquaintance.[14]

The two groups of Allied soldiers that cooperated most closely were the technicians who serviced the planes. Each Soviet crew consisted of three technicians—an assistant crew chief and two helpers—assigned to a given plane. They were led by an American crew chief. Other groups of technicians, including radar operators and weathermen, also collaborated closely. Some Americans were truly impressed with the qualifications of their Soviet partners. Sergeant Franklyn Holzman, the man code-named "Tourist" by the KGB during his 1958 visit, was then a twenty-three-year-old from Brooklyn with a degree in economics from the University of North Carolina. He was assigned as a radar technician to Myrhorod, where he worked alongside a Soviet lieutenant whom he found "brilliant." "Only 27, and he is an electrical engineer," wrote Holzman in a letter home. "We got to talk about music and discovered he was very much interested in Beethoven and Schubert chamber music as I am."[15]

Of course, not everyone on the American or Soviet side was as educated or as fond of classical music as Holzman and his Soviet friend, but they all found ways to communicate and work together. The Americans were initially skeptical about the skills of the Soviets, since Soviet airplanes were hardly a match in technical features: while the Soviets were getting American airplanes through Lend-Lease, Flying Fortresses and Mustangs were not part of the deal. The Soviet mechanics often felt that they were looked down upon by their American counterparts. "Building an air base, providing fuel, loading bombs—that the Russians can do. But the technical side, complex modern aviation technology, is beyond them," wrote Yulii Malyshev, one of the Red Army assistant crew chiefs at the Myrhorod base, trying to describe the American evaluation of Soviet capabilities.[16]

The Soviets were truly impressed by the instruments that the Americans brought along, their abundance of spare parts, and their professionalism, but they considered themselves more resourceful. Malyshev surprised his American supervisor by replacing an engine carburetor single-handed, although the task usually required more than one person. The American showed his appreciation by bringing the rest of the American mechanics, including officers, to show them what Malyshev had accomplished. The Soviets also believed that they were more committed to the job than the Americans. They were surprised to see Americans breaking for lunch and supper without finishing the job they were working on. Soviet standards were different: a mechanic had no right to leave the plane before the job was finished. Before coming to Myrhorod, Malyshev had once spent two days and nights on a plane, sleeping and eating there until the job was done.[17]

Malyshev's colleague at Myrhorod, Vladlen Gribov, who served as an assistant crew chief under an American sergeant named Tommy, shared his friend's opinion about the Americans as good professionals who nevertheless worked "without commitment," and for whom "the supply of food was more important than the task at hand." Given the scarcity of everything in the Soviet Union at the time, Gribov considered the Americans profligate and wasteful. "It turned out that the casing on the nose gun of one of the first planes was torn," recalled Gribov later, "I began sewing it up. When the job was done, Tommy, praising my work, noted that we could have done without it and just changed the casing." That was just the beginning. More than once, Tommy stopped Gribov from doing what he had been trained to do in a Soviet technical school: when a device malfunctioned, to disassemble it, identify the problem, manufacture a new part in the repair shop, and put the device back together. Gribov eventually got used to that.[18]

Both Gribov and Malyshev, young sergeants who had grown up in Moscow and belonged to the first generation shaped by Soviet education, believed in the superiority of their political and economic system. "Almost all of us had been thoroughly propagandized to make us absolutely certain of the rightness, justice, and 'bestness' of our system and cause," recalled Gribov, whose first name, Vladlen, was a combination of the first syllables of the first and last names of Vladimir Lenin. "There was no need for any doubts about us: we could have propagandized anyone at all," echoed Malyshev. Observing what they considered to be American wastefulness and their abundant supply not only of spare parts for airplanes but also clothing, flashlights, snacks, chewing gum, and other things that the Soviets had never seen, the two friends saw this not as an indication of the inferiority of the Soviet economic system but of the impact of the war.

Nevertheless, meeting and working hand in hand with the Americans shook some of the Soviet postulates ingrained in the consciousness of the young Soviet mechanics. "We knew," recalled Gribov, "that in 'their' armies it was the workers and peasants who did the grunt work, while the bourgeois held officer rank." But Gribov soon discovered that his American supervisor, Tommy, came from a farm family that owned as much land and equipment as an entire Soviet collective farm, and yet he was serving in the military as an enlisted man, not as an officer. The young Soviet technicians were also shocked to observe American soldiers talking to their officers as equals without standing at attention, often saluting informally and casually, wearing similar uniforms, and sharing the same food. The army of the bourgeois superpower was more egalitarian in relations between the ranks than that of the first "worker-peasant" state.[19]

Living in a country that had allegedly solved the nationality question but still divided its population into nationalities and singled out entire ethnic groups, such as the Volga Germans, for punishment and resettlement, Gribov was surprised to realize how multiethnic the US Army was. He could not believe that Tommy's friend Bill Drum was an ethnic German. "After all, we were at war with the Germans," explained Gribov later. "But there he was, a German." The only feature that seemingly fitted the Soviet propaganda image of Americans was their attitude toward African Americans. There were no black soldiers permanently stationed at the base. Decades later, Gribov remembered disparaging expressions on the faces of his American acquaintances when they saw the image of a smiling black boy on the cover of a tin of tooth powder—the Soviet designers had wanted to show the effectiveness of the powder by contrasting the boy's white teeth with his dark skin.[20]

Since the effort with the Americans was as much about cooperation as about competition, the Soviet command wanted to show that its soldiers were dressed and supplied as well as, or at least no worse than, the Americans. Old-style military boots worn with cotton puttees were replaced with a new

Soviet product whose inventors got a Stalin Prize—jackboots made of a featherlight material—but it was no match for American army boots, which the Soviet soldiers regarded with envy. Nonetheless the Red Army officers at Poltava did their best to persuade the Americans that jackboots were superior to the American boots, as they were allegedly more comfortable, better protected ankles from moisture, and kept feet and trousers cleaner. After a conference with their Soviet counterparts, the American surgeons requested 400 pairs of leather jackboots from the US Army suppliers.[21]

The Soviet Air Force officers and technicians assigned to the Poltava-area bases were thus better off than at any other of their wartime postings. They received two uniforms—an unheard-of luxury by the standards of the time—and got brand-new linens. They took pride in making their beds in such a way that the straw-filled mattress, shaped by a specially designed wooden box, would keep its shape for a whole day. Neatness and cleanliness in Soviet barracks and tents was enforced by the officers and punctiliously maintained by the soldiers, who were therefore shocked by the messy, cluttered American tents. "The beds were made any old way; things lay about where they were left. Wrapping and packaging, illustrated magazines, pocket books all over the place," recalled Gribov, his disapproval still obvious decades later.[22]

The Americans, for their part, were appalled by sanitary conditions at the base canteens. "[I]t was found that the Russians do not believe in the use of soap for washing dishes and kitchen utensils, asserting that it caused diarrhea," wrote a shocked Major Parton. "Instead they used a 3 percent soda solution and a greasy towel." The Americans sounded the alarm as early as April 1944, when they discovered that the kitchens had no refrigeration facilities and food was stored in open containers, unprotected from dust and myriad flies and insects. The Soviets tried to improve the kitchen and dining facilities but found it a difficult task. In May the US medical officer Captain Robert H. Newell complained about poor ventilation in the kitchens, which were full of smoke from the wood-fired stoves. Another concern was kitchen refuse and food leftovers, which the Soviets collected in huge, foul-smelling wooden barrels and then dumped into a ditch not far from the kitchen. "Rats and rodents have free access and exit to all rooms of the mess," wrote Newell in his report.[23]

Some of the American pilots would refuse to take food after noticing that the kitchen staff failed to wash their hands after visiting the Soviet-style latrines. Captain Newell, who found the beds and bedding perfectly satisfactory, reported that the latrines were in a "deplorable state." He was echoed by Parton, who wrote in June 1944 that "If the Russian kitchen may be termed bad, their latrines can only be called indescribable." The Americans refused to use the Soviet latrines, which consisted of a row of holes in the floor, often covered with excrement. They demanded the construction of new facilities, though the only type of latrine the Soviets could build was already on display. Eventually the Americans gave up and built their own latrines at each of the Poltava-area bases. They could do nothing about the latrine facilities in Kharkiv, Kyiv, and other Soviet-run bases, which the Americans visited from time to time.

For the locals and Red Army soldiers, among whom the American medics frequently observed bad teeth and signs of malnutrition, poor sanitation was coupled with inadequate medical care. According to the chief American surgeon at the bases, Lieutenant Colonel William M. Jackson, it was fifty years behind American standards. Jackson set up separate hospital facilities on each base, staffed by American personnel. Captain Newell wrote in his report of April 1944: "The Soviet standards of diet and sanitation are so vastly different from those of the American people that little change can be prognosticated." Major Parton quipped in his report that "bathing among the local populace appeared to be at best a biennial event."[24]

The Soviets tried hard to deal with the problems pointed out to them by the Americans, although matters of sanitation and personal hygiene were embarrassing to address. Some Americans turned the Red Army soldiers' poor hygiene to their advantage. Private First Class Martin Kloski from Jersey City told American military reporters that "Russian women keep things very clean. They manage somehow, although there's hardly any soap.

Russian men, though, are another story. I figure that the fact that we kept clean, and that our uniforms were neat, is one of the big reasons we made a hit with the gals."[25]

Colonel Kessler was pleased. "GIs walk around the town just as they walk around London," remarked the American commander. Less pleased were the secret-police officers at the Poltava headquarters of the People's Commissariat of State Security (NKGB), the civil security service that monitored the attitude of the local population to the presence of Americans. They spotted some Americans attending church services, which was barely tolerated in the USSR. Others shared with the locals their impressions of comparative living standards in the United States and the Soviet Union, which were anything but in favor of the latter. "You do five dollars' worth of work, and you could live perfectly well on that in America, but here, for that amount, you wouldn't be able to buy a kilogram of bread," one of the American servicemen allegedly told a secret-police informer. He continued: "America is really heaven on earth; here there's nothing but suffering."

■

Especially worrisome to the authorities was the attitude of the locals to the Americans and the hopes they cherished in connection with their arrival. Ukraine had been a problem for the Soviets ever since the Revolution of 1917, when its political and intellectual elites pushed for independence from Russia and created a state of their own. The Soviets managed to crush Ukrainian resistance only by making major concessions to local cadres and agreeing to support the native language and culture. The Soviet Union was created in 1922 as a quasi-federal structure largely to pacify the Ukrainians and Georgians. It gave both rebellious republics and a score of other Soviet nations a degree of autonomy that they would lose with the consolidation of the Stalin regime.

In the early 1930s Stalin starved close to four million Ukrainians, along with millions of other Soviet citizens, in his attempt to collectivize agriculture. As noted earlier, Poltava, Myrhorod, and Pyriatyn were among the areas of Ukraine that suffered most from the famine. Stalin took advantage of the crisis to attack the Ukrainian party cadres and launch an assault on the nation's cultural revival. Ukrainians living outside Ukraine and constituting the largest national minority in Russia proper were reregistered as Russians almost overnight. Contemporaries speak of those events as a Ukrainian genocide.[26]

As the Third Reich invaded Ukraine in 1941, many locals wanted to see the German divisions as portents of the arrival of European civilization and long-awaited liberation from Stalin's brutal rule. Many used the occasion to reclaim their non-Soviet identity and restore a Ukrainian Orthodox Church independent of Moscow. Although the Germans allowed that, they went on to establish a reign of terror in Ukraine. The main victims were Jews: close to a million Jewish men, women, and children, or every sixth Jew who died in the Holocaust, came from Ukraine. Young Ukrainians were hunted down to be sent to labor camps in Germany, producing a huge forced emigration—2.2 million Ukrainians ended up there by 1944. Ukrainian nationalists, briefly tolerated in 1941, also fell victim to the German regime as their leaders were killed and their followers driven underground.[27]

By the time the Red Army came back to Ukraine in 1943, there were few believers in German liberation, but the population did not forget or forgive the Soviet atrocities of the revolutionary and interwar eras. Well aware of this, the Soviet authorities were concerned that Ukrainians had been exposed to anticommunist propaganda during the German occupation and were now anything but loyal to the Soviet regime. With the arrival of the Americans, foreigners of a different brand, the secret police was all eyes and ears.

"The anti-Soviet element, mostly on the list of suspects under surveillance, is trying to establish ties with the Anglo-American aircrew," reported Lieutenant Colonel Chernetsky, the head of the Poltava NKGB (the Commissariat of State Security) to his Kyiv boss, Serhii Savchenko, on June 30, 1944. The locals were impressed by American technological achievement, considering them culturally superior not only to the Russians but also to the Germans. "The Americans have built an airport in Poltava that we could not even dream of," asserted a construction office worker Serhii Ivanovsky. "They have brought special flagstones from America with which they have paved the whole airport. They don't let our people in there for supervisory duties. The Americans, like the Germans, are highly cultured and very rich; even here, they don't deny themselves many trifles and luxuries."

Some even expected an eventual American takeover of Ukraine: the Americans were the second foreign army in the region in the course of the previous three years, and it was easy to imagine that the new foreigners, no matter how rich and cultured, wanted the same as the Germans. Antonina Korsun, a fifty-year-old schoolteacher, allegedly told a secret-police informer on June 3: "The Americans have organized their airports... with a certain purpose in mind. They don't want to fight the Germans on the front but send our fighters there; while our men are on the front, they'll establish themselves all over Ukraine and take it over with no fighting at all. The Germans conquered Ukraine openly, but the Americans are taking it by stealth. Which is better, only time will tell...."

Some of the Poltava-area residents, such as Stepan Kanarevsky, a fifty-three-year-old employee of the Poltava city retail department, welcomed an American takeover as a way of freeing his country from communist rule. "I'm very glad that there will be no communists, and that the Americans will be in charge," Kanarevsky allegedly confided to one of his acquaintances. "I took an interest and rode a bike around the airport myself; our people only have patrols there, but all the rest are Americans who could deliberately kill off our young people raised in the communist spirit and take over themselves." If one believes the secret-police stooges, Kanarevsky was ready for another war, this time between the Soviets and the Americans, and there was no doubt whose side he would take.

Many hoped that the arrival of the Americans portended changes in the Soviet political regime. Olga Smirnova, a woman in her late thirties who studied English and was suspected of anti-Soviet sympathies, stated: "I don't know how the political system of the USSR will change in form after the war, but it cannot remain as it is, for England and America will help us in that regard." Serhii Ivanovsky, impressed by the cultural superiority of the Americans, was more specific about his expectations of change. He told a secret-police informer: "I think the Americans will suggest to us that the party apparatus be prevented from interfering in affairs of state; they will teach us, and they are worth learning from." Others, such as the twenty-five-year-old sports official Anatolii Baev, envisioned a restructuring of the Soviet Union along the American model. "I think it's no accident that the Americans are traveling around Siberia and looking closely at its riches, and the appearance of American air bases on our territory will bring about the end of the existence of the Soviet Union, and completely separate republics (states) will be organized, as in America," said Baev (rather unwisely) to an NKGB informer.[28]

The attitude of the local Ukrainian population to the arrival of the Americans was quite different from that of Red Army officers and soldiers. The latter, especially young officers and technicians, indoctrinated in Soviet class-based thinking and sharing official prejudices against the capitalist West, grudgingly accepted American economic and military prowess, compensating where possible by asserting their sense of their own ideological and cultural superiority. The locals, especially those who had lived in the Russian Empire as children and experienced the German occupation as adults, were not impressed by Soviet propaganda that sought to demean the Americans, viewing their arrival as a change for the better—as heralding reform of the Soviet political system by limiting the power of the party; or the expulsion of the communists altogether; or undoing the takeover of Ukraine.

On the morning of June 11, 1944, the Soviet military and the locals bade farewell to the American pilots as they took over the Poltava, Myrhorod, and Pyriatyn air bases. Altogether there were 129 Flying Fortresses and 60 Mustangs in the formations that assembled above Gribov's Myrhorod air base before flying southwest on a course for Italy. It was the last day and the final mission of Frantic Joe.

To General Eaker's disappointment, weather still did not permit the bombing of the Mielec airplane factory, so he designated the German airfields near the Romanian town of Focşani as the new target. Other airplanes of the Fifteenth Air Force took off from Italian bases to divert the attention of the Luftwaffe and anti-aircraft defenses from the shuttle bombers coming from Poltava. The bombing was a success: at the Focşani airfields six workshops were completely destroyed, as were six barrack-type buildings; the fuel facilities and filling station were set on fire. Also significantly damaged were numerous other buildings and facilities in the area. The bombers did not hit the town itself.

The Germans were better prepared to attack the bombers and their fighter escort this time than they had been on June 2, with flak heavier and Luftwaffe fighter pilots more aggressive. But the losses were still minimal. One Mustang crashed on takeoff, and seven turned back because of technical problems, as did six Flying Fortresses. One more Mustang went down over Yugoslavia because of technical problems, and one B-17 was lost to enemy fire. Unfortunately, that plane was carrying an American photographer who had taken numerous pictures of the Poltava air bases. Those in the know hoped that they would not fall into enemy hands.[29]

Now that it was over everyone considered *Frantic Joe* a stunning success. On June 12, the day after General Eaker's return to Italy, Averell Harriman sent a telegram to Major General Anderson in London, congratulating the deputy commander of the US Strategic Air Forces in Europe, who had overseen the shuttle-bombing operations on behalf of General Spaatz. Arnold was happy to reciprocate with a similar telegram. "I wish you would express my heartfelt appreciation to the General Officers on the Red Army General Staff and the Red Air Force who cooperated with us in making this operation a success, and request them to convey these sentiments to their officers and men." The future looked bright both for the continuation of *Frantic Joe*—or whatever the next name was—and for the Soviet-American alliance. In addition to the Northern France, the Americans were fighting on the Eastern Front. A Grand Alliance had taken its final shape.[30]

Death to Spies

One man who desperately wanted to get on an American plane and leave for Italy with the returning Flying Fortresses was Maurice Reymond. A captain in the French Army before the war, he had been brought to central Ukraine under uncertain circumstances by the Germans and remained there when Soviet forces recaptured the region in the fall of 1943. Reymond made contact with the American commanders in late May 1944. With the second front opened in France on June 6, he hoped that the Americans would fly him to Italy or North Africa, where he could join his compatriots. But the Red Army counterintelligence officers who monitored Reymond's visits to the Poltava base were determined to prevent that by all means possible. They trusted neither Reymond, whom they suspected of being a spy for the Germans, nor the Americans. Reymond would stay in Poltava under secret-police surveillance.[1]

"Allies are allies, but it must not be forgotten that the USA is an imperialist country, and there will probably be spies and saboteurs in the contingent," wrote Vladlen Gribov, recalling the indoctrination he and his colleagues had received before the arrival of the first Americans at the Myrhorod base. They were also told to be careful when talking to one another, as they could be overheard: "among the Americans there will be those who conceal their knowledge of Russian." Finally, they were ordered to "count legs," meaning the number of crew members who arrived with each Flying Fortress. Upon landing, the Americans left the plane through an open hatch in the floor of the aircraft, legs first. The number of crew members was supposed to be ten, therefore the number of legs twenty. Should there be more, the Soviet mechanics were instructed to write down, unobtrusively, the number of the plane with extra passengers and report it to the counterintelligence officials.[2]

Reports filed by Red Army officers and soldiers would eventually reach the desks of the officers of the Soviet military counterintelligence service known as SMERSH (*Smert' shpionam*), which stood for "Death to Spies." The formation of SMERSH was part of a major reorganization of the security services by Joseph Stalin after the Battle of Stalingrad. As the Red Army began to drive out the German occupiers, Stalin decided to improve the counterintelligence work supervised by his security tsar, People's Commissar of Internal Affairs Lavrentii Beria. The dictator apparently feared a drastic increase in the number of spies not only from behind the German lines but also among the population of the newly recaptured territories. A special Commissariat of State Security was formed under the command of Beria's former deputy, Vsevolod Merkulov, and charged with civil counterintelligence. Another part of Beria's counterintelligence empire was subordinated to his other deputy, Viktor Abakumov, and incorporated into the People's Commissariat of Defense. Stalin personally named it SMERSH. Two smaller SMERSH outfits were created within the People's Commissariat of the Navy, and under Beria's command in the People's Commissariat of Internal Affairs, but Abakumov's SMERSH maintained its status as the country's main counterintelligence agency, with its boss reporting directly to Stalin.

The American air bases in Ukraine became the responsibility of Commissar of State Security Second Class Abakumov and his SMERSH outfit, whose main task was combating German spies. The powerful apparatus of SMERSH officers and informers was now turned against the Americans. Whatever the state of Soviet-American relations at the highest level, Abakumov and his men were to act on the assumption that the Americans had come to Ukraine not so much to fight the Germans as to spy on the Soviets.

They built up a huge network of informers, reminding Red Army personnel that their American allies were "capitalists" hostile to the Soviet regime. Ironically, those American officers friendliest toward the Soviets were considered the main threat, as they could not only spy more effectively but disseminate politically harmful views. SMERSH sought to keep the allies separate, trying to disrupt any unauthorized contact between the American airmen, their Red Army counterparts, and the local population. No similar arrangements were ever put in place or even contemplated in the United States with regard to the Soviet officials or the hundreds and thousands of Soviet sailors who visited the American mainland to pick up supplies under the terms of the Lend-Lease program. Soviet suspicion of and spying on the Americans was a peculiar feature of the Grand Alliance.

Given the political importance of the Poltava-area air bases, Abakumov decided to send an officer of the central SMERSH apparatus there. Lieutenant Colonel Konstantin Sveshnikov was the deputy head of the SMERSH department overseeing counterintelligence activities among the Red Army airborne troops. Given the location of the bases, Sveshnikov seemed a natural choice. Now in his mid-thirties, a native of central Russia, he had been recruited into military intelligence in 1932 while serving with the Red Army in Ukraine. He spent the rest of the decade there, rising through the ranks of the military intelligence apparatus. At the time of the German invasion in June 1941, he was in charge of the counterintelligence department of an Air Force division stationed in the city of Uman, on the other side of the Dnieper from Poltava, Myrhorod, and Pyriatyn. He was therefore well prepared for the Poltava appointment and quite conversant with local conditions.[3]

Sveshnikov came to Poltava in the second half of April 1944. On April 30, in his first direct report to Abakumov, Sveshnikov informed his boss of the German bomb uncovered in the basement of the only surviving building at the Poltava airfield. The matter attracted the attention of Stalin himself and Sveshnikov used that to raise matters that required the approval of his superiors. In particular, he wanted to replace the commanding officers of the SMERSH department of the Sixty-Eighth Air Base Region—the entity created by the Red Army Air Force to service the Poltava bases. He also asked for more officers and undercover agents to be posted at each of the three bases. Sveshnikov soon received reinforcements. The new commander of the regional SMERSH department became Major Anatolii Zorin, a counterintelligence officer who had joined the Red Army in 1939 after graduating from an engineering school. By late May 1944, Sveshnikov and Zorin were working as a team, running the SMERSH networks at the Poltava air bases and co-signing the more important reports to Abakumov.[4]

Their first joint report was filed on May 25, a week before the arrival of the Flying Fortresses. They reported on their first successes in carrying out the tasks assigned them by SMERSH headquarters, which included "preventing the penetration of our territory by Allied agents," "uncovering German intelligence agents," and "timely uncovering of subversive activity by anti-Soviet elements." The last two tasks were standard wartime functions of SMERSH units, but the first was unusual. The main foreign power against which Sveshnikov and Zorin were now supposed to work was not Germany but the United States, a partner in the Grand Alliance. Of the 1,090 Americans posted at the Poltava-area bases, 30 had knowledge of Russian and were considered to be potential spies. Four American officers were soon suspected of conducting espionage or anti-Soviet propaganda, simply because of their efforts to establish close contacts with Soviet citizens or sharing American publications with them.[5]

Believing that the best defense was offense, Sveshnikov and Zorin asked permission to employ both experienced and freshly recruited agents to act against these Americans. They were eager to use Red Army officers and technicians in that effort. Sveshnikov and Zorin already had eight agents among the eighty-six Red Army staff officers posted at the three bases and planned to recruit four or five new ones, which would give them roughly one agent for every six officers. Their plans for recruitment among the technicians were even more ambitious. They knew that American planes, as noted earlier, were serviced by four-man crews—a senior American technician and three Soviets—and they wanted one Soviet on every crew to be an agent. The extended network of agents required additional officers to run it, as well as money to pay the agents. Zorin requested an additional 20,000 rubles in a memo that he sent to Moscow on May 24.

Air base security was another SMERSH concern. They planned to recruit agents among the guards securing the bases, soldiers guarding the bomb depots, and local residents. The latter were supposed to be on the lookout for strangers, possible German spies, and any sign of hostile activities. Sveshnikov and Zorin also took measures to deal with unreliable elements among Red Army units serving at the bases and among the general population. They asked for the removal and reassignment of 120 soldiers who had either been in German captivity or lived under German occupation. Local Security Commissariat officers removed any suspicious elements from the entire region of the bases, resettling them to the Stalingrad or Donets industrial basins, where they worked on reconstructing the damaged industrial enterprises and coal mines.

Sveshnikov and Zorin knew that Americans would seek female companionship, and saw this as an opportunity. According to their report, on the weekend of May 20 and 21 more than one hundred Americans had a day's leave in Poltava, where many of them tried to become friendly with local women. "We consider it expedient to lead them [the Americans] into the circle of our female civilian secret service, through whom we would investigate them and their contacts," reported Sveshnikov and Zorin, who were already working with officers of the local branch of the Commissariat of Internal Affairs to recruit women among the local population.[6]

Commissar Abakumov responded to the queries from Sveshnikov and Zorin on June 1, a week after they filed their report. He ordered them to be cautious: "Agents should not be put into contact with the Americans deliberately, but if the Americans become acquainted with our female agents, that should be exploited. In order to take better care of the matter, recruitment of agents among the locals (women) should be intensified." With regard to the other issues raised by the Poltava officers, from finding the best way of registering American crews arriving on shuttle missions to the recruitment of new agents among Red Army personnel and locals, Abakumov advised his subordinates to work with Red Army commanders and the local counterintelligence branch of the Commissariat of Internal Affairs.[7]

The first new agent recruited to work with and against the Americans was the twenty-three-year-old Captain Viktor Maksimov. Maksimov knew some English and had been sent to Poltava from Red Air Force headquarters in Moscow to serve as a key liaison between General Perminov and his American counterpart Colonel Kessler, as well as other US commanders. Maksimov was marked for recruitment as early as April 12, the day SMERSH received its first report on the Poltava-area bases. Maksimov, recruited under the code name "Markov," was handled personally by Sveshnikov and Zorin. He filed numerous reports on his contacts with the Americans that SMERSH officers used as a basis for compiling their profiles.[8]

Sveshnikov and Zorin also activated existing agents, asking their superiors to send their files to Poltava. Agents "Avtomat," "Radiator," "Botkin," and "Konstantinov" were now reporting on their contacts with the Americans and, more important, on the behavior of their comrades. Agent "Botkin," who spoke some English, reported to his SMERSH handlers that on June 13 he had had a conversation with Sergeant Boris Sledin, who suggested that with his knowledge of English "Botkin" could become an interpreter and fly with one of the American crews to the United States, where he would do well for himself. It turned out that Sledin was a SMERSH agent himself, recruited back in 1941 under the code name "Shturman." Agents were now reporting on agents, which seems to have made the SMERSH officers more confident that they were actually in control of what was going on at the bases.[9]

The main targets of the extensive network of agents created by Sveshnikov and Zorin were the Americans, of course. According to Sveshnikov's report filed on June 14, three days after the return of General Ira Eaker and his Flying Fortresses and Mustangs to Italy, there had been 2,703 Americans at the Poltava-area air bases during the first 10 days of June. Of these, 1,236 were permanent personnel—only 36 more than originally agreed in Moscow.

Those who had come on Flying Fortresses and Mustangs as part of *Frantic Joe* numbered 1,477.

Sveshnikov paid special attention to American ground personnel permanently stationed at the bases. In that category he singled out those who spoke Russian or Ukrainian and were therefore, in Sveshnikov's opinion, capable of espionage or at least dissemination of anti-Soviet propaganda. He counted eleven officers born in the former Russian Empire and twenty-seven whose families came from its territory. Those who came to Ukraine to help overcome the language barrier between the Soviets and the Americans were vetted by the US Air Force command to exclude individuals hostile to the Bolshevik regime for ideological, personal, or family reasons. The Americans were not interested in spying of any sort: the only intelligence officers in their ranks were Air Force personnel whose job was to debrief pilots about their targets and the German defenses encountered on their missions. The Americans were in fact engaged in a charm offensive, seeking to persuade the Soviets that they could do business together and open new air bases, particularly in the Soviet Far East. But the SMERSH officers were unaware of that and would not have believed it even if they had been told about it—or perhaps especially if they had been so informed.[10]

Between May 25 and June 14, 1944, Sveshnikov and Zorin identified close to a dozen Americans in the Poltava-area bases whom they suspected of espionage. Close to the top of the SMERSH list of suspects was one of the original planners of *Frantic* and the veteran of the Poltava base Major Albert Lepawsky. As we have seen, Lepawsky had originally called the operation *Baseball*. Born in Chicago in 1907 to a family of Jewish emigrants from the Russian Empire, Lepawsky had had an impressive academic career at the University of Chicago. A student of Charles Edward Merriam, the founder of the behavioral approach to political science, Lepawsky got his PhD at the age of twenty-three and went on to write a number of influential monographs, essays, and reports on city government and management of natural resources. In the 1930s he divided his time between the university and city government, where he held a number of positions. In early 1942, when Lepawsky joined the Air Force in the aftermath of Pearl Harbor, he vacated a number of positions. His former employers in the Chicago city government had to look for a new research director of the Law Department, a new assistant director of the Public Administration Clearing House, and a new director of the Federation of Tax Administrators. The university had to search for a new director of the Institute of Public Service.[11]

A strong proponent of the New Deal, Lepawsky not only believed that he had to serve his country in military uniform in wartime but also welcomed the alliance with his ancestral homeland. The 1917 Revolution had turned the Russian Empire into the Soviet Union, the birthplace of the socialist experiment, with which Lepawsky sympathized without ever endorsing it. For all that he thought his baseball analogy—with home field and visitors and base paths—was useful and effective, Lepawsky was fully aware of the differences between the American and Soviet "teams." He wrote: "The other Ball team is a unique ally with a state of mind and system of politics few of us understand."[12]

Lepawsky probably never imagined how right he was with regard to the Soviet officials' state of mind. As early as May 25, Colonel Sveshnikov put him on the list of suspects for showing too much interest in establishing contacts with Red Air Force officers and local inhabitants. He reported to Moscow what he had learned about Lepawsky so far: that he had studied in Chicago, London, and Berlin, and was currently serving as adjutant to the US commanding officer of the Poltava base. Sveshnikov asked Moscow whether SMERSH officers there knew anything else about Lepawsky. They responded that since Lepawsky's arrival in Moscow with part of the "first echelon" of US Air Force officers to prepare *Frantic* in February 1944, they had kept him and other American officers under surveillance until his departure for Poltava in mid-April.

At 10:20 p.m. on April 14, the day before Lepawsky left Moscow for Poltava, the Soviet surveillance team spotted him leaving the Hotel *Nationale*, where he had a meeting with an unidentified man. After exiting the hotel, the two walked for a while, speaking what the agents identified as a foreign language. Lepawsky then returned to his hotel, while the unidentified man entered a house on Petrovka Street in downtown Moscow. He was soon identified as Isaak Zvavich, a professor of history at Moscow University. Born to a Jewish family in Odesa in 1906, Zvavich had graduated from the University of London and served as a consultant to the Soviet embassy in Britain in the mid-1920s. Since 1928 he had taught at Moscow colleges, researching nineteenth-century Russian diplomatic history and becoming one of the leading Soviet experts on Britain and British history. According to the secret-police report, Zvavich was married, well off, and occupied a large well-furnished room in a communal apartment in downtown Moscow.[13]

That was all that Moscow counterintelligence could offer on Lepawsky. Sveshnikov and Zorin were determined to follow their instincts. Lepawsky's background made him a natural suspect, as did his knowledge of Russian, which, according to the SMERSH officers, he was hiding from them. They received reports that Lepawsky was getting letters from his family in the United States written in Russian, while telling the Soviets that he did not know or understand the language. They also suspected him of using his position as adjutant as a cover for his intelligence work. "He systematically visits our headquarters under the pretext of carrying out certain insignificant assignments," reported Sveshnikov to Moscow. He continued: "Lepawsky carefully studies our officer and civilian staff, taking an interest in those of his military personnel who have any dealings with Russians." For a person of Lepawsky's origins, background, and rank it was virtually impossible to perform any function at the bases without arousing suspicion. He remained on Sveshnikov and Zorin's list of suspects, although they had no hard evidence that he was spying.[14]

A special category of suspects consisted of American officers who had no ancestral ties with the former Russian Empire and did not speak the local languages yet nonetheless, at least in the opinion of SMERSH, held anti-Soviet views and were engaged in spreading anti-Soviet propaganda. The chief surgeon at the US air bases, Lieutenant Colonel William Jackson, a native of Tennessee, was at the very top of that list. Apart from holding and sharing what were considered to be anticommunist views, Jackson showed interest in establishing contacts with locals, especially women. He had arrived in Moscow on March 21 with the "second echelon" of US officers who came to make preparations for the opening of the Poltava-area bases. He made exceptionally productive use of his time in Moscow, visiting hospitals and writing a detailed report on the state of the Soviet health care system and medical profession, which he estimated to be some fifty years behind that of the United States.

Jackson left for Poltava on April 14. Together with his subordinates, he proceeded to set up medical facilities at each of the three bases and provide appropriate sanitary conditions for the resident Americans. He often had to deal with delicate issues, such as persuading Soviet officers to improve the latrines and bathing facilities. But those were not the issues that got Jackson into trouble with the Soviet authorities. On May 25, Colonel Sveshnikov added Jackson to the list of US officers about whom he requested additional information from Moscow, alleging that the American officer was actively seeking contacts with the Soviets. On the same day, Sveshnikov filed another report that named Jackson as one of two US Air Force officers who were purportedly distributing English-language literature deemed to be of anti-Soviet orientation to Red Air Force personnel.[15]

SMERSH headquarters in Moscow had more information on Jackson's stay in Moscow than they had had on Lepawsky. Secret-police surveillance of Jackson's suite in the Hotel *Nationale* in Moscow, where he stayed in March and April 1944, revealed that he was actively seeking contacts with local women. On March 27, less than a week after Jackson's arrival, the secret police intercepted his telephone call to a Moscow apartment. Jackson had called a young woman named Zoia, who did not speak English very well. On April 3, close to 11:00 p.m., a secret-police surveillance team spotted two young women leaving the Hotel *Nationale* after visiting Jackson's suite and that of another US officer. One of them was later identified as the twenty-one-year-old Zoia Guseva. At 10:30 p.m. on April 13, Jackson's last day in Moscow, the surveillance team followed to their homes five young women who had visited Jackson and another officer at the hotel. One of them, Zinaida Pashinina, was eighteen years old.[16]

Lieutenant Colonel Jackson's interest in younger women continued in Poltava. In June, according to later SMERSH reports, he struck up an acquaintance with a local girl, Zinaida Blazhkova, whom he had met through another young woman. Jackson visited Blazhkova on a regular basis and was very generous, according to one of Blazhkova's acquaintances, bringing her a gift every time: "stockings, candy, new pairs of boots, men's and women's shoes, and a military jacket." Women were not the only SMERSH agents to report on Jackson. Information about him was also provided by Jackson's Soviet counterpart, Ivan Lebedev, the chief Soviet medical doctor at the Poltava-area bases. He was recruited by SMERSH under the female code-name "Roza." The Soviet interpreter at the bases, code-named "Soiuznik," also reported on Jackson's contacts with the locals.[17]

The dissemination of anti-Soviet propaganda was at the very center of SMERSH concerns. On June 14, Sveshnikov and Zorin reported to Moscow that after they had warned the American commanders about the inadmissibility of distributing American publications, such incidents came to a halt. But cases in which Americans, while fixing an aircraft engine or being off duty, shared views deemed to be anti-Soviet with their Soviet counterparts continued. Expatriate GIs who spoke Russian or Ukrainian were deemed the main perpetrators in that regard.

These were often ordinary conversations or comments. "Russia is lagging behind: I traveled 200 miles without seeing any factories or plants, while in America there's a plant every 15 miles," said US Air Force Sergeant Michael Lazarchuk to one of his Soviet acquaintances. Lazarchuk confided to the same person, who turned out to be a SMERSH informer, that he was not sure whether he would come back from Ukraine alive, as Stalin might very well order a bombing run on the American bases and blame it on the Germans. In one exchange Odesa-born USAF airmen Peter Nikolaev, all of twenty, told an acquaintance that he was not pleased with the Soviet political order. "Only a small group of communists rule here in Russia and do as they please, but in America it's the other way around; the people have broader electoral rights." He considered the US-Soviet alliance fragile.

As he told a SMERSH agent, "It's hard to have faith in Russia. You are now at war with Germany, but at the slightest opportunity you'll make a treaty with it, and there will be another war." The officers of the local NKGB, the civil security service, reported that Nikolaev was also displeased with President Roosevelt. He told one of their agents: "I don't like Roosevelt's foreign policy, and at the next election I'll vote against Roosevelt."[18]

SMERSH also reported on instances when the Americans made highly positive remarks about the Soviets—their memo on American reaction to the opening of the second front on June 6, 1944, was full of those. But the main task of SMERSH was to uncover spies and curb treason and anti-Soviet propaganda. The reports filed by mid-June indicated that with their agent network fully set up and regular information on the activities of American personnel beginning to flow in, SMERSH operatives were ready to go full force after their American guests. For the time being, however, the "Death to Spies" squad was merely watching.

Pearl Harbor on the Steppes

On the evening of June 21, 1944, General Perminov threw a party for the American officers at the Poltava base. In attendance was his American counterpart Colonel Kessler, recently promoted to brigadier general, and Kessler's new boss, Major General Robert L. Walsh, a cavalryman who had traded his horse for an aircraft while serving in the American Expeditionary Force in France in 1918 and had stayed with the US Air Force ever since, through its numerous incarnations from the US Army Air Corps, the name it acquired in 1926, to the US Army Airforces, as the service commonly known as the US Air Force was officially called after 1941.[1]

Walsh was now commanding officer of Eastern Command, the official name of the American Air Force headquarters at Poltava. The other hat he wore was as head of the Air Force section at John Deane's Military Mission in Moscow. In fact, he became Deane's deputy in charge of the bases. A favorite of the US Strategic Air Forces in Europe commander, General Spaatz, Walsh was sent to the Soviet Union to raise the profile of the shuttle-bombing mission: he had previously served as commanding officer of the US Air Force Transport Command in the South Atlantic, being responsible for the smooth functioning of the air routes between Latin America, on the one hand, and North Africa and then Europe, on the other. While in the Soviet Union, Walsh was spending most of his time in Moscow, leaving Kessler in charge of day-to-day operations at the airfields. He first came to Poltava shortly before the launch of the first shuttle-bombing mission from Italy on June 2, 1944. Walsh was back in Poltava on June 21 to welcome another shuttle mission, this time launched by the US Eighth Air Force in Britain.[2]

The mission code-named *Frantic II* involved a task force, consisting of 163 B-17s and seventy P-51s, and was led to the Poltava-area bases by Colonel Archie J. Old Jr., the commander of the 45th Combat Bomber wing. He was known for personally leading his pilots into battle and had flown forty-six combat missions over Germany, although the original official limit for the bomber pilots was twenty-five. Old would go on to have a spectacular career in the Air Force, rising to the rank of lieutenant general and assuming command of the Fifteenth Air Force, whose pilots had been the first to land in Poltava on June 2, 1944, and would be put on the nuclear alert during the Cold War. In 1957 he would make the first nonstop flight around the world, piloting a B-52 jet.

On the evening of June 21, Old was the guest of honor at Perminov's party. In the company of senior American and Soviet officers, he was happy to share his impressions of the bombing mission. He had no way of knowing that *Frantic II* would result in the largest loss of American planes on the ground since Pearl Harbor.[3]

■

A man more superstitious than Archie J. Old might have seen signs of coming disaster at the very start of the mission. The task force took off from England around 5:30 a.m. under difficult weather conditions, with cloud cover limiting visibility and making it difficult to assemble the task force in the air into effective battle group. Old, in the lead aircraft, was doing his best to speed up the process when he discovered that his Flying Fortress was leaking gasoline. He landed immediately after the last plane of the task force took off, fixed the leaking tank, and took off again without refueling so as to catch up with the rest of the group. By 7:00 a.m. the force had left the

English coast behind and was on course for its target, an oil refinery near the city of Ruhland, south of Berlin and north of Dresden.

Before the planes reached Hamburg, German flak damaged a number of the airplanes, including Old's own B-17, which continued flying with a large hole in the right wing panel. Then forty-five Messerschmitt-109 fighters did their best to drive the task force off course. Twenty-six B-17s eventually dropped their bombs on a different target, but the rest—138 in all—bombed the Ruhland oil refinery as planned. Photos taken later allowed the commanders to rate the results of the bombing as "good." The Flying Fortresses and their Mustang escorts flew toward Warsaw and then turned southeast toward Ukraine. The Messerschmitt fighters attacked the task force again approximately 50 miles before the German-Soviet front line but were repelled by the Mustangs. A German reconnaissance plane tried to follow the Flying Fortresses across the German-Soviet line, but the Mustangs went after it, and it soon disappeared into the clouds. However, that was not the end of the task force's troubles. The Soviet air defenses mistook the Americans for Germans and opened fire, though luckily they caused no damage. The American planes descended to 2,000 feet, identified the Dnieper River, and followed it south to the Poltava-area bases.

While reduced in numbers—Old lost two Flying Fortresses and two Mustangs to enemy fire, five fighters and eighteen bombers returned to England because of technical problems, and five planes landed at an airfield near Kyiv after running out of gasoline—the planes of the Eighth Air Force arrived at the Poltava bases. They assembled in formation and flew over Poltava, as had those of the Fifteenth Air Force two weeks earlier, in a show of American strength and Soviet-American comradeship in arms. Walsh, Perminov, Kessler, and their officers were there, as was a large group of Western and Soviet journalists, who had returned to Poltava to cover the arrival of the new task force, and enjoyed the view of the silver-colored Flying Fortresses and their Mustang escorts glistening in the sun and performing an air show before landing. Among the spectators was a film crew led by Anatole Litvak, a Kyiv-born Hollywood director who had been nominated for an Oscar for his 1943 documentary, *The Battle of Russia*, and was fresh from filming the D-Day landings in Normandy. His footage made a strong impression on Stalin. Now Litvak was at Poltava, filming the arrival of the new echelon of Flying Fortresses.[4]

Seventy planes landed in approximately forty-five minutes, wrote Old in his report on the mission. The crews were debriefed, fed, and sent to tents to sleep after their long and exhausting mission. American losses were more substantial than in *Frantic I*, whose main goal had been to avoid areas heavily protected by the Germans and reach the Soviet bases intact, but *Frantic II* was truly a combat mission. For a mission of that kind, the losses were quite acceptable. Colonel Old agreed to be interviewed by Western and Soviet reporters. The interview, attended by Perminov, Walsh, and Kessler, lasted half an hour. Old was upbeat. "The designated target—war industry installations southeast of Berlin—was hit with a crushing blow. Smoke from the fires started by our bombing rose to a height of 8,000 feet."[5]

Around 11:00 p.m. Old and the other commanding officers accepted Perminov's invitation and gathered around a table to celebrate the success of the new shuttle mission. Like previous dinners thrown by the Soviets, this one was expected to last until early morning, yet turned out to be the shortest of the lot. Some twenty minutes into Perminov's party, a Soviet officer showed up with the news that German bombers were flying in the general direction of Poltava. Perminov dismissed the first warning, as the Luftwaffe did not normally dare to fly so deep into Soviet-controlled air space. But sirens—American Lend-Lease equipment recently installed at the bases at the insistence of General Eaker—sounded shortly afterward. The dinner broke up. Colonel Old later reported that approximately fifteen minutes after midnight the Soviet anti-aircraft batteries opened fire. Fifteen minutes after that the "first German PTF [Pathfinder] airplane dropped flares directly above the field." Kessler recalled seeing a "stick of four flares right over the center." He told an officer who interviewed him about the events of that night: "After that the fun began." In fact, it was more like a nightmare.[6]

Above the Poltava air base were dozens of Heinkel-111 bombers from the Luftwaffe's Fourth Air Corps—the only German air corps that specialized in night bombing and commanded by General Rudolf Meister. In the spring and summer of 1944 its planes regularly attacked Soviet targets, mostly railway junctions immediately behind the Red Army lines. Most of Meister's aircraft were stationed in the vicinity of Brest and Radom on the Polish-Belarusian border, the first city serving as the corps' headquarters. The Brest and Radom airfields were too far from the German-Soviet front line to allow for raids deep into Left-Bank Ukraine—meaning on the left bank of the Dnieper—but Meister also disposed of fields closer to the front line, near the city of Minsk, the capital of Nazi-occupied Belarus. From there, Meister's pilots could fly well past the Soviet front.[7]

The idea of locating and bombing American Flying Fortresses at their Soviet air bases came to Meister during the *Frantic Joe* operation of June 2–11. Ever since, his officers had been on the lookout for another American shuttle-bombing operation. On June 21, a German fighter tried to follow the Flying Fortresses on their way east but was chased away by the Mustangs. A few hours later, a German reconnaissance plane was spotted over the Poltava and Myrhorod airfields soon after the Flying Fortresses landed there. At Myrhorod the American commanders wanted the Mustangs to drive the intruder away, but the Soviets did not allow them to do so, either because every American flight had to be cleared with Moscow or because of a particular Soviet sense of pride: it was their job to protect the Americans. The Flying Fortresses glistened in the afternoon sun and were visible dozens of miles away. The German pilot, who could not miss them, took a number of photos.[8]

News of the Americans at the Poltava bases reached General Meister's Brest headquarters late in the afternoon of June 21. He immediately put together a task force consisting of Battle Wings (*Kampfgeschwader*, or KG) 4, 27, 53, and 55, comprising more than 350 Heinkel-111 bombers and six Junkers-88 light bombers, which were used for target marking, among other things. Meister ordered KGs 27 and 53 to move closer to the front line, relocating to the airfields near Minsk and Białystok. The commanding officer of KG 55, Colonel Wilhelm Antrup, told all his squadrons to be on the alert at 8:45 p.m. They were going to bomb Myrhorod. The task looked ideally simple: the German photographs showed the Flying Fortresses aligned in rows at the edges of small airfields. At 8:30 p.m. the reconnaissance planes were already in the air. By 8:45 Antrup's pilots were in their cockpits. Fifteen minutes later, they began to take off for Ukraine.[9]

Lieutenant Colonel Fritz Pockrandt, the commanding officer of KG 53 "Condor Legion," led the raid on Poltava. His bombers took off immediately after those of Colonel Antrup. The attack was scheduled for midnight Berlin time (1:00 a.m. Moscow time). The most dangerous part of the route was the crossing of the Soviet-German front line east of Minsk. Soviet Yakovlev-9 fighters tried to stop the bombers, but the German planes were protected by squadrons of Messerschmitt-109s and Focke-Wulf-190 fighters that fought off the Soviet attack. The road to Poltava was now open. At fifteen minutes to midnight a Junkers-88 bomber dropped the first flare bomb on a parachute over the Poltava airfield, illuminating the target for the other planes. Soon ten more German planes were over the Poltava base, dropping additional "lights" and attacking Soviet air defenses and lighting stations. Then came the first group of bombers. Wave after wave of Heinkels attacked the Flying Fortresses parked in the open on the edges of the airfield. It was a slaughter.

Pockrandt's bombers were eventually joined over Poltava by those of Antrup's task force. They could not reach Myrhorod on time, as the area was covered with heavy clouds. By the time they made their way to the target, the Ju-88 planes had run out of flare bombs. Antrup turned his bomber wing toward Poltava, where there was no shortage of light because of exploding bombs and burning American planes. The other bomber wings did likewise, whether their target was Poltava or Myrhorod, and together they turned the Poltava airfield into a burning hell. The bombing lasted two and a half hours. Around 2:30 a.m., the Luftwaffe bombers finally began returning to their bases in Belarus and eastern Poland. They left dozens of Flying Fortresses burning, the air base in ruins, fuel and ammunition depots destroyed, and dozens of people killed. Not a single German plane was lost. Later in the morning Meister congratulated his men on their stunning success, praising them for "proven bravery."[10]

The Soviet air defense headquarters in Kyiv had detected the approach of Meister's bombers soon after 10:00 p.m. Moscow time. They soon realized that there were two groups of planes, one heading toward Myrhorod, the other toward Poltava. They alerted air defense batteries and ordered their fighters into the air. That is when the problems began.

Soviet ground-based radar had difficulty distinguishing German planes from Soviet ones. "As our planes rose into the sky and the enemy neared the target, they got mixed up on radar," reads a Soviet report on the attack. "It became completely impossible to figure out which were enemy planes and which were ours." Having no radar at all, the fighter pilots became desperate, getting ready to crash into German planes kamikaze-style. But even that was impossible without searchlights. "Get your lights onto at least one fascist plane, and I'll bring it down with mine!" had demanded Senior Lieutenant Bashkirov. Senior Lieutenant Krasnov made the same request. "I can't see anything. Give me a lead with your searchlight: I'll ram him!" he radioed to the ground. By then, however, the searchlights were gone. The Germans had hit the Soviet lighting stations, and whatever remained of the Soviet air defense batteries, operated largely by young female soldiers, was useless, as the gunners could not see their targets. The Soviet air defenses had failed completely. "The batteries were pounded with incendiary and high-explosive bombs. The bombs exploded in the gun emplacements, wounding the personnel and damaging the equipment," read a Soviet report about the attack.[11]

No matter how bad the situation, for many Soviet officers and soldiers on the ground the failure of air defenses on the night of June 21 was by no means shocking. They were used to the absence of night fighters in the sky and the ineffectiveness of Soviet air defense batteries. Their way of dealing with such attacks was to wait them out in the narrow trenches dug for that express purpose. The airplane mechanic Yurii Dubrovin found his way to one such trench immediately after the alarm sounded at a quarter to midnight: he had just returned to his quarters from a concert in honor of the American pilots of the *Frantic II* task force. In the trench, Dubrovin found himself next to a Red Army captain named Khalturin—rank did not matter much under such circumstances. The captain had his own way of calming his nerves. "So for the whole three hours of the bombardment he sang, 'The old woman had a little gray goat,'" recalled Dubrovin. "And I sang an accompaniment, 'A-na-na, a-na-na, a-na-na, chi ki bri ki shii t' assa-sa, purpurli-murmurli, kurlialia.' Such an idiotic refrain. In the dark, the feeling of fear is dulled."[12]

For the Americans, the absence of effective air defenses had come as a complete and shocking surprise. They had lived through numerous air attack alarms at their bases in Britain but never experienced a real bombardment from the air. The bases there were protected from the Luftwaffe by night fighters and flak artillery. Thus, when the Soviets had sounded such an alarm, many of the American pilots slept through it, either not hearing the alarm or deciding not to react to it. The Americans had seen many flak batteries around the Poltava area air bases and expected night fighters to be on the alert to defend them. They were also dead tired after a long and difficult raid. Their commanders had taken that into account by rescheduling the instructions on how to react to air raids from 9:00 p.m. to 9:00 a.m. the next morning.

Colonel Old later commented that after the sirens went off, his men "merely turned over and cursed because they had been awakened." Old added, however, that when the bombs started falling, "they found the ditches and shelters in record time." As there were 1,100 Americans, and the trenches could shelter only 300 of them, a number of men "elected to lie in depressions along the railroad tracks, while others took shelter behind brick walls," recalled General Kessler. According to Kessler's report, "no one in slit trenches was injured." Those who did not make it to the trenches fared worse. Kessler counted one man killed and thirteen injured—a very low number, given the severity of the attack. Some injuries were minor, like that of the filmmaker Anatole Litvak, who fell and injured his mouth.[13]

Killed on the spot was Joseph K. Lukacek. The twenty-four-year-old second lieutenant, a copilot of a B-17, had arrived earlier that day as a member of the 237th Bomber Squadron of the 96th Bomber Group. Originally from New Jersey, Lukacek was a descendant of emigrants from the Czech lands of the Habsburg Empire. The chief surgeon, Lieutenant Colonel William Jackson, wrote in his report on the consequences of the attack that Lukacek died of shell wounds that caused multiple fractures of his bones. His copilot, First Lieutenant Raymond C. Estle, a

twenty-two-year-old native of Nebraska, initially survived the attack. Estle
had joined the Air Force in January 1942. By April 1943 he was fighting in
Europe, the flight to Poltava being his fourteenth mission.[14]

Lieutenant Colonel Jackson, who treated Estle, recorded his and
Lukacek's Poltava experiences in remarkable detail. "Following the long
mission of that date, he [Estle] was dog tired," wrote Jackson,

> He ate, attended the briefing and then turned in to sleep in the tent
> assigned to him. He slept so soundly that he did not hear any air raid
> alert sounded, and was aware of the situation when he was first
> awakened by the first bombs exploding. He ran out of his tent
> together with his co-pilot, but had no idea where the slit trenches
> were located. He ran aimlessly in the direction which he thought to
> be away from the airfield. In the light of the flares at the edge of the
> hospital he remembers loose bricks stacked in a wall formation.
> At that moment a plane zoomed low and he heard bombs dropping.
> They instinctively flung themselves flat on the ground. A stick of
> three high explosion bombs landed in line about twenty feet apart.
> The nearest one exploded about twelve feet from where he was lying.
> Fragments struck both him and his co-pilot. He realized he was hit
> in many places. He called to his co-pilot, received no answer and in
> the flare light saw that he was dead. He lay there unable to move and
> calling for aid.

Jackson did his best to save Estle's life. Upon finding him on the field, he
gave the young airman morphine, and during a lull in the bombing moved
Estle to a slit trench, where he gave him blood plasma. Estle had sustained
numerous wounds penetrating the left and right buttocks and a severe
wound to the lower right leg, as well as bone fractures. He would die of
those wounds on July 2, 1944.[15]

The morning of June 22 was Jackson's busiest at Poltava. Sometime after
4:30 a.m., while driving a Jeep and looking for wounded officers and
soldiers, he was approached by an ad hoc international team of rescuers,
including US Air Force Captain Theodore Bozard, and Soviet Sergeant

P. A. Tupitsyn. They were returning from the vicinity of an American airplane that had exploded just as a group of Soviets were trying to salvage
it. Some were killed instantly, and Captain Bozard administered first
aid to the wounded survivors. A Soviet interpreter, Lieutenant Ivan
Sivolobov, joined Jackson in his Jeep, which made communication easier.
Communication was essential, as only the Soviet personnel could clear
the way for Jackson to drive to the exploded plane. Since the Germans
had dropped thousands of small bombs that would explode on contact,
scouts had to survey the area in search of unexploded bombs. Sergeant
Tupitsyn and his fellow mechanic Sergeant Georgii Sukhov volunteered
to do the job.

Their bravery and self-sacrifice deeply impressed Jackson. A few days
later, he wrote, "the two Russian enlisted men voluntarily got out in front
and with total disregard for personal safety proceeded to pass the Jeep
through the tall grass heavily sown with bombs and mines where the
wounded lay.... Sgt. Tupitsyn sat on the front of the Jeep, watching for
mines, and mechanic Sukhov Georgy was walking in front of the Jeep, picking up mines and bombs [and] laying them carefully aside. A total of 40 or
more was picked up and laid aside to allow the Jeep to pass safely...." As
they reached the damaged plane, they found two severely wounded Soviet
soldiers, one with his left leg blown away by the explosion, the other with a
fractured leg. Tupitsyn and Sukhov put them in the back of the Jeep and
proceeded to the hospital, again risking their lives to provide safe passage.
Jackson petitioned his commanders, asking them to nominate the two
Soviet soldiers for an award.[16]

Decades later, Sergeant Tupitsyn, who would rise in the ranks to become
a lieutenant colonel, remembered with great clarity the events described by
Jackson. He was one of eight volunteers assigned to salvage airplanes that
had not been destroyed. As they approached one of the lightly damaged
Flying Fortresses, there was an explosion, killing and injuring some members of his group. Tupitsyn did his best to save the lives of the injured, and
it was then that he enlisted the help of the Americans. When they put the
wounded in the Jeep, he recalled, "day began to break, and we could clearly
see the way to drive out of the air base by the shortest route. Sukhov and

I walked 30–40 meters in front of the car, clearing the road of unexploded mines. All that involved great risk but ended well."[17]

"The attitude of the Russians toward the Americans during the raid was rather embarrassing," Colonel Old later wrote about that memorable night. "Their attitude seemed to be: 'Nothing must happen to the Americans or their equipment, regardless of the cost to us.' At the height of the bombing raid, the Soviet military personnel, both male and female, were rushed out of their shelters into an open field trying to extinguish the fire on the B-17s by throwing dirt at the burning machines. Many of these were killed or wounded by the bombing." The Soviet commanders were clearly aghast that they had failed to protect their allies and mobilized the only resource they had in an effort to save face. There was also a principle involved: in the Soviet system of values, airplanes and military equipment, especially those as rare and precious as the ones brought in by the Americans, were more valuable than human lives. Saving them at the risk of one's life was standard operating procedure in the Red Army and its Air Force.[18]

While the Americans lost mainly equipment to the German bombing, the Soviets paid mostly with their lives. Kessler reported the destruction beyond repair of forty-nine B-17s, four C-47s, and one F-5 airplane. Sixteen Flying Fortresses could be salvaged but needed substantial repairs; merely six were operational and three "flyable only." According to the same report, the Soviets lost one Douglas aircraft, the personal plane of General Perminov, and seven Yaks—fighter planes. But their human losses exceeded the American ones many times. The Americans lost one killed and thirteen wounded; the Soviets counted thirty men and women dead and ninety wounded. Those were the losses at Poltava. They also lost a few people at Pyriatyn and Myrhorod, where the bombing was less intensive.[19]

Among the Soviets killed in the attack, none had a higher public profile than Petr Lidov, a reporter for the main Soviet newspaper, *Pravda*. Lidov was a member of the group of Soviet and American journalists who came to Poltava to cover the arrival of the *Frantic II* planes. He had first made a name for himself in January 1942, when he published an essay titled "Tania" about a young Soviet woman with a partisan unit who had been captured by the Germans in a village near Moscow in November 1941. Interrogated by the Germans, she allegedly responded to her captors' question "Where is Stalin?" with the words "Stalin is on duty." The Germans hanged the young woman in front of the entire village. "Tania's" real name was Zoia Kosmodemianskaia. She was an eighteen-year-old student from Moscow who had volunteered to join a partisan commando group.

Lidov was instrumental in discovering the heroine's real name. Together with his friend Aleksandr Kuznetsov, he exhumed Zoia's body. But he either did not know or preferred not to reveal all the circumstances of Zoia's death—as a Soviet commando, she was implementing the policy of scorched earth, burning down villages occupied by the Germans, together with their Russian peasant inhabitants. It was a collective farmer trying to save his house from the partisan arsonist who spotted Zoia and alerted the Germans. Other peasants hurled insults at her before she was hanged by the Germans. Despite the fact that the story turned out to be more complex than the one told by Lidov, a new heroine was born, one of those most celebrated during and after the war, and the *Pravda* reporter was credited with discovering her.[20]

Lidov came to Poltava with a number of other reporters, including Kuznetsov. It was Lidov's second trip to the base—his first, on June 2, had resulted in his article "Flying Fortresses," which was published in *Pravda* and introduced the shuttle-bombing operations to the broad Soviet public. Like the other newsmen, Lidov and his fellow reporters were put up for the night in a sleeping coach parked on the railway line near the outskirts of the Poltava base. When the Germans started to bomb the airfield, Lidov and his companions took shelter in a nearby trench. They survived the first attack, but in a lull between bombings they left the trench and ran in the darkness, apparently looking for a safer place to hide.[21]

The next morning, on June 23, a radio technician named Aleksei Spassky, who had arrived with Lidov and other reporters from Moscow the previous day, was invited by his friends to take a look at the bodies of dead soldiers who were rumored to be German parachutists. The dead were dressed in Soviet uniforms, but a young woman standing guard next to the corpses pointed to them with disgust and called them "fascists." In the pocket of one of the deceased the Red Army soldiers found German currency and a German pin with a swastika. Soviet documents were also found on the corpses. The Communist Party card of Aleksandr Kuznetsov was soon presented to Spassky, who immediately recognized the name and photo of his fellow reporter—certainly no spy. The female sentry told Spassky that they had also documents in the names of Lidov and Strunnikov, another Moscow reporter.

Spassky took a closer look at the bodies. He soon recognized Lidov—the face of the famous reporter was covered with his military jacket, which was missing its shoulder boards—they had been ripped off by the Red Army soldiers who discovered the body. Someone had also removed Lidov's leather boots. Currency found on the corpses was taken and not passed on to officials—Spassky saw bundles of five-ruble bills disappearing into the pockets of the female soldiers who searched the bodies. He was in no position to protest, as he himself fell under suspicion of being a German spy and was taken to the air base headquarters. There Spassky was turned over to a counterintelligence officer who had written a report on what had happened to Lidov.

Petr Lidov and his friends were buried with military honors in a park in downtown Poltava. A street would be named after him and a legend born: that he had been killed while shooting at German airplanes with a machine gun and indeed had managed to down one of them. The plane allegedly crashed close to Lidov, mortally wounding him and his friends. The author of the legend of Zoia became the subject of a legend himself. Regardless of such mythmaking, there was no shortage of true heroism demonstrated by Red Army soldiers in the line of duty.[22]

News of the German attack on Poltava was reported to Stalin, Molotov, and People's Commissar of Internal Affairs Lavrentii Beria, the same day. According to Soviet reports the flak batteries and machine guns fired close to 30,000 rounds without shooting down a single German plane. The night fighters made 17 sorties, also to no avail. Most disheartening was that the losses of the Eighth Army's Flying Fortresses were the largest ever. From the Soviet perspective, the disaster came at the worst symbolic moment—the third anniversary of the German invasion of the USSR on the morning of June 22, 1941.[23]

Who was to blame for a failure of such proportions? The Soviets, while feeling guilty for not having managed to protect their guests, were nonetheless pointing fingers at them. General Perminov had allegedly proposed moving the planes to other airfields after German reconnaissance planes were spotted in the area, but the American commanders had refused, citing the fatigue of their crews. They also had not dispersed their planes around the field, placing them at significant distances from one another—the Soviet "know-how" of dealing with night bombing raids without benefit of night fighters and effective flak batteries. The Americans, in turn, blamed the Soviets, recalling how they had offered their fighters to drive away the German reconnaissance planes and the Soviets had allegedly refused. More than anything else, the Americans complained about the absence and ineffectiveness of night fighters—the main defense of British airfields against German raids.[24]

Perminov pointed out that Soviet bombers had attacked German airfields in retaliation. He also ordered the removal of still operational airplanes from the Poltava-area bases to Soviet airfields further east. That was all the Soviets could do in anticipation of the next night and another German air raid. Indeed, as expected, the Germans showed up the following night and bombed the Myrhorod air base to devastating effect, though the Flying Fortresses were no longer there. Major Marwin Bower of the 100th Bomber Group stayed at Myrhorod with the few remaining planes, one of them in disrepair, and witnessed the attack. "[A]bout 01:00 hours from 75 to 100 Ju-88s plastered the field with everything except the kitchen stove and live fish. Many Russian soldiers were wounded and some were killed," wrote Bower in his diary. "Our damaged B-17 was practically destroyed but the two others escaped with only minor damage, probably from falling flak." The following day Bowman flew to the air base near the city of Kirovohrad (present-day Kropyvnytskyi in central Ukraine), where he "was royally entertained by three Russian generals and the whole post for that matter."[25]

Radio operator Palmer Myhra was also stationed at Myrhorod and re-membered later that he had learned about the coming attack on his base from German radio. The GIs in Ukraine entertained themselves by listen-ing to the "Axis Sally" show, a German program that mixed popular music and propaganda. It was hosted by an American-born actress named Mildred Elizabeth Gillars, who had been in Germany before the war and agreed to broadcast Nazi propaganda aimed at American troops fighting in Europe. (She would be arrested in 1946, convicted of treason by the United States court and spend more that fifteen years in prison.[26]) "Of all the women we knew when in Operation Frantic, the most discussed and familiar was Axis Sally," remembered Myhra. "She came to us most every night with her sexy insinuating messages." The program would end with her words: "Don't forget to listen again tomorrow and kisses for all of you from Sally."

That evening, recalled Myhra, Axis Sally was on the air earlier than usual, "telling us at Myrhorod that we were next." Indeed, around midnight they had heard Soviet anti-aircraft batteries and machine guns opening fire. They waited for Soviet night bombers to appear, but none did. Once again the German bombers had a field day, bombarding the air base without much opposition. The only difference was that the American planes were now gone, relocated the previous day to other airfields. "The big loss was fuel supply and bomb dumps," recalled Myhra.[27]

The Soviets did their best to make Americans forget the terrible experi-ence of June 22 and 23. It was no easy task. Morale at the bases was deterio-rating quickly. SMERSH agents picked up rumors among the Americans that the bombing raid had been caused by the Soviet newspaper announce-ment of the arrival of the Flying Fortresses. First Lieutenant Albert Jaroff, the US Air Force intelligence officer at Myrhorod, whose job was to debrief the US pilots about the German targets and air defenses, and whom the SMERSH commanders suspected of espionage, expressed the feelings of many of his comrades when he told one of the SMERSH informers: "I con-sider your anti-aircraft defense system very weak: during the attack, the shooting was very poor; there were no night fighters; the searchlights pro-vided very poor illumination; our artillery and our night fighters should have been put into service, then all would have been well."[28]

The American commanders Walsh and Kessler approached General Perminov, informing him of the suspension of shuttle-bombing operations. A Soviet counterintelligence report summarized their complaints as follows: "The Germans are bombing us [the Soviets] scot-free, our artillery is not powerful enough, our fighters are not equipped for night fighting, which means that they cannot do their job properly, and military operations will begin when they [the Americans] are confident that they will not be bombed here and will be adequately covered with anti-aircraft artillery and fighters." The Soviets could do little to accommodate those demands, as they had no radar-equipped night fighters, and their flak batteries were all but useless at night.[29]

In Moscow the American commanders, backed by the US embassy, asked permission to bring in American night fighters and air defenses, but the usually accommodating General Nikitin was not enthusiastic about the idea. His political bosses did not want more Americans on the Poltava air bases. Following Nikitin's negative response, the American commission investigating the matter suggested a number of provisional measures to avoid disasters like the one of June 22. These included keeping as few American aircraft as possible on the Poltava-area fields at any given time and replacing the silver-painted Flying Fortresses with camouflaged ones. The time to show off American air power had passed: the priority was now to preserve and secure it.[30]

Meanwhile, General John Deane at the US military mission was in damage-control mode, doing his best to reduce tensions, avoid finger-pointing and, most importantly, prevent Allied journalists from reporting about the bombings—even as Berlin radio was triumphantly broadcasting news of the Poltava raid. He succeeded in convincing Western reporters who had been at Poltava and those who had stayed behind in Moscow not to report on the disaster and to focus instead on the heroism of the Soviet and American comrades-in-arms. Having organized a joint press conference for Soviet and Western reporters, Deane managed to avoid a public-relations disaster. Nonetheless, there was little he could do to bridge the gap in Soviet-American relations that began to widen after the Poltava raid.

Deane later wrote that the Poltava disaster "sowed the seed of discontent, the Russians smarting and sensitive because of their failure to provide the protection they had promised, and the Americans forgiving but determined to send their own anti-aircraft defenses as protection for the future." The spirit of cooperation at the Poltava-area bases was rapidly deteriorating, tensions were growing. It did not help matters that the Western media would refuse to follow Deane's instructions.[31]

9

Forbidden Love

"**Y**ou will remember the unprecedented shuttle bombing of June 21st to July 5th in which American B-17 Flying Fortresses flew from England to Russia," wrote Howard Whitman in his opening line in an article for the New York *Daily News*. Whitman was referring to the *Frantic II* shuttle mission. To General Deane's relief, there was no mention of the German raid on the US air bases and the damage it had done to the American Air Force and more generally to Soviet-American relations. Still, Whitman's article, which first appeared on July 19, 1944, was soon picked up by numerous US newspapers, created a public-relations disaster of a different nature. He wrote about relations between American men and Soviet women at the Poltava-area bases—a topic previously taboo in American, to say nothing of Soviet, coverage of the shuttle-bombing operations.

Whitman was a fairly well known reporter at the time. Before starting to write for the *Daily News*, he had covered the world war for the *London Daily Express*. After the war he published a number of popular books, including *Let's Tell the Truth about Sex* (1948), on the need to educate children about sexual life. Sex was also the main subject of his July 1944 *Daily News* article. The title left no doubt about its content: "Nude Welcome to Russia

Shocks U.S. Bomber Pilots." Other newspapers ran the article under equally provocative titles. The one chosen by the *Chicago Tribune* editors was "See Russia and Blush, Verdict of U.S. Flyers." "You join the air forces and you expect to see the world, but you probably don't expect to see it in the nude," read the opening sentence of the piece.[1]

Whitman filed his dispatch from Britain, where he interviewed American pilots who had just returned from Poltava. One of them recounted how he and his comrades had stumbled into a pond full of naked men and women taking a bath. The Soviets were not ashamed of their bodies and invited the Americans to join them in the warm water. "Finally a girl comes up to one of our fellows and motions him to take his shorts off," one of the pilots allegedly told Whitman. "It was funny seeing her walk up like that without a thing on." Other pilots had juicer stories to share. According to one of them, a Soviet officer approached the Americans with a question: "How many women do you want?" Whitman wrote that the officer "was prepared to provide the customary contingent of registered camp followers" and was disappointed by the pilots' answer: "I'm afraid we don't do things that way." One of the pilots explained to Whitman the norms of sexual life in the Red Army. "In Russia each soldier is allowed to visit official army brothels every so often, more or less like we go to the post exchange. Russian soldiers do not pay anything if they stick to the regular ration, but if they want to make more frequent visits they have to pay a fee."[2]

Whitman never named his sources, and it is not clear whether he invented parts of his story or whether the pilots had played a prank on a naïve reporter, but the article had an explosive effect at the US mission in Moscow. Everyone there, from General Deane to the lowest clerk, knew that the Red Army did not have brothels for its officers and soldiers, and the story about regular visits to brothels came straight from Wehrmacht practice. With no brothels or "registered camp followers" available, the Soviets could not have offered the Americans a "customary contingent," although some Americans reported that in the early days at the bases Red Army officers encouraged them to dance with Soviet women.

The bathing story had some factual basis but was apparently exaggerated either by Whitman or by his informants. Franklyn Holzman, who was stationed at Myrhorod, described his bathing experience there in a letter sent home to Brooklyn on June 30, 1944: "I went swimming this afternoon. A lot of Russian fellows and girls were there. The fellows mostly went in nude. Some would hold themselves, but others made no attempt to hide." He added: "The girls are a little more careful." Holzman's fellow radar operator at Myrhorod, Palmer Myhra, recalled that he and his friends watched local women coming to the river to wash their clothes and take a bath. "As we would slowly glide by we could see many of them didn't bother with swimming suits," wrote Myhra decades later. "Why waste cloth on a swimming suit? They probably had been bathing in the river this way for a long time."

Myhra was not there to judge local customs. Writing that he and other Americans "wore swimming trunks or cut off old trousers," he also remarked: "most of us farm boys remembered that wasn't always necessary back home." He drew no conclusions about mixed bathing, which was rooted in medieval and early modern traditions of Slavic village life and became a cliché in Western travel literature about Russia. Neither Myhra nor Holzman made any connection between nude bathing and sex. A day earlier Holzman had written to his parents, describing the town of Myrhorod: "This town is fine, although the women are a little too moral for your son."[3]

Whitman's article threatened to aggravate growing tensions in Soviet-American relations, and Deane's subordinates in Moscow rushed to call a press conference debunking his account. The State Department in Washington issued a press release, citing American officers who had been stationed at the bases and now denied the story, stressing the "utmost hospitality and courtesy" offered to the Americans by their Soviet hosts.

Ironically, Whitman's article appeared at a time when relations between American men and Soviet women at the Poltava-area bases actually were becoming a problem, though not of the kind imagined by Whitman or his sources. On the contrary, the Soviets were doing their best to disrupt any liaisons that the American airmen had managed to establish with Soviet women.[4] At Poltava and other American bases, SMERSH officers alternated between the roles of chaperones and puritans, allowing local women to date American allies when this was found useful and preventing it when it was not. The Americans resented such restrictions. Conflict over dating rights became a key factor in disenchanting GIs with their Soviet allies.

On Monday, July 10, about a week before the publication of Whitman's article, Major Albert Lepawsky, now the commandant of the Eastern Command headquarters, sat down to write a memo to Major General Walsh. As noted earlier, Lepawsky, the most senior American officer of "Russian" descent at the bases, was on the SMERSH watch list. This was in part because, as described in a Soviet counterintelligence report, he "is carefully studying our officer and civilian staff and taking an interest in those of his enlisted men who have ties of any kind with Russians." Such ties were indeed the main theme of Lepawsky's memo, the subject line of which read: "Reported Incidents Involving American Soldiers and Russian Personnel."[5]

Lepawsky reported on a number of incidents that had taken place in Poltava over the previous weekend. On Friday, July 7, First Lieutenant Edward A. Coutts had been conversing with two women who were suddenly attacked by a Soviet man in civilian clothing. The attacker kicked them, shouted something in Russian, and chased them away. On the same evening, Technician 4th Class Judson J. Sorrell had a date with a local woman in the Poltava Corpus Park, the city's main attraction and site of the recent funeral of Petr Lidov and his fellow reporters. Mindful of a briefing from his superiors, Sorrell did not dismiss the possibility that the girl he was meeting might be a Soviet spy seeking information about the Americans, but his suspicions were almost completely dispelled fifteen minutes into the date. As Sorrell, who spoke no Ukrainian or Russian, tried to communicate with the Ukrainian woman, who spoke no English, a man in Red Army uniform suddenly attacked his date. As Sorrell told Lepawsky, "after saying a few words to her, this man kicked her, thereby pushing her a distance of several feet." After that, the attacker and the victim walked in different directions, leaving Sorrell on his own to make sense of what had happened.

The attacks continued the next day, Saturday, July 8. As Staff Sergeant T. H. Northway was speaking to his Ukrainian date in a Poltava park, a man and a woman in civilian clothing approached the couple. As Northway described what happened to Lepawsky, "The man had some heated words with…[his] friend, and then slapped her, continuing to talk to her in a scolding manner." As in Sorrell's case, the girl and her attackers then went off in different directions. Like Sorrell, Northway did not get into a fight: both were under instructions not to engage in conflicts with the Soviets. Also like Sorrell, he did not know what to make of the incident. His first guess was that the couple who had approached them had been the girl's parents, and then noticed that the woman was too young to be the girl's mother. Northway had already arranged another meeting with the girl later that day and hoped that she would explain what had actually happened, but she did not show up for the second date. Northway "does not blame her in the least," wrote Lepawsky in his report.[6]

Lepawsky got a better understanding of what was going on after interviewing Corporal Peter Nicolaeff, a Russian-speaking native of Odesa who, like Lepawsky himself, came from a family of émigrés from the Russian Empire and was on the SMERSH espionage suspects list. Nicolaeff and Technician Sergeant Ralph Mowery met in the park with two Red Army women, one a lieutenant, the other a private. They were sitting on a bench when a woman in a Red Army lieutenant's uniform approached them and "spoke to the girls in an insulting tone." Then three men passed by, two of them in military uniform and one in civilian clothes, making similarly insulting remarks. The words they used were "whore" and "German whore," but at some point "uncomplimentary" references were made with regard to the "American Allies" as well. Nicolaeff stated that one of the men involved in the incident was a member of the secret police—he was carrying a pistol and was identified as such by Nicolaeff's date. When Nicolaeff and Mowery left the bench and walked their dates away from the trouble spot, local boys followed them, verbally assaulting the girls.[7]

Everyone Lepawsky spoke to was under the impression that the Soviets had issued a ban prohibiting local girls from dating American GIs. He received similar reports from Myrhorod, where the American commander,

Major Callahan, had demanded an explanation from his Soviet counterpart. He was assured that these were isolated incidents and not sanctioned by the authorities. Lepawsky was eager to give the Soviets the benefit of the doubt and wanted to believe that the same applied to Poltava. But he also asked General Walsh to conduct a special investigation of the incidents while imposing a temporary ban on GI visits to Poltava and asking the Soviet Air Force commanders for proof that the incidents had not been coordinated. He passed on the information to his superiors, leaving them to decide those matters.[8]

The American commanders knew all along that the Soviets were opposed to personal relations between US airmen and Red Army women. On April 25, General Perminov had declared to his US counterparts: "the temper of the local population is important. The question of vodka, brothels—all these things must be liquidated. These problems must be decided soon." In May he had complained to Colonel Kessler that unwanted advances from the Americans had so embarrassed one of the local girls working at the base camp that she stopped coming to work. Kessler found the accusations unfounded, but the American commanders did whatever was in their power to avoid upsetting their Soviet hosts. They instructed the GIs to stay away from Red Army women.

American troops arriving at the Poltava-area bases in May had already been instructed not to "expect the usual social freedom in their relations with Russian girls," as Lepawsky noted. The Fifteenth Air Force pilots were warned before their first shuttle-bombing mission to Poltava in early June: "Russian women are quite friendly and open. Do not mistake the friendliness as an invitation to further intimacy." The Americans were advised that Red Army women were prohibited from dating them and would be punished if caught violating that rule. Many believed that this policy was the reason for the transfer of the most attractive Soviet woman at Poltava, who held the rank of lieutenant, to the Myrhorod base. The logic behind the American indoctrination effort was that men were honor-bound to protect Soviet women in uniform by not dating them.[9]

US military commanders also wanted their men to forget the possibility of marrying a Soviet woman. In Moscow, General Deane spelled out the policy in a memorandum that he forwarded to Colonel Kessler, at the very beginning of shuttle-bombing operations in early May 1944. The memorandum read: "If a member of the Forces of the U.S. on duty in the USSR marries a citizen of the Soviet Union while in Russia, he will be immediately relieved of his assignment and be transferred to a station outside of the USSR. Experience of the State Department and the U.S. Army and Navy, while serving in the USSR, has shown that complications and differences have arisen when an American marries a Russian. To eliminate these embarrassments, marriage will be discouraged. In previous instances the American citizen has never been able to depart with his wife."[10]

While recognizing as legitimate Soviet efforts to prevent airmen from dating women in uniform, the American commanders were not prepared to prohibit their subordinates from dating civilians. They considered such a policy neither fair nor enforceable. The curfew hour was 11:00 p.m., after which no American soldier was supposed be in the cities, but Soviet sentries would occasionally catch Americans staying overnight at the homes of their dates. The Americans found civilian women more attractive than those in military uniform. "The local girls...were mostly Ukrainian and had opportunities to dress up some and look more attractive," remembered Palmer Myhra, who was stationed at Myrhorod. "Most of the girls were a little husky and strong, but not all. Most had dark hair and blondes were rather rare except those in the Army as many Russians especially from the North were blond." Myhra did not date any Soviet women. Others did, however. In June, when American troops were moved from Pyriatyn to a camp at the airfield seven miles away, they managed to visit their girlfriends despite a temporary prohibition on visiting the city. "How this was done at a distance of 12 kilometers, without transportation being made available, is one of those secrets that only the GI in the American Army in Russia can answer," wrote an historian of the American mission at Poltava.[11]

At first the Soviets, who were strict about preventing contacts with women in uniform, seemed much more relaxed when it came to dates with civilians. Throughout May and June, there were almost no reports of Soviet military personnel or civilians approaching Americans and verbally or physically abusing their dates. An investigation into the matter launched by Major Lepawsky's report and conducted by Inspector General Major Ralph P. Dunn of Eastern Command showed that such incidents increased drastically in early July: there were thirteen attempts to disrupt dates between July 3 and 14, almost all of them took place in Corpus Park in Poltava. It looked as if all and sundry took part: of the thirteen reported cases, five involved civilians, four Red Army officers, and three Red Army soldiers.

In one case, a Russian-speaking American sergeant was approached by two Red Army lieutenants while on a date with a local woman named "Viola." "Without anything being said," the sergeant later reported, "both lieutenants struck Viola with their clubs, one hitting her on the back of the right hand and the other hitting on the back of the left wrist." The sergeant stepped between the attackers and his date. One lieutenant then took Viola aside and discussed something with her. The other told the sergeant that they simply wanted to protect him and other Americans from venereal disease, as many of the girls whom the Americans were dating had also dated Germans and become infected. Then a woman in civilian clothing approached the sergeant and Viola; on hearing what had happened, she made one of the lieutenants apologize. Surprising everyone, she introduced herself as a Red Army lieutenant.

Given the tensions aroused by these incidents, it was not surprising that Soviet attacks on women who dated Americans produced conflict between servicemen of the two armies. On the evening of July 14, a fight broke out between Soviet and American servicemen in Myrhorod. Two Red Army officers approached an American NCO and his girlfriend sitting on a bench in the park. One of the officers hit the girl, the American hit him back, and then one of the Soviets hit the American on the head with his pistol butt. When the American came to his senses, he found himself in a hospital. The US commanders sounded the alarm, issuing an immediate order prohibiting American personnel from leaving the bases after dark, which was significantly earlier (about 8:45 p.m. in July) than the established curfew of 11:00 p.m. The order also stated that "American troops will not be subjected to insult and injury with impunity."[12]

On July 17, three days after the incident, Colonel Paul T. Cullen, who was commanding the bases during Kessler's temporary absence, approached General Perminov and demanded explanations. Perminov, reported Cullen the next day, "stated officially and solemnly that neither Soviet military nor government authorities have issued any prohibition or restriction upon the association of Soviet women with US personnel." Cullen, whose main concern, apart from the safety of his troops, was the maintenance of good working relations with the Soviets, asked the officers under his command to pass Perminov's words on to their enlisted men. He also used the occasion to appeal to his men's sense of loyalty to their own women back home. He asked the GIs to imagine that the situation was reversed, with Soviets stationed on US territory. In that case, suggested Cullen, "individual members of this command would be irritated and provoked that their wives and sweethearts permitted themselves to be courted by others." Further, Cullen tried to educate his men in the basics of Soviet law, instructing subordinates that "the Soviet government does not tolerate prostitution and does everything in its power to stamp it out, usually by exile or confinement."[13]

Colonel Cullen was right: the Soviets were out to eradicate prostitution. In the course of the 1930s they had reversed their early postrevolutionary policies, which treated prostitution as a social problem generated by capitalist society, and had begun to treat it as a crime, imprisoning prostitutes and pimps and declaring them class enemies. The official position was simple. The Soviet regime had liquidated the social condition that caused prostitution, and it had ceased to exist as a social phenomenon. Now the Soviets were eager to prevent a recurrence of prostitution with the arrival of the Americans, whose society, according to their interpretation of Marxism, was more than capable of generating it.

At first glance, the US Army was in agreement with the Soviets on the issue. In France after D-Day, the French authorities wanted to regulate the sexual activity of American soldiers by creating army brothels to remove it from public sight in streets and parks. The US Army commanders, apprehensive about a possible outburst on the part of wives and girlfriends of GIs at home, refused to comply. The Americans and the French agreed that sexual activity was essential to keep military morale high and soldiers fighting but disagreed on the role of the army in making provision for such activity. Like the Americans, the Soviets also made no such provision. They tried to control the spread of venereal disease, but otherwise their army was left to its own devices.

Of course, there was no less hunger for sex in the Red Army than in any other. As a Soviet Army veteran recalled, "death, food, and sex" were the soldiers' most common subjects of conversation. But if there were funeral detachments to deal with the first and field kitchens to take care of the second, the third was not addressed by any service of the Red Army. Sex was not discussed in Stalinist society, which meant in wartime that the army was supposed to take care of the soldiers' desires at the expense of the civil population. Once the Red Army crossed the Soviet border in the summer and fall of 1944, women, especially German women, were considered legitimate trophies, with Soviet commanders turning a blind eye to the sexual crimes of their subordinates or even encouraging rape, as in East Prussia.

Then there were the army's "internal reserves," or women who served in the army and were considered legitimate objects of sexual advances by their male counterparts. There were close to a half million such women—Air Force pilots, flak operators, machine gunners, medical doctors and nurses, telephone operators and construction workers, to name some of the most popular occupations in which the Red Army employed women during the war. No matter what position they took and what functions they performed, most Red Army officers and soldiers saw them first and foremost as sex objects. The situation of women in mixed units—and most Red Army units were—was especially difficult. Given the predominance of men in the army, there was intense competition for the affections of women, with higher-ranking commanders emerging victorious over their subordinates. In some cases, women themselves referred to their military barracks as harems.[14]

When it came to sexual liaisons with foreigners on their territory, however, the Soviets tried to prevent them in any way possible. In the settlements retaken from the Germans, the Soviet officials, unlike the French, never publicly humiliated women who had "collaborated horizontally" with the Germans during the occupation—since it raised the issue of political loyalty on the most intimate level, the subject seemed too potentially wounding to the pride of the regime to be addressed in public. The authorities preferred to maintain their puritan façade, refusing to recognize sexual desire as a legitimate subject of government policy in the military and civilian contexts alike.

With regard to sexual encounters between American servicemen and their Soviet dates, a policy was adopted but not publicly disclosed. SMERSH officers at the Poltava-area bases were specifically instructed to limit contacts and break those not controlled by the secret police. The rationale given to the Americans by those who attacked their dates—that they were trying to protect the Americans from venereal disease—was not credible, as some Americans noticed that Soviet men did not react when Americans dated women who "would go with anyone" but became aggressive when GIs dated attractive girls. Those Americans who could understand Russian heard attackers reproaching girls for not going out with Soviets, who apparently were not good enough for them, but dating Germans or Americans instead.

The young women who were prevented from meeting with Americans thought that there were cultural reasons behind the prohibition. One of them confided to a Russian-speaking American officer that after spending two years under German occupation, the local Ukrainian girls had seen that "the Germans were much more cultured and civilized than the Russians, and if these girls were allowed to see that the Americans were even more cultured and civilized than the Russians in their way of living, they obviously would prefer the Americans to the Russians, and the Russians would not want that to happen."[15]

The American commanders believed that they could recognize a pattern. The jealousy expressed by local men toward Americans who were dating pretty girls, and attacks on women who allegedly had dated Germans, resembled behavior that American servicemen had already encountered elsewhere in Europe at the time.

Envy of Americans was part of everyday experience in Britain, the launching pad of the American-led invasion of Europe. The Americans had better uniforms, which made them all look like officers, had more money than their British counterparts and, no less important, had access to such scarce goods as American cigarettes and nylon stockings, highly valued in wartime. All that made them popular with British women—that, at least, was the opinion of British men. "They think they can buy them body and soul, if they take them into a pub and buy them a drink," wrote one British soldier. "What chance has a poor Tommy with a couple of bob jingling in his pocket?"[16]

American soldiers' success with women created even more anxiety among British soldiers stationed overseas than those at home. By the fall of 1942, the British military command in the Middle East had handled more than 200,000 divorce cases initiated in Britain by the wives of soldiers stationed in the region. Whatever the reason behind the wave of divorce, it was easy to imagine that British women were leaving their husbands to marry Americans. The "American problem" even affected the family of Winston Churchill. His daughter-in-law, Pamela Churchill, spent her nights in the company of Averell Harriman, then the administrator of the Lend-Lease program in London, while her lawful husband, Major Randolph Churchill, served in North Africa. Pamela Churchill did not marry Harriman until twenty-eight years later, but many GIs married their British girlfriends right away despite the numerous obstacles created by their commanders, who wanted their soldiers to stay single and focus on their duties.[17]

In July 1942 the US Army journal *Yank*, distributed among GIs in Britain, ran the headline: "Don't Promise Her Anything—Marriage Outside the U.S. Is Out." It was probably welcomed not only by British soldiers concerned about competition on the home front but by the wives and girlfriends of GIs back in the United States. Interviewed for *Life* magazine in September 1944, Sonya Nansen, a seventeen-year-old counter girl whose boyfriend was serving in Australia, asked the magazine reporter whether he knew anything about "two shiploads of wives of American soldiers" who had allegedly come from Australia. She was not far off the mark. Altogether about 30,000 war brides came to America from Britain, and about 70,000 from Europe as a whole.[18]

In France, ravaged by occupation and war, the Americans seemed even more popular with local women than they were in the United Kingdom. The language barrier was minor compared to the dire financial conditions in which many women found themselves after the Germans left the country. "In France everything was in short supply except alcoholic beverages, bread as only the French could make it, and women," remembered one GI. The Americans wanted all three and had much to offer in return. US Army supply stores had cigarettes, coffee, chocolate, and, last but not least, soap, which could readily be exchanged for sexual favors. Prostitution, with sex exchanged for money obtained by selling American goods on the black market, flourished in French towns and cities—to the outrage of French civilians, who had seen prostitutes thriving from liaisons with the Germans a few months earlier and were now appalled to see them doing even better with the arrival of the Americans.

Even so, few French were prepared to condemn liaisons with Americans as harshly as "horizontal collaboration" with Germans. In 1945, when a writer for the *Journal de la Marne* compared the women walking the streets of Reims with Americans to the whores who had populated the very same streets during the German occupation, he was heavily criticized by his readers and forced to apologize. Americans were regarded as liberators, not occupiers. Yet the humiliation that came with the German occupation continued to influence public attitudes toward women who had chosen to sleep with foreigners in uniform. Once again, the reputation of the entire nation was at stake.[19]

Parallels with Britain and France aside, the Americans found themselves in a unique situation in the Soviet Union. What had been spontaneous manifestations of insecurity, jealousy, and national pride by citizens in Western Europe took on the characteristics of state policy in the Soviet Union, where government agencies claimed the right to monitor interaction between

their citizens and foreigners. "The usual problems of social and sexual relations were given a special twist in the Russian project, largely as a result of
unique Russian reactions on this subject," wrote Albert Lepawsky later.[20]

American airmen who dated Soviet women or were suspected of facilitating such dates found themselves under the watchful eye of SMERSH.
Among the main figures on the Soviet list of espionage suspects was Albert
Jaroff. The first lieutenant was under suspicion because of his position as
head of the intelligence unit at Myrhorod and because of his outgoing personality, which led him to befriend Red Army personnel and locals alike.
There was also the allegation that Jaroff and his Jewish family had been
linked with the White movement during the Russian Revolution. Jaroff had
come to the Myrhorod base in May via the Middle East route. Fluent in
Russian, Jaroff was eager to establish contacts with the Soviets. He enjoyed
a drink or two with Red Army officers and, by all accounts, was happy to be
among people whose language and culture he shared. "I have never seen a
more friendly attitude," confided Jaroff to Raymond Davies, the Canadian
reporter who had come to Poltava to report on the landing of the first Flying
Fortresses on June 2.[21]

Jaroff had aroused the suspicion of the SMERSH officers early on. His
openness to contacts with his Soviet counterparts was interpreted as an
attempt to develop trust and potentially recruit agents; his visits to Soviet
commanders in the area with offers of showing American movies were
perceived as an unobtrusive way of spying on Soviet military installations. He was also suspected of eavesdropping on Red Air Force officers'
conversations. His inquiries about areas outside the Poltava-area bases
seemed even more suspicious. On May 25, Jaroff told a Soviet commander visiting Myrhorod that in 1936 he had visited the Soviet Union
as a tourist, with stopovers in Vladivostok, Moscow, and his native Odesa.
He asked the visiting officer for assistance in locating a certain employee
of the Soviet consulate in San Francisco in 1936–1937 who apparently
had helped him arrange the trip. In early June in Myrhorod Jaroff asked a
Soviet acquaintance, Captain Ivanov, who happened to be an undercover
SMERSH officer, to check the address of a woman he had apparently met
in Moscow in 1936.[22]

Predictably, Jaroff did not get far with either of his requests. His inquires were viewed with suspicion as a way of acquiring information about Soviet citizens or recruiting agents. Sveshnikov and Zorin increased surveillance of Jaroff and came up with new "proof" of his espionage activities. "Surveillance of his behavior among the Americans has established that despite his insignificant service occupation and rank, the commanders of the American Air Force group reckon with him," reported Sveshnikov and Zorin to Moscow. In their experience, only a secret-police or counterintelligence officer could be respected or even feared by his superiors. The two regarded the US Air Force from the perspective of Stalin's police state. They had no other perspective to rely on, nor the power of imagination to suggest that things might work differently in the United States.[23]

In mid-July, around the time when that Soviet lieutenant attacked an American NCO and sent him to hospital, the Soviets demanded that the US commanders recall Jaroff from the Soviet Union. His superiors in the Eighth Air Force in Britain were not happy, not being aware of the SMERSH tactics. They blamed him for the problems with the Soviets and wanted him gone. "Return this officer to the Ninth [Air Force], the Eighth does not want him," went the cable to Myrhorod. The reason for the Soviet demand that remained unknown to the Americans was spelled out in great detail in SMERSH internal documents.

Jaroff, claimed the SMERSH officers, was trying to use the Soviet command's prohibition on dating between Red Army women and Americans, along with the resulting dissatisfaction among the GIs, to incite conflicts between the two sides. According to the SMERSH report, during the first half of July, at the height of attacks on the American dates, Jaroff had arranged to bring sixty-five Soviet nurses from the nearby military hospital to the American camp at Myrhorod. They watched a movie with the Americans and ate and danced at their restaurant before being taken back to the hospital. SMERSH considered that a provocation, suggesting that Jaroff expected the Soviet authorities to order the Soviet nurses back to their hospital, which would provoke an outburst among the Americans. SMERSH gave itself credit for handling the provocation smoothly and allowing the evening to proceed as planned, But they wanted Jaroff out of the country.[24]

With Jaroff out of the picture, the Myrhorod SMERSH officers turned their attention to Jaroff's assistant in the base's intelligence unit, Sergeant Philip Tandet. Like Jaroff, Tandet was a fluent Russian speaker and, having been born to Russian parents in the Chinese city of Harbin, was thought to have had links with the White movement. According to SMERSH reports, Tandet not only spread "fabrications to the effect that Russian girls were not allowed to meet with Americans" but also dated some of those girls himself. He was spotted on a date with Yekaterina Stankevich, an employee of Voentorg, the Red Army retail department that ran the restaurant for the Americans and sold them Soviet-made goods. The young woman, originally from Moscow, was, like her colleagues, a civilian employee in Voentorg. While military personnel were under strict orders not to date Americans, civilian employees at the bases fell into a gray area. SMERSH considered them to be under the same restrictions as the military but had trouble enforcing the prohibition.[25]

What made the SMERSH officers especially nervous about Tandet's liaison with Stankevich was that, according to their informers, Tandet wanted Stankevich to find a rental apartment in Myrhorod where he could live with her. He also promised to take her with him to the United States. Stankevich confided to her friends at Voentorg that she was ready to go, but only if she could take her young daughter along. The SMERSH officers demanded that Stankevich's superiors fire her and send her back to Moscow, which was done on July 21. Before her departure, Stankevich apparently told Tandet that she had been fired for dating him and named the counterintelligence officer she believed responsible for her dismissal, Captain Ivanov.

Tandet promised to teach Ivanov a lesson. Ivanov, who knew about the threat, decided to get Tandet first. On the night of July 23 he learned that Tandet had visited another woman, named Boldyreva, who had previously shared a rented room with Stankevich. The Americans were supposed to be back in camp by 11:00 p.m., but Tandet spent the night in Boldyreva's room. At 1:30 a.m., Ivanov showed up at Boldyreva's building and arrested Tandet for violating the curfew. He was duly reprimanded and sentenced by his US commanders to six days of manual labor. Ivanov had a victory but wanted more. He asked the Red Army officers running Voentorg to dismiss Boldyreva. Interestingly, he received an unexpected rebuff from General Perminov himself.[26]

What SMERSH saw as a victory was considered a complete disaster by the Soviet military commanders. The arrest of Tandet, the firing of Stankevich, and the requested dismissal of Boldyreva only worsened Soviet-American relations at the bases, already tense because of the attacks on women dating the Americans. If anything, such attacks supported the accusations made by Tandet and others that the Soviets were prohibiting their women from dating Americans and undermined the solemn statements to the contrary Perminov had made to Colonel Cullen. Moreover, the Myrhorod Voentorg was losing staff at a record rate, and if the tendency to fire female employees implicated in dating Americans continued, Perminov might soon be left without civilian help at the bases.

General Perminov complained about Ivanov's actions to Sveshnikov, but to little avail. Sveshnikov told him that he had "directives from Moscow to break off relations between all Russians, especially girls, and the Americans." Perminov realized that his only hope was to appeal to the higher-ups. In the growing conflict between the Air Force commander and SMERSH officers, only one authority had the power to intervene decisively—the Communist Party. On July 26, Perminov sent a report to the supreme party official in the Red Army Air Force, General Nikolai Shimanov, who was both a political appointee in the Military Council of the Red Army Air Force and head of the Aviation Department in the party's Central Committee in Moscow. In his report to Shimanov, Perminov described the arrest of Tandet, the firing of Stankevich, the SMERSH demand to fire Boldyreva, and an earlier episode at the Myrhorod base in which a SMERSH officer had ordered two women from Voentorg to get out of a car driven by Americans.

Perminov did not dispute Moscow's orders to Sveshnikov but questioned the way in which SMERSH implemented them and went about its work. In Perminov's view, SMERSH tactics played into the hands of enemies— supporters of the Revolutionary-era anti-Soviet "White Guards," as the

Soviets now referred to American personnel born in Russia or elsewhere to Russian parents. The "Whites" allegedly wanted to undermine relations between the allies. "Obviously, one must know how to go about 'breaking off' acquaintances and not just shoot from the hip, as that affects working relations, creates new conflicts, and helps the White Guards develop their activity," wrote Perminov. He also requested permission not to fire Boldyreva, "as no other compromising materials about her have been presented to me." He added: "Following that line would mean dispersing all civilian women employees in the immediate future."

In the same report he condemned even more strongly SMERSH efforts to threaten the local population into breaking off their contacts with the Americans. "I consider such a manner of solving the problem politically harmful," argued Perminov. "If that's the way it goes, then repressive measures will have to be taken against half the population of Poltava, Myrhorod, Pyriatyn, and surrounding villages."[27]

The report addressed to General Shimanov eventually ended up on the desk of SMERSH head Viktor Abakumov in Moscow, along with a memo signed by Sveshnikov, who wrote that the actions of his subordinates had caused no trouble at all: Tandet did not complain about his arrest, while Boldyreva allegedly decided on her own not to date him again. Sveshnikov was clearly on the defensive. He claimed that Perminov himself was warning civilian employees that liaisons with the Americans were prohibited. Abakumov gave his orders to subordinates orally, leaving no trace in the documents of what they actually were, but after Perminov's intervention, attacks on women dating Americans ceased. In August, Americans were able to date their Ukrainian girlfriends and stay in Poltava-area parks during hours of darkness until the 11:00 p.m. curfew. SMERSH changed its tactics, putting more emphasis on monitoring liaisons between American men and Ukrainian women and less on brutal suppression.[28]

The July crisis over dating endured in the memory of Americans at the Poltava air bases, changing their initially positive attitude toward the Soviets. If the Luftwaffe bombing in June had alienated the base commanders, the July events left the rank and file disaffected. August and September would add fresh concerns.

Picking a Fight

On Sunday, August 6, 1944, the Ukrainian airfields came to life once again with the arrival of seventy-eight Flying Fortresses and their escort of sixty-four Mustangs. This was part of the first shuttle-bombing raid to be carried out since late June, when the Flying Fortresses of the Eighth Air Force had descended on the Poltava-area airfields, only to be destroyed by the subsequent German attack. After that disaster, it took the US commanders almost a month and half to launch a new raid, dubbed *Frantic V*. *Frantic I* had begun the operation in early June; *Frantic II* was the unfortunate mission that all but ended during the German attack of June 22 on the bases; and *Frantic III* and *IV* had been conducted in July by the Fifteenth Air Force in Italy, involving fighters alone. *Frantic V*, in contrast, was carried out by three bomber wings accompanied by one fighter wing—all part of the Eighth Air Force based in Britain.

The mission was undertaken as a result of a Soviet request. Moscow wanted the Flying Fortresses to bomb targets in Upper Silesia in Germany and in the Krakow area of Poland, and it wanted the job done quickly—before August 5. But bad weather postponed *Frantic V* and led to a change of target: the Flying Fortresses bombed installations near the Polish city of

Gdynia on the Baltic coast. On the next day, August 7, they achieved part of their original goal by attacking the Krakow-area targets from the Poltava bases. On August 8, instead of flying back to Britain, the airplanes of the Eighth Air Force flew to Italy; on the way they bombed targets in Romania, which the Soviets were preparing to invade later that month.[1]

The operation was considered generally successful, although the number of Flying Fortresses involved, the importance of targets hit, and the damage recorded could not compare to *Frantic II*, undertaken in June. This time, however, no planes were lost on the ground after the raid. The Americans never succeeded in convincing the Soviets to allow them to bring in their own night fighters and anti-aircraft defenses, a move that would have increased the number of Americans in the Poltava area fivefold. It no longer seemed necessary. The Soviet-German front line had moved too far west for the Germans to undertake the kind of attack they had mounted only a few weeks earlier. The Red Army offensive, "Operation Bagration" (named after a Russian military commander of Georgian origin who had fought in the Napoleonic wars) began on June 22, the same day the Germans bombed the Poltava air bases. By mid-August, Red Army troops were approaching East Prussia in the north, the Vistula River in the center, and the Carpathian Mountains in the southern sector of the front. Belarus and Ukraine were now almost entirely under Soviet control.[2]

The rapidly advancing front line presented the Poltava-area bases with a new challenge. The number of targets that the Americans could reach from those bases was decreasing dramatically as they either came under Soviet control or became part of the Red Army's theater of operations. The Americans on the ground in Poltava and the military mission in Moscow began to notice that the Soviets were showing less and less enthusiasm for the shuttle-bombing operations. The same was true of the American commanders in London and Washington, who were becoming increasingly interested in acquiring new bases closer to the fast-moving Soviet-German front line.[3]

In Moscow, American requests for new bases farther west and closer to the front fell on deaf ears. The Soviets kept delaying the approval of targets for new operations; thus *Frantic VI*, a new mission that would bring

American planes from the United Kingdom to Ukraine and to Italy did not take place until mid-September—the longest gap in the history of *Frantic* operations. Faced with the lull in bombing operations and receiving conflicting signals from Moscow about their future, the officers and GIs at the Poltava bases began to feel confused and unwelcome. Their conflicts with the Soviets multiplied, some degenerating into fistfights. The Alliance was developing a major crack, one that went right down to its foundation—servicemen who were supposed to fight side by side were turning against one another.

In mid-August the bases were visited by the US Strategic Air Forces in Europe (USSTAF) deputy commander for administration, Major General Hugh J. Knerr. On his arrival to the Soviet Union, Knerr visited Averell Harriman and General Deane. He spent almost a week—from August 15 to 21—at the Poltava bases. He left them highly skeptical about the Soviets' commitment to continuing the project, and doubtful whether it made any sense to go on with the shuttle-bombing operations. Knerr also did not think much of the possibility of establishing American bases in the Far East—which has been one of the key American objectives in launching *Frantic* in the first place.

On the Soviet attitude toward the bases, Knerr commented in his report: "The Devil [is] no longer sick and not interested in becoming a Monk for the defeat of Germany." That memorable assessment reflected the views of American officers and GIs at the bases. The Soviets, emboldened by their recent victories, were showing steadily declining enthusiasm for cooperation with their American allies. After all, by this point the Americans were bogged down in France, still far from the German border, while they, the Soviets, were on the move, liberating their own territories and now crossing into Central Europe and the Balkans. Knerr criticized the Soviets for doing very little to improve air defenses after the German attack of June 22. He also noted that cooperation between Americans and Soviets technicians who serviced the planes was breaking down, and that "the Russians steal all the tools that they can get their hands on."[4]

Knerr believed that under the circumstances General Walsh was failing to maintain morale and discipline. He saw a sign of "lack of leadership" in the weeds growing around the American tents at Poltava. Morale at the bases was indeed in free fall. Seeing the writing on the wall, the GIs talked of little else than returning to their bases in Europe or home to the United States. Discipline also deteriorated, with a sharp increase in cases of illicit trade in American goods and drunken conflicts between fellow Americans, as well as between them and the Soviets.

There could hardly have been a more striking indication of the apathy that was afflicting the American bases than an episode that occurred in the course of Knerr's inspection—a drunken brawl in the Soviet-run restaurant at the American base in Myrhorod all but resulted in shooting between the Americans and Soviets. On the night of August 17 First Lieutenant Philip R. Sheridan, a bomber pilot whose plane was under repair in Myrhorod, had too much to drink. Heavily intoxicated, he hurled two bottles through the window of the restaurant and got into a quarrel with Soviet officers. In the confusion caused by Sheridan's behavior, two American NCOs outside the restaurant heard the sound of a Soviet soldier loading his weapon. Apprehensive that he was about to start shooting the Americans, the two NCOs attacked the Red Army soldier and disarmed him, causing a minor cut to his face. No shots were fired, but in the resulting confusion the American officer on duty, apparently trying to break up the brawl, struck another American on the head with a flashlight, sending him to the hospital. General Perminov demanded that the perpetrators be punished. Sheridan was sent back to England to face court-martial.[5]

Restaurants like the one at the Myrhorod base were run by Voentorg, and were opened in late June at Poltava and in early July at the other bases. From the start, they were a focal point of the growing tensions between American and Soviet personnel at the bases. They sold drinks and food, especially pastries. The restaurants were established with the support of General Perminov, who pleaded in late May 1944 for the authorization of shops at the bases. While the Americans were well fed, they needed a place to spend their spare time, and the Soviets not only had no pubs available to them but had restricted their access to the locals. Perminov needed restaurants to stop the Americans from wandering into the towns and villages to buy liquor. The restaurants became a meeting place for the two groups and should ideally have strengthened rapport between them. In fact, as friction developed and morale declined, especially on the American side, they had the opposite effect.[6]

The Americans found the food and drink of good quality and the waitresses "personable and attractive." As the restaurants were open to both Americans and Soviets—the former were allowed to invite guests from the bases but not from among the local population—the Americans had to learn quickly how to drink glasses full of vodka bottoms-up, as the Soviets insisted, without immediately becoming intoxicated. When one American officer emptied a glass of vodka under the table, his action was noticed, and General Perminov demanded that he drink another glass as punishment. The Americans soon learned to neutralize the effect of vodka by eating rye bread, onions, and greasy food, but newcomers to the base, such as Lieutenant Sheridan, had to learn the hard way.[7]

Downing vodka in quantity was not the only challenge facing the Americans at the Soviet restaurants. For them, those establishments soon came to exemplify all that was wrong with economic conditions in the Soviet Union. The Americans believed that the restaurants encouraged corruption and illicit trade in military goods. As the Voentorg restaurants sold goods for both dollars and rubles, they solved part of Perminov's problem by stopping GIs from going to nearby towns for liquor but aggravated it in another way—by increasing GI traffic to the same towns to sell American goods in order to acquire rubles needed to buy liquor in the restaurants.

At the core of the Americans' problems was the USSTAF decision to pay them only part of their salaries in Soviet rubles and the Soviet-imposed exchange rate used to convert their dollar allowances into rubles. Lieutenant Arthur Cunningham, who was stationed at Myrhorod, explained to a Soviet acquaintance that out of his monthly salary of US $165 he received only $18.00 in rubles; the rest was sent to his American bank account. At the official Soviet exchange rate of 17.35 rubles per dollar, Cunningham's

Myrhorod salary amounted to 315 rubles, which was far less than Soviet officers earned and put the Americans at a disadvantage.

The decision to pay only a small part of US military salaries in rubles was probably influenced by the assumption that there was little to purchase in places such as Poltava and Myrhorod. The opening of the restaurants changed the situation. Now there were drinks, food, and cigarettes to buy but little money to spend. With 315 rubles in his pocket, an American could buy little more than two bottles of vodka priced at 150 rubles each. Beer went for 15 rubles a bottle. And no sooner had the restaurants opened than the Soviets changed the exchange rate, offering Americans only 5.30 rubles to the dollar and thus reducing their already meager buying power by two-thirds. With less than 100 rubles to spend per month, the Americans were unhappy and had no inhibitions about expressing their dissatisfaction.

Soviet counterintelligence was quick to pick up on the displeasure voiced by the Americans. "If you have few goods, then there was no need to open up that trade," complained First Lieutenant Elias Bacha. "Our Americans are considered the wealthiest in any country, considering the high exchange value of the dollar," said Lieutenant Jaroff, soon to be sent out of the country for allegedly provoking conflicts with the Soviets, to one of his Soviet contacts. Jaroff added that the American commanders were discussing plans to buy liquor in Iran and bring it to the bases. Indeed, on July 8 the Americans in Myrhorod opened their own store, selling goods to Americans only—a pack of American cigarettes for one ruble, while in the Soviet-run restaurant a pack of low-grade Soviet cigarettes went for more than a dollar. General Walsh complained to Perminov, who in turn petitioned Moscow, as did Lieutenant Colonel Sveshnikov.[8]

Moscow said nothing. The new exchange rate remained the same for the rest of the summer, encouraging American GIs to look for other ways of obtaining rubles. Poor in currency, they were rich in goods that were plentiful on their bases but unavailable in Soviet stores, from instruments and technical equipment to uniforms, shoes, blankets and, last but not least, sweet-smelling soap. Almost overnight, the markets of Poltava, Myrhorod, and Pyriatyn were flooded with American merchandise, including cigarettes and chewing gum. Two bars of soap went for 120 rubles,

American-made shoes for 6,000 rubles, blankets for 2,000, and watches for 5,000. The Americans investigated cases of black-marketeering to the best of their ability but could not root out the illicit trade fueled by the demand for rubles.[9]

Franklyn Holzman, stationed at Myrhorod, recalled that during the first month after deployment in June the Americans gave things away free of charge, moved by the scope of wartime destruction and the general poverty of the population. Later they began selling goods for rubles. According to Holzman, everyone was doing so, but GIs were upset when they saw their chaplain drive away from the base with a supply of blankets for sale. Some American officers with access to cars, dissatisfied with the prices they could get in the towns, turned into itinerant salesmen, traveling to nearby villages and selling goods according to price lists they distributed among the population. Rubles were not only spent at restaurants but also used to purchase goods available in local markets and stores. Soviet-made cameras, replicas of German Leicas, were especially popular, and some of them had German lenses. Items of Ukrainian folk art were especially sought after, embroidery in particular. Holzman purchased quite a few embroidered blouses and sent them home.[10]

Red Army soldiers tried to steal whatever they could from the Americans. In June, in Myrhorod, they stole two wallets from a safe in the office of the intelligence unit. Soviet drivers transporting American supplies stole 39 cans of food, 4 parachutes, 125 boxes of candy, and 40 packs of cigarettes from one of the American warehouses. Someone removed the ignition system, one light, a spare tire, and instruments from an American car parked at an airfield. Personal belongings of a female nurse, including an alarm clock, a flashlight, and gold pins were stolen from an American hospital.

Perminov sounded the alarm on July 26. He ordered his subordinates, as well as SMERSH officers, to investigate cases of theft among Red Army personnel. The Air Force commanders followed the order. The SMERSH officers, on the other hand, protested it all the way to Moscow. They argued that Perminov had no authority over them, and that it was not their job to deal with petty crime. The SMERSH bosses in Moscow agreed with their subordinates in Poltava that the task of counterintelligence was to look for spies and deserters, not to deal with property crimes against the Americans. Perminov was left to deal with the crime on his own.[11]

SMERSH became involved in larceny investigations only when Red Army servicemen were engaged in criminal schemes with Americans. The latter supplied the goods, while the former took care of the sales. That was one area in which Soviet-American cooperation encountered few setbacks. In September 1944, three boxes of American goods were found by SMERSH officers in a Red Army auto shop on one of the bases. The person charged with taking them for resale was Lieutenant Ivan Kuchinsky. He testified that the boxes, which included eight packages of photo paper, a leather jacket, clothes, cans of meat, sausages, and packages of sugar and chewing gum belonged to an American acquaintance, a technician in a photo laboratory, who had asked him to sell the goods. Kuchinsky's acquaintance, who was preparing to leave the base, was apparently selling either personal belongings or items obtained from military stores to which he had easy access, such as photo paper.

Kuchinsky admitted to his guilt. He also confessed that in the past he had sold merchandise for his American friend while on a business trip to the city of Kharkiv. Back then, he had sold the goods for slightly more than 2,000 rubles, ten times the monthly allowance of an American soldier at the bases. While pleading guilty, Kuchinsky asked for clemency. He told the SMERSH interrogators that he was not a "lost man" but needed money to help his family, which had fallen on hard times. The plea was of no avail. The merchandise was discovered on September 12, and on the following day Kuchinsky was expelled from the Communist Party—a clear sign that they were putting him on trial. SMERSH was eager to show its zeal in fighting American illegal trade.[12]

By later summer of 1944 the rubles that the Americans received from illegal commerce abruptly changed the symbolic balance of power in the Soviet-run restaurants, where Americans were now the equals of their Soviet counterparts or could even outspend them. The cash-rich Americans, who also had access to Air Force shops and could ask pilots to bring them goods from Britain, Italy, and Iran, also had a clear advantage over the Soviets when it came to courting local women. Almost all cases of sexual liaison between American men and local women investigated by SMERSH involved some form of material benefit to the women. That was true even in cases when the Americans were not looking for sexual favors but simply wanted to enjoy the company of younger women. According to SMERSH reports, such was the motive of William Jackson, the surgeon who praised the bravery of the ordinary Soviet soldiers during the June 22 German attack on the bases. He had dated Zinaida Blazhkova of Poltava. The relationship, which began, according to the SMERSH reports in June 1944, involved gifts of stockings and perfume.

In most cases, however, gifts of American goods smoothed the way toward sexual encounters between American GIs and Soviet women. Around 2:00 a.m. on the morning of August 30, a Soviet officer on duty in Myrhorod discovered that two female soldiers from his department, the nineteen-year-old Taisia Nesina and the twenty-one-year-old Liubov Abashkina, were absent from their night shift at the local bakery. The officer soon found them in their rented room, "sleeping in the nude with two Americans." A search of the room turned up "630 rubles, 5 bars of American toilet soap, a package of American chocolate, a brooch with American stones, 4 packets of expensive face powder, 2 bottles of perfume, and 2 photos of those Americans." The girls were arrested, and one of them was expelled from the Young Communist League. The women in their unit were treated to a lecture "on Soviet morals."[13]

As the future of the bases became murkier, the Soviets showed less and less interest in accommodating the Americans, who in turn were growing ever more frustrated with the limitations imposed by their hosts on their freedom of movement and contacts with locals. The result was a sudden spike in conflicts between them. Especially "productive" in that regard were the first two weeks of September, when word spread among the Americans that they were about to leave the bases. With nothing to lose, they became ever more open in venting their frustration with what General Knerr referred to in his memo of August 25 to General Spaatz as "political control," which he found "neither friendly, nor cooperative."[14]

Events planned as ways of improving and strengthening relations between the allies tended increasingly to result in quarrels. On September 1, a group of American officers celebrating their newly received promotions invited their Soviet counterparts to celebrate the occasion at the Poltava air base restaurant. They apparently had too much to drink and, according to a SMERSH report, one of the Americans, Captain Hiller, got into a fight with a Red Army Lieutenant named Savchuk. Hiller told the Soviet interpreter, First Lieutenant Ivan Sivolobov, that he "hated Russians like dogs and wanted to beat someone up." Lieutenant Colonel Sveshnikov interpreted such conflicts as deliberate provocations intended to worsen relations between the allies and took credit for preventing fights from escalating. He was happy to report to his superiors that one such fight between Soviet officers and American sergeants at the Pyriatyn base restaurant had been prevented. The Americans had allegedly broken into the restaurant after hours to get drinks and food.[15]

As Soviet-American conflicts grew in number and intensity in the first weeks of September, the SMERSH agents of Sveshnikov and Zorin kept a close watch on certain American personnel. As Sveshnikov noted in his report to Moscow in mid-September, "in most cases the provocations are initiated by American intelligence personnel who know the Russian language and have relatives in the USSR." In September the SMERSH officers insisted on prosecuting one such Russian-speaking officer, Second Lieutenant Igor Reverditto, who got into a fight and shouted anticommunist insults.[16]

Reverditto provides an interesting case. Despite his Italian name, he was born in 1919 in Ulan-Ude, then Verkhneudinsk, the capital of the Russian Baikal gubernia, to the family of an actor and theater director named Konstanin Petrovich Arkazanov and his wife, Kharkiv-born actress Marina Mikhailovna. Arkazanov's name was a stage one, "borrowed" from a leading character of a popular 1886 Russian play "Arkazanovs." The theater company Arkazanov ran was real. It traveled around before and during World War I, and Konstantin and Marina Arkazanov were constantly on the move. The Russian Revolution caught the family in the Siberian city of Tomsk, where in July 1917 the theater staged performances in Polish and in

Russian, suggesting Polish origins of some of the members of the group, if not Arkazanov himself.

Judging by the place of Igor's birth, by 1919 the theater and the family moved further east and ended up in Ulan-Ude. In 1920 the city became the capital of a Bolshevik-controlled but formally independent Far Eastern Republic. The Arkazanov family left Verkhneudinsk for China in 1923, the year in which the Bolsheviks incorporated the republic into the Russian Federation. Igor's father died in China. His mother immigrated with young Igor to the United States, where she married again and changed her and Igor's surname. The left-leaning Albert Jaroff, under whom Reverditto served in the Intelligence Department of the Myrhorod base, distrusted Reverditto and called him a "White Guardist," suggesting his family's anti-Bolshevik leanings. There was little doubt that they had left Russia in order to flee from the Bolsheviks.[17]

Like all Russian-speaking Americans, Reverditto found himself under the eye of the SMERSH officers soon after his arrival at the Poltava base. They discovered that the handsome, tall, and blond American was interested in dating local women. They did not know this, but before joining the US Air Force Igor had spent some time in Hollywood, where, according to family legend, he had dated up-and-coming stars Alexis Smith and Donna Reed. In late June 1944, Igor was seeing a Ukrainian woman named Valia, and SMERSH naturally sought more information about her. In July Igor met and dated an attractive Poltava woman named Zinaida Belukha. She had a child from a previous marriage, and her father, a Soviet police official, had been executed before the war. Reverditto told Belukha that the Americans on the base were unhappy. They had been advised that while local women were not officially banned from socializing with Americans, these women had been discouraged from doing so. When they did meet up with Americans, they did so in secret. Reverditto shared the general resentment over this.[18]

On Friday, September 8, Reverditto made his displeasure known to his SMERSH watchers. Sveshnikov's agents spotted him at the Poltava restaurant in the company of a fellow Russian speaker, First Lieutenant William Roman Kaluta. According to the SMERSH report, the two "were trying to cause a quarrel with members of our officer staff, spreading provocative rumors that Russian officers were trying to prevent Americans from going out with girls." The next time SMERSH agents reported on Reverditto, they said he was not only spreading anti-Soviet propaganda but had been involved in a fight with a Red Army officer. According to the report, on September 12 Reverditto and Kaluta beat up Red Army Lieutenant Fedor Grishaev and tried to assault other Soviet officers. "During the uproar," read the report, "Reverditto shouted obscene anticommunist abuse and declared that 'It's not you who are helping us but we who are helping you.'"[19]

The American investigation found Reverditto, though not Kaluta, guilty as charged. It all began with a remark made by First Lieutenant Michael Dubiaga, another American officer of East European ancestry, to Reverditto, who was drinking heavily and using foul language. Later Dubiaga and Reverditto got into a fight, which was joined by Reverditto's drinking buddy, First Lieutenant Cherry C. Carpenter. The cause of the fight was Reverditto's assault on an American corporal. Reverditto and Carpenter then attacked Dubiaga. Kaluta appeared on the scene and tried to break up the fight and instead exchanged blows with Reverditto. At some point in this brawl, Reverditto, speaking Russian, assaulted the Soviet manager of the restaurant, saying the words that were picked up in the Soviet report. As always, the Soviets refused an American request to interview their people, leaving gaps in the investigation, but the overall story was clear—bored beyond endurance and fed up with Soviet tactics, the American officer cracked under pressure.[20]

Two days after the fight, Sveshnikov presented General Perminov with a long list of American "provocations," headed by the fight. Others included an unsubstantiated claim that two American officers had tried to rape a female Red Army officer at the Pyriatyn air base; an accusation that Americans in Myrhorod were deliberately taking pictures of poorly dressed people; and a claim that the Americans were making anti-Soviet comments in public and private. Perminov in turn protested to generals Walsh and Kessler. They promised to investigate all the cases mentioned by Perminov. In Reverditto's case they acted almost immediately. He was fined half a month's pay, his promotion was withdrawn, and he was transferred from

Poltava on September 15, less than three days after the incident. The American commanders had to restore discipline, if not morale, among their officers and soldiers as soon as possible before the situation got completely out of control. Nevertheless, they felt sympathy for the officers they had to reprimand.

On September 15, the same day Reverditto was ordered out of Poltava, General Kessler wrote him a glowing letter of recommendation that made no reference to the incident and recommended Reverditto as a "loyal, sincere and conscientious officer."[21] Kessler and his deputies at Poltava no longer trusted their Soviet counterparts. Not so for their commanders in Moscow. In a further attempt to appease the Soviets, Walsh ordered Corporal Peter Nicolaeff, the Russian-speaking officer whom SMERSH and General Perminov considered anti-Soviet, to be transferred back to the West European theater. He also issued an order prohibiting GIs from taking photos outside the bases. The last thing Walsh and Deane wanted was to give the Soviets any pretext for shutting down the bases before the US Air Force was able to complete its last mission over Eastern Europe: the raid on Warsaw, which was in the middle of an all-out uprising against the Germans.[22]

11

Fall of Warsaw

In the last week of August Master Sergeant Estill H. Rapier and Corporal Leroy G. Pipkin flew from Ukraine to the Soviet capital. They were housed in Moscow's main hotel, the Metropole, and invited to a US embassy reception for Soviet officers decorated with American awards. They were truly impressed by what they saw in Moscow.

At the Metropole the airmen were shocked to see Japanese diplomats in the restaurant—the Soviet Union was not at war with Japan. "I stared right at the bastards but they deliberately avoided my eyes," recalled Rapier. "I kept it up until they raised their newspapers in front of their faces." At the embassy reception hosted by Averell Harriman on August 22, 1944, Rapier and Pipkin rubbed shoulders with Soviet dignitaries and senior commanders. "All of a sudden I found myself getting a big handshake from Molotov, the commissar for foreign affairs," remembered Pipkin, "and then from Marshal Rokossovsky [the commander of the First Belarusian Front, advancing at that time in central Poland], who had been called to Moscow to be decorated. And from Ambassador Harriman, the British ambassador, the Chinese ambassador, the Soviet commissar of public health and lots of other Soviet and diplomatic big shots." Pipkin was especially impressed by

Molotov and his frank replies to "blunt" questions addressed to him by the Americans.[1]

The American airmen did not come to Moscow to receive an award or prepare for a special mission. They were part of a tour group organized by the US Air Force commanders at the Ukrainian bases. As relations with the Soviets grew ever tenser, and daytrips to Poltava and other towns in the vicinity of the bases had become more problematic, American officers came up with the idea of taking officers, GIs, and nurses from Poltava to Moscow on a fairly regular basis. Along with Rapier, Pipkin, and their fellow airmen, one such group included nurses who had struck up an acquaintance with Kathy Harriman in June 1944. She repaid the hospitality offered her a few weeks earlier by inviting the group to the embassy reception and arranging a tour of Moscow. "We stayed around for a while and then Kathleen told us the dinner to follow the reception would get pretty dull, so we took off for town to see the Moscow night life," recalled Pipkin.

The GIs and nurses left Moscow full of admiration for the Soviet Union, a sentiment they would share with fellow soldiers and nurses at the Poltava-area bases. They had no idea how tense Soviet-American relations had become during their brief visit to Moscow or of the problems faced by their hosts in dealing with the Kremlin over the Ukrainian bases. "Life here at Spaso [House] functions at an ever increasing tempo," wrote Kathy Harriman to Mary on August 30. Their father had "almost nightly excursions to the Kremlin, the last one at two a.m...." The previous night the ambassador had approached Molotov with an appeal to save at least one of the three American bases in Ukraine. The Soviet foreign commissar made a noncommittal reply. He wanted all the Americans out.[2]

A new crisis in Soviet-American relations began in early August 1944, when an uprising broke out in German-occupied Warsaw. It involved tens of thousands of Polish patriots led by officers of the clandestine Polish Home Army.

The uprising began soon after Soviet troops under Rokossovsky approached the suburbs on the right bank of the Vistula, across the river from the city center and its main quarters. The Germans sent an armored division into battle and managed to stop the Soviet advance. The Red Army, which had been on the attack for weeks, with its supply lines severely overextended, was unable to cross the Vistula and occupy the main part of the city. The offensive that had brought the Soviets from the Dnieper in Belarus to the Vistula at Warsaw had run out of steam. For the lightly armed Polish insurgents, that was a disastrous turn of events. They were never able to establish full control over the city and lacked the heavy weaponry required for battle against the German tanks. After the euphoria of the first days of the uprising, its progress stalled, and it soon became clear to everyone in London, Washington, and Moscow that the insurgents would be slaughtered unless they received immediate help.[3]

Of the three Allied powers, the Soviets were best positioned to render such assistance with artillery fire and supplies. But Stalin refused. The reasons, as the Western powers suspected, were political rather than military. The insurgents reported to the Polish government-in-exile in London, whose members were mostly representatives of prewar democratic political parties. Stalin, who considered the London Poles anti-Soviet, created his own Polish government, controlled by his secret police and by the Polish communists in Moscow, in preparation for a takeover of Poland. The Soviet media announced the creation of Stalin's Polish government on July 22, 1944, soon after the Red Army had moved into Polish ethnic territory. But the new Polish government was allowed to assume some semblance of power under Soviet military control only after it signed an agreement recognizing the Soviet territorial acquisitions of 1939—the transfer from Poland to the Soviet Union of western Ukraine and Belarus. That was a concession that the Polish government in London and its supporters in Warsaw were not prepared to make.

For Stalin, lending assistance to the London-backed uprising in Warsaw meant creating a rival to his own hand-picked Polish government and jeopardizing the Soviet territorial acquisitions of the war years. The Polish insurgents, their political leaders in London, and the Western allies led by Roosevelt and Churchill were up against a calculating and ruthless practitioner of realpolitik who would stop at nothing to achieve his goal. The pro-Western insurgents being slaughtered by the Germans in Warsaw would make his takeover of Poland all the easier. As events would show, that was actually his preferred scenario.[4]

■

On August 3, as the first news about the successes of the uprising began to come out of Warsaw, Stalin met in the Kremlin with Stanisław Mikołajczyk, the head of the London government-in-exile. On the agenda was the political future of Poland, and Mikołajczyk, who had given the go-ahead for the uprising before flying to Moscow, hoped that the start of the insurgency would strengthen his hand in negotiations with Stalin. It did not. Stalin dismissed the Polish Home Army as an ineffective fighting force. "What kind of army is it—without artillery, tanks, air force?" he asked Mikołajczyk. He then continued: "I hear that the Polish government instructed these units to chase the Germans out of Warsaw. I do not understand how they can do it." Mikołajczyk did not disagree: the rebels needed help, and he asked Stalin to provide it. The Soviet leader graciously agreed to look into the matter. They would try to parachute a liaison officer into the city, he told Mikołajczyk.[5]

The Polish Home Army could not hold out long against a technically and numerically superior enemy. The Germans threw armored divisions, SS detachments, and police battalions recruited among anticommunist Russians and Ukrainians into the battle. The leaders of the revolt appealed to London for help. On August 4, Churchill cabled Stalin about the help being offered by the British and asked for further assistance. "At the urgent request of the Polish underground army we are dropping subject to the weather about sixty tons of equipment and ammunition into the southwestern quarter of Warsaw where it is said a Polish revolt against the Germans is in fierce struggle," wrote Churchill. "They also say that they appeal for Russian aid which seems very near. They are being attacked by one and a half German divisions. This may be of help to your operations." Stalin responded the next day, questioning the reliability of Churchill's information and the insurgents' claim that they had captured Warsaw. Making no definite response to Churchill's cry for help, Stalin played for time,

which was on his side. Every passing day without significant assistance reduced the insurgents' chances of survival.[6]

In Washington, President Roosevelt watched the developing situation in
and around Warsaw with growing concern. He came up with an apparent
solution: the Allies would not ask the Soviets to risk their pilots' lives in
facing German flak to drop supplies on Warsaw. The Americans would do
so themselves, using the Poltava-area bases as a launching pad for the operation. Roosevelt's military advisers signed off on the plan, which Harriman
proposed to Molotov on August 14. He also encouraged the Soviet foreign
commissar to consider a similar operation by the Soviet air force. Molotov
could easily decline the latter request, citing the danger of the operation,
but it was more difficult to turn down the American proposal to use the
bases. He therefore temporized and instructed his first deputy, Andrei
Vyshinsky, the former government prosecutor at the infamous Moscow
show trials of the late 1930s, to rebuff Harriman on both counts, which
Vyshinsky did in writing.[7]

Harriman requested a meeting with Vyshinsky and was joined by the
British ambassador, Sir Archibald Clark Kerr. He came up with an additional argument to convince the Soviets to allow the use of the Ukrainian
air bases. If the British were already trying their best to help the Poles by
making air drops, and the Soviets had done their best by trying to put a liaison officer into the city, why were the Americans not allowed to participate
as well? In response, Vyshinsky repeated the statement made in his earlier
letter to Harriman: the Soviets did not want to be seen as participating in an
adventurous act. "Mr. Harriman pointed out," reads the American protocol
of the meeting, "that he was not seeking the participation of the Soviet government but merely permission to drop arms. Mr. Vyshinsky interjected—
and to land on Soviet bases. That would constitute participation." Vyshinsky
was under orders to yield nothing, and indeed he did not.[8]

The meeting produced no results, disappointing the American military
commanders. Soon afterward General John Deane informed General
Walsh in Poltava and General Spaatz in London that the planned mission to
Warsaw would have to be postponed. The cable read: "The Soviet Foreign
Office informed Harriman that the Soviet government does not, repeat,

does not, concur in using Frantic Six to drop supplies to Poles in Warsaw." Harriman kept pushing. On August 16 he wrote to Vyshinsky that the mission had been postponed until August 17, but if the Soviet government reconsidered its position, the aircraft could still be used to drop the supplies. Vyshinsky stuck to his guns, restating his earlier position: "the Soviet government does not wish to associate itself either directly or indirectly with the adventure in Warsaw."[9]

The presence of American air bases on Soviet soil, which the Soviets had had to tolerate in the previous weeks, now became intolerable. The Soviets could offer no valid excuse for preventing the Americans from helping the Polish insurgents. Stalin apparently decided that the bases had to be closed down. On August 17 Molotov used his meeting with Harriman and Clark Kerr to deliver an unexpected blow to the Americans: the Soviets not only objected to the use of the Ukrainian bases to resupply the Poles but wanted the Americans out altogether. "After a long discussion on the supplying of arms to Polish resistance groups in Warsaw," read the American protocol of the meeting, "Mr. Molotov suddenly stated, in the British Ambassador's presence, that he wished to warn Mr. Harriman that the Red Air Force was proposing to revise the question of the 'Frantic' bases. The summer season during which the fields were to have been available to the United States Air Force had ended and it was improbable that many flights would be made in the winter. The airfields were now needed by the Soviet Air Force."

Harriman pushed back. He told Molotov that the fields had been made available to the US Air Force for the duration of the war, not for the summer, and that the plan was to move the bases westward, not to shut them down altogether. He proposed further discussion and offered to demonstrate to the Soviet foreign commissar how successful the shuttle operations had been. Molotov interjected that not much action was taking place at the fields, to which Harriman responded that flights had been suspended for a while after the German attack of late June, hinting at the Soviet failure to protect the bases. He also pointed out that the Soviets were delaying their decisions on opening air bases in the Far East.

The conversation ended with Molotov slightly softening his position. He suggested that his comments about the bases were of a preliminary nature, and that the question of their continuing use by the Americans could be raised later. The future of the Poltava-area bases, as well as prospective American air bases in the Far East, was suddenly in question. The Soviets were punishing the Americans for taking the British side in the dispute over the Warsaw Uprising. They were also determined to get rid of the American presence on the bases, which made their policy of suffocating the uprising by denying help indefensible. It was one thing to say that the Soviets were trying to help but had decided that it was too dangerous and ultimately useless, and another to prevent their allies from rendering assistance.[10]

Harriman, agitated and ever more frustrated by the reaction he was getting from the Soviet leaders, appealed to Roosevelt. Apparently under the influence of Harriman's messages, Roosevelt decided to add his signature to a letter that Churchill had proposed they send to Stalin about the uprising. It was a desperate cry for help. "We are thinking of world opinion if anti-Nazis in Warsaw are in effect abandoned," read the cable. "We believe that all three of us should do the utmost to save as many of the patriots there as possible. We hope that you will drop immediate supplies and munitions to the patriot Poles of Warsaw, or will you agree to help our planes in doing it very quickly? We hope you will approve. The time element is of extreme importance."

Stalin once again responded in negative. Roosevelt was disappointed, but did not think he could do much to change the Soviet leader's mind. "The supply by us of Warsaw Poles is, I am informed, impossible, unless we are permitted to land and take off from the Soviet airfields," he wrote to Churchill, who pushed for further action. "Their use for relief of Warsaw is at present prohibited by the Russian authorities," Roosevelt continued. "I do not see what further steps we can take at the present time that promise results."[11]

Roosevelt decided to retreat. He would need Stalin's good will in the future, especially with regard to the war in the Pacific, and did not want to burn his bridges on account of the Polish uprising. Whatever Roosevelt's caution may have done to secure his long-term objectives in dealing with Stalin, it did little to ensure continuing American use of the Poltava-area bases. On August 25, the day Churchill wrote to Roosevelt proposing another joint message to Stalin, Molotov delivered on his earlier threat and demanded the closure of the American bases in Ukraine. He informed Harriman and Deane that the Soviets needed the bases for their own missions, while the coming winter would make the continuation of shuttle bombing all but impossible.

Harriman was extremely upset. In a cable that he sent Secretary of State Cordell Hull but did not dare to send to the White House, he argued that the Soviet refusal to allow the Americans to help the Poles was the result of "ruthless political considerations in order that the underground may get no credit for the liberation of Warsaw and that its leaders be killed by the Germans or give an excuse for their arrest when the Red Army enters Warsaw." Harriman was right. Stalin's refusal to help the Poles was based on "ruthless political considerations," and he did not relent until September 1944, by which time the uprising had been almost crushed by the Germans.[12]

On September 2 the Polish Home Army abandoned the Old Town, the symbolic center of power in the capital. The Germans intensified their attacks on areas near the Vistula still controlled by the insurgents. In desperation, the Polish commanders opened surrender negotiations with the commander of the SS units fighting against them in Warsaw. Surprisingly, they achieved their main objectives: the Germans promised to treat them not as rebels but as combatants and give them the status of prisoners of war as defined by the Geneva Convention. News of the impending surrender reached Moscow as the First Belarusian Front, led by Rokossovsky, resumed its advance on the city. Based in Praga, a district of Warsaw on the right bank of the Vistula, Rokossovsky's units were now resupplied and ready to strike. Under his command were the officers and soldiers of the First Polish Army, formed by the Stalin regime out of Polish military detachments that swore allegiance to the Stalin-controlled Lublin government. They were eager to cross the Vistula, capture the Old Town, and raise the flag of the pro-Stalin government in the Polish capital.

It suddenly became in Stalin's interest to prevent or delay the surrender of the insurgents in Warsaw and make them fight as long as possible, in order to distract the German troops along the Soviet front line. The Soviets began flying their own supply missions to Warsaw. This, along with the dramatically increased artillery barrage of German positions in the city and the Soviet advance in Praga, made the leaders of the Polish uprising increase their demands on the Germans, requiring surrender to regular German troops and not the hated SS units. This demand led to a break in negotiations, and the Poles continued to fight. The slaughter of Polish patriots would continue for the rest of the month, while the Soviets remained on the Praga side of the Vistula. Stalin and his aides nevertheless did their best to convince the Western Allies that they were doing everything in their power to save the insurgents.[13]

On September 9, the day the Soviets began to resupply the insurgents from the air, they also withdrew their objections to the use of the Poltava-area bases for resupply purposes by the US Air Force. Soviet permission to use the Poltava bases for Warsaw airdrops was granted to the British in an offhand manner, and they passed the news on to the Americans. Around the same time the Soviets also approved the long-delayed shuttle-bombing mission designated as *Frantic VI*. It had no relation to Warsaw.

The *Frantic VI* task force, put together by the Eighth Air Force in Britain that bombed German industrial targets near the cities of Chemnitz and Breslau (present-day Wrocław), consisted of seventy-seven Flying Fortresses and sixty-four Mustangs. They landed at the Ukrainian bases after completing their mission on September 11 and spent the next day at the bases, waiting for Soviet approval of targets to be bombed on the way back to Europe. Oblivious to the high level of tension between the Allies, the American airmen enjoyed the day and were impressed by the attitude of ordinary Red Army soldiers and locals toward them. Captain Edward Martin, who came to Poltava with the *Frantic VI* task force, found the Soviets "as friendly as any people I've seen."[14]

On September 13, after finally receiving approval from the Soviets, the *Frantic VI* planes flew to Italy, bombing targets in Hungary. The mission was considered moderately successful—only one Mustang was shot down by the Germans on the way to Ukraine, and there were no losses on the flight to Italy. As for the results of the bombing, the outcome was estimated as "fair to poor." It was only much later, after the end of the war, that *Frantic VI* was characterized as the most successful raid ever undertaken by the shuttle bombers. It turned out that the machine-building factory near Chemnitz bombed by the Flying Fortresses on their way to Ukraine produced all the engines for the German Tiger and Panther tanks. Its destruction set back German production of tank engines for half a year—an eternity in a war quickly nearing its end.[15]

News of Stalin's change of heart regarding Warsaw caught the American Air Force commanders by surprise. Major General Anderson, as deputy commander of operations of the US Air Force in Europe, raised his concerns about the Warsaw airdrops to Roosevelt's special adviser Harry Hopkins, whom he visited on September 7 at the White House. Anderson suggested that a cost-benefit analysis did not favor such operations. He pointed out the difficulties of dropping supplies with precision in a battle zone and the risks that crews would incur by flying at low altitudes. Anderson was also concerned by the political cost of pushing for the airdrops—the possibility that the bases might be denied to the Americans altogether. But that was two days before the Soviets finally granted permission for the drops, removing the political factor. The logistical problem and the risk to airplanes and crews from enemy fire still had to be dealt with. The American pilots would soon learn that the odds of conducting of a successful mission in the skies over Warsaw and staying alive were not in their favor.[16]

General Eisenhower gave permission to start the airdrops on September 11. On the following day, he informed Army Chief of Staff George Marshall of a mission planned for September 13, and Marshall cabled General Deane in Moscow, ordering him to clear and coordinate the mission with the Soviet commanders as soon as possible. Time was of the essence, and the first sentence of the cable stressed that: "Conditions [of the] Polish patriots in Warsaw so critical that urgent action is required." The last sentence carried the same emphasis: "delivery of supplies must be accomplished at earliest possible date."[17]

Deane made haste to carry out the new mission. On the night of September 12 he, Averell Harriman, and Archibald Clark Kerr were in

Molotov's office in the Foreign Commissariat asking that the mission be allowed to go ahead the next day. Molotov called the deputy chief of the Red Army General Staff, General Aleksei Antonov, who told him that they had already approved the airdrop—a surprising demonstration of efficiency compared to previous missions, which had been postponed for days and even weeks. However, bad weather got in the way, forcing USSTAF to move the date of the operation first to September 14, then to the fifteenth, and eventually to the eighteenth, the first day when the skies were finally clear over most of northern Europe.[18]

The mission to Warsaw, code-named *Frantic VII*, involved 110 Flying Fortresses and 73 Mustangs of the Eighth Air Force. They took off from airfields in Britain on the morning of September 18 and headed in the direction of Warsaw. Morale was high, as the pilots knew that this time they were going on a humanitarian mission instead of a bombing run. Yet humanitarian mission or not, it was fraught with greater danger than a typical bombing raid. The German air-defense coordinators had figured out in advance where the task force was headed, and their fighters and anti-aircraft gunners were at the ready. As the planes had to descend to an altitude of 18,000 feet or lower to make precision drops of supplies, they became easy targets for German flak. The planes appeared over Warsaw and began dropping canisters of weapons and supplies around noon.[19]

Later that afternoon, when the Frantic VII Flying Fortresses began to land on the airfields of Poltava and Myrhorod, American and Soviet mechanics could not believe their eyes. One Flying Fortress and two Mustangs had been lost in battle, as well as nineteen Fortresses heavily damaged, one of them beyond repair. An additional thirty bombers reported minor damage, as did some Mustangs. By *Frantic* standards, these were heavy losses.

The results of the mission were no less disappointing. Out of close to 1,300 containers of weapons, ammunition, food, and medical supplies dropped by the task force, only a quarter got into the hands of the insurgents—the rest landed on German-held territory or sank in the Vistula. The airdrop lifted the spirits of the Polish fighters and prolonged their struggle but did little to change the situation on the ground. Moreover, the insurgents reported that after the American raid of September 18, the Soviets had scaled down their own airdrop operations. The cost-benefit ratio was hardly in favor of continuing airdrops, whether the pilots and planes were American or Soviet.

On September 21, Deane wrote to the Red Army General Staff, asking for information on the results of the Soviet airdrops. The original request had come from Hap Arnold, who was trying to determine (as Deane noted) "whether or not additional American assistance is required in this respect." Arnold clearly had his doubts. So did General Anderson, who wrote to his superiors in Washington that the Poles had recovered only one-tenth of the supplies dropped by the Americans. Anderson called the airdrop operations impractical and thought that they "should be discouraged in the highest U.S. circles."[20]

The British, however, insisted that the operations continue, and Roosevelt went along. On September 30 General Spaatz informed Eastern Command that Washington had approved *Frantic VIII*, with a mission to Warsaw. He wanted General Walsh and his subordinates to secure the requisite Soviet permission. The Soviets advised against airdrops, suggesting that the supplies would fall into German hands, but approved the mission for October 1. Bad weather delayed it until October 2. Early that day, Anderson received word that the Soviets had withdrawn their approval. The logic was as realistic as it was grim: whatever remained of the Polish resistance in Warsaw was on its last legs.[21]

The Warsaw Uprising was drowned in the blood of its participants, who fought for 63 long days with little outside help. More than 15,000 fighters died in battle, with approximately 5,000 wounded. The remaining 15,000 combatants were captured or surrendered at the end of the uprising on October 5. Losses among the civilian population were far greater—in excess of 150,000; approximately 700,000 were expelled from the city, which was leveled by the Germans in a symbolic act of punishment inflicted on the entire Polish nation. When the Red Army and its Polish units finally entered Warsaw on January 17, 1945, there was little left of the Polish capital, which had to be rebuilt almost from scratch in the decades to come. But Stalin could now claim Warsaw for himself. [22]

For Averell Harriman, Stalin's refusal to allow the use of the Poltava-area air bases to help the Polish insurgents early in the uprising constituted a turning point in his relations with the Soviets. It was the last straw for the US ambassador, just as it was for many American officers at the bases, convincing them that they could not do business with their Soviet hosts. Stalin's sudden change of heart or, more properly, of political calculation, only worsened the situation. In their last-minute effort to save the Poles, the Americans suffered their greatest combat losses since the start of shuttle bombing. The mission that had begun with high hopes ended in profound disappointment. With the *Frantic VIII* mission to Warsaw canceled and no new ones in the offing, the Americans in Ukraine prepared for the inevitable—evacuation.

Part III

STRANGE BEDFELLOWS

Forgotten Bastards of Ukraine

T he radar operator Palmer Myhra and his friends left Myrhorod early in the morning of October 5, 1944. Ahead was a long and exhausting trip, first by railway to Tabriz, the capital of Iranian Azerbaijan, and then on trucks and ships back to England. In his diary Myhra wrote, "At Myrhorod it was the best I ever had in the Army despite all the dangers and problems." Judging by his memoirs, Myhra appreciated his contacts with the locals, and probably expected to see grateful crowds bidding farewell to the departing Americans. But on his last day in Myrhorod, the city streets were empty. "I am sure the whole town was aware of it and probably wanted to bid us good bye but no one even ventured out to wave to us as we passed through town." He had noticed a change in the official attitude toward the Americans in the weeks leading up to the departure: "By now Russian and Ukrainian women were no longer permitted to talk or associate with us." Myhra recalled that the usually friendly guards were no longer smiling at the Americans, and generally that the Soviets were trying to steal everything they could in the American camp. Fights erupted on a daily basis. "Sometimes we were wondering if we would ever get out of this place alive," wrote Myhra years later.[1]

The first echelon of American airmen leaving the Ukrainian bases departed from the Poltava railway station on October 7. There were 395 officers and enlisted men in all, accompanied by three Soviet Air Force officers and one representative of SMERSH. The train left for the city of Kharkiv and went on from there to Rostov, Baku, and Tabriz. The Soviets had furnished the coaches with soft seats and two restaurant cars, while the Americans provided their hosts with written statements of gratitude for the care they had received in the Soviet Union.

Four days later, on October 11, two more trains came to Poltava to pick up another four hundred officers and soldiers. The first train reached Tabriz on October 18. A long road lay ahead through the Middle East to Port Said, on the northern end of the Suez Canal, from where the next convoy of ships was scheduled to leave for Britain during the second week of November. Altogether around eight hundred US airmen returned to the United Kingdom by the Middle Eastern route. Fewer than two hundred others departed by air.[2]

The evacuation of Myhra and his fellow soldiers from the Ukrainian air bases was a direct outcome of Molotov's demand the previous August to vacate the bases, as the Soviets needed them for their own purposes. It also came as a result of the recommendation of Major General Knerr, who visited the bases in mid-August and sensed that the Soviets wanted the Americans out as soon as possible. In his report to USSTAF he recommended "that Frantic be terminated as of September 15, and all equipment and supplies now en route be embargoed." Knerr repeated that recommendation at a meeting later that month at Allied headquarters in Italy attended by General Spaatz, General Eaker, and the commander of the Ukrainian bases, General Walsh. They all agreed with the proposal but wanted to keep the Poltava base going through the winter months and decided to await the outcome of Harriman's negotiations with Molotov regarding their future.[3]

By the end of August, Averell Harriman had found himself caught between two crises—one started by Molotov, the other by Knerr. Both threatened to destroy what he and General Deane had spent so much time building—an American presence on Soviet soil and the hope that the Alliance they envisioned would continue to work. On August 29 Harriman approached Molotov with a compromise. He offered to give up the bases at Myrhorod and Pyriatyn while retaining the one at Poltava for American use. He also proposed to reduce the number of personnel stationed there and to limit their mission. Those remaining at Poltava would service American planes engaged in reconnaissance missions and keep the base operating for the possible resumption of shuttle bombing in the spring. Molotov agreed to consider the proposal. The immediate shutdown of the bases was prevented but they remained in limbo, contributing to the decline of morale there.[4]

The Americans acted on the assumption that they would be allowed to stay at least in Poltava but made preparations to leave Myrhorod and Pyriatyn, dumping some of their surplus equipment into the rivers—an activity not overlooked by SMERSH. Uncertainty about the future of the Poltava base depressed commanders on the ground and unnerved USSTAF planners. On September 27, Air Force commander Hap Arnold gave vent to their exasperation about the lack of clarity on the issue of the Poltava base in a telegram to Moscow. On the following day Harriman wrote to Molotov, reminding him of the request made a month earlier. Again, there was no answer. Deane for one believed that Soviet agreement to help the Americans winterize their quarters at Poltava indicated that approval was forthcoming. The experienced Kremlin watcher got it right. On October 7, the Soviets approved the continuing operation of the Poltava base, putting a cap on American personnel there at three hundred officers and GIs.[5]

In all approximately two hundred Americans stayed at the Poltava base, about thirty of whom were officers. Those who remained were volunteers. In fact, there were more volunteers at first than spots available for them. Given the political importance of the mission, only those with little previous communication with the Soviets were selected, in order to deflect any suspicion that they harbored anti-Soviet attitudes. As in the selection of candidates for the *Frantic* mission in Britain in the spring of 1944, individuals suspected of anti-Russian or anti-Soviet attitudes were weeded out.[6]

SMERSH officers in Moscow were suspicious of the official American explanations for staying on at Poltava. In their internal correspondence they noted that the Americans had been left in Poltava "on the pretext that in time 'shuttle' operations would be revived." Their subordinates shared the same concern. Soviet commanders on the ground remained in the dark with regard to the American intentions. "The purposes of the continuing existence of the American base in Poltava are unknown to our commanders," read a SMERSH report of the time. The counterintelligence officers were doing their best to collect information from the American personnel, both those leaving and those staying, about those purposes. Most of the Americans they interviewed believed that they were being left in Poltava to await Soviet entry into the war with Japan. After that they would be moved to the Far East.[7]

That was indeed one of the hopes shared by Harriman and Deane in Moscow. Nonetheless, USSTAF commanders still had to define a new mission for the reduced personnel that would go beyond the promise of the Far Eastern bases. Their desire to keep the base going in order to "avoid any interpretation of the termination of our activities as an incident," as stated at the high-level meeting in Italy in late August, hardly constituted such a mission. American commanders discussed the issue among themselves throughout September. Among the tasks to be handled by the remaining personnel were support for reconnaissance flights, salvaging of damaged American aircraft, assistance to American prisoners of war liberated by the Red Army from German camps in Eastern Europe, and upkeep of the base should shuttle-bombing operations be resumed in the spring.[8]

Because the shuttle-bombing operations were suspended, and the rationale for remaining in place still under discussion and debate, the American airmen selected to stay in Poltava were not entirely sure what they were doing. They felt abandoned by their government, their USSTAF commanders, and the public at large. No acknowledgment of their existence was made in the media, and Americans at home did not know that their compatriots were still behind the Soviet lines. In their own words they became "forgotten bastards of Ukraine."

The Poltava base needed a new commander. General Walsh became a special assistant to General Arnold in Washington, while the recently promoted General Kessler became an Air Force attaché in Stockholm. At Poltava he was replaced by Colonel Thomas K. Hampton, a thirty-five-year-old experienced commander, who had served with distinction in the Panama Canal Protection Zone and the Eighth Air Force in Britain before coming to Ukraine in the spring of 1944. By the end of the summer he was in charge of operations at the Poltava base.

Though a veteran of the base, Hampton lacked knowledge of Russian and needed considerable help in dealing with the Soviets. The SMERSH officers, who carefully studied the new command infrastructure that the Americans set up at Poltava, noticed that Hampton appointed at least one officer who could speak Russian to all key departments and areas of operation—they counted sixteen such officers in all. The American assessment of those who spoke Russian was more modest. It was reported that four had native fluency in Russian and three had picked up enough of the language over the summer to be able to communicate. The commanders made a conscious effort not to take too many Russian-speaking enlisted men, as it was now understood that they were the first to get into trouble with the Soviets.[9]

The most important position at the US base at Poltava from the point of view of contact with the Soviets went to an officer whose Russian was better than his English. First Lieutenant George Fischer was Hampton's adjutant and responsible for the day-to-day running of the colonel's office. The bespectacled, serious-looking twenty-one-year-old Fischer had been born in Berlin but spent most of his childhood and adolescence in Moscow. He adopted the Russian name Yurii, attended an elite Soviet school, and befriended children of European communists then exiled in Moscow. His closest friend was the future head of foreign intelligence of the East German Ministry for State Security (or Stasi), Markus Wolf, who would become known to Western intelligence services as the "man without a face," since they could not locate any photograph of him. Fischer gave Markus his nickname, "Mischa," by which Markus would be known to his Soviet and Russian friends until his death in 2006.

Fischer was a true believer in communism during his years in Moscow. His father, the prominent American journalist Louis Fischer, born in Philadelphia into a family of Jewish emigrants from the Russian Empire, had strong socialist convictions, though never became a communist. George's mother, Bertha Mark, who came from a Jewish merchant family in the Russian-controlled Baltics, was a card-carrying communist with extensive connections among the Bolshevik elite during the early postrevolutionary years. Bertha, known as "Markoosha"—an affectionate Russian rendering of her surname, Mark—stayed with George and his younger brother, Victor, in Moscow throughout the 1920s and 1930s. Meanwhile Louis, who long served as Moscow correspondent for *The Nation*, traveled the world, writing and advancing the leftist agenda. He joined the International Brigades during the Spanish Civil War and served as a liaison between the Soviet government and leftist circles in the West.

An ideological freelancer or, in the parlance of Stalinist propaganda, a "fellow traveler" of the regime rather than its devoted soldier, Louis Fischer soon got into trouble with the increasingly authoritarian Stalin regime, which demanded that he promote Stalin's policies in his writings. His refusal to do so made life difficult for his family in Moscow, and he wanted to arrange their departure. Bertha Mark was even more anxious. With the start of the Great Purge in 1937, she abandoned her loyalty to the Stalin rule and grew terrified as her friends and neighbors—foreign communists and Soviet officials she had befriended in Moscow—were arrested. The authorities kept Bertha and her children in Moscow as hostages, hoping to influence the tone of Louis's publications abroad.

Soviet officials were not the only ones opposed to the family's departure from the Soviet Union. The seventeen-year-old George (or Yurii) Fischer also objected to the move. A Young Communist League activist and devotee of the Stalinist system, he dreaded the idea of leaving the communist paradise and moving to the capitalist West. It took Bertha a great deal of effort to convince him to join the family on their way out of the USSR. George finally agreed, but only on condition that he be allowed to return if he wished. The family managed to leave in the spring of 1939—the result of lobbying efforts of no less a figure than Eleanor Roosevelt, an old acquaintance of Louis Fischer.

In New York, where the Fischer family found temporary home after traveling through Europe, George did not abandon his leftist beliefs but became critical of the Stalin regime, especially because of the Great Purge. In 1942, he enlisted in the US Army in hopes of becoming an intelligence officer. His family's communist leanings stood in the way, however, and he was assigned to work as an Army censor in London, where he made friends with politicians and writers representing the left wing of the Labour Party. Among his new acquaintances was George Orwell, who wrote for the *Tribune*, the newspaper representing that current of opinion. It was in London that a US reporter and old friend of George's father recommended him to one of the officers overseeing preparations for *Frantic*.

Young as he was, George Fischer played a key role in selecting US officers and GIs with a knowledge of Russian to serve as interpreters and liaisons at the Ukrainian bases. "Tried to choose the right people," he wrote later in his memoirs, "with good Russian and apt to work well with the Soviets." The trick was to select Russian speakers who were not anti-Soviet and would not be regarded as White Guardists. It was no easy task, as most of the Russian speakers were refugees from the Soviet regime, or their children, but Fischer did what he could. "I interviewed hundreds, picked a dozen," he recalled. Altogether he selected more than twenty interpreters who were sent to the Poltava camps.[10]

Fischer himself was assigned to the intelligence unit at Pyriatyn and spent most of the summer of 1944 there. In his memoirs, written close to the end of his life in 2005, Fischer called the Soviet Union, which he equated with Russia, his "motherland," a reference to his mother's birthplace, and the United States, the birthplace of his father, "fatherland." Landing in Ukraine led to an attempt to reconcile his two loyalties. At first he was glad to be back in the USSR. "I was happy to be on Soviet soil with Soviet people," he wrote later. "To hear and talk Russian. To eat hearty native food in the Soviet mess hall for their Poltava officers." He was glad that the Grand Alliance was working and delighted that the Americans regarded the Soviets as "a noble people with a great leader." "I choked on the praise of Stalin," added Fischer—he considered Stalin guilty of betraying the Revolution. "Otherwise I shared the warm glow and postwar hopes."[11]

Fischer's Moscow past naturally caught the attention of Sveshnikov and Zorin. The SMERSH agents compiled a file on Fischer and tried to collect

more information through a female classmate of his in Moscow, now a lieutenant serving as an interpreter at Poltava and a SMERSH agent code-
named "Moskvichka." A SMERSH report characterized Fischer's father as
a "Trotskyite"—a follower of Stalin's nemesis, Leon Trotsky.

Fischer's excitement about returning to his beloved "motherland" began
to change as time passed and he began to notice that the Russian-speaking
liaison officers whom he had selected with such care in Britain started
disappearing one by one. "The Soviets picked one interpreter at a time.
Complained about each. Our Eastern Command honored the complaints.
It shipped out the accused. To me that felt like a Stalin purge, like the '37
cleansing." In July they transferred Albert Jaroff from Myrhorod. In
September they sent away Igor Reverditto, who had become a close friend
of George's despite his "White Guard" origins—they dated women together in Poltava and partied together.[12]

Fischer later remembered that of all the people he had selected in Britain,
only one continued to serve at Poltava after the reduction of personnel in
October—Major Michael Kowal, whom Fischer remembered as "Mike, a
pal of mine from New Jersey." Kowal was born in 1917 in Paterson, New
Jersey, to a family of Slavic immigrants (SMERSH documents identified
him as Ukrainian) and had a good knowledge of Russian. Before coming to
Poltava, he had piloted Flying Fortresses in the Eighth Air Force, completing
twenty-five daylight bombing missions over Germany—without benefit of
fighter protection, as at that stage in the war the Allies still lacked long-
range fighter aircrafts capable of protecting the bombers on their raids over
Germany. In the fall of 1944 he inherited Colonel Hampton's old job as
operations officer at the Poltava air base.

Fischer and Kowal managed to stay at Poltava partly because Soviet authorities did not consider them White Guardists or anti-Soviet. Another
factor was the inept manner in which SMERSH tried to remove them from
the base, leading Eastern Command to refuse to send unwanted American
personnel back to Britain, as it normally did. During the second week of
September 1944, in the midst of American preparations to evacuate the
bases, General Perminov complained to Kessler that on September 7, at the
communications center of the Pyriatyn air base, Major Kowal and First

Lieutenant Fischer had allegedly quarreled with a Soviet officer, created a scandal, and tried to assault a female switchboard operator. Sveshnikov included the incident in his report to Moscow at the end of September, describing it as a provocation on the part of the Americans that was resolved by the Soviet command.[13]

Major Ralph Dunn, the inspector of the bases, immediately investigated the incident. Kowal and Fischer testified under oath, claiming that there had been no altercation whatever. Dunn interviewed the Soviet commander of the base, Major A. Yerko, to whom the initial complaint had allegedly been lodged. Yerko had heard nothing about the incident. Dunn filed a report stating that there were no grounds to reprimand the American officers. He also concluded that there was a Soviet campaign to discredit Americans of Russian background or those associated with the Soviet Union by family origin. Both Fischer and Kowal, who of course volunteered to continue at Poltava, were allowed to stay. The Soviets did not protest. SMERSH had nothing on file about the two officers except their background and the trumped-up charge about the quarrel at Pyriatyn.[14]

The first weeks after the evacuation of the Myrhorod and Pyriatyn bases passed with no major Soviet-American conflict. False reports about American misdemeanors, such as the one involving Kowal and Fischer, became matters of the past. At Poltava, the Soviets helped American crews to build new housing from prefabricated parts shipped from the United Kingdom and generally showed a better attitude toward their guests than in late summer. American morale improved as well with the lifting of uncertainty about the future of the Poltava base. George Fischer was probably glad to report, in his capacity as adjutant to the chief of Eastern Command, that "the month of November was marked by a complete friendliness between the officers of the Russian and American headquarters both at work and in personal relations."[15]

Friendship and solidarity between the two armies and peoples was demonstrated during the celebration of the twenty-seventh anniversary of the Bolshevik Revolution in 1917, marked on November 7 with a military parade and a rally in Poltava that involved Red Army personnel, locals, and Americans. The Americans marched to Poltava for a ceremony, including speeches by party and military officials that lasted about two and a half hours. American photographers took dozens of pictures of the ceremony and those who attended it.

Nonetheless, the solidarity captured by the photos had its limits. After the rally was over, the Americans returned to the base, as the city was declared temporarily off-limits to GIs. The Soviets were concerned that fights might be started by drunken Red Army soldiers, and their commanders worried that they could not restrain their subordinates. Once at the base, the Americans celebrated the holiday with a dinner in the mess. The day ended without incident, though the Americans were not exactly happy. "They were given a day off, then forced to attend a celebration at which they understood nothing of what was said and finally restricted to the airdrome for the evening," reads an American account of the event by William Kaluta, the author of the history of the Eastern Command at its final stage, after the evacuation of the Myrhorod and Pyriatyn bases in the fall of 1944.[16]

On November 7, the same day as the celebration in Poltava, Americans in the United States voted in a presidential election, choosing between Franklin Roosevelt and his Republican opponent, Governor Thomas E. Dewey of New York. Discussion of the election at the Poltava base exposed the political and cultural gulf between the Soviets and the Americans. The Soviets, following the lead of their media, strongly supported Roosevelt and could not understand how American newspapers could publish portraits of Dewey, whom the Soviet propaganda portrayed as an enemy of the Soviet Union. It was probably an even greater shock to the Soviets that the Americans could openly criticize their president and vote for his opponent. For the Soviets, official ceremonies like the one held on November 7, began and ended with praise of Stalin; political discussions were infrequent and brief. "The Americans refused to talk politics with people who knew nothing about our political set-up," wrote Kaluta.[17]

According to Fischer's reports, Soviet-American relations on the base had a new and positive start in October and November but began to deteriorate in December 1944. He listed three main reasons for growing dissatisfaction among his fellow officers. The first was the slow processing of their requests to clear flights from Poltava to Moscow, Teheran, and airfields in western Ukraine and Poland, where damaged American airplanes were now landing. The second was the struggle between American and Soviet pilots for control of the two American Douglas C-47s used to fly to and from the Poltava base. Finally, there was Soviet petty theft of American property that had begun in the summer months and continued.[18]

On the first issue, the Soviet commanders were indeed in no rush to facilitate flights requested by the Americans, whom they continued to regard with suspicion, especially now that the shuttle bombing operations were over. Nor did they trust the Americans to make flights on their own, having insisted from the beginning that Soviet pilots take charge, with Americans as copilots. During the summer months, the Douglasses were used largely for flights between the Ukrainian bases. While the Americans complained generally about Soviet pilots taking unnecessary risks and flying too low, that did not seem to be a major problem on short flights mostly between the bases. It became one when the Myrhorod and Pyriatyn bases were returned to exclusive Soviet control and Red Air Force pilots took charge of long-distance flights, such as to Lviv in western Ukraine and airports in the Krakow area. The Americans began to complain loudly about their hosts' reckless flying techniques.

One episode in particular illustrates the basis for such complaints. According to an official report compiled later by Mike Kowal, in November a Soviet pilot named Kvochkin returned from a trip to Lviv and almost crashed his airplane while trying to land it at Poltava. Low scud above the airfield prevented a landing at Poltava, so he proceeded to Myrhorod. American passengers told their colleagues that the aircraft hit the surface twice but failed to land. Kvochkin then returned to Poltava, where he landed the aircraft perpendicular to the runway. The Americans later found that the airplane's "oil filters were full of wheat and leaves, twigs were lodged in the control surfaces, and ears of corn were found in the wheel wells." Moreover, the gas tanks were empty, as Kvochkin had burned gas in his attempt to land at Myrhorod before returning to Poltava. Kowal wrote in his report: "After questioning the pilot it was deduced that he was flying by the seat of his pants, and did not attempt making approaches with the available radio facilities. The night lighting facilities were all displayed and all radio facilities were on, which, if they were used, should have lowered the risk of safe landing." He concluded, "It seems that the Russians are not very well trained in instrument flights and the navigators are not capable of doing more than pilotage."[19]

The greatest cause of tension between the Americans and the Soviets in the autumn of 1944, however, was that petty theft. The issue was as complicated as it was controversial. Neither side was wholly innocent. While the low exchange rate of the American dollar had been offset by a per diem introduced in late August, the Americans continued to engage in barter, using their access to American stores and Air Force supplies either to acquire local goods or to engage in black-market activity. Cameras, including Leica and Contax models, remained popular and were available in Poltava for between 2,500 and 5,000 rubles, bargain prices. The Americans sold items of their clothing; pilots' leather jackets were especially popular. The American command clamped down on barter in its own ranks, making officers and enlisted men personally responsible for equipment and supplies entrusted to their care. This put them on a collision course with Red Army thieves.[20]

The US motor pool at Poltava was a particular locus of stealing. On October 24 a Red Army soldier tried to drive an American vehicle off the base; on November 4, another soldier tried to steal antifreeze, probably for drinking; on November 14, tires were stolen by unknown individuals, though some were later recovered at the Soviet motor pool. American supplies were guarded by Soviet sentries, who were either complicit in theft or negligent of their duties. Americans vented their frustration on the sentries, causing conflicts.

Close to midnight on November 20, a US sergeant on duty at the motor pool discovered that two Soviet guards had left their post and, in a complete dereliction of their duties, were sleeping in a nearby tent. The sergeant and two other US officers entered the tent and confronted the guards. One of them ran away but the other resisted. One of the Americans, Warrant Officer Roy Cannon, who had spent part of the evening in the restaurant, fired warning shots from his pistol into the ground. The Red Army sentry surrendered but refused to cooperate. When he declined to write down his name, Cannon struck him twice on the face. This physical abuse of a Soviet

Americans behind Stalin's lines: The first thing that was constructed in the war-ravaged Poltava upon its recapture by the Soviets in the fall of 1943 was the monument to Joseph Stalin. (Library of Congress)

Frantic I: Boeing B-17 Flying Fortresses of the Fifteenth Air Force overflying the fields of Eastern Europe on the way to Poltava, June 2, 1944. (Library of Congress)

The Ambassador: Averell Harriman, before his appointment as the US Ambassador to Moscow, London, 1942. (Library of Congress)

The Man in Charge: General John R. Deane, the head of the US Military Mission in Moscow, and the man ultimately responsible for opening, running, and closing US air bases in the USSR. Here he enters the residence of Averell Harriman, the US Ambassador to Moscow, July 1945. (US National Archives and Records Administration)

The Hosts: Joseph Stalin and Viacheslav Molotov, awaiting members of Western delegations at Yalta, February 1945. The two Soviet leaders agreed to the American request to open US air bases on Soviet territory, but barely tolerated their presence behind the Soviet lines. (State Archive of the Russian Federation)

The Counterparts: (left) Chief Air Marshal Aleksandr Novikov. (right) Novikov and his deputy in charge of the formation of new units, Colonel General Aleksei Nikitin, pictured with the US award of the Legion of Merit for his role in setting up US air bases in the USSR. Both Novikov and Nikitin did their best to help their American allies. (Library of Congress)

Poltava airfield: Pictured at center is the apartment building mined by the retreated Germans in the fall of 1944. The bombs in the basement of the building were discovered in preparation for the American arrival to the base in April 1944. The airplanes are visible at the airfield beyond the building. (Poltava Museum of Long-Range and Strategic Aviation)

■ The Poltava women: Dressed in embroidered blouses and Ukrainian folk costumes for what seems to be a market day, summer 1944. The war created a gender disbalance in Poltava and other places in Ukraine with women and children constituting the majority of the population, while the men were drafted in the Red Army. (Franklyn Holzman Collection, Davis Center, Harvard University)

■ The air bases come to life: The Soviet commander of the bases, Major General Aleksandr Perminov, with Soviet commanders to his right and American officers to his left. Second from his left is Major General Robert L. Walsh, the commanding officer of the Eastern Command of the US Strategic Air Forces in the USSR, the official name for the US shuttle operation in the Soviet Union, June 1944. (Library of Congress)

Getting to know each other: A Soviet mechanic gets familiar with the Flying Fortresses, June 1944. (Library of Congress)

Tasting Ukrainian borshch: Local women were employed at the American canteens. GIs picked up some Ukrainian and Russian words and in return taught kitchen staff some American words. Not all of them could be used in a polite society. (Ukrainian Museum-Archives, Cleveland, OH)

Welcoming US pilots to Poltava: Second from left is General Perminov. Next to him on his left, translating for the general, is Second Lieutenant Igor Reverditto. Second from the right is the US commander of the base Colonel (later Brigadier General) Arthur Kessler. (Courtesy of Tony Reverditto)

Enjoying a concert at the base: From left to right: Major General Ira Eaker, General Perminov, Moscow Mission Interpreter Captain Henry Ware, General Walsh, Colonel Kessler, and a Soviet interpreter. (Library of Congress)

The Americans were impressed by the number of medals the Soviets wore on holidays and festive occasions. Here, a GI tries to break the language barrier by making medals the subject of conversation. The Soviets prohibited GI liaisons with the Red Army women. June 1944. (Library of Congress)

Volleyball at the base: The teams are mixed, consisting of the US and Red Army servicemen. Fifth from the right is General Ira Eaker. (Library of Congress)

■ Comrades in arms: Soviet pilots and their US counterpart next to the US built P-39 Airacobra fighter aircraft, supplied to the USSR through the Lend Lease and highly valued by the Soviet pilots. (US Air Force)

■ Getting ready for the flight back home: While on the way back to their British and Italian bases, the Flying Fortresses refueled and reloaded at Ukrainian bases before embarking on another bomb run on their German targets. (FORTEPAN/National Archives)

▨ Chewing gum or "zhvachka" became the best-known American import at Poltava. The Americans were shocked by the number of orphans on the streets of Ukrainian cities and villages, and were originally giving out food and supplies for free. (Library of Congress)

▨ The Ukrainian market: The place where the Americans would learn to sell army merchandise to get rubles and buy Soviet-made cameras, Ukrainian embroidery, and last but not least, local alcohol. (Library of Congress)

■ Pearl Harbor on the Steppes: On June 22, 1944, as the Luftwaffe made a night attack on the Poltava air base, the US Air Force suffered the largest losses on the ground since Pearl Harbor. As the Americans assessed the damage, the Soviets tried to blame the losses on the American's reluctance to disperse the planes on the airfield, as recommended by the Soviet commanders. The Soviet-American relationship began to deteriorate. They never again reached the level of trust they had before June 22, 1944. (American Air Museum in Britain)

■ Ready to go home: The evacuation of the Pyriatyn and Myrhrod bases and the downsizing of the Poltava base came as a result of changes in the front lines in Europe, and rapid deterioration of US-Soviet relations. Stalin refused to allow US and British Air Forces to use Ukrainian bases to resupply during the anti-Nazi uprising in Warsaw, October 1944. (Poltava Museum of Long-Range and Strategic Aviation)

Forgotten bastards of Ukraine: Americans, with Soviet assistance, building winter quarters at Poltava. Stalin allowed a small contingent of GIs to stay in Poltava to help with American air traffic in the Soviet Union. (Franklyn Holzman Collection, Davis Center, Harvard University)

Averell Harriman on one of his visits to the Poltava base. Apart from being a stopover for American diplomats during their flights from Moscow to Southern Europe and the Middle East, Poltava became a major intelligence gathering point. It is one of the very few places where information was exchanged about Soviet policies being overtaken by the Red Army, Eastern Europe, fall 1944. (Poltava Museum of Long-Range and Strategic Aviation)

Kathleen Harriman on her return visit to Poltava in the fall of 1944. She gave a detailed description of her initial visit there on June 1-2 when she came to greet the first wave of the Flying Fortresses to arrive in Ukraine. To the left of Kathleen is the new Soviet commander of the base, General Stepan Kovalev. (Poltava Museum of Long-Range and Strategic Aviation)

President Roosevelt arrives at the Saki airfield in the Crimea on his way to Yalta, February 3, 1945. He confers here with his closest advisor, Harry Hopkins. Viacheslav Molotov is third from left. The American operations at Saki were run by the Poltava air base personnel. (FDR Library)

Viacheslav Molotov confers with British Foreign Secretary Anthony Eden after signing an agreement on the exchange of prisoners of war. The Soviet treatment of the American POWs in their custody became one of the most contested issues in Soviet-American relations after the Yalta Conference. This put Poltava pilots and ground crews at the center of US efforts to bring the POWs back to the United States. (State Archive of the Russian Federation)

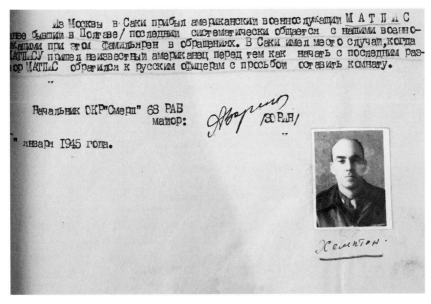

As Soviet-American relations deteriorated, the Soviet security apparatus (in particular, SMERSH - the Red Army counterintelligence service), stepped up its surveillance of the Americans. Here is a report on the American activities at the Saki airfield, signed by the head of the Poltava SMERSH Major Anatoly Zorin. The photo of the US commander of the Poltava base Colonel Thomas Hampton is attached to the report. (Archives of the Security Service of Ukraine)

■ One of the Americans who flew to the Crimea with Colonel Thomas Hampton was his adjutant Russian-speaking and Moscow-raised First Lieutenant George Fischer, pictured here in a 1945 photo. (Courtesy of Vic Fischer)

■ Sergeant Franklyn Holzman, whose letters home tell a day-to-day story of American life in Ukraine. His stay first at Myrhorod and later at Poltava instilled in him an appreciation of the Soviet war effort and set him on the path of becoming a lifelong student of Soviet society and economics. He received graduate training in Soviet affairs at Harvard, where he crossed paths with another aspiring academic with Poltava roots, George Fischer. (Franklyn Holzman Collection, Davis Center, Harvard University)

■ Here, Holzman is pictured with one of his Ukrainian girlfriends, Nina Mozhaeva, in Myrhorod. Holzman's liaison with another woman in Poltava was broken by the Soviet secret police, who tried to recruit women into spying on the Americans. (Franklyn Holzman Collection, Davis Center, Harvard University)

■ Second Lieutenant Igor Reverditto, a Russian-speaking officer and friend of George Fischer, was shipped back to the US in September 1944 after a quarrel with Soviet officers. With his outgoing personality and fluent Russian-speaking abilities, Reverditto was considered to be a spy by the Soviets, and was fed up with SMERSH and secret police surveillance and harassment. (Courtesy of Tony Reverditto)

■ In this 1945 photo, Igor Reverditto is portrayed with his first-born son, Michael. He and his family settled in California after the war, while the KGB kept harassing the women he had previously dated or had acquaintances with at Poltava trying to get information on Reverditto's whereabouts in the United States. (Courtesy of Tony Reverditto)

■ First Lieutenant William Kaluta became extremely skeptical of the Soviet regime when he was asked to use his knowledge of Russian to help fellow officers protect their Ukrainian girlfriends from the secret police harassment. Here, Kaluta is portrayed playing the accordion at one of the Soviet-American social gatherings at Poltava. On the far left is the US commander of the base Colonel Hampton, immediately behind Kaluta is another Russian-speaking officer Major Michael Kowal. Sitting to the left of Kaluta is the commander of the Poltava SMERSH, Major Anatoly Zorin. (Poltava Museum of Long-Range and Strategic Aviation)

■ US officers and nurses dressed for the 1944 Christmas party. William Kaluta is on the far right, sitting next to his future wife, Second Lieutenant Clotilde Govoni. Their marriage was registered in Poltava in May 1945. (Poltava Museum of Long-Range and Strategic Aviation)

■ Disheartened, disoriented, defiant: The US troops march for the memorial service for President Roosevelt, Poltava, April 1945. (Poltava Museum of Long-Range and Strategic Aviation)

■ Americans made many memories in Poltava and the region. Stalin's secret police tried its best to preclude GI contacts with the locals. For decades to come, they harassed women who had the "misfortune" of meeting Americans. (Library of Congress)

soldier by an American went all the way to General Deane, who assured the Soviet commander at Poltava that the perpetrator would be court-martialed. Cannon was indeed shipped out of Poltava on November 23.[21]

Things would become much more tense as the "forgotten bastards of Ukraine" continued serving at the Poltava base into the late fall and early winter of 1944. Those who opted to stay at the Poltava base tended to be sympathetic toward the Soviet Union and its people, if not toward communist ideology, and in fact that had been one of their reasons for volunteering to take part in the new stage of the mission. However, SMERSH officers were growing increasingly concerned about what they deemed the spread of anti-Soviet sentiment among the Americans, many of whom had become highly critical of the Soviet regime. Ironically, it was SMERSH activity, which became considerably more intrusive as counterintelligence officers and agents investigated the remaining Americans with greater scrutiny, that helped to turn allies first into skeptics and then into adversaries.[22]

13

Watchtower

John Deane got a chance to question Stalin directly about the future of the air bases on October 14, 1944. The occasion was a meeting of Soviet, American, and British military commanders with Stalin and a visit from British Prime Minister Winston Churchill to the Kremlin. The main agenda items were the conduct of the war in Europe and the future of Eastern Europe and the Balkans. The Pacific war was included as well, and Deane seized the opportunity to ask Stalin a series of questions about Soviet participation in the war on Japan. One question concerned the opening of US air bases in the Soviet Far East. "Young man," said Churchill to Deane after the meeting, "I admired your nerve in asking Stalin those last three questions. I have no idea that you will get an answer, but there was certainly no harm in asking."[1]

To everyone's surprise, at the next day's session Stalin gave direct answers to all Deane's questions. He approved the idea of American bases in the Far East but noted that the Americans would have to find a way of supplying them via the Pacific route, as the Trans-Siberian railway would be used to full capacity in moving Red Army troops to the region. Responding to a follow-up question from Averell Harriman, Stalin assured the ambassador that the Soviet Union would enter the war with Japan three months after the end of the war with Germany, assuming that conditions were met. The conditions that Stalin had in mind were Soviet territorial claims to the Kurile Islands, Southern Sakhalin, and Port Arthur, as well as the establishment of a de facto sphere of influence in Manchuria. Harriman and Deane were delighted. "We adjourned with the conviction that progress was being made," recalled Deane.[2]

In the opinion of Harriman, the promises extracted from Stalin on Soviet participation in the Pacific war and US air bases in the Far East were easily the most successful outcomes of Churchill's visit to Moscow. The rest was much more problematic. As far as the future of Europe was concerned, Harriman had reason to be unhappy both with Churchill, who had arrived in Moscow on October 9 for a ten-day visit, and with his own president, who was interested in a Big Three meeting but could not come because of the imminent American presidential election and had asked Harriman to represent him, though merely in the role of observer. Harriman attended some of the meetings between Stalin and Churchill but not others and was unable to present and defend the American position as much as he deemed necessary. At a reception in honor of Churchill, Maxim Litvinov, the former Soviet foreign commissar and now deputy to Molotov, asked Deane, referring to an article in *Look* estimating Harriman's wealth: "How can a man with a hundred million dollars look so sad?"[3]

Harriman was particularly unhappy with Roosevelt's refusal to take a more active part in deciding the future of Poland—a thorny issue in Allied relations and an emotional one for Harriman after Stalin's refusal either to help the Polish insurgents in Warsaw or to allow the Allies to use the Poltava bases to render assistance on their own. Churchill flew to Moscow with the Polish question at the top of his agenda, and Harriman believed that it should headline the American agenda as well. If Roosevelt could not come, perhaps Harry Hopkins could fly in and help Churchill save the country from Soviet domination, reasoned Harriman. It did not happen. Harriman was left on his own.

Churchill had first outlined his plan for Poland at the Big Three conference in Teheran in late November and early December 1943. According to that plan, Stalin was supposed to keep the former Polish eastern territories that he had seized in 1939 on the basis of the Molotov-Ribbentrop Pact, under the pretext of defending fellow Ukrainians and Belarusians. The Polish government in London was expected to accept a new eastern border following the Curzon Line, proposed back in 1920 by then–British Foreign Secretary George Curzon that more or less coincided with the Polish ethnic boundary in the east. But the Poles refused. Now Churchill brought to Moscow Stanisław Mikołajczyk, the Prime Minister of the Polish London government in exile. That did not help either. Mikołajczyk refused to play along and accept the Curzon Line as Poland's new eastern border. In particular he objected to giving up the city of Lwów (Ukrainian Lviv), a major urban center surrounded by the Ukrainian settlements but largely settled by Poles. Harriman knew that the deadlock in negotiations benefited Stalin.

The issue of Lviv and the Polish eastern border was postponed until the next Big Three meeting, which would not take place until February 1945. Meanwhile, with no agreement in place, Stalin could do as he wished in the Polish territories conquered by the Red Army and which remained out of reach to the Western Allies. The closest outpost to the region that the Americans had at that point was Poltava. The only US military personnel with access to Lviv and the region around that contested city were the airmen who flew there to salvage downed American aircraft. This new situation unexpectedly thrust the Poltava air base into a new role—that of watchtower for US military and diplomatic interests in Eastern Europe.[4]

Captain William Fitchen was the chief of the Poltava air base intelligence section, and only twenty-six years of age when he embraced a new role for himself and for the base. It happened on October 21, 1944, when a C-47 with American pilots that had been damaged while flying in Central Europe landed at Poltava en route from Lviv.

A graduate of the University of California at Berkeley, where he had earned a degree in entomology, Fitchen spent the summer months interviewing crews and collecting information on the German Air Force, anti-aircraft defenses, and the results of American bombing. The end of bombing runs in September meant there were no more crews to interrogate, unless they came from western Ukraine and eastern Poland. With the arrival of the plane from Lviv, Fitchen and his people began to do what the SMERSH officers had suspected them of doing all along—collecting information not only on the Germans but on the Soviets as well.[5]

The C-47 from Lviv brought to Poltava two US airplane crews that had been forced to make emergency landings on now-Soviet-held territory near the cities of Lviv and Tarnów. Given that the Red Army was advancing into Poland, American crews flying from Britain and Italy on missions to bomb German targets could make emergency landings behind the Soviet lines, as these two crews had done. They ended up in the hands of Red Army commanders who shipped the Americans off to Poltava.

Fitchen did his own debriefing, though it was not of the usual kind. Next to him was Colonel George A. McHenry, the deputy chief of the Air Force division of the US military mission in Moscow, who flew to Poltava to take part in the debriefing of the pilots. According to one of the US Air Force historians, McHenry "was primarily interested in those points that were of a political nature." He wanted to find out about the situation on the ground in the Soviet-controlled areas of what had been eastern Poland before the war. The pilots reported that once in Soviet custody they were kept under constant surveillance, but that their personal liberties had not been constrained in any way and they were well treated by Red Army personnel. According to their observations, there were clear signs of tension between the Soviets and the Poles, with the latter regarding the Red Army as little better than the Germans.[6]

This first information on the situation in the Soviet-occupied territories was soon confirmed by other American pilots who were flown to Poltava in November 1944, and by members of the Poltava base's own staff. The Soviets allowed American technicians based in Poltava to fly to places where downed planes had landed in order to repair them and fly them back to Poltava. Some would spend weeks in those areas on repair missions; others would visit for shorter periods. All of them turned out to be important sources of information on the situation in western Ukraine and eastern

Poland. Their reports would be sent fairly regularly to the military mission in Moscow, and some would make it onto Harriman's desk.[7]

Among the latter group was a report filed by Colonel Hampton, the commander of the Poltava base. On November 14 Hampton, in the company of a number of Russian-speaking officers and technicians, including his chief operations officer, Mike Kowal, the intelligence officer Sergeant Samuel Chavkin, and the technician Philip Mishchenko, visited Lviv, where they spent four days before returning to the base on November 18. They took off from Poltava on one of the base's two VC-47 Douglasses and flew to Lviv to provide fuel for a B-24 Liberator that landed there. (The B-24 was a heavy bomber with a longer wingspan than the B-17, though many believed that it was not as good, or as reliable, as its predecessor.) On their way back they took on board Captain Joe R. Johnson, who had been in the area of Lviv helping the downed American crews since October 6 and was a fount of information. Johnson and US officers from the Poltava base had noticed NKVD surveillance and seen Red Army soldiers harassing local girls who were interested in meeting the Americans, and were able to gather a fair amount of information on the situation in Lviv simply on the basis of their observations and occasional contacts with the locals.

Like the crews Fitchen had debriefed in October, Hampton and his companions found the Poles, who constituted a majority in the city, highly dissatisfied with the Soviets. They all filed individual reports, concurring that the Poles actually preferred German rule to Russian. Hampton wrote that the locals had found the German city administration more efficient than the Soviet. "Evidently the Germans left the Poles pretty well alone and they carried on their own way of life while the Soviets are poking into everything and making life generally unpleasant." Besides, according to Hampton, the Soviets were trying to reduce the standard of living in order to bring it into line with that of the Soviet Union. They forced the locals to work for meager salaries of 200 rubles per week (a black-marker equivalent of one American dollar). The Soviets were busy selling cans of food received from the United States through Lend-Lease at inflated prices. The Poles, for their part, were selling their belongings in order to survive. "Food was more scarce and expensive under the Soviets than under the Germans," wrote Hampton.[8]

Hampton had a very different story to tell about the Jews of Lviv. He reported that he had met many witnesses of the atrocities committed by the Germans, including two university professors. "Almost always the Jews were sufferers at the hands of the Nazi," he wrote. "Surprising to me was the fact that those Poles who had lived with and seen these atrocities committed apparently had little or no sympathy to the Jews. In fact I think some of my informers were in accord with the Nazi policy against the Jews." This was probably the first account of the mass extermination of Jews in Lviv and the role of the local population in the process to reach the American military command and officers of the US embassy in Moscow.[9]

When Hampton and his crew flew to Lviv in November 1944, what would become known as the Holocaust was still not revealed to the general public. In late August 1944, the Soviets arranged for American and other Allied correspondents to go to Majdanek, the German extermination camp near Lublin in eastern Poland, allowing the Western world for the first time to see gas chambers and furnaces in which the bodies of the inmates were burned. One of the reporters, Bill Lawrence, published an article in the New York Times about his trip to Majdanek. "I have just seen the most terrible place on the face of the earth—the German concentration camp at Majdanek, which was a veritable River Rouge for the production of death, in which it is estimated by Soviet and Polish authorities that as many as 1,500,000 persons from nearly every country in Europe were killed in the last three years." (Lawrence was referring to the Henry Ford's best known plant, located in River Rouge, west of Detroit.) The conveyer-belt extermination of Europeans, but not yet of European Jewry, was first revealed to the world.[10]

Kathy Harriman, who spoke with Lawrence upon his return to Moscow from Majdanek, saw tears in his eyes. Still, neither Lawrence nor any other Western reporter pointed out that Jews were the main victims of the atrocity, and that what they had seen was evidence of the planned extermination of an entire people. They simply did not know the truth. The Soviets organized the trip partly to legitimize the Stalin-backed Polish government in-the-making, and the reporters had a chance to interview Edward Osóbka-Morawski, the nominal leader of the Lublin Poles, who promoted the view that the Germans had killed people of all nationalities. In a letter to Mary, Kathy gave the number of those nationalities as twenty-two. That figure apparently came from Lawrence, who took it from his Soviet and Polish guides. Lawrence's report was originally met with disbelief. While new reports on Majdanek published in the fall of 1944 confirmed his story, there was still little understanding of the ethnic composition of the victims—as late as November, they were characterized as "Jews and Christians alike."[11]

No other member of Colonel Hampton's crew in Lviv was more traumatized by the story of the city's Jews, and left a more detailed account of their plight, than Samuel Chavkin, the Air Force intelligence officer, who was a native of Kyiv and a Jew himself. In his report, Chavkin recounted a story told to him by a Jewish woman who had survived the German occupation of the city. "Just soon as the Nazis had entered the city they began to round up Jews or anybody who resembled a Jew. Through the local Fifth Column, they contacted the pro-Nazi Poles who acted as their guides. She claims that in the space of six months of German occupation all of Lwow's 100,000 Jews were massacred. Approximately 3,000 who managed to hide in the provinces remain alive." Captain Johnson, who had been in the region since October 7, wrote in his report about 160,000 Jews of Lviv killed "by methods ranging from mass executions to killing children in the streets."[12]

Estimates of the number of Jewish victims of the Holocaust in Lviv given by Hampton and his crew were neither inflated nor unrealistic. The city had been home to approximately 110,000 Jews before World War II; 100,000 more Jewish refugees found safe haven there after 1939 and saw the German takeover of Lviv in late June 1941. Present-day estimates of the number of Jews killed in the city and its environs exceed one hundred thousand. The fate of the rest is unclear, though only a few hundred survived the occupation of the region to see the arrival of the Red Army in July 1944. The reports were also correct about the role played in the Holocaust by the locals. Many non-Jewish residents, not only Poles, as mentioned in the reports, but also Ukrainians, helped carry out the Holocaust in the city.[13]

The horrors of the Holocaust were only part of the story told by Hampton, Chavkin, and their comrades. Their attention was focused mainly on Soviet policies in the city and region, and they saw clear signs that the Soviets were not going to return Lviv to Poland. The Poles were given a choice of becoming Soviet citizens or moving to central and western Poland. "Lwow has been declared a Ukrainian city by the Russians and the Russians do not want the Polish people there," wrote Johnson. Major Kowal noted that the NKVD had terrorized the city, and Poles were afraid to speak to members of the US team. Privately they would tell the Americans that their only hope was American intervention. Hampton wrote that the Polish citizens of Lviv were determined to "hang on until Roosevelt and Churchill intervene on behalf of the Polish people." Chavkin noted that many hoped to immigrate to the United States.[14]

A letter from Mieczysław Karol Borodej, a British Air Force officer of Polish descent, that Hampton was asked to pass on to the British embassy in Moscow left no doubt that the Soviets were prepared to crush any attempt to keep the city in Poland. A native of the city of Stanyslaviv (present-day Ivano-Frankivsk, in western Ukraine), Borodej had just completed his training as a pilot when the Germans attacked Poland in September 1939. He escaped to Britain, where he became a pilot in the Royal Air Force. Shot down by the Germans in the fall of 1941 during a mission over Europe, Borodej ended up in a German prison camp but escaped and joined the Polish underground in Lviv. He was arrested by Soviet counter-intelligence in July 1944, soon after the Soviets entered the city, and charged with membership in the underground Polish Home Army, which had staged the Warsaw Uprising. While in captivity, Borodej wrote a letter to the British ambassador in Moscow, pleading for help. The letter was smuggled from the prison and found its way into Hampton's hands. The Allies were unable to help. In January 1945, Borodej was sentenced to twenty years' hard labor and sent to the Kolyma gold mines in Siberia.[15]

Colonel Hampton's team was not the last to visit Lviv. Others would follow in the weeks and months to come. Among them was a team of officers led by a medical doctor from the Poltava base, Major Robert Wiseheart, who flew to Lviv on December 6. During his four days in the city Wiseheart noticed among the locals "a marked lack of appreciation of the efforts of their Russian liberators." The desperate Poles pinned their hopes on the Americans and on a future American-Soviet war. He and his men were greeted with questions: "When will you clear the Russians out of Poland?" "Will the Americans and Russians fight after Germany falls?" Wiseheart returned to Poltava not only with fresh impressions of the situation in Lviv but in the company of American airmen who had made forced landings in the area and spent significant time in the countryside. They provided first-hand intelligence on the situation in the region.[16]

One of those brought to Poltava from Lviv was the B-17 nose-gunner Sergeant John R. Dmytryshyn, who was of Ukrainian descent and could understand discussions going on around him. He recounted the story of his adventures after his airplane had been shot down to Fitchen once he got to the air base. Dmytryshyn was making the first parachute jump of his life, and his parachute opened without a problem, but he found that he had no sensation of falling and was seized by panic at the thought that he would remain floating in the sky until he died there. He tried to unbuckle the parachute straps; fortunately he did not succeed. When he finally started his descent, Dmytryshyn realized that he was in danger of another kind: someone from the ground was shooting at him. After landing, he found three bullet holes in the canopy. Dmytryshyn hid the parachute in the bushes, covered himself with leaves, and prepared for an encounter with the Germans.

Dmytryshyn had lain quietly in his hideout for roughly half an hour when he heard someone addressing him in his native Ukrainian. It was an unarmed farmer, who took him to his village, where Dmytryshyn was discovered by Polish police loyal to the Soviet-controlled Lublin government rather than to the Germans who used to control the area. The policemen initially treated him in friendly fashion when he told them that he was an American. However, after hearing him speaking Ukrainian, a Polish captain decided that Dmytryshyn was in fact a German. The Poles took him to the neighboring town, where they turned him over to a Red Army colonel who interrogated him for more than four hours, claiming that he was a German who had learned English and Ukrainian specifically for the mission in which he was now engaged. About 2:00 a.m., Dmytryshyn told Fitchen, he broke down and started crying. The Soviets then left him alone. The next day he was reunited with his commander, Lieutenant R. E. Beam, and another member of his crew who had also parachuted from the plane. They had been picked up either by the Soviets or by their Polish allies.[17]

Fitchen debriefed Dmytryshyn upon his arrival in Poltava on December 10. Another group of pilots arrived there on December 18, and Fitchen also wrote down their stories. Their experiences had been fairly similar, although some had ended up in the hands of members of the Ukrainian Insurgent Army, who were fighting both the Soviets and the Poles and operating in the Peremyshl (present-day Przemyśl) region, with its mixed Polish-Ukrainian population. The insurgents turned out to be quite friendly toward their American guests. Some of them had family members who had immigrated to the United States, had visited the country, and spoke some English. They were playing a cat-and-mouse game with the local Polish police but arranged for the Americans to be picked up by that police. The Poles in turn passed the Americans on to the Soviets.

One of the new arrivals, Sergeant E. G. Kelly, testified that upon landing he had encountered a Ukrainian insurgent who had been to Scranton, Pennsylvania. Kelly noted that the Poles were unhappy with the Soviets but followed their orders, as they were allied against the Ukrainians. A Soviet officer interrogated Kelly in particular detail about the time he had spent with the Ukrainian "bandits." Another fresh arrival, Sergeant R. G. Stubaus, had also fallen into the hands of Ukrainians armed with machine guns, and again, one of them spoke some English, having visited New Jersey— Stubaus's home state, as it turned out. In one of the villages where Stubaus stayed, he was informed that the Russians were getting ready to post notices ordering Ukrainians out of that particular village.[18]

The reports of the US airmen collected by Fitchen and sent to the American embassy in Moscow in December 1944 left no doubt that the Soviets were creating a new reality on the ground. They were determined to keep Lviv for themselves, forcing the Poles out and declaring that the city belonged to the Ukrainian SSR. But west of the Curzon Line, which passed through the Przemyśl (Peremyshl) region, they allied themselves with the local Polish militias against the Ukrainian insurgents and were pushing the

Ukrainians eastward, into the territory they wanted to keep for themselves. By the time Roosevelt, Churchill, and Stalin met in Yalta in February 1945, the ethnic composition of the region would be dramatically changed by the Holocaust, still unknown to the world, as well by Soviet policies introduced immediately after the takeover of the region in the summer of 1944. In the fall of that year, the Lublin government and Stalin's lieutenant in Ukraine, Nikita Khrushchev, signed an agreement on "population exchange" between Poland and Ukraine.[19]

Major Anatolii Zorin replaced Lieutenant Colonel Sveshnikov as the chief SMERSH official in charge of the reduced US personnel at Poltava after the "downsizing" of American operations in Ukraine in October 1944. He was first alerted to American information-gathering activities in Lviv after the visit of Colonel Hampton and his team to the city in November 1944. Zorin believed that the whole trip was nothing but a pretext to spy on the Soviets. On the basis of testimony given by the Soviet members of the Douglas C-47 crew that accompanied Hampton to Lviv, Zorin concluded that neither Hampton nor Kowal was needed to deliver fuel—the official purpose of the trip.

Zorin learned that the American airmen had spent their time in Lviv shopping and meeting with the locals, who sold them trinkets. Among the locals were a Hungarian actress and four Polish women. It was learned subsequently that the Hungarian actress had been arrested at some point by the Soviet secret police. The Polish women were suspected of harboring anti-Soviet views. Some Americans were accused of holding and even spreading anti-Soviet views of their own. Sergeant Chavkin had allegedly asked his Soviet teammates why Ukraine and other Soviet republics were not independent, and suggested that the Poles in Lviv were more friendly toward the Germans than toward the Russians, while the population of Poltava was not happy with the Russians either.[20]

Zorin reported on Hampton's trip to Lviv to the Soviet Air Force commanders along with the request that Americans flying to the region to salvage airplanes be accompanied by senior Soviet officers. From then on,

SMERSH would also try to place its agents among the interpreters on American flights in order to supervise American contacts with locals. The interpreter who accompanied Hampton on the November 14 flight to Lviv, Second Lieutenant Galina (Galia) Ganchukova, apparently was not a SMERSH informer and did not file a report on the trip. But after the next American flight to Lviv, which included Major Wiseheart and Sergeant Chavkin, SMERSH officers got a detailed report from an interpreter code-named Olia. The agent reported on a meeting that Wiseheart and Chavkin had with a professor of the local university, who had a brother in the United States and was trying to reestablish contact with him.[21]

The Americans complained bitterly to their superiors in Poltava and Moscow about the surveillance conducted almost openly by Soviet liaison officers and interpreters on their flights to western Ukraine and Poland. They called them "Bird Dogs" and blamed them for much more than spying on them. The Soviet minders gave false weather reports in an effort to stop flights from leaving or returning to Poltava, and prevented American contacts with the local population by forcing the crews to sleep in their aircraft. At Poltava the Soviets increased their activity, monitoring relations between GIs and locals and trying once again to prevent contacts between GIs and Ukrainian women.[22]

14

New Year's Dance

The arrival of 1945 was celebrated in the Soviet Union as the beginning of the end of a long and devastating war. The Red Army was completing preparations for a major offensive that would bring its units into the heart of Germany, a few dozen miles from Berlin, and everyone believed that the war would end with the capture of the capital. On New Year's Day one of the leading newspapers, *Izvestiia* (News), published a front-page cartoon showing Hitler, Himmler, and Goebbels celebrating the New Year in Hitler's bunker with a bottle of Valerian drops—which are supposed to help with insomnia—at the head of the table. Under the table were Hitler's remaining allies, including Mussolini. The accompanying verse read: "The inescapable judgment / Hangs over that criminal rabble / The enemies tremble before the New Year / It will put an end to them in good time!"[1] Unlike Hitler and his allies, the Big Three had good reason to look forward with optimism.

But there were clouds on the horizon as well, most notably the future of Poland. Stalin was ready to recognize his Lublin Poles as the only legitimate government of the country. Roosevelt asked him to postpone the recognition; Stalin refused. On January 1, 1945, he sent Roosevelt a note that, along with the New Year's greetings of "health and success," conveyed Stalin's regret that he had failed to convince Roosevelt of the soundness of the Soviet position on the Polish question. Most disingenuously, Stalin told Roosevelt that he could not postpone recognition because the matter was out of his hands: the Supreme Soviet has already assured the Lublin Poles of their recognition. On the same day, Churchill publicly refused to extend recognition to the Lublin Poles. He also approached Roosevelt, suggesting a separate meeting on Malta prior to the forthcoming Big Three conference in Yalta. Churchill believed that they had to coordinate their positions before facing Stalin.[2]

The Grand Alliance found that the holiday season brought both joy and aggravation. The end of war was in sight, but the existing cracks in their relations deepened, indicating problems ahead. Nowhere was discord among the Allies more pronounced in the first days and weeks of 1945 than at Poltava, where their cooperation was ostensibly closest.

The Americans on the base were in a celebratory mood on New Year's Eve. The city of Poltava was declared off limits to the GIs in order to prevent possible drunken brawls with Red Army soldiers and locals, but the Soviets allowed local women to come to the New Year's dance at the base. "They had a big celebration at the post last night, and I hated to miss it," wrote Franklyn Holzman in a letter home. "Fellows were even allowed to invite girls to the post to our club."

Sergeant Holzman was on duty on New Year's Eve. Most of the American personnel got two days off, but he was one of the skeleton crew who worked through the night. Unable to take part in the dance, Holzman and two of his friends visited their female acquaintances in Poltava on New Year's Day. They brought along an impressive assortment of drinks: four bottles of champagne, a bottle of cognac, and a bottle of port along with some food. The girls roasted chicken and prepared potatoes and cabbage. With food ready, the GIs opened a bottle of champagne right away. It was Holzman's first drinking party in Ukraine, and as he wrote later to his parents, he had been "feeling high as a kite."[3]

Overall, Holzman was quite satisfied with his time in Poltava. His Russian, which he had begun to learn in Myrhorod, had improved significantly, as had his chances to meet local women. In Myrhorod, Holzman had two girlfriends. One of them, a high-school student named Nina Mozhaeva, was his platonic love; he had a real affair with the other, an older woman. After his transfer to Poltava, Holzman found yet another girlfriend and had plenty of opportunity to spend time with her. On some occasions, he remembered later, almost half the personnel did not sleep at the base, staying with their girlfriends in Poltava. Holzman remained oblivious to Soviet harassment of women dating the GIs. His girlfriend, Nina Afanasieva, was detained and interrogated by the secret police two months later, on March 12, 1945. They forced her to sign two documents, the first swearing her to secrecy about the detention, the second obliging her to break off relations with Holzman.[4]

The secret police would probably have confronted Afanasieva sooner and ruined the romance had Holzman not been on duty on New Year's Eve and thus unable to invite her to the dance at the club. "Following New Year's Holidays a story was widely circulated around the camp to the effect that some four Russian girls who had visited the American Enlisted Men's Club over the New Year Holiday were detained in town by the Russian Secret Police for questioning," reported George Fischer in his capacity as Hampton's adjutant. "The girls were reported to have been asked during the interrogation why they associated with the Americans instead of their own people."[5]

This once again put to the test Soviet–American relations at Poltava. Attacks on women dating Americans, which as noted had spiked in the summer of 1944, had become quite rare by the end of the year, partly because there were fewer Americans around, and partly because the cold weather did not encourage the lovebirds to stroll along the streets and alleys of city parks. They met instead at the women's homes, as did Holzman, or at the American premises, where the US personnel, with Soviet assistance, had built two clubs—one for officers, the other for enlisted men—and a theater. The Americans would invite their girlfriends to visit, and that raised the contentious question of access to the base.

The Soviets, who controlled that access, were in a position to decide whom to admit. They introduced a pass system, limiting the number of Soviets with permanent passes to eight—mainly liaison officers and interpreters. Everyone else had to apply for a pass. American officers and GIs had to submit a request for their guest's visit to the base forty-eight hours in advance. The guest's full name, home address, and purpose of visit were to be recorded on the form. The Soviets, especially SMERSH and the Poltava secret police, needed time to study the applications and, as the Soviet officer responsible for issuing passes, Lieutenant Colonel Arsenii Bondarenko, once told Fischer, to "weed out... undesirables who had no business looking around American installations."[6]

The new rules were introduced in mid-December, ahead of the Christmas and New Year holidays. To avoid possible conflicts between American and Soviet servicemen, Colonel Hampton, in consultation with the Soviet commanders, declared Poltava off limits to American servicemen on New Year's Eve and New Year's Day. Thus contacts between GIs and their girlfriends were allowed only at the American base, and the women had to apply for a pass, which caused panic among Ukrainian women dating Americans. They knew that their names and addresses would end up on secret-police lists and that they would be accused of association with foreigners. Some American boyfriends refused to request passes for their girlfriends; others decided to take the risk. Quite a few women from Poltava attended both the Christmas and the New Year's dances at the American base.

Very soon, the Americans began to hear from their girlfriends about the consequences of attending the dances. George Fischer wrote in his report that rumors about Soviet secret-police interrogations of women who had come to the base remained unconfirmed, but an American officer undertook his own investigation into the matter. William Kaluta, a construction engineer at the base and its future historian, had a good knowledge of Russian and often served as an intermediary in dealings between his English-speaking colleagues and Soviet officials. He had plenty of opportunity to see how intrusive Soviet surveillance could be and how brutal the secret-police attempts to break up relationships between Americans and locals, especially women.

Like Fischer, Kaluta had been a Sovietophile when he came to Poltava in May 1944. Also like Fischer, he came from a family that had deep roots in that part of Europe and proud of its leftist leanings. They came to the United States immediately before World War I from the Pinsk region on the border between Ukraine and Belarus. Kaluta senior was probably active in the workers' movement in the Russian Empire and, as an immigrant, became a labor activist in New York. He served as chair of a workers' club and member of the editorial board of the pro-Soviet newspaper *Russkii golos* (Russian Voice).[7]

SMERSH informants reported that at a dinner with Red Army officers in July 1944, Kaluta, whom they identified as a Ukrainian but called "Vasilii," using the Russian form of his first name, told those around the table: "If my father in America knew that his son is now in Russia, partaking of a festive dinner at table with Russian officers, he would weep tears of joy. After the war I will certainly arrange a visit to Russia for my father and sister, sparing no effort to get passports for them." The SMERSH agents described Kaluta as very friendly and happy to socialize with the Soviets. He played the accordion, often sang Russian and Ukrainian songs, and was popular with the Red Army officers. Some of his songs caused concern among his SMERSH minders, however. One of them allegedly included the words, "The Soviet land is free, but one sees no freedom in it." From their perspective Kaluta's acceptance of the Soviet regime seemed partial at best.[8]

Kaluta's favorable attitude toward the Soviets began to change in late 1944 and early 1945, when fellow servicemen asked him to help their girlfriends in their dealings with the Poltava local branch of the NKGB. When Kaluta asked secret-police officials why the women were arrested, interrogated, and had had their passports confiscated, the answer he got was pretty standard by that time: that the women were prostitutes. The Soviets were doing the Americans a favor by protecting them from venereal disease. After talking to the women involved, Kaluta learned that upon being arrested they were usually asked why they were dating Americans. The women would then be ordered to spy on their American friends and collect as much information as possible on what they did and said. The secret police would make them sign forms pledging to remain silent about what had happened to them at the police station, subject to legal penalty.

The women were careful not to refuse directly, Kaluta noted, but pointed out that there was little going on between them and their lovers except sex. The only English they knew was "love me" and "kiss me," while their Americans friends spoke little Russian. Kaluta later wrote that the GIs' language skills were limited to "bedroom Russian." The NKGB officers seemed to have a solution to that problem. After a month they would order the girlfriends to dump their lovers and date other Americans, hoping those would be able to speak Russian or Ukrainian and be of more use to the intelligence services. Some did, while others refused. When Kaluta asked those women who continued to date their American boyfriends despite the orders from NKGB why they did so, he learned that they seemed resigned to their fate and psychologically ready to go to prison if necessary. Their hope was that the American servicemen and their commanders could intervene successfully on their behalf.[9]

The SMERSH and Poltava secret police stepped up their efforts to recruit women who dated Americans, with varying success. In February 1945 the Poltava division of the NKGB reported that it had recruited one informer among the women who attended the Christmas party at the American base, and another who had attended the New Year's party there. The first of these they convinced to cooperate was a seventeen-year-old schoolgirl named Irina Roginskaia. She had been invited to the Christmas party by a chaplain, Major Clarence Strippy, who was in charge of organizing it. Roginskaia was already on the list of Ukrainian women dating Americans and confirmed that she had first become acquainted with an American serviceman in June 1944. In fact, she had a couple of meetings with Lieutenant Colonel William Jackson, who was in charge of the medical services at the bases. Since the secret police had no other compromising information on Roginskaia, they decided to recruit her and put on their agent list under the code-name "Mikhailova."

The secret police were interested in information not only about the Americans but also about the Soviet women who dated them and Roginskaia fit the bill, as she had extensive contacts in both groups. Faina Ageeva, a few years older than Roginskaia, dated the American sergeant Ray Mongjow and was invited by him to attend the New Year's party. She was recruited under the code-name "Matsulevich." The secret-police report indicated that both women were willing to collaborate. They would probably have told a very different story about their recruitment had they been asked by an independent party. As far as they were concerned, their future and per-haps their freedom were on the line once they were spotted dating Americans.[10]

Kaluta had another brush with the Soviet security services in early February 1945, when he and Major Kowal negotiated with Soviet officers about inviting female students at the Poltava medical institute to a party and dance at the American base. The two American officers promised to drive the women home after the party. The Soviets offered to issue passes but refused to contact the institute. Kaluta and Kowal took the matter into their own hands, drove to Poltava, where they met a female student whom they knew socially, and asked her to invite up to twelve of her friends to attend the dance. She promised to do so but warned that many of her girl-friends were reluctant to provide their names and addresses to Soviet offi-cials. Still, they put together a list, submitted it to the Soviet authorities, and got ready to celebrate. The Soviets issued the passes, and everyone was looking forward to the party.[11]

However, when Major Kowal drove to Poltava on the afternoon of February 3 to collect the girls and bring them to the base, he was in for a surprise. At the home of one of the girls, whom Kaluta called "Valia" in his account, Kowal found both Valia and her mother crying. They had just re-ceived a visit from Captain Maksimov. Most likely it was the same Maksimov who served as the base's chief liaison officer and was among the first officers on the base to have been recruited by SMERSH as an agent under the code-name Markov. Doing his masters' bidding, Maksimov told Valia that she should refuse to go to the dance, pretending to be busy with exams. She also should decline any future invitations. If she ever told the Americans about his visit and instructions, she would be arrested and sent to Siberia. The last words terrified Valia's mother, who, according to a later report, was "in a frenzy during Major Kowal's visit."

Now that plans for the party at the base had been ruined, a number of American airmen organized a separate small party at Valia's place that was attended by a few of her friends. Kowal soon learned that other women had received similar visits and the Americans, upset by the cancellation of the original plans, protested. Major Zorin of the Poltava base SMERSH department denied responsibility for what had happened. According to his report, the women had been persuaded not to attend the dance by agents of the Poltava department of state security (NKGB). The Poltava security officers simply ordered the director of the medical school to prohibit her students from attending the dance. They now wanted General Kovalev, the new Soviet commander of the Poltava base, to react to the American protest, but he refused, wishing to maintain working relations with the Americans.[12]

Stepan Kovalev, a native of the Poltava region who had served as General Perminov's deputy during the summer months and now assumed the command of the base with the rank major general, did not mind attending American parties. A Valentine Day's party at the US base was scheduled for February 14 and Kovalev was looking forward to it.

According to his later report, Kovalev noted that the Americans turned the reception into a costume party. Lieutenant Kaluta was dressed as a German, sporting a Hitler-like hairstyle and moustache and shouting "Heil!" Others responded to him accordingly. Major Wiseheart marched with Kaluta, showing how the Germans were fleeing the Allies. The American nurses were dressed in costumes modeled on the clothing of ordinary Russian women. Pilots who had arrived from Poland a few days earlier showed up in female attire, wearing bathing suits and lipstick. Everyone was drinking except Major Kowal, Captain Nicholson, and the duty officer, who were maintaining order.

Kovalev ended his report on the party with a statement that was perhaps unsurprising from a communist zealot dedicated to the conservative values of Stalin's USSR. "In general, that party, like some other festivities, took place in disorderly fashion, spontaneously, with everyone doing as he pleased. Uninhibited by the presence of women, they allowed themselves the most vulgar actions, thereby manifesting the shortcomings and even the absence of elementary rules of culture in the behavior of American officers at their officers' parties, even in the presence of Russian officers and Russian women."

For unknown reasons, Kovalev filed his report two weeks after the event, on March 1. He may have been forced to do that because rumors about his participation in the party reached his superiors. Although Kovalev presented his report by way of educating and entertaining his superiors about American customs, the SMERSH officers found fault with his conduct at the party. "Instead of immediately leaving the vulgar orgy described above, and then making an official representation to the Americans, Kovalev, together with his wife and other Red Army officers, who were also present with their wives, remained witnesses of the scandalous behavior that was going on," wrote a high-ranking SMERSH official in Moscow.[13]

Soviet interference with the American parties at Poltava leaves little doubt that SMERSH and security officers like Major Zorin were acquiring more and more power at the base, sidelining military commanders like Kovalev. Many Americans knew that they were under surveillance, and that knowledge, coupled with frustration gathering over the previous weeks and months, contributed to their growing desire to have as little as possible to do with the Soviets.

In February, Zorin filed a report decrying the deterioration of Soviet-American relations at the base and citing numerous examples to show that the Americans were limiting Soviet officers' access to their base and were under orders not to socialize too much with the Soviets or tell them anything.

The SMERSH officers blamed the American change of attitude not on their own actions, but on the anti-Soviet views of the American commanders. "Changes of attitude on the part of the American command," wrote Zorin, "are to be explained by the hostility of the remaining leadership to the Soviet Union." The report quoted no less a figure than Colonel Hampton, who had allegedly told one of SMERSH's informers: "You are trying to impose your Marxism everywhere, but it's already out of date for America. We have people who refuted Marx long ago."

Zorin also cited an episode in which Hampton took off from the Poltava airfield in a Douglas aircraft even though General Kovalev had refused to clear the flight, as he was waiting for a go-ahead from Moscow. Hampton refused to wait. He had just returned from the Saki airport in the Crimea, where he was making preparations for the arrival of the Big Three for the Yalta Conference, and had to fly back to continue his work. Fed up with Soviet delays and obstructionism, he was in no mood to tolerate them any longer.[14] The fraying of the Grand Alliance continued apace.

15

Yalta

Averell Harriman was the first to propose the old tsarist playground of Yalta on the Crimean peninsula as the venue for the meeting of the Big Three. On December 6, 1944, in the middle of preparations for the meeting, he cabled Roosevelt: "Two of our naval officers visited Yalta and Sevastopol during last summer. They report that Yalta has a number of large and well-built sanatoriums and hotels undamaged by German occupation. By Russian standards, town is extremely neat and clean. The winter climate is reasonable." The ambassador was looking forward to seeing the place he had heard so much about but never visited himself.[1]

Yalta, or for that matter the Crimea, was far from Roosevelt's first choice for a conference venue. His health was clearly in decline and he had only a few months to live. Had he known how short his time would be, he would probably have chosen another destination for his last trip abroad. The road to the Crimea involved a voyage across the Atlantic, infested by German submarines, and a long flight in an unpressurized airplane cabin over the Balkans, still occupied by the Germans. Roosevelt had asked Stalin for a meeting closer to the United States, but the Soviet leader would not budge.

He was in no hurry to meet his allies, who would want to discuss Poland and his oppressive policies in Eastern Europe.

Roosevelt gave in because he felt he could not wait. He wanted to see Stalin as soon as possible to discuss the war in the Pacific and plans for the creation of the United Nations Organization. Churchill, disturbed by developments in Poland and Stalin's diplomatic recognition of his Lublin puppets, was eager to see both Roosevelt and Stalin. As noted earlier, he wanted to meet with Roosevelt on Malta to agree on a joint position before the conference. On January 1, 1945, the day he refused to recognize the legitimacy of the Lublin government, Churchill sent Roosevelt a cable asking for a private meeting and adding lines of doggerel of his own composition: "From Malta to Yalta. Let nobody alter." He found the prospect of going to Yalta extremely unwelcome. "[I]f we had spent ten years on research we could not have found a worse place in the world," he told Harry Hopkins, an early champion of the Crimea as a possible venue for the meeting.[2]

Harriman may have regretted his own advocacy of Yalta when in mid-January 1945 he began looking for a way to get there. His original plan was to fly to the Crimea either via Poltava or directly to the town of Saki on the southern shore of the peninsula, but bad weather made that impossible. In his original suggestion of Yalta to the president, Harriman had written: "Average temperature in January and February 39 degrees Fahrenheit. The town has good southern exposure and is protected from the north winds by high mountains." During the last weeks of January 1945, the weather refused to cooperate. After waiting in vain for flight clearance from the Soviet Air Force command, Harriman and his always energetic, curious, and observant daughter decided to take the train.[3]

"A long affair—three days and three nights—most of the time spent standing in bombed out stations," wrote Kathy Harriman in one of her letters. The railway from Moscow to Simferopol, the largest city in the Crimea, passed sixty miles to the east of Poltava, giving her a chance to observe the now snow-covered landscape familiar from her summer trip to the city. "The Ukrainian peasants seem far more prosperous than those around Moscow. Their cottages are painted, with thatched roofs and quite picturesque," she wrote Mary. At one of the stations, Kathy and her companions bought fresh eggs and made punch out of canned milk, bourbon and butter. Still, it was a long journey. By the time they finally reached Simferopol late in the afternoon of their third day of travel, her father was so impatient to get to Yalta, which was about fifty miles away, that he disregarded the advice of his Soviet hosts, who counseled against a night drive through the mountains in a snowstorm, and insisted on departing immediately. After a drive of three and a half hours, during which one of the cars became stuck in the snow, they made it to Yalta.[4]

The Harrimans would spend the following days making sure that everything was ready for the visit of the dignitaries, Roosevelt and Churchill in particular. The Western leaders of the alliance were scheduled to arrive at the Saki air base in the Crimea on February 3. The American officers charged with ensuring that the arrival would come off without a hitch were flown to Saki from Poltava. They would do their best to make the conference a success.

■

Arrangements for the American arrival at Saki, the airfield closest to Yalta, were entrusted to Poltava base commander Colonel Hampton. Soon after January 10, the day on which Churchill gave his final approval to the Yalta venue, Hampton and his subordinates put all other projects on the back burner and focused on the Crimea. As an officer wrote at the time, the Poltava staff was under orders "to furnish a nucleus of service people for a secret mission in Crimea." No longer "forgotten bastards of Ukraine," the Poltava airmen found themselves involved in a political event of world— and as it turned out historical—significance. By the time the Yalta conference ended, it would provide the base with a new mission, one involving not merely observing Soviet actions in Eastern Europe but helping American prisoners of war on Soviet-controlled territory get home.

Hampton went to Saki in the company of two of his Russian-speaking aides, his adjutant George Fischer and First Sergeant John Matles, a native of Bessarabia in the former Russian Empire who had worked on a number of American projects in the Soviet Union during the 1930s. Others would soon follow, either dispatched on short visits or seconded to Saki and Sarabuz airfield near the peninsula's main city of Simferopol for the duration of the conference.[5]

Hampton and his people were intent on doing all they could to ensure the smooth running of the conference. It turned out to be not an easy task. As before, the Soviets insisted that the first pilot on all American flights between Poltava, Saki, and Sarabuz airfields be one of their own airmen. Given that the Americans did not trust the Soviet pilots, whom as we have seen they considered prone to take unnecessary risks, relations between the two sides over Yalta immediately grew tense.

The level of mistrust was illustrated by an episode involving the head of the Allied Expeditionary Air Force in Europe, British Air Chief Marshal Arthur Tedder, who came to Moscow to negotiate with Stalin. On January 17, Hampton brought Tedder from Moscow to Poltava and flew him to Saki the next day. His Soviet copilot insisted on being the first pilot on the plane. Hampton refused and Tedder backed the American, taking over as second pilot himself. The Soviets were upset but did not venture to contradict a senior British commander fresh from a meeting with Stalin. Once in the Crimea, however, Tedder discovered that a briefcase he had with him on the plane had disappeared. By that time the plane, piloted this time by a joint US-Soviet crew, had returned to Poltava.

Tedder turned to Hampton for help. On January 19, Fischer approached a Soviet radio operator at the Saki air base, asking him to contact the Poltava base by radio and find out whether the crew had found Tedder's briefcase. General Kovalev, who received the request, was informed that the briefcase had been found and offered to fly it to Saki, but the Americans insisted that one of them deliver it. The US military mission in Moscow was in agreement; Kovalev maintained that it should be delivered by Soviet personnel. Contrary to established procedure that prohibited him from interrogating American officers, the general questioned the American sergeant who had found the briefcase on the plane after it landed at Poltava. Kovalev's action was protested by the American officers at Poltava, and ultimately the briefcase instead of being turned over to the Soviets was delivered to Tedder by the Americans.[6]

The lack of trust made Hampton's task of flying between the Poltava base and the Saki and Sarabuz all but impossible. American planes could take off from the Poltava airfield only with clearance from the Soviet authorities, clearance that had to be requested a day in advance. In the summer and fall of 1944 it normally took only a few hours to clear an American flight, but as relations between the two sides at Poltava deteriorated, delays grew longer, and sometimes flights were not cleared at all. That was the case on December 22, 1944, when Hampton and Major General Edmund W. Hill, the commander of the US military mission's Air Division, were scheduled to fly from Poltava to eastern Poland.

The Soviet commanders at Poltava gave a simple explanation for the delays: they had no authority to clear flights on their own. Final approval had to come from Moscow, and Moscow was often silent for days, if not weeks. The Red Air Force commanders in Moscow issued a blanket order prohibiting any flights from Poltava between January 20 and 28, 1945, at the height of preparations for the Yalta conference, giving bad weather as the reason. The weather that week was terrible indeed, with constant heavy snowfalls. American weather officers at Poltava reported that there were breaks in weather conditions during that period. Nevertheless, the blanket prohibition remained in effect as the opening date of the conference, February 4, drew near.[7]

Moscow's refusal to clear flights even after the weather improved provoked an open conflict at Poltava, the first that directly involved Hampton and Kovalev, the two commanding officers. On January 29, Hampton flew an American C-47 from Saki to Poltava. He then requested clearance to return to Saki, a flight that he claimed to have been cleared by Marshal Semen Zhavoronkov of the Soviet Air Force, the commander of Soviet naval aviation, who was also responsible for air communications pertaining to the Yalta conference. Kovalev asked Moscow for permission to clear the flight and was informed that General Nikitin had canceled all flights for the day. Hampton protested that he had to bring some American officers back to Saki and had permission from Zhavoronkov.

According to the SMERSH report, an hour and a half after landing at Poltava Hampton again took to the skies in violation of direct orders from

Kovalev. The Soviet general was furious. He tried to establish radio contact with the aircraft, but it was already out of range of the transmitter. Kaluta, who was then at the air base's control center, witnessed Kovalev's outburst. "I would have believed that a young fighter pilot would disobey my instructions, but not Colonel Hampton," said Kovalev, making no effort to hide his frustration. He added that he was the base commander, and no aircraft was allowed to take off without his command.[8]

Kovalev had every right to be upset, though he had never given Hampton or any other American a plausible explanation of the Soviet refusal to clear flights. The reason was given by Major General Slavin, the assistant chief of the Red Army General Staff in charge of liaison with the Americans, in a letter to the chief of staff of the Soviet Navy, Admiral Vladimir Alafuzov, the direct superior of Marshal Zhavoronkov, who had ordered Hampton's flight. Slavin told Alafuzov that the entire crew of the C-47 flown by Hampton was American. "They could use flights from the Crimea to Poltava without our navigators and radio operators aboard to photograph sites of interest to them," wrote Slavin. He also pointed out that American officers were using the special Soviet government line for communications between Poltava and Sarabuz airfield. Slavin asked Alafuzov to warn his subordinates at Saki against allowing the Americans to use government communication lines or making flights without Soviet personnel on board.

Slavin's letter was written on February 8. By that time the American and British delegations were already at Yalta, negotiating with their Soviet counterparts. The tone of the letter and the policies it introduced differed sharply from the friendly attitude that Stalin displayed toward his American guests, in particular President Roosevelt, whom he tried to charm and separate from Winston Churchill physically, mentally, and politically.[9]

Roosevelt and Churchill landed at Saki airfield as planned on the afternoon of February 3. If Churchill's main concern was Soviet behavior in Eastern Europe, where Stalin was continuing to crush democratic opposition, represented in the first instance by forces loyal to the Polish government-in-exile in London, Roosevelt's main objectives, as noted earlier, were to ensure that the Soviets would not renege on Stalin's earlier promise to enter the war with Japan after victory in Europe and to convince the Soviet leader to join the United Nations Organization—the key institution Roosevelt envisioned of the postwar world order.

The American delegation to Yalta, originally meant to number no more than seventy, grew tenfold as the summit meeting approached, partially because Roosevelt invited so many American military commanders. This was a ploy to push for the opening of negotiations on Soviet participation in the Pacific war, which the Soviet side had kept postponing. The American brass was eager to broach the issue. Major General Laurence S. Kuter, representing the commander of the US Air Force, General Henry Anderson, who had fallen ill and could not attend the meeting, was especially interested in discussing US bases in the Pacific. In the months leading up to the conference, General Deane had been frustrated by the refusal of the Red Army General Staff to make any progress on the matter. The hope was that Roosevelt's presence would induce the Soviet commanders invited to Yalta to begin discussions.[10]

The question of the bases came up on the third day of the conference, February 8, when Roosevelt, accompanied by Harriman, met Stalin to discuss the war in the Pacific. The president began indirectly, noting that with US troops entering Manila, the time had come to intensify the bombing of Japan, and the US Air Force was establishing new bases on islands south of Japan. Stalin got the hint. He told the president that he was prepared to allow US Air Force bases in the Amur region. It was a breakthrough of enormous proportions. Stalin also agreed to new US military bases in the vicinity of Budapest and approved another request: to allow American officers to go behind the Soviet lines in Eastern Europe to survey the results of recent US Air Force bombings.

Stalin was clearly on his best behavior. Although Harriman knew from experience that Stalin's oral approval was not the end of the story, he also knew that it was essential to make something happen in the Soviet Union or in the parts of Eastern Europe occupied by the Red Army. Roosevelt reciprocated, saying that he saw no problem with the USSR taking over southern Sakhalin and the Kurile Islands in the Far East. They agreed that the consultations could take place later. A deal had been made: American bases and Soviet participation in the war in exchange for Soviet territorial acquisitions. Stalin was happy with it, as were the US military in general and the Air Force commanders in particular. If they could establish new air bases in Eastern Europe and the Far East, they would be able to make use of the experience gained at Poltava at the new bases and shut down the existing ones.[11]

The American hopes turned out to be premature. Soviet insecurity about the Western presence behind their lines was demonstrated by the long and largely fruitless negotiations on the future of Poland, the issue most discussed at Yalta. It had become central to US-Soviet relations ever since the Warsaw Uprising, and reporting on developments there continued to be one of the tasks of the American airmen who traveled from Poltava to Lviv and back. Roosevelt made his last attempt to convince Stalin to leave the city of Lviv in Poland. Stalin refused. With the Red Army in control of much of Eastern Europe, Stalin had little incentive to compromise. He was also a master at playing the nationalities card, which counted for much in deciding the future of that ethnically and religiously mixed region.

Stalin brushed aside Roosevelt's proposal to return Lviv to the Poles by presenting himself as an advocate of Ukrainian national interests. "What would the Ukrainians say if they [Stalin and Molotov] accepted the Allies' proposal?" Stalin asked Roosevelt and Churchill. "They might say that Stalin and Molotov had turned out to be less reliable defenders of the Russians and the Ukrainians than Curzon and Clemenceau." The former reference was of course to the Curzon Line of 1920, created in the wake of the Paris Peace Conference. As Harriman knew by then from Poltava intelligence reports, the Soviets were already moving people from one side of the Curzon Line to the other in order to create homogeneous ethnic communities—Ukrainians to the east and Poles to the west. Both Roosevelt and Churchill had to accept the new border, with Lviv remaining under formal Ukrainian and actual Soviet control.[12]

Stalin was equally uncooperative on the question of the Polish government, which he staffed with his own people, and on the future Polish elections, which he promised to arrange but was intent on controlling. When

the issue of the forthcoming Polish elections came to the fore, Stalin assured Churchill that as far as the Red Army was concerned, British and
Western diplomatic representatives would be free to travel in the country to
observe the elections but would have to negotiate directly with the Polish
government. With Stalin's representatives now running key sectors of the
Polish government, he could easily take away with one hand what he had
given with the other. The Poltava base would remain one of very few places
where the Americans could gather information on the Polish situation after
the conference.[13]

The question on the Yalta agenda that would be of greatest importance
to the Poltava airmen in the weeks and months to come was settled on the
last day of the conference, February 11, when General Deane signed an
agreement on the exchange of prisoners of war. It had been long in the
making, and Deane had reason to celebrate. He had first raised the question
of American POWs with the Red Army General Staff in June 1944, days
after the first American planes landed on the Poltava-area airfields. This was
also the period of the run-up to Operation Bagration, the Soviet offensive.
The American commanders expected that the Soviet advance would free
the Allied POWs held by the Germans in that part of Europe and wanted
Soviet cooperation in bringing them home as soon as possible. The Soviets
had then shown no interest in the subject. Now they were finally ready to
accommodate the American request and sign a formal agreement.

The basic principles of the agreement were laid out by Molotov in a letter
sent to the US embassy in Moscow on November 25—almost five months
after the POW question had first been raised. Molotov agreed "in principle"
to the American proposal, which provided for the free access of American
representatives to liberated American prisoners of war. He also raised the
question of Soviet POWs and former Soviet citizens enrolled in the
Wehrmacht and auxiliary German formations captured by the Americans
and British in Western Europe. Molotov wanted them placed in separate
camps and sent back to the Soviet Union. Deane did not object. He agreed
to the deal, which obliged the Americans to send all Soviet citizens from
the territories occupied by the US Army back to the USSR. In exchange,

the Americans would be allowed to evacuate their own citizens from territories controlled by the Red Army.[14]

Deane signed the agreement he had helped to negotiate on the last day
of the Yalta conference. That was probably also the last day on which he was
satisfied with its content. The deal would create more problems in US-
Soviet relations. "The agreement was good one," he recalled, "but, so far as
the Russians were concerned, it turned out to be just another piece of
paper." The document failed to address profound differences between
American and Soviet political and military culture. If for US servicemen
there was no higher duty than to rescue their own prisoners of war, Stalin
regarded his POWs as deserters and traitors to the socialist fatherland. As
far as he was concerned, they were criminals deserving the harshest possible punishment. Former Soviet citizens, captured in German uniform,
knew that and refused to go back, claiming German citizenship on the basis
of their service in the Wehrmacht. They preferred that the Americans treat
them as Germans rather than Soviets. Some would even commit suicide in
American custody to avoid deportation to their home country.

American military commanders such as Deane either did not understand the situation or did not want to understand it. At the top of their
agenda was the welfare of US prisoners of war: if the Soviets wanted to reclaim their nationals and made that a condition of helping the American
POWs return home, they were prepared to accept it. Deane also underesti-
mated the depth of Soviet paranoia about the American presence behind
their lines in Poland and other countries of Eastern Europe, where they
were installing communist-led governments while cracking down on independent political activity and basic elements of the democratic electoral
process. The agreement that Deane signed did not specify that the Soviets
were to provide access to the American POWs as soon as possible after
their liberation in areas close to the front lines, and the Soviets refused to
allow American representatives anywhere near their front.[15]

In the next few months—which he called his "darkest days"—Deane
would become thoroughly acquainted with the traps and loopholes of
the document he had signed at Yalta, as well as the cultural difference in
the Soviet and American treatment of POWs. The American personnel

at the Poltava base would become essential to Deane's efforts to make the agreement work, as they were the only American detachment with access to parts of Eastern Europe, where thousands of American POWs were being held.[16]

■

"In an alliance the allies should not deceive each other," said Stalin at a dinner that he hosted at Yalta for Roosevelt and Churchill on February 8. "Perhaps that is naïve? Why should I not deceive my ally?" continued the dictator, who had successfully bugged the premises of the American and British delegations and was receiving reports on their conversations. He went on: "But I as a naïve man think it best not to deceive the ally even if he is a fool." The Western leaders, who Stalin had just suggested might be dupes, listened in silence to their interpreters. Stalin, for his part, could not stop playing with the idea of double-dealing. "Possibly our alliance is so firm just because we do not deceive each other." He then had another thought: "Or is it because it is not so easy to deceive each other?" He finally proposed a "toast to the firmness of our Three Power Alliance. May it be strong and stable; may we be as frank as possible."[17]

Many in the American camp believed that Stalin meant what he said in his final toast. The conference ended with high hopes. The Americans got what they wanted on Soviet participation in the United Nations and in the war on Japan and found Stalin unusually accommodating on other issues, including the establishment of US air bases on territory that he controlled. There were problems, especially in Poland, but given the good will Stalin showed at Yalta, they believed that they could be worked out as well. Harry Hopkins expressed the feelings of many when he recalled after the war: "We really believed in our hearts that this was the dawn of the new day we had all been praying for and talking about for so many years."[18]

The Poltava airmen seconded to the Crimea for the duration of the conference knew the Soviets and their methods better than anyone else in the American delegation, and were therefore less impressed by their Soviet hosts. That was certainly the case with George Fischer. Before the conference, Hampton's adjutant had been concerned about prospects of a new world war and was afraid that if the US government, which kept making concessions to the Soviets, did not start asking for something in return, "the Russians will learn to despise us, and we will learn to hate them." Fischer's time at the Saki air base did nothing to dispel those worries despite the fact that he enjoyed company of his Soviet counterparts. "Having fun together eased the jelling and blending," he wrote later. It helped that the Allied officers were given the same rations as the top brass. "Loads of good food," recalled Fischer before turning somber and admitting that "on starving land we drank and ate like kings. We had a Feast in Time of a Famine."[19]

Not all Poltava airmen's reminiscences of their free time in the Crimea were as favorable as Fischer's. William Kaluta, who flew to Saki on February 1, recalled that five days later, the Soviets arranged an evening of dance and some American pilots invited local women to the event. The women began to leave the hall after being approached by Soviet officers. The explanations they gave the Americans may have been true in some cases but could not have applied to all. One woman allegedly had to go home, another to work, a third suddenly felt ill. Soon the rest of the locals who had had a chance to talk to the Americans were gone, putting an end to the evening. For visitors from Poltava such as Kaluta, the pattern was unmistakably clear: the Soviet secret police was doing in Saki exactly as it had done in Poltava.[20]

The Poltava airmen helped the conference become the success it was judged to be, but their Poltava experience made them much less optimistic about the prospects of the Grand Alliance than were Roosevelt and Churchill. They knew that there was a huge gulf between what the Soviets said and did. The American leadership would soon appreciate that hard-earned truth of the Poltava veterans. Their base would soon become not only the main American window on the rapidly deteriorating situation in Soviet-controlled Eastern Europe, but also safe haven and last hope for American POWs freed by the Red Army advance in the region and facing confinement in Soviet transit camps.

Prisoners of War

On March 4, 1945, Roosevelt gave his approval to one of the harshest telegrams he had ever sent to Stalin. Their previous exchange, around February 23—Red Army Day in the USSR—was full of courteous gestures, with the president sending Stalin his "heartiest congratulations" and the Soviet leader answering in kind: "I beg you, Mr. President, to accept my thanks for your friendly greeting." This March telegram struck an entirely different tone. "I have reliable information regarding the difficulties which are being encountered in collecting, supplying and evacuating American ex-prisoners of war (POWs) and American aircraft crews who are stranded east of the Russian lines," began the message, omitting the usual salutation.[1]

Roosevelt was clearly angry. Thousands of American POWs liberated from German camps by the Red Army were de facto left to their own devices, even hitchhiking to Moscow to get medical help and support. Contrary to the American interpretation of the Yalta agreements, the Soviets were not informing the Americans about the number or location of liberated POWs and refused to allow US contact teams to move into Eastern Europe to assist them. General Deane and his aides in Moscow offered a solution. They wanted to use the Poltava base as a logistical hub for rendering assistance as well as an assembly point and hospital facility from which the POWs could be flown to the United States via Teheran. The Soviets would not allow the use of the Poltava base for those purposes, just as they had not allowed its use for airdrops to Warsaw six months earlier.[2]

Roosevelt, who had been rather diplomatic on the issue of Warsaw, showed no such restraint when it came to American POWs. "It is urgently requested," read his cable, "that instructions be issued authorizing ten American aircraft with American crews to operate between Poltava and places in Poland where American ex-prisoners of war and stranded airmen may be located." The cable continued: "I regard this request to be of greatest importance not only for humanitarian reasons but also by reason of intense interest of the American public in the welfare of our ex-prisoners of war and stranded aircraft crews." Reports about the mistreatment of Americans in Soviet custody made Roosevelt worry not only about their fate but also about the future of the Grand Alliance itself.[3]

The question of Soviet treatment of American POWs produced the first major crisis in Soviet-American relations after the Yalta conference. The Soviet refusal to admit Americans to the original assembly points of POWs in Eastern Europe not only worsened existing tensions over the future of Eastern Europe but also exposed a profound cultural difference between the allies. The Americans of course regarded their POWs as heroes who deserved all possible assistance to save and repatriate them, and the Soviet regime, as noted, considered soldiers captured by the enemy as traitors. If the Soviets were prepared to imprison and occasionally shoot their own soldiers upon finding them in German camps, they regarded it as a courtesy to their overseas ally that they allow captured Americans to go free. Taking care of the liberated Americans' needs was not their responsibility. Thus, what the Americans regarded as barbaric treatment by their Soviet allies was seen as humane enough by the Soviets. Once again, the Poltava airmen found themselves in the middle of a clash.

The American officers in Moscow got the first indication that something was going wrong with the agreement on the treatment of POWs on the day after Deane signed the document at Yalta.

On February 12, a representative of the pro-Soviet government in Poland informed the US mission in Moscow that there were close to one thousand American prisoners in Poland, with no one to take care of them. The message originated with two American ex-POWs who had managed to convince a local Polish official to send word to Moscow about the plight of their comrades. Deane learned the news on February 14, soon after his return from the Crimea. The mission sprang into action, and on the same day Major General Edmund Hill, Deane's Air Force deputy, instructed Eastern Command at Poltava to prepare the base for processing as many as fifteen thousand liberated POWs in groups of one hundred at a time. The POW contact officers were supposed to reach Poltava from Britain. Food and other supplies were to arrive from Teheran. At Poltava, medical personnel got busy preparing hospital facilities for new arrivals.[4]

On February 16, the prisoner contact team headed by Lieutenant Colonel James D. Wilmeth—a three-man crew that included a doctor and an interpreter—arrived in Poltava from Moscow. They were ready to go to Poland and start helping American POWs there. All that was needed was Soviet permission to leave Poltava. Deane applied for permission on February 14, but the Soviet Commissariat of Foreign Affairs was silent. Poltava Soviet commander Kovalev did not allow any member of the Wilmeth crew to board the plane leaving Poltava for eastern Poland on February 17. "A plane took off for air rescue this morning, but we remain here," cabled Wilmeth to Deane.

American commander Colonel Hampton tried in vain to persuade Kovalev to let at least the doctor from the Wilmeth team go to Poland. He then proposed to send an interpreter instead of a doctor, only to be rebuffed again. Next day Deane informed Wilmeth that the Red Army commanders were opposed to using Poltava as the POW processing center and proposed Odesa instead. From there the American ex-POWs could go by ship to the Mediterranean and join the Americans there. Meanwhile the Soviets continued to refuse to clear Wilmeth's flight to Poland. He suspected that they were buying time to prepare exemplary conditions for handling the POWs.[5]

The Soviets had first come into contact with American POWs on January 23, when troops of the First Belarusian Front under the command of

Marshal Rokossovsky overran Oflag 64, a German concentration camp near the Polish village of Szubin, between Gdańsk and Poznań. The camp housed close to fifteen hundred American officers captured in North Africa and Western Europe. The Germans had managed to evacuate most of the inmates before Soviet troops arrived, but close to one hundred sick or injured officers remained. They were soon joined by dozens of others who had managed to escape during the forced march westward. The Red Army soldiers who overran the camp paid little attention to the inmates or their needs, and it took days for a Red Army officer, who introduced himself as a liaison with the command of the front, to show up in Szubin. The Americans were moved east, away from the front line, split into smaller groups, and ordered to wait for a transport to Moscow or Odesa.[6]

The Soviets failed to inform Deane and his mission about the American POWs in their custody prior to signing the Yalta agreement or afterward. Deane, who as noted first learned of Americans behind the Soviet lines on February 14, received a full report on the fate of the Szubin inmates three days later. On February 17, three former POWs knocked on the door of the US Mission. Captain Ernest M. Gruenberg and his two colleagues had left Szubin on January 21 as part of the POW march westward but escaped two days later and made their way to the Soviet filtration camp for Americans west of Szubin. With the Soviets silent about plans to move the ex-prisoners, the three officers left the camp and headed east on their own, concerned mainly about avoiding the Soviet repatriation camp for Americans on the outskirts of Warsaw. Other Americans they met en route had terrible stories to share about hardships that awaited the former POWs there. Hitchhiking on Soviet trucks during the day and spending nights in the homes of Polish peasants, the Americans had finally got on the train and arrived in Moscow.

Members of the mission greeted them as heroes. Captain Gruenberg told Deane that there were dozens of Americans in need of medical help and hundreds of others uncared for in Poland. While Polish peasants helped the Americans as best they could, the Red Army commanders and soldiers could not have cared less about them. In some cases, Red Army soldiers took their wrist watches and other possessions they had managed to retain in the German camp. Similar stories were told by other escapees.

On February 21, three other US officers formerly imprisoned in the Szubin camp were brought to Poltava by an air rescue crew returning from Poland. They were debriefed by Lieutenant Colonel Wilmeth. "The Soviet attitude toward liberated American prisoners is the same as the Soviet attitude toward the countries they have liberated. Prisoners are spoils of war won by Soviet arms. They may be robbed, starved and abused—and no one has the right to question such treatment," wrote Wilmeth, summarizing what he had heard from the ex-POWs and drawing on his own experiences of dealing with the Soviets.[7]

Wilmeth was growing ever more desperate at Poltava. Deane received word from his Red Army contacts that the Soviet Foreign Commissariat had cleared Wilmeth and his team to go to Lublin in eastern Poland on February 18, but General Kovalev kept dragging his feet. Wilmeth began exploring the possibility of taking a train either to Lublin, where all Americans were supposed to be sent before being put on a train to Odesa, or to Odesa itself. In Poltava local Soviet and party officials promised to assist with the ride, but Wilmeth was afraid that, as he wrote to Deane, the promises were nothing but the "usual run around." It was on the evening of February 24, the day Wilmeth revealed his plans for a train journey to Deane, that Kovalev finally told Hampton that Wilmeth had been cleared to leave for Lublin by air. On February 27, after a delay caused by bad weather, Wilmeth and his party departed. Another group of American officers left Poltava, also by air, for Odesa, two weeks to the day after the first news about American ex-POWs had reached the US mission in Moscow.[8]

Wilmeth, as noted earlier, assumed that he had been delayed so long to give the Soviets time to prepare exemplary conditions for the Americans in Lublin. He was in for a surprise. The Soviet officers in charge of the American repatriation camp told Wilmeth that his presence in the city was unnecessary, especially as the headquarters of the Soviet repatriation commission had moved the previous day from Lublin to the Warsaw suburb of Praga. When Wilmeth told them that he wanted to see the American ex-prisoners, he was given the reply that he would need permission, which could only be obtained in Warsaw. When Wilmeth announced that he was going to Warsaw, the Soviets told him that they would first have to get permission from Moscow. It was a master class in Soviet cynicism.

Wilmeth was able to break out of this run-around only when he produced a letter from General Deane stating that his mission was to help the American ex-POWs get home. The Soviets probably did not want to create any trouble on the Moscow level. They took Wilmeth to the barracks, which housed 91 American and 129 British ex-POWs. Before ending up in Lublin, some of them had been housed in Majdanek, the German concentration and extermination camp on the outskirts of Lublin. Close to eighty thousand people had been killed there, three-quarters of them Jews. The Soviets did their best to publicize the Nazi atrocities but could not resist the temptation to use the camp facilities to incarcerate soldiers of the Polish Home Army, which had launched the Warsaw Uprising. Eventually they put the Americans and British in the same barracks where victims of the Holocaust had awaited their end.

Wilmeth found the ex-POWs angry with the treatment they had received. They had been hastily moved to another facility three days before Wilmeth's arrival, but the new housing had no warm water, toilets were overflowing, and there were no outside latrines. There was a shortage of beds; many slept on the floor. There was no bedding or clean clothing available: all they got was a blanket. A number of the ex-POWs had lice. They were fed twice a day with black bread and thin gruel. If that was the main repatriation camp, one can only imagine what was going on in the smaller ones. Not surprisingly, the ex-POWs tried to avoid such camps at all costs, though the Soviets did not seem to be concerned or unduly embarrassed. The conditions in which their own soldiers lived and fought were not much different, and now they were expected to divert scarce resources to house and feed liberated POWs who, as far as they were concerned, deserved to be punished for surrendering to the enemy, not hailed as heroes and pampered by the victorious Red Army.[9]

The Soviets wanted Wilmeth to go back to Poltava and wait there for an answer to his request to visit the repatriation camps established for the Americans in Krakow, Łódź, and Warsaw. Wilmeth refused. Instead he presented a top Soviet commander, Colonel Vlasov, with a copy of the Yalta agreements. Vlasov declined to take it. Given the stalemate, Wilmeth stayed in Lublin. On March 1 he bade farewell to the American and British ex-POWs, who were put into boxcars and shipped to Odesa. According to the Soviets, there were already more than 2,500 ex-POWs assembled in Odesa. The American contact group that went there from Poltava found local conditions tolerable. They were not up to American standards but quite different from those in Lublin, and the main complaint they heard was about the trip to Odesa: the boxcars had no toilet facilities, and trains waited forever for their turn to use the tracks.[10]

By early March 1945, when Roosevelt sent his terse cable to Stalin about American POWs, the Soviets already had in place a rudimentary system of collection points, camps, and railway connections that they used to ship the ex-prisoners to the relative safety of Odesa. That allowed Stalin to respond to Roosevelt on March 5, the day after receiving his message, with assurances that any problems with the POWs were a thing of the past.

Stalin's main objective was to convince Roosevelt to keep his officers out of Eastern Europe—his war trophy and new political playground. "[T]here is no necessity to carry on flights of American planes from Poltava to the territory of Poland on matters of the American prisoners of war. You may feel assured that the appropriate measures will be properly taken also in respect to crews of American planes having a forced landing," read Stalin's cable. While the Soviets did all they could to preclude or limit American access to their ex-POWs before they reached Odesa, they did not stop US Air Force operations intended to help downed crews.[11]

There have been a number of reasons the Soviets treated Poltava-based air rescue missions differently from those intended to evacuate ex-POWs. First, air rescue missions were limited in number and could be controlled with little expenditure of resources, while the permanent presence of American officers at the numerous POWs concentration points made it more difficult for the Soviets to cover up the real situation in the region from their Western allies. There was also a cultural and political component. The crews of planes that made forced landings had never surrendered to the enemy, and therefore deserved better treatment. They were served food on plates. Ex-POWs had to eat their food from buckets. The members of one US crew testified at Poltava that they had received from Red Army officers "the best treatment that it was possible for people to give."[12]

Unable to help POWs as originally envisioned by Deane at Yalta, the US airmen at Poltava did their best to assist them while conducting air rescue missions. In February 1945 the Poltava base meteorologist, Major Donald Nicholson, and Sergeant Major Wiseheart visited Lviv as members of an air rescue team and found close to one hundred US ex-POWs in local hospitals. The reports they got from the ex-POWs in Lviv left no doubt that there were many more wounded and exhausted American ex-POWs in newly Soviet-occupied areas trying to survive under terrible conditions. Nicholson and Wiseheart could not help all of them but insisted on bringing back three officers, former POWs of Oflag 64, Lieutenants William R. Cory, Peter Gaich, and Hill Murphy. The Soviets refused to give permission, arguing that ex-POWs were supposed to go to Odesa. Wiseheart insisted, and the Soviets gave in. The lieutenants were flown to Poltava on the afternoon of February 21.

The lieutenants told their saviors a disturbing story. One of them had escaped from the forced march to the west, while two others hid in the Szubin camp and never joined the march. They were among the 233 Americans (83 of whom were sick) that the Soviets moved to the town of Rembertów near Warsaw. Those were the early days of the POW crisis, when the Soviets had not yet decided what to do with the Americans. After six days in the camp, they were told that they could proceed eastward on their own, and that Red Army officers would help them get on trucks going in that direction. One hundred twenty-eight sick or wounded Americans stayed in the Rembertów camp. The rest started their journey east without money, food, or knowledge of local languages.

Captain Fitchen, the Poltava intelligence officer, was appointed POW contact officer at the base. He summarized the three officers' reports on their treatment at the hands of the Soviets as follows: "the men were just allowed to wander around, being told that they would be taken care of in the next town." The lieutenants took advantage of Soviet assistance and then did their own hitchhiking to get to Lublin, which they reached on horseback, and Lviv, arriving there on February 15, more than three weeks after the Soviet takeover of Oflag 64. They were taken for questioning by Soviet officers dressed, strangely enough, in Polish uniforms. The interrogation lasted from 3:00 p.m. to 11:00 p.m., with Gaich, who spoke Russian, agreeing to serve as interpreter. It ended only when the officers refused to answer any more questions about their personal background and training.

The Americans were then put up at the Hotel George in Lviv, where they befriended the Moscow Radio reporter Vladimir Beliaev, who was in town as a member of the Soviet commission investigating German atrocities. According to a later report, Beliaev "personally saw to it that the men were treated as white men." (The rest of the POWs, given the conditions they endured, probably were viewed by Fitchen and his informants as "blacks.") Beliaev also "briefed the men...and warned that there were many in the town who were still very pro-German." Whether Beliaev befriended the Americans on his own or did so on behalf of the NKGB, with which, some believed, he was closely associated, was not entirely clear, but the Americans appreciated the help he offered them.[13]

On February 22, the day after the arrival of the three lieutenants brought by Nicholson and Wiseheart, three more former POWs, one captain and two lieutenants, reached Poltava via Moscow and were debriefed by Captain Fitchen. On February 28, another ex-POW arrived from Moscow. On March 6, a Poltava air rescue crew brought eleven more American and two British ex-POWs picked up in eastern Poland and western Ukraine. The plan was to fly them to Teheran, but by then the Soviets were insisting that all ex-POWs go to Odesa and prohibited the Poltava air rescue crews from bringing any more of them to the base. The Soviets took custody of the British and wanted to send the Americans to Odesa. The American commanders refused, asking General Deane for instructions. Deane secured special permission to fly the eleven ex-POWs to Teheran.[14]

▪

The American sergeant Richard J. Beadle and the British private Ronald Gould were among the lucky ex-POWs who managed to reach the safety of

Poltava at the height of the Soviet-American crisis. They were brought to the base on March 17 by an air rescue crew headed by Captain Robert Trimble, the Poltava base's assistant operations officer. Trimble, along with the Russian-speaking Sergeant Major John Matles from the Poltava base, met Beadle and Gould near the Lviv railway station. They were part of a group of five American and British ex-POWs who had left the Lublin collection camp, were caught by the Soviets and then escorted by Red Army soldiers to the city commandant after escaping from one of the Soviet repatriation camps for American and British POWs.[15]

Trimble took the men to the Hotel George, where they ate, bathed, and checked into rooms. The two British officers in Beadle's group of five had papers to be delivered to General Deane from Lieutenant Colonel Wilmeth, who was still holding on in Lublin despite Soviet attempts to send him back to Poltava. Trimble put the two on a train to Moscow, while Master Sergeant Matles took Beadle, Gould, and one more member of the party to the Soviet repatriation camp in Lviv, from where they were supposed to go to Odesa. The Red Army officer in charge of the camp assured Matles that he was ready to take the ex-POWs and had warm quarters, bathing facilities, clothes, and even a barber shop to take care of them before their departure. Matles left the three in the officer's custody, giving them his telephone number at the Hotel George in case they needed assistance.[16]

Three days later Beadle and Gould were back. The Red Army officer with whom Matles left the POWs arranged for them to have showers, but only after a three-hour wait. They were then taken to another building, where they shared a room with ten French soldiers and two civilians. They slept on the wooden floor in a cold room without blankets. Beadle and Gould, who had no overcoats, could not fall asleep because of the freezing cold. Next day they received some additional clothing. However, during the night a group of Red Army soldiers woke them up and took from Beadle his two woolen shirts, giving a Soviet one "in exchange." Next day the Soviets moved sixteen civilians of both sexes (one of the women was ill) to the already overcrowded room. Altogether the room housed twenty-four men and six women. The food they got consisted of soup, tea, and a piece of black bread.[17]

Beadle and Gould had had enough and went to see Captain Trimble at the Hotel George. To their relief, he was still there. Shocked by what he heard, Trimble decided to take the two to Poltava. He and Major Sergeant Matles arranged a room in the Hotel George. Soon afterward, more exhausted and needy ex-POWs showed up. The night before Matles left Lviv, he arranged a room for five more desperate Americans. Next day, just as Matles was ready to get on a truck that would take him to the airfield, seven more American officers and a number of enlisted men, all ex-POWs, showed up at the Hotel George. All Matles could do was buy them some beer and tea and wish them luck on their way to Odesa. In the report that Matles helped Captain Trimble to file on their return to Poltava, he urged the commanding officers to station a US representative in Lviv to help arriving ex-POWs. He found those whom he met in the city "in the most horrible condition; hungry, dirty, lousy, and with no one to receive them, guide them, or take care of them, or to offer them a cup of tea or a piece of bread."[18]

On March 17, the day Captain Trimble returned to Poltava with Beadle and Gould on board his plane, Roosevelt fired off another cable to Stalin. "In your last message to me you state that there was no need to accede to my request that American aircraft be allowed to carry supplies to Poland and evacuate the sick. I have information that I consider positive and reliable that there are a very considerable number of sick and injured Americans in hospitals in Poland and also numbers of liberated US prisoners in good health who are awaiting entrainment in Poland to transit camps in Odessa, or are at large in small groups that have not yet made contact with Soviet authorities."[19]

The last sentence was taken almost verbatim from a cable sent to the president from Moscow by Averell Harriman on March 12. The ambassador informed him that after forty-eight hours of delay, the Soviet authorities had denied General Deane's request to be allowed to travel to Poland personally to investigate the ex-POWs' situation. They wanted Deane to apply for permission to the Soviet-controlled Polish government. Deane found the demand ridiculous, as the Lublin government was completely dependent on Moscow. The Soviet commanders also demanded the termination of Lieutenant Colonel Wilmeth's mission in Lublin and did not allow a plane with medical and other supplies to leave Poltava for Lublin. The claim was made that there were no more American ex-POWs in Poland. "It seems obvious that the Soviets have been attempting to stall us off by misinformation from day to day in order to hold up the sending in of more of our contact officers until they get all of our prisoners out of Poland," wrote Harriman.[20]

The ambassador urged the president to send Stalin another cable, a draft of which he provided. Roosevelt agreed, adding a few words of his own to heighten the emotional impact of his appeal. "Frankly I cannot understand your reluctance to permit American officers and means to assist their own people in this matter," wrote the president. "This government has done everything to meet each of your requests. I now request you to meet mine in this particular matter." He added: "Please call Harriman to explain my desires in detail."[21]

Stalin never called Harriman. Instead, on March 22 he cabled Roosevelt, suggesting that the information he had received was wrong. There were only seventeen sick Americans remaining in Poland; all the rest were on their way to Odesa, and those who were ill would be flown there. Given that situation, Stalin claimed that American officers stationed behind the Soviet lines would only be an impediment to Red Army commanders, who would have to busy themselves with arranging meetings for them and protecting them from German agents. That would divert the commanders from their main tasks, and they, wrote Stalin, "pay with their lives for the state of matters at the front and in the immediate rear." He then went on the offensive, asserting that conditions for American ex-POWs were better than those for Soviet ex-POWs in the American camps, where they were kept together with Germans, "often mistreated and even beaten up."[22]

Harriman, who received a copy of Stalin's cable, was outraged. He wrote to Roosevelt, stating that the suggestion that the American POWs were in good condition was "far from the truth... until arriving in Odesa the hardships undergone have been inexcusable." He added that Polish civilians helped the ex-POWs more than the Red Army officers, a statement echoed by almost every ex-POW who made it to Poltava. Harriman wanted

Roosevelt to tell Stalin all that in a new cable. The president refused. "It does not appear appropriate for me to send another message now to Stalin," he wrote to Harriman, asking him nevertheless to ensure the best possible treatment of Americans through available diplomatic channels.[23]

Meanwhile, the Soviets pushed for the prompt departure of the remaining American representatives from Poland. With the Lublin repatriation camp closed on March 17, the Soviets, as noted, wanted Wilmeth to end his mission there and to leave for Moscow as soon as possible. On March 23, the day after Stalin's response to Roosevelt, Deane ordered Wilmeth to depart. With no plane available to take him to Poltava, the Soviet authorities threatened to put him on a train. He finally left for Poltava by plane on March 28. In Moscow he faced an unhappy Deane, who believed that Wilmeth had unnecessarily alienated the Soviets by refusing to leave Lublin when ordered to do so. Wilmeth disagreed. In his report to Deane he listed twenty-seven cases of friction and unprovoked hostility toward him on the part of the Soviets, making it clear that they had never wanted him in Lublin in the first place.[24]

On March 31, the Soviet command ordered a halt to all flights from Poltava. By that time twenty-seven American and four British former POWs had passed through the base, which had played a more important role in supplying information on their sorry state in Soviet custody than in taking them to safety and medical care in Teheran or the United Kingdom. In his account of Eastern Command, First Lieutenant Kaluta appropriately put the blame for that not on lack of effort by his Poltava comrades but on the Soviets and their attitude toward POWs.[25]

All of the Americans considered that treatment baffling, and even those in the Poltava bases who had been pro-Soviet found their last reservoirs of good will diminishing.

Rupture

O n the afternoon of March 31, 1945, the Poltava Soviet commander
Major General Kovalev called an emergency meeting. Once his
lieutenants were all present, Kovalev shared with them recommendations
he had just received from Moscow. Lieutenant General Korolenko, a deputy
chief of staff of the Red Army Air Force, advised Kovalev that given worsen-
ing Soviet-American relations there was a possibility of armed conflict at
the Poltava base—an eventuality for which Kovalev and his men had to be
prepared. "You see that things aren't working out here with the Americans."

After two battalion commanders at the base reported on the number of
soldiers at their disposal, Kovalev ordered his chief of staff to prepare a plan
of operation in case of armed conflict. According to that plan, in case of
emergency one of the battalions was to encircle and seal off the American
base, while the other took control of the airplanes and bomb depots.
A counterintelligence platoon was to secure the US headquarters and take
possession of the radio station, preventing the Americans from transmit-
ting any information about developments at the base. The attack was to
begin with a horn signal. Americans who happened to be in the city of
Poltava at that point were to be detained there. Preparations for a possible

attack on the American quarters began immediately, as the commanders of the two battalions under Kovalev's command went to reconnoiter the base. Soldiers in the engineer battalion, who normally were not armed, were issued guns. A horn player was assigned to the duty officer to be ready to sound the attack as soon as he received an order.[1]

Kovalev was preparing for the worst. So was his American counterpart Colonel Hampton. Hampton took measures to secure Eastern Command files, and the most sensitive of them were placed in a steel box that was moved to the office of his adjutant, George Fischer. The normally unarmed Fischer began to carry a pistol. He assembled a group of clerks seconded from different departments who would spend long evenings copying the most important documents. That meant retyping more than a thousand pages of correspondence. The documents were supposed to be shipped to Teheran at the first opportunity or destroyed in case of emergency.[2]

There is no indication that Hampton knew about Kovalev's preparations to take over his headquarters, though there was little doubt in his mind that relations with the Soviets were taking a dramatic turn for the worse. They stopped clearing any flights from Poltava. Order no. 011050 from the headquarters of the commander in chief of Soviet military forces to halt Americans flights to and from Poltava came from Stalin himself.[3]

The chain of events that led to the new crisis began on March 8, 1945, when Allen Dulles, the head of the Office of Strategic Services station in Switzerland, met with the commander of SS troops in northern Italy, Obergruppenführer Karl Wolff, to discuss the possible surrender of German troops in Italy. Wolff, who was on a Hitler-approved mission of sowing discord among the Allies, had no mandate to speak on behalf of the German military command, so little came of the meeting. Nevertheless, Dulles's report about it to the Allied military commanders in Italy raised high expectations about a possible German surrender in Italy. The American and British commanders sent representatives to Italy, and Averell Harriman was instructed to inform Molotov about the forthcoming negotiations.

Molotov asked for the inclusion of Soviet representatives at the forthcoming meeting in Switzerland.[4]

Harriman conveyed Molotov's request to Washington. He was personally skeptical, to say the least, as was General Deane. They both suggested that the Soviets would not have invited the Allies to negotiate a German surrender on the Eastern Front, nor would the Western Allies have asked to participate in such negotiations. The Chiefs of Staff in Washington agreed with that reasoning and suggested to the Soviets that they send representatives to Caserta, the Allied headquarters in central Italy, where the actual negotiations would take place, treating the talks planned in Bern, Switzerland, as preliminary. Molotov protested, demanding that the Swiss negotiations be terminated. The "Bern incident" was now an inter-Allied crisis.[5]

Stalin accused Roosevelt and the Western Allies of negotiating a separate peace with the Germans behind his back. He allegedly had information to the effect that the Germans had agreed to open the Western Front to the Allies, who would march into the "heart of Germany" while continuing to fight the Red Army on the Eastern Front. Although he hinted that the information came from military intelligence, his statement had no factual basis. More than anything, it betrayed Stalin's phobias about the Western Allies and the possibility of a German-British-American deal to stop him from moving farther into Europe. Roosevelt responded with a message that opened and closed with sentences containing the word "astonishment." In his cable of March 29 to Roosevelt, Stalin stated that the American position "is irritating the Soviet command and creates ground for mistrust." In his response of March 31, Roosevelt referred to an "atmosphere of regrettable apprehension and mistrust." In another message dispatched the same day, Roosevelt wrote: "I cannot conceal from you the concern with which I view the development of events of mutual interest since our fruitful meeting at Yalta."[6]

The Alliance was clearly in trouble, and no one knew that better than John Deane in Moscow, who was barraged by Soviet protests over the conduct of American airmen on Soviet soil. On March 30, 1945, two days after General Kovalev stopped clearing American flights to and from Poltava, and one day before he called his emergency meeting to plan an attack on the American base, the chief of the Red Army General Staff, General Antonov, forwarded to Deane a letter replete with denunciations of American conduct on Soviet soil. Antonov complained bitterly about three occasions on which American personnel had refused to follow Soviet orders and caused friction in relations.

The first episode concerned Lieutenant Colonel Wilmeth's refusal to leave Lublin as ordered by Soviet commanders on March 11. Wilmeth, who was taking care of American ex-prisoners of war, managed as we have seen to stay in the city until the end of the month. The second involved Captain Donald Bridge, who landed his aircraft at the Soviet air base near Mielec in Poland on March 22. He took off after refueling but without Soviet clearance. The incident led to the suicide of a Soviet captain named Melamedov, who was probably held responsible for the incident by his superiors and SMERSH officers.[7]

General Antonov was especially bitter about the third case, which involved First Lieutenant Myron King, the pilot of a Flying Fortress. King's aircraft was hit by German flak over Berlin in early February 1945, but he managed to land at a Soviet base near Warsaw. The Soviets fixed the plane and cleared it for return to Britain. As the plane stopped for refueling at a Soviet air base near Szczuczyn in northeastern Poland, however, the Soviets discovered that King and his crew were trying to smuggle a Polish citizen in British uniform out of their zone. King listed the man as a "waist gunner" (aircraft side gunner), but the deception was uncovered by a Red Army major, who shouted at King and threatened to shoot him. King tried to bribe his way out, offering the major his wrist watch. The major took the bribe yet still refused to clear the flight. For seven long weeks, King and his crew remained in Soviet custody. They managed to free themselves only on March 18, after the Soviets gave King permission to fly to Kyiv; he headed for Poltava instead.[8]

Colonel Hampton conducted his own investigation into the King incident and informed General Deane of his findings on March 29. Hampton's report arrived the day before Antonov's letter, giving an unexpected spin to the affair. Antonov accused King of having taken on board "a terrorist-saboteur brought into Poland from England." According to Antonov, King had tried to bring back to Britain a spy sent to Poland by the Polish exiles in London who was involved in Home Army activities against the Soviets. "The facts listed are a rude violation of elementary rights of our friendly mutual relations," wrote Antonov. He demanded that Deane not only prevent any more such cases but report to him on actions taken with regard to those who had committed the violations listed in the letter.[9]

That was not all. The next day, March 31, Deane received another protest, this time from his main liaison at the Red Army General Staff, Lieutenant General Slavin. It concerned an incident in Hungary, where the crew of a B-24 bomber had made a forced landing at a Soviet-held airfield. It then flew to Italy with a thirty-seven-year-old Red Army captain named Morris Shanderov on board. A native of Ohio, Shanderov was born into the family of a Russian revolutionary who had immigrated to the United States after the Revolution of 1905. Shanderov returned to the Soviet Union in 1925 and stayed there. In the spring of 1944 he was stationed at the Poltava air base, where he attracted the attention of SMERSH officers because of his contacts with the Americans. On the evening of April 23, 1944, a few weeks after the arrival of the US airmen, Shanderov was detained while trying to make his way to the American base. A few days later he asked his commander for permission to hold a party to which he wanted to invite the Americans. Lieutenant Colonel Sveshnikov, the SMERSH commanding officer at the time, ordered Shanderov out of Poltava.[10]

In March 1945, Shanderov met American pilots again, this time at the airfield in Hungary. He told his life story to Lieutenant Charles Raleigh and informed him that he wanted to go back to his native land, the United States. Raleigh took Shanderov, then working with a crew of Soviet engineers who helped to repair the American plane, on board, ostensibly for a test flight. Raleigh flew to Italy, landing in Bari, where Shanderov requested asylum and was interrogated and detained by the US military command. The American crew's takeoff without clearance from the Soviet airfield, especially with a Red Army officer on board, infuriated the Soviet commanders. Now Slavin was accusing the American crew of violating the trust shown to them by the Soviets as they helped to repair Lieutenant Raleigh's plane. He demanded the return of Shanderov and the punishment of Raleigh and his crew.[11]

Generals Antonov and Slavin peppered General Deane with accusations that the Americans had violated their Soviet allies' trust at the same time as they ordered General Kovalev at Poltava to halt all American flights to and from the base. On March 28 Kovalev issued his own order grounding the American airplanes. Twenty-two American technicians were then at various locations in western Ukraine and eastern Poland, repairing US aircraft. They could not return to the base, and the base commanders could not send them food supplies or spare parts to continue their work. Three repaired planes remained where they were, as there were no available crews to fly them to Poltava. Flights to and from Poland were grounded, as were Poltava-Moscow and Poltava-Teheran flights. Three American nurses from the Poltava base were on leave in Moscow and could not return. A far more disturbing effect of the grounding was that six wounded Americans who badly needed operations in Teheran could not be flown there.[12]

Kovalev's order took the Americans completely by surprise. Since he gave no reason for it other than to say that the order had come from Moscow, the Americans at Poltava were at a loss as to what to think. Soviet counterintelligence agents picked up signs of displeasure in American dealings with their Soviet counterparts. They would refuse to give information the Soviets wanted from them, either claiming that the workday was over or questioning the reason for the inquiry. They complained about transit crews left at Poltava without sufficient food supplies, asked why the Soviets refused to evacuate their wounded, and demanded the return of the nurses from Moscow. The Soviets would not allow the nurses to return even as they continued to bring food-service personnel from Moscow to Poltava.[13]

The US airmen at the base could not understand the sudden change in Soviet behavior. Franklyn Holzman told a SMERSH informer: "It's not clear to me why flights are not being allowed because of personal disputes. Your armies and ours are at the gates of Berlin, and this is no time for disputes, as flights are needed to secure military operations." Sergeant Major

Matles, who had been involved with helping British and American prisoners of war, believed that flights had been grounded because of tensions between the US military mission in Moscow and the Soviet authorities. Sergeant Chavkin told a SMERSH informer that the US mission in Moscow blamed the American commanders at the base.

The base, in turn, blamed Moscow. George Fischer, now promoted to captain, wrote in a report that the Americans at Poltava were unhappy both with the Soviets and with their own commanders in Moscow, who apparently "gave in to the Soviets too much," provoking such behavior on their part. "It is hard to cram a true picture of the feelings that pervaded through the base through that painful frustrating and sad period in the history of this command," wrote Fischer later. "It changed from apathy to despair, from disgust to short hopefulness, from trying to forget the outbursts of angry accusations of the Soviets and higher headquarters, and again and again so."[14]

The "higher headquarters" meanwhile did their best to reduce the intensity of the conflict that had resulted in the grounding of American planes at Poltava. On March 31, the day after General Deane received General Antonov's indignant letter, and the day on which General Slavin wrote to Deane complaining about American pilots smuggling Polish and Soviet officers out of Eastern Europe, General Hill, Deane's deputy in Moscow in charge of the US Air Force, wrote to Colonel Hampton at Poltava. Hill informed Hampton that Soviet-American relations had been severely strained by a series of incidents in which US personnel had failed to comply with Soviet demands and regulations. He instructed Hampton to enjoin his subordinates at Poltava "to preclude the possibilities of friction and arguments, to conduct themselves with dignity and avoid slurs to the end that present strain will be corrected and that there will be no recurrence."[15]

Caught between his cautious superiors and belligerent underlings, Hampton was becoming increasingly irritated and no longer attempting to hide his attitude toward the Soviet regime. Major Zorin was getting considerable information on Hampton's attitude from the Soviet interpreters, who doubled as SMERSH informers. One of them, Lieutenant Sivolobov, who used the code-name "Kozlov," repeated to Zorin on April 1 what

Hampton had allegedly told another Soviet interpreter, Galina Shabelnik: "You have freedom only in words, but in fact there is the dictatorship of the NKVD. Your whole population has been cowed, and you are forbidden to associate with foreigners."

Shabelnik, who informed on the Americans under the code-name "Moskvichka," and a former classmate of Fischer, added more details. Hampton had allegedly told her: "Your people live badly. Our unemployed, about whom your newspapers have written so much, live better than those who are employed in your country." Hampton was also involved in what SMERSH described as anti-Soviet propaganda. He supplied Shabelnik with English-language publications, which included an article by Aleksandr Barmin, a former Soviet diplomat and intelligence officer who had defected to France in 1937 to avoid Stalin's terror and whom Zorin called a "traitor to the motherland."[16]

The secret police were not the only ones to notice Hampton's growing irritation with his Soviet counterparts at Poltava. He made no secret of his hostility in the numerous reports that he submitted to his Air Force commanders and the US military mission in Moscow. George Fischer, wrote in his memoirs about his boss: "We both got the anti-Soviet fever.... Together [Hampton and I] went on a holy crusade. All we could, we pushed our own higher-ups. The U.S. air [force] headquarters in Paris, the U.S. Military Mission in Moscow. We flooded them. Fired off oodles of messages. Sent one coded cable after another. Spelled out the Poltava crisis, the Soviet misdeeds and broken promises. We never stopped urging action. To heed the ally/foe much more. To take a much, much tougher stand. No response came. That didn't matter. It even egged us on. To spread the word, build a crusade."[17]

Meanwhile, the Soviet authorities decided that things had gone too far and it was time to alleviate tensions. Stalin wanted the alliance to survive at least until the end of the war. On April 5 he ordered Molotov to denounce the Soviet-Japanese Neutrality Pact, signed in April 1941. It was a clear signal to the United States that the Soviet Union was honoring its obligations under the Yalta agreements concerning the war with Japan and preparing the diplomatic ground for an alliance with Washington in the Pacific. In a message dated April 7, Stalin assured Roosevelt that he had never questioned his "honesty or dependability." The dictator believed that he had pushed far enough, having obtained from Roosevelt the reassurance he wanted: the Americans were not contemplating a separate peace on the Western Front.[18]

Measures were also taken to calm things down at Poltava. A high-level commission arrived from Moscow in early April to look into General Kovalev's preparations for a possible armed takeover of the headquarters of Eastern Command. On April 2, two days after Kovalev ordered the preparation of a plan for a possible attack on the American headquarters, Major Zorin, whose task was to seize the headquarters in case of a crisis, sent a report to the commanding officer of SMERSH in Moscow. Zorin expressed his concern that Kovalev's plan might lead to open conflict with the Americans. The SMERSH commanders sounded the alarm, and the report was forwarded to Stalin on the same day. His resolution on the report read: "Please calm Comrade Kovalev and forbid him any unauthorized actions." On April 3, Lieutenant General Fedorov, a deputy chief of staff of the Red Army Air Force, and a Lieutenant Colonel Belov, a high-ranking SMERSH official, flew to Poltava to investigate the situation.

The investigation confirmed all the facts presented by Zorin. Kovalev had indeed ordered the preparation of a plan of attack. It seemed that he was simply overzealous, though SMERSH was fully prepared to assume the worst. Could Kovalev be an enemy within, trying to provoke a conflict between the Allies to benefit the Germans? SMERSH dug into its files for all possible information about Kovalev. Zorin soon discovered that in 1938, at the height of Stalin's Great Terror, Kovalev, an ethnic Ukrainian and a native of the Poltava region, had been investigated for possible membership in a Ukrainian nationalist organization. The organization had allegedly worked among cadets of the Red Army officers' school in the eastern Ukrainian city of Kharkiv, where Kovalev worked as an instructor. Two other officers under investigation testified that between 1928 and 1937 Kovalev had been involved in spying on Red Army cadres and installations. He was also accused of indoctrinating cadets in the spirit of Ukrainian nationalism. Kovalev pleaded complete innocence. Luckily for him, the key figure in the investigation, the commander of the school, Onufrii Nahuliak, refused to implicate Kovalev and was eventually shot for his role in the alleged conspiracy. Another officer who testified against Kovalev subsequently withdrew his testimony. Kovalev was left alone.[19]

Another piece of potentially compromising information on Kovalev had been his report on the Valentine's Day party at the American base. The party, which SMERSH officers believed to have denigrated the honor of Red Army officers, took place on February 14, and as we have seen Kovalev filed a report about his participation on March 1. The SMERSH memo about Kovalev's report was produced on March 27, only a few days before his order to prepare plans for an attack on the American base. SMERSH found Kovalev to have been too understanding of the Americans one day and too eager to start a fight with them the next. Apparently, in the minds of Kovalev's superiors, neither of these attitudes constituted a crime, and they canceled each other out. The high commission from Moscow reprimanded Kovalev for overzealousness but left him in command of the base. His political loyalty to the regime was never questioned. Still, Kovalev got the message: open confrontation with the Americans was to be avoided at all costs.

At the US military mission in Moscow, John Deane and his deputy General Hill were also looking for ways to smooth things over at Poltava. They decided to change commanding officers at the base. While the Soviets reprimanded but kept Kovalev, the Americans decided to send Thomas Hampton away in peace, if not with honor.

On April 7, in the midst of the ban on flights to and from Poltava, Hill informed Hampton that he was removing him from Poltava and reassigning him to US Air Force headquarters, now located in Paris. He was about to be dismissed "without prejudice." The same applied to his second in command at the base, Lieutenant Colonel Marvin L. Alexander. On April 10, Hill issued an order reassigning both officers. There was a feeling at the base that Deane was sending Hampton away not just to ease tensions but because he blamed the colonel for the crisis that had led to the grounding of flights. While the letters that Deane received from Generals Antonov and Slavin at the end of March listed no violations of discipline, the halting of flights from Poltava made American commanders there easy targets for the wrath of their superiors. Their removal signaled to the Soviets that the Americans were listening and prepared to clean up their act.[20]

On April 11, the Americans notified General Kovalev about Hampton's imminent departure. However, with flights still grounded, Hampton would stay at the base for a few more days, waiting for a chance to leave the Soviet Union. His duties were taken over immediately by the new American commander, Hampton's former chief operations officer and George Fischer's close friend, Major Kowal. Kowal managed to stay in his new position for less than a day, as Hampton received a new order from Hill on April 12. It turned out that Kowal's appointment was protested by General Slavin, who suggested that Kowal "had shown himself to be unamiable and frequently hostile to Red Air Force officers and was a source of deterioration of relationship." Kowal, who of course spoke Russian fluently, had as we have seen found himself in the middle of many conflicts with the Soviets and was repeatedly listed by SMERSH among the US officers suspected of spying on them. Slavin demanded Kowal's dismissal. Deane and Hill were quick to oblige. Hill reassigned Kowal to the Paris headquarters and cabled Hampton, ordering him to take Kowal along when he departed. Command over the base then passed to Captain Trimble, the Air Force officer who had arrived less than two months earlier and worked with returning American prisoners of war in Lviv.[21]

The American military diplomats in Moscow were doing their best to appease the Soviets and put the crisis behind them. Removing the Poltava base commanders was one element of the plan; going after US officers guilty of transgressions was another. Court-martial procedures were initiated against First Lieutenant Myron King, who had tried to smuggle a Polish citizen to Britain, and Captain Donald Bridge, who had flown the Soviet major Morris Shanderov from Hungary to Italy.

On April 12, when Hill reassigned Kowal and appointed Trimble the new commander, a B-24 made a landing at the Poltava airfield. It was one of the few planes allowed to land at Poltava since the official grounding of flights in late March. The plane was on a top-secret mission to Moscow.

Soviet officers armed with pistols guarded it during the stopover, prevented American personnel from approaching, and made an exception only for the maintenance crew, which helped to refuel the aircraft. Inside the plane, guarded by American military police, was Shanderov, on his way from Italy to Moscow to what seemed certain death. Information about the plane's destination and its passenger was withheld even from Captain Trimble. He learned the truth only after refusing to clear the plane's departure. Trimble then reluctantly gave his approval. The order had been given from above, and there was little that he could do.

On the same day, Trimble welcomed another American plane carrying Generals Deane and Hill, who were flying from Moscow to the United States for a meeting with American commanders there. Hill took Trimble aside and told him to do everything in his power to cooperate with the Soviets, which meant the sacrifice of Shanderov.[22]

In the United States, where Deane and Hill were heading, President Roosevelt began his day on April 12 by talking to Dewey Long, the White House travel officer, with whom he discussed the best route to San Francisco. The founding conference of the United Nations Organization was scheduled to open there later that month. The president was in Warm Spring, Georgia, still recuperating from the impact of the Yalta trip on his health and demeanor. He wanted to attend the conference both to bask in the glory of his greatest foreign-policy achievement and to ensure that everything went smoothly.

Soviet-American relations were at a difficult pass, and the agreements made at Yalta appeared to be in jeopardy. Stalin was doing everything in his power to prevent the formation of a representative government in Poland. The crisis over American prisoners of war and the Bern incident were behind Stalin's decision not to send Molotov to the conference, thereby lowering the level of Soviet representation at the founding conference of the body whose creation had been at the top of Roosevelt's agenda at Yalta. Nonetheless, the Soviets were still coming, which was essential.

At 10:50 a.m., as Roosevelt worked on his papers, his chief of staff, Admiral William Leahy, cabled from Washington to Warm Springs a draft message to Averell Harriman in Moscow. On the previous day Leahy had forwarded to Harriman the text of the president's letter to Stalin that the ambassador was to deliver to the Kremlin. Roosevelt wanted to put an end to the controversy surrounding the Bern incident. His message read: "There must not, in any event, be mutual mistrust, and minor misunderstandings of this character should not arise in the future." Harriman delayed the delivery of the message, suggesting that the word "minor" be dropped with in reference to the Bern incident. That was not what Roosevelt wanted, and Leahy, who could read the president's mind better than anyone else, drafted a response: "I do not wish to delete word 'minor' as it is my desire to consider the Bern misunderstanding a minor incident." The president wanted to avoid anything that would jeopardize Soviet-American cooperation.

At 1:06 p.m. Roosevelt approved the wording of his cable to Harriman. Nine minutes later he told those next to him: "I have a terrific pain in the back of my head." He soon lost consciousness. The president was declared dead at 3:30 p.m. on April 12. It was afternoon in Warm Springs and late evening in Moscow and Poltava.[23]

18

Last Parade

N ews of the death of Franklin Roosevelt reached Spaso House in
Moscow early in the morning of April 13, 1945. It came via a public
broadcast that was picked up by the embassy's duty officer, who immediately called Averell Harriman's residence. It was around 1:00 a.m., but no one
was sleeping—a farewell party for John Melby, a diplomat in the embassy
who had been recalled to the United States and would soon be taking part
in the San Francisco conference for the formation of the United Nations,
was in full swing.[1]

Kathy Harriman, who picked up the phone, listened to the report and re-
layed the news to her father. Both of them approached Melby and informed
him. The rest of the guests were dismissed with no explanation of why the
party was suddenly over. After they left, the Harrimans, Melby, and a number
of other key staffers gathered in the ambassador's office to discuss the situation. They decided to call Molotov immediately and inform him of Roosevelt's
death. Stalin, with long-standing insomnia, used to work into the early hours
of the morning, forcing his subordinates to do the same. Molotov was indeed
in his office when Harriman called him to break the news. Molotov insisted
on coming to Spaso House immediately to offer his condolences.[2]

Stalin seemed equally moved. That was the impression Harriman received when he visited the Kremlin on the evening of April 13, and Stalin told him: "President Roosevelt has died, but his cause must live on." At Harriman's request Stalin decided to reverse his earlier decision and appoint Molotov (instead of the Soviet ambassador to the US, Andrei Gromyko) to head the Soviet delegation to the opening conference of the United Nations Organization. That was what Roosevelt had wanted him to do, and now, on receiving the news of the president's death, Stalin decided to honor his wish. He probably also wanted Molotov to size up Roosevelt's untested replacement, the former vice president and now president Harry Truman.[3]

Getting to Truman quickly was also at the top of Harriman's agenda. In the weeks before Roosevelt's death, Harriman had been planning to fly to Washington to see the president and convince him to take a tougher stand on Stalin and the Soviets. Now he decided to speed up his preparations, go to Washington as soon as possible, and offer Truman his help in shaping the new administration's policy on the Soviet Union. Before leaving, Harriman met with Stalin once again on April 15. He was accompanied by the US Ambassador to China, Patrick J. Hurley, who was on his way from Washington to Chongqing, the capital of Generalissimo Chiang Kai-shek's government.

It was not a friendly meeting. In Hurley's presence, Harriman clashed with Stalin over the recent developments in Soviet-controlled Eastern Europe. The main subject of discussion was the composition of the Polish government, but the most heated disagreement involved the American Air Force. Stalin accused US airmen of siding with the Polish underground against the Red Army. The reference was to First Lieutenant Myron King's attempt to smuggle a Polish underground operative out of Poland. Upset, Harriman told Stalin that by making such an allegation he was questioning the loyalty of General George Marshall himself. Stalin responded that he was questioning the judgment of a junior officer, adding that the Americans lacked discipline. Harriman preferred to speak about an "act of stupid soldiers, brave men perhaps, but somewhat stupid." Hurley was surprised by this intense and undiplomatic turn of the conversation. He did not know how important the US pilots had become in the day-to-day dealings of the American diplomats with the Soviets.

On April 17 Harriman left for Washington, taking with him all the frustration that he and his fellow Americans, including the Poltava officers recently ordered out of the USSR, had built up over the last few months in dealing with the Soviets. He was also intent on conveying to Washington their understanding of Soviet politics and ways of doing business. The briefings Harriman gave Truman and other US government leaders would prove influential in bringing about a change of the American attitude toward the Soviet Union in the new administration.[4]

■

At the US base in Poltava, the news of Roosevelt's death was received on the morning of April 13 via British and German broadcasts. It came as a fresh blow to already low American morale. Flights had been grounded for more than two weeks, leaving the personnel with little to do. The crews of downed airplanes who had been flown to Poltava and stranded there felt abandoned if not forgotten. The continuing presence at the base of Colonel Hampton, Lieutenant Colonel Alexander, and Major Kowal, who had been dismissed from their positions but could not leave because of the grounding, added to the generally depressed atmosphere. Everyone was angry at the Soviets. Some believed that the president would still be alive had Stalin not obliged him to make the dangerous and exhausting trip to Yalta a few months earlier.[5]

Upon receiving the news of the president's death from Moscow, General Kovalev once again gathered his subordinates. He ordered them to form a column and march toward the American quarters in a show of solidarity. Not unlike Molotov the night before, Kovalev surprised his American counterparts with this unexpected demonstration of sympathy. The arrival of the Red Army column shook the Americans out of their apathy, and on the following morning they held a parade of their own. They marched in formation, with the American flag carried at the front of the column by a color guard—the first such display of the flag at the base. Earlier initiatives to display it prominently had been abandoned in order not to alienate the Soviets. Now, with little if anything to lose, the Americans were not shy about showing the colors.[6]

When the American officers gathered that day for a memorial service in honor of the president, they were all dressed in Class A uniforms—the first time Franklyn Holzman had seen his superiors so attired at Poltava. Captain Trimble, the new commanding officer, spoke at the ceremony. "Today the United States has lost a great leader," he declared, "and Eastern Command too has lost a leader." The reference was to Colonel Hampton, who was seated in the front row next to General Kovalev, the head of the Soviet group at the ceremony. Holzman recalled that Trimble mentioned Hampton first and Roosevelt second, eliciting a gasp from the audience. A university graduate, Holzman considered Trimble, who had little schooling, a good but simple man who had to fill the big shoes of a base commander under difficult circumstances, and had trouble rising to the occasion.[7]

On April 15, Trimble visited General Kovalev in his new capacity as commanding officer of the base and told him that he was under instructions to do everything possible to improve relations with the Soviets. Kovalev suggested that relations were being strained because the Americans could not send stranded crew members from downed airplanes on their way from Poltava. A few hours later, he gave permission for them to be flown to Teheran. Problems with clearing flights would continue, but the siege of the Poltava base was effectively over. Kovalev, or, rather, his bosses in Moscow were eager to use the occasion of Roosevelt's death to show their willingness to cooperate with the new leadership, both in Washington and in Poltava. The only question they had for their counterparts at Poltava was: "Who is President Truman?" The Americans themselves were not sure of the answer.[8]

The partial lifting of the flight ban helped raise the morale of the American airmen at Poltava, but few were optimistic about the prospects of cooperation with the Soviets. That attitude was shared by the commanding officers of USSTAF in Paris, who by now saw little reason to keep the Poltava base open. By late March, it was clear that the advance of American troops in the Pacific was making it possible to establish American air bases on captured islands near the Japanese mainland. The need for Soviet air bases, involving political problems and logistical difficulties because of long supply lines, was diminishing. Soviet procrastination with the opening of new bases in the Budapest area clouded the general prospect of using bases in

Eastern Europe, and the rapid advance along the Western Front was making them unnecessary. The Americans could now use newly captured airfields in Western and Central Europe to support their bombing operations.

With plans for Far Eastern and Budapest-area bases effectively canceled by mid-April, USSTAF decided to shut down the Poltava base. The proposal to do so was sent to George Marshall on April 13, the day on which Trimble assumed full command of the base and presided over the memorial service for Roosevelt. Marshall gave his approval on April 19. The Soviets officially lifted the ban on all flights to and from Poltava on April 27. By that time they knew that what they had long wanted had been achieved: the Americans were leaving.[9]

A page in Soviet-American wartime relations was about to be turned, but the bitterness it helped create on the American side would live on. In Washington, Harriman told Truman on April 20 that the Soviets were launching a "barbarian invasion of Europe" and that they mistook American generosity for softness. The president was receptive.

Harriman got a chance to develop his ideas in another meeting with Truman and his advisers on April 23. Among those present in the Oval Office was General Deane. It turned into a brainstorming session to advise the president on the eve of his meeting with Molotov, who was stopping in Washington on Stalin's orders before proceeding to the San Francisco conference. The key question was the formation of the new Polish government. The Soviets had proposed a formula according to which communists would outnumber noncommunists by three to one. Harriman, backed by Deane, insisted that the Soviet position was a violation of the Yalta agreements, in which the Soviets had agreed to form a new government.

Not everyone agreed with Harriman's interpretation of the Yalta agreements. Among the skeptics was Secretary of War Henry L. Stimson. The military believed that the Soviets had actually delivered on all their promises in the military sphere. Stimson suspected that Harriman and Deane's experiences in Moscow had prejudiced them. "They have been suffering personally from Russians' behavior on minor matters for a long time," wrote

Stimson in his diary. He was sympathetic but also concerned that their anti-Soviet argument had won the day. "[T]hey moved for strong words by the President on a strong position."

Stimson read the situation right. Later that day, when Truman met with Molotov, he demanded that the Soviet Union fulfill the Yalta agreements on Poland. "I have never been talked to like that in my life," he protested to the president. "Carry out your agreements, and you won't get talked to like that," retorted Truman. Harriman remembered that he too was taken aback by Truman's treatment of Molotov, as it might allow Molotov to report to Stalin that Roosevelt's policy of cooperation with the Soviets was being abandoned. Nonetheless, his actions at the time show little concern about the president's general position. Harriman believed that the United States had to use whatever leverage was available to influence Soviet behavior in Eastern Europe.

At a private meeting with Truman on May 10, Harriman suggested threatening to curtail Lend-Lease shipments to send Moscow a signal that he meant what he said about Poland and Eastern Europe. The president signed a directive that was interpreted as an order to stop shipments immediately. It was implemented on May 12, provoking Soviet and British protests, as shipments to Britain were affected as well. The directive was immediately recalled, as the Americans still needed the Soviets to fight in the war on Japan, and the Soviets needed fresh supplies of armaments, ammunition, and food.[10]

The change in the White House was looking more and more like a change in the nature of Soviet-American relations. Truman was signaling that he was prepared to risk losing Soviet participation in the United Nations to ensure that they did not create a sphere of influence in Eastern Europe—something his predecessor would never have considered. Harriman played an important role in instigating that change, convincing Truman that concessions were a road to nowhere and that the Soviets needed the Americans more than the Americans needed the Soviets. That belief was also deeply held by the US officers at Poltava, who knew only too well that the Soviets were flying American airplanes and driving Lend-Lease cars and trucks while treating Americans as unwanted guests who had outstayed their welcome.[11]

By early May 1945, the two allies could hardly agree on anything, including Victory in Europe Day. News of the German surrender reached the Americans at Poltava by radio broadcast at 5:00 p.m. on May 7. Celebrations, accompanied by the firing of guns into the air, began immediately but involved only the Americans. The Soviets had received no official announcement from Moscow about the surrender and refused to take part.

The victory celebrated by the Americans had been declared in Reims, France, in the early hours of May 7. General Eisenhower signed the documents stipulating the unconditional surrender of Germany on behalf of the Western Allies. General Alfred Jodl signed on behalf of the German government. The Soviets were represented by General Ivan Susloparov, who put his signature on the document next to those of the representatives of the British and French governments and armed forces. The Germans were surrendering on both the Western and the Eastern fronts, but the Soviets felt that they had been robbed of the victory by their Western partners.

The Soviet government declared the Reims surrender a preliminary one and arranged for another ceremony in the Berlin suburb of Karlshorst on May 8. The key figure on the Soviet side was Marshal Georgii Zhukov and, on the German side, Field Marshal Wilhelm Keitel. On behalf of the Western Allies, the document was signed by two airmen, British Air Chief Marshal Tedder and the American commander of the Strategic Air Forces in Europe, General Spaatz, both involved the Eastern Command's operations at Poltava. The Soviets could now openly celebrate as well.

News of the German surrender in Berlin was received by General Kovalev at Poltava around 2:00 a.m. on May 9. Celebrations began immediately, leading to the joint Soviet-American parade the following day. Sergeant Chavkin wrote an article published in an army newspaper describing "a colorful parade and carnival in which American air corpsmen marched shoulder to shoulder with their Soviet comrades in arms." In fact, they marched in separate columns. The Americans noticed that some of the German prisoners of war working on the reconstruction of Poltava under Soviet guard removed their hats when they saw the American flag. The American reaction was dismissive. "It's too late now to show your respect for the United States," said one of them. It soon turned out that many of the so-called Germans were in fact Poles exiled to the Soviet Union. They hoped for a better future with the Americans and showed no similar respect for the Soviet flag.[12]

On May 9, Victory Day in the Soviet Union and the day of the Soviet-American parade, General Spaatz, fresh from the signing of the German surrender documents at Karlshorst, issued an order to close the Poltava base by transferring most of the equipment and supplies to the Soviets under the Lend-Lease program. Captain Trimble and his subordinates got busy with preparations for departure. Relations between the two sides had improved once again. Soviet-American parties celebrating the victory would continue throughout May, and the Soviets would reserve seats for the Americans at performances by Soviet theater groups. "Though in line of duty, frequent conflict and friction arose," wrote Lieutenant Kaluta, now appointed official historian of Eastern Command, "personal relations were very friendly." He then added: "It was EASCOM's diplomatic mission."[13]

The "diplomatic mission" was that of strengthening the Grand Alliance and improving Soviet-American relations that the planners of *Frantic* had put forward back in early 1944. Many officers and sergeants of Eastern Command left transformed by their experience. The face-to-face encounter with their Soviet allies had made a strong impression on the Americans at the base, though for many of them it was not transformative in the way envisioned by their commanders or welcome to their Soviet hosts. Having come to Ukraine with high expectations and great sympathy toward the Soviets, they were leaving utterly disillusioned and, more often than not, even openly hostile to the regime. Others maintained their initial pro-Soviet views or developed sympathy toward the people.

Captain Fischer, ordered out of Poltava on April 28, was leaving Ukraine, where he had spent almost a year, with a new sense of his American belonging. He flew to Paris, the headquarters of USSTAF to which he had been assigned, via Teheran, Greece, and Italy, arriving in time to celebrate V-E Day there. Fischer imagined that he had been summoned for a high-profile job as liaison with the Soviets, possibly for Eisenhower himself. He was in for a disappointment, as there was no such prestigious appointment in the offing. Colonel Hampton, now out of Poltava himself, was concerned about the well-being of his adjutant and fellow conspirator in their joint anti-Soviet crusade. He simply wanted Fischer out of the USSR before he got into real trouble with the Soviets.

Before Hampton left Poltava, Fischer had given him *My Lives in Russia*, a memoir by his mother, Markusha Fischer, to read. The book, issued in the United States the previous year, candidly described the Fischer family's experiences in the Soviet Union, including during the Great Terror. Markusha documented the Soviet attempts to prevent her and her American children from leaving the promised land of communism. Hampton felt that had the book, numerous copies of which Fischer kept in his footlocker at Poltava, been discovered by the Soviets Fischer would have found himself in hot water, possibly unable to leave the USSR.[14]

For Fischer, his year at Poltava had not shaken his love for what he still called his "motherland"—Russia, or the Soviet Union—his mother's birthplace and the country in which he had grown up. That year had strengthened his disgust with the Stalin regime—an attitude he had first developed after encountering the democratic societies of the West. "Old hate," wrote Fischer in his memoirs. "The Poltava year boosted it. The hate began soon after I left Moscow. It went back to the unthinkable year 37. My shock got renewed now, the memory of it brought up-to-date. That wed me to Uncle Sam. To the new main foe of the motherland, the new leader of the Free World. Near the end of my Poltava stay I caught it."[15]

Even more striking was the evolution of Kaluta, the new official historian of the mission. As noted earlier, Kaluta began his tenure at Poltava with a sense of excitement. He was critical of his more conservative or suspicious countrymen, including Lieutenant Reverditto, Major Kowal, and even Colonel Hampton. But day-to-day encounters with the Soviets transformed his way of looking at things. "I have sharply changed my view of Russia," Kaluta told a SMERSH informer in May 1945. "I imagined that there was complete freedom in Russia, but in fact the NKVD dictatorship holds sway here," he continued. "I do not see your officers feeling free. People cannot say what they think here." In the last weeks of his stay at

Poltava, the usually gregarious Kaluta tried to stay away from his Soviet contacts.[16]

According to SMERSH reports, probably the only US officer at Poltava who had not been disillusioned by the Soviet Union was Chavkin, who arrived later than the others, in August 1944. If one believes SMERSH reports, Chavkin volunteered information about the attitudes of his fellow officers and was even upset when the Soviets took no action on that basis, so that those officers remained in place. He complained that almost everyone around him, including Fischer and Kaluta, was anti-Soviet.[17]

Even so, Chavkin was not trusted by the Soviets. Given his Jewish-Ukrainian origins, knowledge of Russian, and the fact that he was assigned to the intelligence unit at Poltava, he was immediately entered on the SMERSH list of possible spies. His seemingly naïve questions—why, for example, Soviet republics such as Ukraine were not free to leave the Soviet Union—gave SMERSH grounds to suspect him of spreading anti-Soviet propaganda. His desire to meet Soviet officers in order to write a book about the Battle of Stalingrad was regarded as an attempt to spy on the Red Army.[18]

Franklyn Holzman remained oblivious to the SMERSH efforts to keep him and his comrades under surveillance and chase away his girlfriends. He left Poltava rather pessimistic about the future of the Soviet-American alliance, but feeling friendlier than ever toward the Soviets. He was now quite proficient in Russian, enjoyed attending Russian and Ukrainian performances in the local theater, and thoroughly enjoyed listening to Soviet musicians. Unaware that his former girlfriend had been prevented from dating him by the secret police, he struck up a relationship with another woman named Natalia. He had no plans to marry Natalia, who for reasons unknown to Holzman avoided being photographed with him (a clear sign that she did not want to leave any evidence of her liaison with an American), but did later consider marrying a woman of Russian descent in the United States, partly to keep up his conversational Russian. That plan came to nothing, but the Russian that Holzman picked up in Myrhorod made a profound impact on his life and decided his future career.[19]

Some of the Americans left Poltava heartbroken: in Ukraine they had met the love of their lives but were unable to marry. Among those was

Sergeant Mishchenko. The son of Ukrainian émigrés to the United States (his father came from the Russian Empire and his mother from Austria-Hungary), Mishchenko was an airplane mechanic selected for *Frantic* thanks to his knowledge of Russian and Ukrainian. Language skills were in high demands at the bases and Mishchenko helped translate conversations between US officers and Soviets, as well as facilitating contacts of fellow GIs with local girls. His facility in languages naturally and immediately put him under suspicion as a possible spy. SMERSH recruited a Soviet counterpart, one of Mishchenko's fellow mechanics, to keep an eye on him.[20]

SMERSH agents soon uncovered Mishchenko's liaison with Yelena Semizhenova, an attractive young blonde who worked at the local post office. As the Soviets began harassing local women who dated Americans, Semizhenova became a prime target of the secret-police campaign. In the eleven months that they dated, she was arrested by the NKVD five times, told that Mishchenko was a spy, and ordered to report on him. She refused, saying that he was not a spy, and there was nothing to report on. They kept arresting her for failure to cooperate. After the fifth arrest, when they locked her up for two days, Mishchenko, deeply upset, went to the local NKVD headquarters to inquire about her. The duty officer told him that his fiancée, a member of the Young Communist League, was in fact a prostitute, had slept with Germans, and had a venereal disease.

The NKVD refused to release Yelena. When her mother begged them to let her daughter go, they suggested that it was all Mishchenko's fault. "Today our allies, tomorrow our enemies," was the explanation they gave Yelena's mother, who claimed that her daughter was dating a friend, not an enemy of the Soviet Union. Mishchenko turned for help to General Kovalev, who assured him that Yelena had been arrested by mistake. Indeed, she was soon released. She told Mishchenko that before the secret police let her go, they awakened her in the middle of the night for interrogation and told her that her boyfriend had abandoned her. They then told Yelena that the American was not worthy of her and threatened her with ten years' imprisonment if she continued dating him. Finally they made her sign a pledge that she would never tell anyone what had happened to her in custody.[21]

Despite ongoing NKVD harassment, Mishchenko and Yelena decided to marry. Mishchenko's father in America gave his blessing; the US embassy in Moscow did not. When Mishchenko flew to Moscow to petition the embassy for permission to marry, his plea was rejected: it was the policy of the US military mission to discourage such marriages, given the Soviet government's refusal to allow Soviet wives to leave the country with their American husbands. Mishchenko returned to Poltava with the bad news, sending Yelena into a depression. According to SMERSH reports, she was afraid that with Mishchenko gone, the secret police would be free to do with her as they pleased. SMERSH was concerned that Mishchenko might try to smuggle his fiancée out of the country by placing her on a flight to Teheran. He made no such effort. Heartbroken, Mishchenko left the Poltava base in June 1945. Yelena Semizhenova stayed in Poltava, the subject of an ongoing secret-police investigation.[22]

Kaluta, who tried to help Mishchenko in dealing with the Soviets and included the story of his relations with Yelena in his history of Eastern Command, was the only American who managed a successful romance in Poltava. In April 1945, Kaluta married a fellow American, Second Lieutenant Clotilde Govoni, a nurse stationed at the Poltava base. Their wedding took place at the Poltava City Hall in the presence of numerous onlookers. Captain Trimble, the senior officer at the base, took the place of Clotilde's father. Red Air Force officers were happy to bring gifts to the wedding. The newlyweds spent a few weeks of their honeymoon in Egypt, their departure from Poltava delayed by the April ban on flights.[23]

In May 1945, Kaluta returned to participate in the closing of the American base in Poltava. On June 23, Trimble and Kaluta became the last American officers to leave the base. Trimble boarded a Douglas C-47 Skytrain to Moscow, from where he would fly to USSTAF headquarters in Paris. Kaluta took a similar plane to Cairo. Being fully committed to his new role of the official historian of the mission, he took along a precious cargo—the Eastern Command records that would serve as the basis for his history and one of the key sources of this book. The story of the Poltava bases was effectively over. Their history was about to begin.[24]

Part IV

COLD WAR LANDING

Spoils of War

T he departing Americans left behind more than their illusions, broken hearts, and memories at Poltava. The metal mats used to build runways a year earlier remained in place, as did a great deal of equipment and ammunition. It was too expensive to remove all that equipment from Poltava, and the Soviets agreed to take it as part of the Lend-Lease shipments to the USSR. The guests also left food supplies. The Soviets later calculated that altogether two metric tons of wheat flour, one metric ton of jam, and at least a couple of sacks of sugar were distributed among the Soviet officers and soldiers remaining at the base. Red Army personnel had no compunctions about selling the surplus American goods and keeping the profit. Chewing gum, which was popular among adults and children alike, as well as candy bars and cigarettes, promptly appeared on the Poltava market.[1]

General Kovalev and his deputies divided the lion's share of food supplies among themselves. For Kovalev and some of his top lieutenants, these were their last days at the base. Many of them would be posted to occupied Germany. On June 26, 1945, a few days after the last Americans had left Poltava, Kovalev was appointed deputy commander of the Air Force division of the Soviet Military Administration in Germany (SMAG), which was in charge of Soviet-occupied German territory and handled relations with the Western Allies, who controlled the rest of Germany. In a few short years, the Soviet part of the country would become the German Democratic Republic, or East Germany, while the western part would be known as West Germany, its official name being the Federal Republic of Germany. The commanding officer of SMAG, Marshal Zhukov, became Stalin's pro-consul in Soviet-occupied Germany, with his headquarters in the divided Berlin, and Kovalev's new supreme commander.

The troops of the First Belarusian Front under Zhukov's command had played a key role in the Battle of Berlin in late April and early May 1945. More than eighty thousand Soviet soldiers and officers were killed and more than three times as many wounded. It was now their time to take re-venge—victors' justice at its worst. By late June, the murder of civilians, gang rape, and robbery that had been ubiquitous immediately after the Red Army's entrance into Germany slowly diminished. The SMAG command-ers now presided over the much more orderly and systematic plunder of the conquered country. A few months earlier, at Yalta, Stalin had convinced the reluctant Roosevelt and Churchill to allow the Soviets to take up to 10 billion dollars in reparations from the defeated enemy. It was SMAG's task to make sure that industrial equipment, works of art, antique furniture, and valuables of every kind were shipped to the USSR.

Most of the equipment and goods taken in lieu of reparations were shipped to the Soviet Union by rail, but some were transported by air—the responsibility of Kovalev's division. His immediate superior, the com-mander of the SMAG Air Force, Lieutenant General Timofei Kutsevalov, was a long-time acquaintance and subordinate of Zhukov. Both men had cut their teeth as military commanders in 1939 at the Battle of Khalkhin Gol in Mongolia, where they defeated the Japanese and were awarded the order of Hero of the Soviet Union. Zhukov and Kutsevalov needed people who could communicate effectively with the Americans, British, and French. As agreed at Yalta, the occupation of Germany was a joint enter-prise, as was the occupation of its capital, Berlin, and many assets that the Soviets wanted were outside the Soviet zone of occupation—which consisted largely of the agricultural areas of eastern Germany—and in the industrial Ruhr region controlled by the Allies.[2]

Few in the Red Army had more experience of day-to-day cooperation with the Americans than Kovalev and his Poltava colleagues, who were accordingly posted to Germany. By the end of the war the first commander of the Poltava air base, General Aleksandr Perminov, had become commander of the 18th Air Army, which specialized in long-range bombing. He had learned a thing or two about it from the Americans. The chief operations officer of the Poltava air base, Captain Viktor Maksimov, was also sent to Germany. Scores of interpreters were dispatched there as well, including the twenty-two-year-old Second Lieutenant Andrei Sachkov, who would interpret for General Kovalev at four-party meetings with Allied air force commanders. Kovalev's responsibilities at the SMAG Air Force division included negotiations with the Allies, and he would often attend sessions of the Allied Air Directorate along with his superior, General Kutsevalov.[3]

In November 1945, Kovalev played a key role in establishing air corridors to West Berlin, which would assure the survival of the city during the 1948-49 blockade. To use them, the allies were not required to notify the Soviet authorities who controlled the air space around Berlin. Kovalev also negotiated the establishment of Soviet air bases in western Germany. Probably because of his experience at Poltava, he asked the Allies to assign their own technicians to help Soviet personnel at the Western bases. A problem arose with this request. Unlike the Soviets, the Americans and British were not troubled by the presence of foreigners on their turf, while the British lacked sufficient technical personnel to assist the Soviets. The Soviets were therefore allowed to bring in as many technicians as they needed to service their aircraft.[4]

Kovalev's many responsibilities included the coordination of efforts to acquire German technological know-how in areas of interest to the Soviets. The USSR was both cooperating and competing with the Western Allies in Germany, especially when it came to hunting down German experts in rocket science, aviation, tank-building, and other branches of arms production in which German scientists and engineers were often ahead of their Soviet, American, and British counterparts. But Kovalev's tenure in Berlin did not last very long. In August 1946 he was recalled to the Soviet Union and took a teaching position at the Air Force Academy in Moscow, a clear demotion for a general on active duty. Kovalev would be remembered in Berlin for his considerate and humane attitude toward his subordinates.

It was not his relations with staff members that caused his recall. Kovalev left Germany in the middle of a major purge of Red Army commanders initiated by Stalin. Marshal Zhukov himself was recalled a few months before Kovalev, in April 1946, and assigned to a second-rate command in the Ukrainian city of Odesa. The "Marshal of Victory," as Zhukov was known to the Russian public, was accused of enriching himself by robbing German mansions and museums of their most valuable pieces of art and furniture. Kovalev would be investigated for embezzlement of Lend-Lease supplies and food that the Americans had left at the Poltava base. Times were changing. If in March 1945 Kovalev had been reprimanded for belli-cosity toward the American allies, he would now find himself under scru-tiny by the secret police for being too friendly with them and benefiting from that liaison.[5]

The purge began in February 1946, when Stalin delivered a speech in the course of elections to the Soviet parliament, the Supreme Soviet. He took stock of the war that had just ended and reminded the Soviet people of Lenin's words about the inevitability of war as long as capitalism ruled the world—a statement understood by many in the West as a sign that the Soviets were preparing for a new conflict. In fact, he was simply setting the stage for reclaiming powers that he had temporarily relinquished during the war to his civilian and military aides. "They say that victors are never judged; that they are not to be criticized or checked. That is wrong," Stalin told the audience gathered in the Bolshoi Theater in Moscow. "Victors can and must be judged, can and must be criticized and checked. That is useful not only to the cause but also to the victors themselves."[6]

Which victors Stalin had in mind and what kind of judgment he had prepared for them became clear in April 1946, when he approved the arrest of the minister of the aviation industry, Aleksei Shakhurin. Later that month the commander of the Red Army Air Force, Marshal of Aviation Aleksandr Novikov, found himself behind bars. In February 1944 Stalin had ordered him to accommodate American requests for the establishment of US air bases in the USSR. General Deane had characterized Novikov as the "General Arnold of the Red Air Force"—comparing him to Hap Arnold, head of the USAF. Both Shakhurin and Novikov had been in conflict with Stalin's son, Air Force General Vasilii Stalin, who complained to his father about the high death rate of pilots caused by malfunctioning planes. Novikov was accused of deliberately causing the deaths of pilots by putting into service defective airplanes produced by Shakhurin. Both were blamed for the inferior quality of the Soviet aircraft industry as compared with its Western competitors.

There were indeed problems, as Soviet pilots who saw Flying Fortresses at Poltava and compared them with Soviet-built aircraft could attest. Out of more than eighty thousand airplanes lost by the Red Air Force during the war, 47 percent were lost not to enemy fire but to accidents caused by technical defects. Still, Stalin unleashed his secret police on the captains of the airplane industry and Air Force for reasons other than the deficiencies of Soviet aircraft, which he had tolerated during the war, knowing perfectly well that the Soviet air industry was inferior to the American. For years the Soviets had replicated American C-47s under license and B-29s illegally after a few of them made emergency landings in the Far East and fell into Soviet hands in 1944. There was more on Stalin's mind than the desire to punish officials and commanders who had failed to catch up with the Americans. He was after the military brass, which he regarded as having become too powerful during the war and thus presenting a potential threat to his power.[7]

Stalin's main investigator in the "case of the aviators" was Viktor Abakumov, the long-serving head of SMERSH, appointed minister of state security in May 1946. Who could do a better job of prosecuting generals than the former head of army counterintelligence? Abakumov wanted Novikov to testify against Marshal Zhukov, who had already been recalled from Berlin. Novikov had eventually signed the document prepared for him. "They arrested me in the Military Air Force case but interrogated me about another," Novikov recalled later. "I was interrogated day and night and returned to my cell at 6:00 a.m., when prisoners were obliged to rise.... After two or three days of such treatment I fell asleep standing or sitting but was immediately awakened. Deprived of sleep, in a few days I was reduced to such a state that I was ready to give any testimony at all to put an end to the torture."[8]

In a letter addressed to Stalin, Novikov claimed that Zhukov had shown disrespect to the nation's leader. "Stalin is envious of my fame," Zhukov had allegedly told Novikov. "He has not forgotten my capacity to contradict him sharply and argue with him, to which he was unaccustomed." That was not all. "Novikov asserts that this is not merely brazen and mendacious blather but that Zhukov might head a military conspiracy," stated Abakumov's report to Stalin. The dictator was clearly afraid of Zhukov's popularity and the power acquired by the top echelon of the military during the war. It was there that he saw the primary challenge to his leadership. The potential threat had to be eliminated before it could become actual.[9]

In August 1946 Stalin learned that customs officials had impounded seven railcars taking German-made furniture from Germany to the USSR for Zhukov. Vsevolod Merkulov, the minister of state security, and his staff were ordered into action. With Zhukov in Odesa, Abakumov's investigators searched his apartment in Moscow and his country house near the Soviet capital. They found a treasure trove of jewelry, sculptures, paintings, and furniture looted from German private houses, collections and museums. In due course, Abakumov reported to Stalin on the findings at Zhukov's country house: "large and expensive rugs and tapestries taken from Potsdam and other German palaces and homes—44 items in all... large, valuable classical paintings in artistic frames—55 items in all hung in various rooms, with some awaiting removal for storage." The charges were not made up. Zhukov's weakness for "trophies" was an open secret, and he himself would admit later to his transgressions.[10]

The arrests of generals closely associated with Zhukov, including a number of his top aides in the Soviet Military Administration in Germany, uncovered a web of organized theft and corruption that included not only Red Army military commanders but also counterintelligence officials in

Germany. What began as a case against aviators turned into a case against generals, or the so-called "trophy case." In early 1948 the Politburo considered the results of the investigation. The document adopted by the supreme party institution asserted: "Having been provided with every necessity on the part of the state, Comrade Zhukov abused his official position and gave himself over to looting, appropriating and taking out of Germany a large number of diverse valuables for private use. To that end Comrade Zhukov, giving free rein to his unrestrained inclination to greed, exploited his subordinates, who, truckling to him, engaged in obvious criminal activity."[11]

Zhukov, still in Odesa, was sent into more distant exile in the Ural Mountains to command a third-rate military district. He would be joined there by his longtime ally, Kutsevalov. Recalled from Germany in 1947, Kutsevalov had been sent to head a second-rate pilots' school in the provincial town of Taganrog, and then, after becoming a student in a military academy, assigned to the Urals. Like Zhukov, Kutsevalov was never arrested but could have said a great deal about the goods looted from Germany by Zhukov and his fellow generals—many of them were shipped to the Soviet Union by transport planes under Kutsevalov's command.[12]

Zhukov and Kutsevalov were lucky to keep their ranks, medals and, most important, their freedom. Many of their colleagues and subordinates were sent to prison. Among them was a confidant of Zhukov's, General Vladimir Kriukov, who had been the uncrowned king of Königsberg and East Prussia before being recalled in December 1945. The investigators searched Kriukov's three apartments and two country houses, uncovering two Mercedes automobiles, one Audi, 107 kilograms of silver objects of high artistic value, 87 suits, and 312 pairs of shoes. Ten days later they arrested Kriukov's wife, Lidiia Ruslanova, a popular Soviet folk singer and the darling of every Soviet soldier during the war. Kriukov and Ruslanova would spend almost five years in prisons and camps, released only after Stalin's death in 1953.[13]

■

General Kovalev's turn came in October 1947, fourteen months after his recall from Germany. That month Lavrentii Beria, the deputy head of the

Soviet government in charge of the Interior Ministry and the Ministry of State Security, received a letter from Major Pavlo Bondarenko, an Air Force officer who had overseen supplies of gasoline, spare parts, and technical supplies for American airplanes at the Poltava air base. Bondarenko accused his former superior of suspicious contacts with the Americans and misappropriation of goods and food supplies left by the Americans after their departure from Poltava. Kovalev allegedly had two co-conspirators, Lieutenant Colonel Nikolai Shchepankov and Lieutenant Colonel Pavel Demin.[14]

Bondarenko was unlikely to have made things up. A native of the Sumy region in northern Ukraine and a professional military officer, he had fought in the Soviet war against Finland, for which he received his first military decoration, the Order of the Red Star, in 1940. He was awarded the Order of the Red Banner for the defense of Leningrad and the Medal of Military Merit for his role in the campaign to retake western Ukraine and Belarus in 1944. He also distinguished himself at Poltava, while staying in the shadows, never making it into the SMERSH reports, and remaining of little interest to the Americans.

Bondarenko's superiors credited him with providing support for 1,100 flights of transport planes, 900 flights of B-17 bombers, and 138 reconnaissance flights. Between December 1944 and March 1945, he had played an important role in salvaging US airplanes that made forced landings on Soviet-held territory in western Ukraine and eastern Poland. He had made seven trips to help American crews repair damaged aircraft. In short, he was an excellent officer, and on May 31, 1945 Lieutenant Colonel Shchepankov, whom Bondarenko would later accuse of corruption, signed papers recommending Bondarenko for a high government award, the Order of the Great Patriotic War second class.[15]

Bondarenko was deadly serious in his accusations against his former superiors, ranging from corruption to treason. He claimed that Kovalev had taken possession of the two tons of wheat and one ton of jam left at the base by the American airmen. The food supplies had been divided among Kovalev, Shchepankov, and Demin. The three officers had allegedly gained possession of American cars, and Demin had even given a Willys Jeep to a local collective farm. Another car allegedly went to a Poltava regional official. Bondarenko also attached two photographs to his letter, showing Kovalev partying with the Americans. He suggested that in exchange for the gift of a leather suit Kovalev had supplied the Americans with secret Soviet air maps. The implication was clear: now that the Americans were no longer considered allies, those maps could be used to guide American airplanes in operations against the Soviet Union.

With investigations into the "aviators' case" and the "trophy case" involving Zhukov and other generals going full blast, the military counterintelligence directorate of Abakumov's state security ministry ordered an investigation into Bondarenko's allegations. They interrogated Kovalev himself and scores of witnesses, completing their work by the end of December 1947. Abakumov's agents established that Kovalev had indeed had numerous official and private meetings with American officers at the Poltava air base. Bondarenko's claim that Kovalev had caroused with the Americans at drinking parties, however, found little corroboration. The investigators established that Kovalev had helped organize and attended dinners given at the air base in honor of Ambassador Harriman, President Roosevelt's son Elliott, and generals Deane, Walsh, and Hill. With Lieutenant Colonel Shchepankov he had also attended weekend parties at the American officers' club on the Poltava base. The investigators did not regard such receptions and courtesy calls as drinking parties. They were not interested in the amount of alcohol Kovalev consumed.

The investigators were also soft on Kovalev with regard to gifts he had received from the Americans. They were unable to establish that he had received this "leather suit," an allegation that he apparently denied. American items that Kovalev did not deny receiving were presented in exchanges of gifts between the two parties. When visiting the base, Generals Walsh and Deane had presented Kovalev with an automatic hunting rifle, a fountain pen, and boxes of perfume, and in exchange he had sent them gifts of fruit. Kovalev received a silk sleeping bag from General Hill, but that was in return for leather boots he gave the general on one of his visits to Moscow. Kovalev also received cigarette lighters and other trinkets from the Americans. The investigators clearly did not consider them significant.

The investigation established that topographic maps were indeed passed on to the Americans, but that was officially approved, as they needed maps of the routes to Poltava from Teheran and Moscow, as well as areas in western Ukraine where emergency landings were made. The foodstuffs left by the Americans at the Poltava base were, as noted earlier, distributed among the officers and soldiers there, and some were sent to the headquarters of the Kyiv military district. Still, it was established that Kovalev and his aides had received larger shares than anyone else. As for cars, it appeared that Kovalev and Demin had benefited from Red Army requisitions in Germany rather than from American generosity. Kovalev's car was brought to Poltava from Germany on a transport plane, while Shchepankov and Demin got their cars from among those seized from Red Army officers who had driven them to the USSR from Germany without obtaining official clearance.

The matter of prime interest to Abakumov's investigators was whether Kovalev had ever been alone with the Americans. They found that most of Kovalev's conversations with Colonel Hampton had taken place in the presence of Soviet interpreters. His inability to speak English seemed a blessing under the circumstances. More suspicious were meetings between Kovalev and Hampton in the presence of American interpreters, George Fischer and Samuel Chavkin, whom the investigators identified as employees of American intelligence services. Nevertheless, there was no indication that anything untoward had happened at those meetings. By this point Major Bondarenko could not be interviewed, as he had died of unspecified causes in a military hospital on June 27, 1947, a few months before his letter reached Beria's office. It is not clear how he died.

The investigators' report ended on an unpromising note for Kovalev and his assistants at Poltava: "Thus the facts set forth in Guard Major Bondarenko's statement are basically confirmed by the investigation." In reality, the findings supported only some of Bondarenko's assertions. Nonetheless in the charged atmosphere of the aviators' and trophy cases, the investigators preferred to err on the side of the government in their official conclusions. The last thing they wanted was to be accused of a cover-up. They reported their findings to Abakumov's deputy, General Nikolai

Selivanovsky, who decided to pass on the results of the investigation to General Ivan Moskalenko. Like Selivanovsky himself, Moskalenko was a former SMERSH officer now in charge of a department of the military counterintelligence division.[16]

This was good news for Kovalev. Moskalenko was a fellow Ukrainian from the agricultural heartland of the republic; he had also started his career in aviation. More importantly, Moskalenko's daughter, Second Lieutenant Halyna Hrynko-Okolovych, had served at the Poltava air base as one of Kovalev's interpreters. If Moskalenko investigated Kovalev aggressively, he might endanger his own daughter. Kovalev, by then already in semi-exile in Moscow, where he taught at the Air Force Academy, apparently avoided arrest. His name does not appear among those prosecuted in the aviators' or trophy case. He died a free man in 1964 after a successful second career in Soviet missile engineering—a specialization that he probably acquired in Germany while trying to help Soviet scientists gain access to German technological secrets.[17]

Kovalev was lucky to have survived the purge. While Abakumov's investigation focused on his contacts with the Americans, the main concern of the secret police was to uncover possible corruption. In 1947, the year in which General Moskalenko apparently closed Kovalev's case, his Ministry of State Security began to review the SMERSH Poltava files in search of possible spies. As the Cold War set in, rendering all aspects of Soviet-American relations suspect, mere contact with Americans would be considered sufficient grounds to launch an espionage investigation. The files of the Poltava bases were to be further mined for incriminating evidence.

20

Poltava Suspects

For many American veterans of the Poltava bases, postwar Berlin brought a sense of déjà vu. It was induced not so much by the bombed-out streets of the two cities as by familiar faces among their counterparts on the other side of the Soviet-American divide and, more importantly, by familiar thoughts, attitudes, and patterns of behavior. The Soviets were not the only ones who relied on their Poltava air base officers to staff their administration of occupied Germany. The Americans were there as well, placing their own "Poltava experts" in the heart of Europe.

Soviet-American encounters that had begun in Poltava continued in Berlin, a city divided into four occupation zones but dominated by representatives of the two postwar superpowers. Americans and Soviets who had met in Poltava found themselves dealing with one another again, ostensibly as allies but more and more as adversaries. The Americans showed little trust in Soviet intentions. The Soviets, for their part, distrusted both the Americans and their own Poltava veterans, investigating all those who had been in contact with the Americans at Poltava or in Berlin. Even Soviet officers who had spied for SMERSH at Poltava now fell under suspicion. The Cold War, a conflict of spies par excellence, was heating up. In Berlin the wartime allies were slowly but surely turning into rivals.

■

The former commanding officer of the Poltava-based Eastern Command, Major General Robert L. Walsh, who had left Moscow for Washington in November 1944, was back in Europe by the fall of 1946, two years later. Walsh took over the Twelfth Tactical Air Command, stationed in the West German town of Bad Kissingen, and moved to Berlin in April 1947 to become director of intelligence of the European Command under General Lucius D. Clay, the new military governor of Germany. Walsh would remain at that post until his return to the United States in October 1948. As a key advisor to Clay, he played an important role in shaping American policies toward the Soviet Union in the first months of the Cold War.[1]

As Walsh assumed his post in Berlin, US-Soviet relations were going from bad to worse. Earlier in the year President Truman had announced a shift in foreign policy that became known as the Truman Doctrine— Western containment of Soviet geostrategic aspirations. He promised money and military assistance to Turkey and Greece, then under pressure from Moscow and its communist satellites. The United States thus took over a role in the Mediterranean that the rapidly imploding British Empire could no longer sustain. In the same year, in a commencement speech at Harvard, Secretary of State George Marshall announced a program of economic assistance to war-torn Europe that came to be known as the Marshall Plan. In Germany, the United States sought to create a West German state by fusing the American, British, and French zones of occupation. The Soviets opposed that policy.[2]

In Stalin's view, the Marshall Plan meant the consolidation of American economic, political, and military power in Western Europe and an attempt to lure his new East European dependencies away from the USSR. Well aware that he could not compete with the world's largest economy, Stalin had little to offer Eastern Europe besides propaganda and coercion. The Kremlin launched military maneuvers in its occupation zone of Germany, provoking rumors that the Allies would have little choice but to leave Berlin.

The Soviets soon began to interfere with Allied trains bound for Berlin. The writing seemed to be on the wall: sooner or later the Americans and their allies would have to leave their sectors of Berlin, a city completely surrounded by the Soviet zone of occupation.[3]

General Clay first began to notice the changes in Soviet behavior in August 1947, when Marshal Vasilii Sokolovsky, Zhukov's replacement as Supreme Soviet Military Commander in Germany, rejected a proposed American monetary reform that would have affected occupied Germany as a whole and helped it overcome rampaging inflation. Clay did not think that Sokolovsky wanted a military confrontation in Germany but feared that he might be overruled by his superiors. For some time Clay kept his thoughts to himself. In March 1948, however, he spelled out in writing his concerns about a possible military conflict in Berlin. He did so under General Walsh's pressure and with his assistance.[4] "Lucius, if you feel there is a good chance of war, we had better get the word to Washington," said Walsh, a seasoned Soviet hand, to Clay, who had no wartime experience of dealing with the Soviets.

To show that he meant business, Walsh sat down with pen and paper, ready to record Clay's thoughts. "For many months, based on logical analysis, I have felt and held that war was unlikely for at least ten years," read the final version of Clay's memo, cabled to Washington, coincidentally, on Stalin's birthday, March 5, 1948. "Within the last few weeks, I have felt a subtle change in Soviet attitude which I cannot define but which now gives me a feeling that it may come with dramatic suddenness. I cannot support this change in my own thinking with any data or outward evidence in relationships other than to describe it as a feeling of a new tenseness in every Soviet individual with whom we have official relations."[5]

Clay's telegram was forwarded to Secretary of Defense James Forrestal and helped launch an investigation into the possibility of a military confrontation with the Soviets. Most intelligence officials, with the exception of General Walsh, believed that war was unlikely because the Soviets were not ready for a major confrontation. Nonetheless, their political challenge to the Western presence in Berlin was quite apparent. Soon Clay and Walsh got the proof they had lacked in order to make their case about the coming confrontation with the Soviets stronger. On June 24, 1948, in response to the Allies' announcement of their plans to create a West German state, the Soviets imposed a ground blockade of West Berlin, arguing that given that the country was no longer to be jointly occupied but partitioned, Berlin, located in the Soviet sphere of occupation, would have to be placed under sole Soviet control.

Some in Washington agreed with that logic. Not General Walsh, however, who argued along with Clay against abandoning Berlin. On June 26, two days after the start of the blockade, the US government ordered its Air Force to start providing supplies to besieged West Berlin, using the air corridors negotiated back in 1945 with the help of General Kovalev. The logic of the decision was explained in Walsh's telegram on the eve of the blockade: "There is no practicability in maintaining our position in Berlin and it must not be evaluated on that basis.... We are convinced that our remaining in Berlin is essential to our prestige in Germany and in Europe. Whether for good or bad, it has become a symbol of the American intent." Two days after the start of the airlift, which produced the first indications that it might work, President Truman gave it his official blessing.[6]

In October 1948, three months after the airlift started, Walsh was recalled to Washington to become the US Air Force representative to the joint boards of defense for the United States and Canada and the United States and Mexico. The airlift continued, lasting in all for 321 days, with 272,000 flights carried out by American and British cargo planes, mainly C-47 Skytrains and C-54 Skymasters, landing at Tempelhof Airport every 45 seconds. The Soviets retreated in the face of American resolve, superior air power, and sheer economic strength demonstrated by the capacity to supply the besieged city with food, fuel, medicine, clothing and other necessities for almost a year. On May 11, 1949, Moscow announced the end of the blockade, and West Berlin remained under joint American, British, and French control.[7]

General Walsh was not the only US officer with Poltava experience to find himself in Berlin at the start of the Cold War. Another was the former adjutant to the commander of the Poltava air base, Captain George Fischer. He had joined General Clay's staff in the summer of 1945, when Clay was a deputy to General Eisenhower serving as US military governor of Germany. Fischer's immediate superior in Berlin was General Clay's chief of staff, Colonel William Whipple, a graduate of West Point and Princeton and a Rhodes Scholar at Oxford who would end his military career with the rank of brigadier general. Whipple's true passion was civil engineering. His main achievement in Germany was helping Clay to scrap the Morgenthau Plan, once backed by FDR and named for Henry Morgenthau, his Secretary of the Treasury, and which envisioned the deindustrialization of Germany. Rebuilding Germany instead of punishing its civil population was also Fischer's approach, and he received high praise from Colonel Whipple when George's journalist father, Louis Fischer, came to Germany to interview American military commanders there. "When I was about to go, Whipple delivered a speech about you. He said you are a wonderful fellow, full of enthusiasm," wrote Louis to his son after his visit to Berlin.[8]

Fischer's approach readily found allies among Americans as well as among those Germans who had belonged to the left wing of the German Social Democratic Party, many of them former prisoners of Nazi concentration camps, whose basic beliefs were unshaken by imprisonment. Upon their release by the Allies, they resumed their prewar activities and sought to organize German workers in order to oppose both American capitalism and Soviet communism. Fischer helped the Social Democrats in every possible way, such as by arranging to sell cigarettes and other goods he could acquire at the American headquarters on the black market and then turning over the proceeds to them. Eventually he got into trouble with some of his fellow officers, who suspected him of profiteering. Even his mother stopped sending him American-made watches, which he would sell to the Soviets in order to help fund his cause.[9]

In Berlin Fischer reconnected with two old acquaintances from Moscow. They were friends of his younger brother, Victor: Konrad Wolf, known to his friends as "Koni," and Lothar Wloch, the son of a German communist who resided in Moscow. Koni and Lothar had fought on opposite sides in the war, Koni with the Soviet forces and Lothar with the Nazis. In 1943, at the age of seventeen, Koni had enlisted in the Red Army, becoming an officer in the foreign propaganda unit of the political directorate of one of the Soviet armies. After the fighting was over, Koni's close friend, a fellow German interpreter named Vladimir Gall, invited him to join the Culture Department of the Soviet military administration in the city of Halle. Lothar, for his part, returned to his native Germany after his communist father was executed in Stalin's 1937 purge. He became a Luftwaffe pilot, fighting on the Eastern Front against his former communist friends.[10]

As noted, George Fischer's experiences at Poltava helped change his worldview, leading him to abandon the communist beliefs of his youth. Nothing demonstrated that better than his meeting in Berlin with Koni's elder brother, Markus "Mischa" Wolf. "He'd been my close chum in 30s Moscow, my best friend among the Red German exiles," recalled Fischer. They met in 1945 for the first time since George, his brother Victor, and their mother had left the Soviet Union in 1939. Wolf came to Berlin to work for the Free Germany Radio service and write for the *Berliner Zeitung*, a pro-Soviet German newspaper whose first issue appeared in the Soviet zone of Berlin on May 21, 1945. He would become the newspaper's reporter at the Nuremberg trials of Nazi war criminals. George and Mischa met often in Berlin, but their former cordiality was gone. "He and I talked of nothing personal, only high-up politics," remembered Fischer. "For Germany, the birth land we had in common, Mischa urged what he called limited democracy. I disagreed, held out at least for a capitalist democracy."[11]

Wolf later wrote that he and Fischer were "delighted to see each other again, but it was hard to ignore the prickle of distrust that had entered the relationship." Wolf criticized his old friend for his contacts with anti-Soviet and anticommunist "schismatics" in the workers' movement and for the fact that he felt at home among the old social-democratic rebels. Years later, Wolf came to believe that Fischer had ties with American intelligence. In 1949 Mischa Wolf would join the East German diplomatic service, and in 1952 he would become one of the founders of the Stasi foreign intelligence directorate. As noted earlier, he became one of the Cold War's most cunning and successful spymasters, known in the West as the man with no face, as Western intelligence services struggled to find recent photos of him.[12]

Even without Wolf, Fischer's presence in Berlin was noted by the Soviet intelligence services, which left no stone unturned in their search for American spies once the Cold War set in. They knew that after leaving the Poltava air base in early May 1945, Fischer had gone to Cairo. In July of that year they spotted him in Berlin, where a former Soviet interpreter at the Poltava base, Second Lieutenant Andrei Sachkov, had visited him in his apartment in the American sector of the city. According to Soviet agents, after his return from Poltava, Fischer bragged "in a circle of American Trotskyists that he had made friends with a Soviet general while he was in the Soviet Union." Soviet spies failed to establish the identity of this general, who had allegedly spent time in London and then taken Fischer with him to the Yalta Conference.[13]

Red Army military counterintelligence investigated Sachkov in 1953, after his return from Germany to the USSR. Officers at Sachkov's new place of service, the city of Voroshylovhrad (present-day Luhansk) in eastern Ukraine, wanted to check Sachkov's bona fides and were especially interested in his relations with George Fischer. They do not appear to have gotten very far in their investigation, and Sachkov survived the ordeal. An alumnus of a prestigious Institute of Military Interpreters (Voennyi institut inostrannykh iazykov), he eventually landed a job in the Foreign Policy Department of the Central Committee of the Communist Party in Moscow. Sachkov's career rise notwithstanding, Fischer would remain at the top of the Soviet list of American Poltava suspects for years to come.[14]

The hunt for American spies associated with the Poltava bases began with the first signs of cooling relations between the USSR and the Western Allies. The first orders to focus on Americans who had served at Poltava were issued by the leadership of the Soviet Ministry of State Security in February 1947. It was then that former SMERSH officers working at the ministry compiled a list of American officers and Soviet citizens suspected of espionage on behalf of the United States. In addition to George Fischer, it included Albert Jaroff, William Kaluta, Peter Nicolaeff, Philip Tandet, Igor Reverditto, and Alex Bebenin. Prominently featured on the list was Samuel Chavkin.[15]

With Fischer and other American officers now beyond their reach, Soviet counterintelligence turned its attention to Red Army officers who had been in touch with the Americans and thus might have been recruited as spies. The first to be suspected of spying for the West was an acquaintance of Lieutenant Kaluta's named Daniil Babich (a Ukrainian, Danylo Babych), the deputy chief navigator of the Soviet 4th Air Force Army. Kaluta was listed in American records at Poltava as a construction engineer, though SMERSH officers considered that he had scarcely been involved in any engineering work, while his fluency in Russian and Ukrainian, along with his outgoing personality, had allowed him to establish numerous contacts with Russian-speaking Red Army officers and local Ukrainians, making him a prime suspect for espionage activities.

In August 1944, SMERSH had gained access to Kaluta's notebook. There they found the address and office telephone number of Babich, whom Kaluta had first met in Britain. According to SMERSH records, Babich had been there on a "special mission," inspecting and taking possession of American-built airplanes supplied to the USSR under the Lend-Lease agreement. After his return from Britain, military counterintelligence agents noticed a change in Babich's attitude toward the Soviet regime. It appeared to them that he had been unduly impressed by the quality of life in wartime Britain, which he compared unfavorably to what he had seen at home. "Babich has expressed dissatisfaction with service, discipline, and the living conditions and provisioning of the officer staff of the Red Army, casting aspersions on the Soviet people and the officer staff of the Red Army. At the same time Babich is praising the living conditions of the English people and their officer staff in particular, asserting that the English officer is a highly cultured, competent individual."[16]

This information was passed on to the counterintelligence officers of the 4th Air Force Army, an Air Force division stationed in Poland and with which Babich had served in 1944, but caused no particular alarm at the time—the Americans and British were still Soviet allies. The situation had changed quite dramatically by the summer of 1947. In June, those counterintelligence officers wrote to their counterparts in the Kyiv Military District asking for information on Babich's contacts among the Americans.[17]

The Kyiv Military District officers were happy to help. They soon reported to the headquarters of the 4th Air Force Army that according to their records William Kaluta had indeed recorded Babich's address and telephone number in his notebook. Moreover, Kaluta, serving at Poltava, had passed on greetings to Babich, who was then apparently in Moscow. The Kyiv officers supplied a photo of Kaluta with his future wife, Clotilde Govoni, taken at Poltava during Christmas celebrations in 1944. They could not figure out the exact nature of relations between Babich and Kaluta, but Babich's stay in Britain and what he had said about it to his colleagues made him a prime suspect as a spy for the British. We do not know how the investigation turned out. However, it must have caused Babich a great deal of anxiety and did not help his military career. His name is nowhere to be found among the luminaries of the postwar Soviet Air Force despite his outstanding war record.[18]

With the Cold War picking up speed, Soviet military counterintelligence investigated scores of Air Force pilots and technical officers who had served at Poltava. As a rule, such investigations began upon their return to postings in the USSR after having served in Germany. Even those who had been SMERSH informers at Poltava were not above suspicion in the eyes of investigators eager to prove themselves.

One of the suspects was SMERSH's most active agent at Poltava (indeed the first to be recruited into the SMERSH informant network in April 1944 because of his daily transactions with the Americans)—Captain Viktor Maksimov, an officer in the operations department of the Poltava air base. Maksimov was handled personally by the heads of the SMERSH department at Poltava, Lieutenant Colonel Sveshnikov and Major Zorin. After the war Maksimov was transferred to Berlin, where he worked under General Kovalev in the Air Force department of the Soviet Military Administration in Germany (SMAG) and often represented the Soviet side in negotiations with the Western Allies concerning air traffic and air corridors.[19]

Maksimov's subordinates in Germany remembered him as a competent officer, with a good knowledge of English, who was tough on his Russian-speaking American liaisons, whose emigrant families had a Russian background. He also had important connections, including an elder brother, who was thought to be an Air Force attaché in the Soviet embassy in Washington and who held the rank of colonel. None of that seemed to matter to the Army Counterintelligence Department in the city of Kazan, where Maksimov was posted after his return from Germany in January 1953. They were especially interested in his contacts with Fischer, Mishchenko, and Alexander Bebenin. The latter, a captain in the US Air Force and a Poltava veteran, had taken part in the same negotiations in Berlin as General Kovalev and then Major Maksimov.[20]

Maksimov tried to prove his innocence as best he could, pointing out that he had worked for SMERSH throughout his service at Poltava. His main task, he told the investigators, was collecting information on Americans with whom he came in contact. The Poltava SMERSH opened special files on all of Maksimov's contacts, which included their profiles. They were updated monthly, and Maksimov claimed to have taken an active part in preparing and updating the profiles. That assertion, checked against the existing Poltava files, appears to have cleared him of suspicion. He retired from the Soviet Army in 1963 with the rank of lieutenant colonel after twenty-five years of service. His postmilitary career was dedicated to teaching the basics of civil defense, an important subject during the Cold War. For almost twenty years he taught civil defense to students of the Kazan Institute of Architecture and Construction before taking full retirement in 1993 at the age of seventy-two.[21]

Military counterintelligence combed the SMERSH Poltava files mainly for evidence of espionage by male officers and civilian personnel employed at or visiting the American bases. Women, however, were not excluded from the hunt for spies. In October 1948, counterintelligence officers of the 12th Air Force Army requested information on Lidia Romashevskaia, who worked as a waitress at the Red Army canteen on the Poltava air base and was suspected of ties with American intelligence because of her contacts with US airmen in 1944–1945.[22]

Wives of Red Army Air Force officers also came under suspicion. Counterintelligence officers dug up whatever they could from the SMERSH files on a former nurse at the Poltava base, Maria Solodovnik, a young woman who was married to a senior officer at the base, Lieutenant Colonel

Arsenii Bondarenko, and allegedly showed undue interest in the official documents and affairs of his fellow officers. By 1950 Bondarenko, who served with the Soviet Air Force in the Arkhangelsk military district, was under investigation.

At the same time, military counterintelligence began to look into allegations that Natalia Lavlinskaia, who had been only fifteen years old in 1944, was allegedly detained by the Poltava SMERSH for dating an American serviceman. The counterintelligence officers were particularly interested in Lavlinskaia because after the war she married a star pilot and Hero of the Soviet Union, Major Yefim Parakhin. The investigation turned up nothing but probably did not help Parakhin's career. He retired in 1957 without having been promoted from major and settled in Poltava, where he died in 1997.[23]

Maksimov, First Lieutenant Sachkov, and scores of other officers investigated because of their own or their wives' contacts with Americans at the Poltava-area bases were all exonerated of espionage by secret-police investigations. Still, there is no doubt that their service at Poltava, which brought them face to face with their American counterparts and seemed so promising for their further military careers, turned from an advantage into an impediment as the Cold War began. As many of them were deployed to Berlin in the summer of 1945, their skills were in demand in the new world that the United States and the Soviet Union were supposedly committed to building as allies. As hopes of cooperation dwindled, so did expectations that the diplomatic skills acquired by Soviet officers and interpreters with such effort at Poltava would serve them and their country well in the future. Instead of trusted commanders and experts, the Poltava men became suspects—and remained so for years to come.

The same was true for local Ukrainians who came into contact with Americans in and around the Poltava-area bases. The most difficult fate was the one awaiting women who had dated Americans. The secret police continued to be interested in the love affairs of Stalin's subjects, nominally entitled to be treated as citizens, long, long after the American pilots had left the bases.

Witch Hunt

For anyone who read Soviet newspapers or listened to Soviet radio in the late 1940s and early 1950s, there was little doubt that the Americans had become the main adversaries in the Kremlin's undeclared war on the West.

Behind the scenes, impervious to media investigation, Stalin and the Central Committee demanded that the Ministry of State Security (MGB), the postwar incarnation of the People's Commissariat of State Security, intensify its unmasking of Western, especially American, spies. The latter task fell to the Second Division of the Second Department of the ministry, charged with counterintelligence work against the Americans. The department had a difficult task: few Soviet citizens had ever encountered any Americans (as opposed, for example, to Germans) and could be plausibly accused of working on their behalf. In the republic of Lithuania, newly annexed to the Soviet Union, officers of the Second Department of the Ministry of State Security managed, in the first ten months of 1950, to arrest fifteen alleged agents of German (Nazi) intelligence and counterintelligence, seven British agents, yet only one accused of working for the Americans.[1]

In the atmosphere of rising hostility to the United States and the attendant espionage mania, anything related to the American air bases at Poltava became prime terrain for Soviet counterintelligence, whose Ukrainian agents were in a privileged position compared to their Lithuanian counterparts. All three US air bases had been located within Poltava administrative region (*oblast'*) and thus were under the jurisdiction of the Poltava regional MGB headquarters and its American counterintelligence section.

In their search for American spies and their agents, the Poltava officers paid special attention to the local women who had dated US officers suspected of espionage. At the very top of the list of suspects was Lieutenant, later Captain, George Fischer. Number 7 on the same list was his friend, the flamboyant Russian-speaking Lieutenant Igor Reverditto, who as we have seen had been sent packing to Britain in September 1944 for a quarrel in a restaurant and verbal insults against Red Army officers and the Soviet regime in general. The list of US officers suspected of intelligence work, first compiled by the MGB in February 1947, listed not only Fischer and Reverditto but also the woman they had allegedly befriended in Poltava.

An attractive Poltava blond, Zinaida Belukha, who met both Fischer and Reverditto, became the prime target of a lengthy secret-police investigation. Belukha came from the Soviet elite. Born in 1922, she grew up in the family of a senior police officer who oversaw the Poltava regional penitentiary system. He was arrested and shot at the height of the Great Terror, his sentencing and execution taking place on the same day, October 17, 1938. Andrii Belukha left two daughters, Zinaida and Olena. Neither felt much loyalty toward the regime that had killed their father and had no qualms about dating first Germans and then Americans.

The MGB files contained the details of the first meeting between Reverditto and Belukha. Zinaida was bathing at the local beach when Igor approached her with a friend and asked whether they could take a picture of her. She agreed, and Reverditto's friend photographed the two of them. That evening Igor and Zinaida, who came with her friend Hanna Manko, met in the local theater. They agreed to meet again on the evening of

Saturday, July 15, 1944. Soviet attacks on local women dating Americans were then at their height, and the date did not go as planned.[2]

Igor came with his friend, US Air Force Lieutenant Aleksandr Bibenin, another Russian émigré to the United States, and Zinaida brought along a friend named Lida. No sooner had they met in a local park than a drunken Soviet approached the group and kicked Lida. Bibenin reacted immediately by punching the attacker in the face, drawing blood. A Red Army military patrol summoned to the scene told Reverditto and his friends that after sunset all Americans had to be in their camp. Reverditto later admitted to Zinaida that American relations with the Soviets were anything but good. Fights were taking place, mostly because of girls. Some Americans were being mugged. They would be asked for a cigarette and then threatened with a gun and robbed of flashlights and other valuables.[3]

The Soviet secret police opened an investigation of Belukha in November 1944, a few months after Reverditto's departure from Ukraine. An agent code-named "Lily" reported that during the German occupation of Poltava, Belukha had dated German officers. That seemed to be of secondary importance, as the investigation had been opened on the suspicion that she was an American spy. More important was "Lily's" assertion that Belukha not only had dated Reverditto in July and August 1944 but also had been introduced to Fischer, who had proposed an evening meeting. Belukha had never mentioned to "Lily" whether the meeting actually took place.[4]

At the time, the Poltava Pinkertons showed little interest in Belukha and her encounters with the Americans. Years passed without their paying attention to the matter. By 1950, however, with the renewed interest in Fischer and Reverditto, Belukha was again under suspicion. So was Hanna Manko, whom Belukha had brought with her on her first date with Reverditto at the Poltava drama theater in July 1944.[5]

■

Manko was born in 1924 into the family of a committed communist. Her father, Terentii Manko, was a poster child of the revolution—a former peasant boy whom the Communist Party appointed rector of the Poltava Institute of Agricultural Construction even before he had a chance to graduate from that institution. But what the party could give, it could also easily take away, and that is indeed what happened to Terentii Manko in the summer of 1938. "I was awakened by pounding on the door," remembered Hanna, recounting the fateful day of June 22, when she was fourteen. "My father went to open the door; two uniformed men came into the room with him and our neighbor, who was summoned as a witness. A search began. They ransacked everything in the home, digging into books and my father's papers. My mother and grandmother wept bitterly, and my father, looking as if he had been taken down from the cross, stood and protected them. It was already light outside when they took my father out of the house and led him away."

In September 1938 they also arrested Hanna's mother. A month later, Terentii Manko was sentenced to death for anti-Soviet activities. "Terrible black days followed," recalled Hanna. "I graduated from the seven-year school in a state of fear. I decided to enroll in a medical college... which I completed in 1941. It was hard, very hard: I was regarded as the daughter of an 'enemy of the people.'" Hanna's graduation took place in the month that Hitler's armies invaded Stalin's Soviet Union—a year before he expected the attack. After all that Hanna had endured, she felt no attachment to the retreating Soviet forces. The agent code named "Dmitrieva" believed that Manko welcomed the arrival of the Germans. Later reports suggested that she dated German officers who visited her apartment. She was also friendly with Zinaida Belukha, also a daughter of a persecuted Soviet official who did not mind dating German officers, and later introduced her to Reverditto.[6]

The Poltava MGB officers first heard about Manko's acquaintance with Reverditto in January 1951. Agent "Bocharova," who was being investigated by the MGB for links with the Nazi police and thus eager to prove her usefulness to the MGB, reported that Hanna had confided to her that on one occasion in the summer of 1944, when she was walking with her friend Zinaida Belukha, they were approached by Americans and "spent a couple of hours in conversation." Later Bocharova saw Manko together with Belukha and Reverditto at the theater performance. Bocharova witnessed Manko approaching Belukha and then chatting with her and Reverditto.[7]

The MGB officers, eager to make a case against Igor Reverditto, were interested in recruiting Manko as an agent, but some aspects of her behavior seemed suspicious. Could she have been recruited by the Americans to spy on her Soviet motherland? An MGB informer code-named "Tishchenko" who had studied in medical school with Hanna before the war and now worked with her in the city's epidemiological department told the MGB that Manko had lived well under the Germans and after the war as well. "Manko still dresses stylishly now. As soon as a new fashion appears, she has everything," reported Tishchenko. The sources of Manko's perceived wealth remained a mystery. "She has no father, only her mother, and works at an unenviable job; I know that it's impossible to dress like that on a medical assistant's salary," continued Tishchenko. In postwar Ukraine, it was indeed considered nothing short of a luxury to have more than one dress. MGB officers ordered their agent to continue observing Manko and her behavior.[8]

The MGB grew more suspicious as it learned that Manko had a boyfriend, Mykhailo, who was currently serving in the Soviet Army. One of the MGB female agents, "Kuznetsova," asked Manko whether she was interested in marrying Mykhailo, but Hanna told her that there were many reasons why they could not marry. This raised new questions for the MGB, which were partially answered by agent "Bocharova." In March 1951 she reported on a discussion with Manko about her fiancé. It turned out that Manko wanted to marry him but was afraid that he would turn her down once he learned that her father had been arrested and executed by the MGB.

She had reason to fear this. Right after the war she had fallen in love with a Soviet Army officer named Pavel. They were about to be married when Pavel asked about Hanna's father. Once he learned that her father had been arrested and had never come back, and that her mother had also been imprisoned for half a year, he told Manko that as a counterintelligence officer he could not marry someone who had lived under the German occupation and whose father was in prison (Hanna did not know at the time that her father had been executed). She told "Bocharova" that recalling what had happened between her and Pavel often made her cry. She hoped it would be different with Mykhailo, who was an officer in the medical service and not, like Pavel, in counterintelligence.[9]

With the fiancé puzzle cracked, the MGB was ready to move ahead with recruiting Manko as a new informer. In the report asking permission to approach her, the MGB case officer stated as a fact that she and Belukha had dated Fisher and Reverditto. He pointed out Manko's contacts with other women who had dated Americans were an asset. "She is politically aware, cultured, well-developed, good at making new acquaintances quickly, and well informed about the international situation," read the MGB report. The plan was to summon Manko to the police station and interrogate her about her ties with the Americans. "If she frankly relates what she knows, she will be given a proposal to work with the organs of the MGB and an appropriate document to sign," continued the report. The request was approved on September 7, 1951.[10]

We do not know whether Hanna Manko agreed to answer the MGB officers' questions and convinced them of her sincerity, or, if so, whether she proposed that she work for the MGB. What we do know is that Manko worked her entire life at the same job in the same hospital where she had worked during the war. After the fall of the Soviet Union in 1991, when local journalists investigating Stalinist purges turned to her in search of material on her father, Hanna told them of his arrest and her life as the daughter of an "enemy of the people," a political and social outcast in postwar Soviet society. She also showed the journalists her father's senior thesis, which he had been scheduled to defend on the day of his arrest. "Now I keep that file of his calculations and computations as my sacred and dearest relic."[11]

Whether or not the MGB officers succeeded in recruiting Manko, they managed to recruit Zinaida Belukha. They employed all agents who had access to her to collect information about her activities and attitudes, but that seemed insufficient. Eventually they recruited Belukha's husband, Boris, who was forced to report on his wife under the code-name "Fedotov." The information gathered by the MGB in the early 1950s suggested that despite Belukha's extensive record of dating Germans and Americans, she was not working for US intelligence. They could go ahead with her recruitment.

In September 1952, after lengthy interrogation, Belukha agreed to work for the MGB. She admitted having dated German and Hungarian officers and soldiers during the war. "I must admit that during the German presence in the city of Poltava I did not conduct myself with the dignity befitting a Soviet citizen: in particular, I spent time with German officers, and parties repeatedly took place in our home with drinking, music and dancing. I was at the theater several times. . . . I was acquainted with a pilot named Hans who held the rank of noncommissioned officer, an officer named Richard who worked in food supply, a soldier named Hans, and Hungarian pilots." Zinaida also admitted having dated Igor Reverditto in July and August 1944. The newly recruited MGB agent was given the code-name "Taiga."[12]

Who was exploiting whom in that game of recruitment is not entirely clear, as Belukha turned out not to be the kind of agent the MGB had been hoping for. She volunteered little useful information, and in 1955, less than three years after recruitment, she was removed from the agent roster of the MGB, which by then was renamed the KGB. But in November 1958 her name popped up again in the KGB files. The reason was quite simple: George Fischer was visiting the Soviet Union and seemed likely to come to Poltava. The Poltava residents who had met him in 1944 and 1945 were regarded by the KGB as possible assets in spying on the American visitor. The local KGB officers were ready to contact her when a memo came from Moscow informing them that Fischer was not after all going to visit Poltava.[13]

Belukha again ceased to be an object of KGB surveillance, though, ironically, the United States never fully disappeared from her own horizon. She refused to give up on the hope of finding Igor Reverditto in faraway America and making contact with him. In the fall of 1959 she asked an acquaintance named Yevgenii Chuchko, a former prisoner of German concentration camps who had spent some time in Europe after the war and had relatives in the United States, to ask them to look for Reverditto. Chuchko duly wrote to his uncle Petro, who lived in Passaic, New Jersey. Belukha knew only that Reverditto was living in California, information that turned out to be insufficient. In late December 1959, Chuchko received a letter from New Jersey informing him that attempts to find Reverditto in California had failed. The uncle suggested that Reverditto might have changed his surname.[14]

The Poltava KGB renewed its interest in Belukha in May 1964: Fischer now code-named "Mustang" by the KGB, was about to revisit the Soviet Union. They expected him to visit Poltava, and the KGB looked into the possibility of using Belukha to contact him. KGB officers met with "Taiga" in late May 1964 to review—yet again—her wartime contacts with Reverditto and Fischer. With regard to Fischer, Belukha told the officers that she had met him just once—when Reverditto introduced him to her. She had more to say about Reverditto, claiming that she had dated him for two and a half months and that their "association" had been "of a purely intimate character." Reverditto had told Zinaida that he was from California. They had not been in touch since he left Poltava in September 1944.

Belukha admitted that she had tried to find Reverditto through her acquaintance Chuchko. The KGB officers suggested that Belukha ask Chuchko once again to look for Reverditto through his relatives in the United States. Belukha did as ordered. The KGB files are silent on the outcome of that attempt. Most likely, Chuchko's relatives proved to be of little help. Belukha was never able to get in touch with her wartime boyfriend.[15]

The Poltava KGB was clearly disappointed. Still, their belief that Reverditto was an American spy was far-fetched at best. So were Zinaida Belukha's hopes for a future with Igor. From Poltava he had been sent back to England, where he joined the 13th Combat Wing of the Eighth Air Force. Before the war ended, Igor married Pauline Nan Millard, a sergeant at the Royal Air Force Academy in England. In 1946, with their son, they took a steamship to San Francisco. They had settled in Anaheim, in 1955, the year that Disneyland opened its gates there.

Three more sons were born to them in subsequent years. Reverditto worked as the manager of Boys Market, playing cards at night to earn extra money. In 1987 he and his son Tony, a theater director and later a food critic, founded the "Way off Broadway" playhouse in Santa Ana, California. The family tradition of devotion to theater and arts that had begun in the Russian Empire before 1917 survived in California. Reverditto lived a long life. He divorced his first wife after twenty-nine years of marriage and married again. He died in February 2015 in Fullerton, California, at the age of ninety-five.[16]

We do not know what became of Zinaida Belukha. In 1968 someone denounced her to the KGB for her wartime liaisons with Germans. She had given birth to her child in a German hospital, claimed the author of the denunciation, who was upset that at the time of writing Belukha was employed by the Poltava regional prosecutor's office. The KGB investigated but apparently did nothing. They never gave up hope that she would help to lead them if not to Reverditto, then to George Fischer, who for his entire life remained at the very top of the KGB list of suspected American spies at Poltava.[17]

Washington Reunion

One man's trash is another man's treasure, goes a proverb equally cherished by archeologists and spies. FBI agents going through the trash bins of the Soviet embassy in Washington in early January 1955 found many things that might well qualify as treasures by intelligence standards. With the start of the New Year, Soviet diplomats were discarding their old loose-leaf calendars. Either shredders were unknown to them at the time or the calendars were considered insignificant. In any case some of their leaves ended up in the trash.

One, dated August 7, 1954, had a name and address written on it that caught the attention of the FBI agents. "Professor and Mrs. George Fischer, Brandeis University, Waltham 54, Massachusetts." The Washington FBI field office informed headquarters about their find. The news was passed on to Boston, where local agents visited Brandeis, a nonsectarian institution founded in 1948 by the Jewish community in the Boston suburb of Waltham. A woman from the university's admissions office informed the FBI agents that there was indeed a Professor George Fischer on the faculty. He was thirty-one years old, born on May 5, 1923, and married to Katherine

Hoag. The family resided not in Waltham but at 39 Walker Street in the nearby city of Cambridge.

Fischer's identity was now established, yet the question of why his name had been written on a Soviet embassy calendar leaf remained unanswered. Was he a spy? Or was there an innocent explanation? The FBI agents were determined to uncover the truth. Times were uncertain. The French, defeated in Vietnam, were leaving Indochina, the Chinese communists were intent on taking over Taiwan, and Senator Joseph McCarthy of Wisconsin was claiming that communists had infiltrated the US nuclear industry, and even the CIA. It was not only Soviet counterintelligence officers who were falling prey to Cold War paranoia; Americans were also susceptible. Anyone who had been involved with the wartime allies turned enemies became subject to suspicion on both sides of the Iron Curtain.[1]

As noted, George Fischer's name was at the very top of the Soviet list of Americans suspected of espionage activity and remained there from early 1947 all the way into the mid-1950s. Anyone who had had even a chance encounter with him became prime suspects in their own right and subjected to intense MGB investigation, as in the case of Zinaida Belukha.[2]

None of that was known to the FBI agents who looked into Fischer's contacts with the Soviet embassy in the first months of 1955. Had they known what Soviet counterintelligence thought about Fischer, they would have been very surprised. Nothing they discovered about him supported the SMERSH and MGB theories. On the contrary, he seemed to be a perfect candidate for recruitment as a Soviet spy. Had the Soviets succeeded in turning him against the country he had served with honor during World War II? Perhaps he found the wartime alliance more compelling than the postwar enmity.

■

The investigators began by checking their old files and requesting Fischer's service record from the US Air Force archives in Denver and found that he had been stationed overseas until April 29, 1946, holding the rank of captain at the time of his discharge. Further investigation showed that soon thereafter Fischer returned to the University of Wisconsin, which he had left in 1942 to join the US Army. On May 31, 1946 he had already resumed his studies at the university, from which he graduated in September 1947. With his bachelor's degree in hand, Fischer went to Harvard to study for a master's degree in Slavic Languages and Literatures. He graduated from the program in 1949 after taking a summer course in Prague in 1948, the last year before the complete communist takeover of the country.

In 1951 Professor Clyde Kluckhohn, the director of the newly opened Russian Research Center at Harvard, invited the young graduate to work on the Center's joint initiative with the US Air Force, a project on the Soviet political and social systems. The research was based on interviews with former Soviet citizens, largely post–World War II refugees. These had to be conducted in Displaced Persons' camps in Germany and required participants like Fischer to travel there. It also required security clearance. The Office of Special Investigations (OSI), the counterintelligence branch of the US Air Force, which was directed to provide the necessary clearance, had reservations about Fischer. It turned out that he had been brought up by Hede Massing, the wife of the known German communist Paul Massing, while his father was Louis Fischer, a "member and an affiliate of numerous communist front organizations" and the subject of an espionage investigation completed in 1943. George Fischer himself "was reported to have evidenced strong Communist beliefs," read the OSI report. The reference was to views that Fischer had allegedly expressed in 1942, when he had tried to join US Navy intelligence.[3]

Not sure of what to make of their findings, the OSI asked the FBI to investigate. The FBI officers, in particular Special Agent Thomas F. Sullivan of the Boston FBI, smelled blood. In New York they found and interviewed Fischer's one-time guardian, Hede Massing. Massing had actually previously cooperated with the FBI. In 1949, at the second trial of the alleged Soviet spy Alger Hiss, she testified against him, recalling an episode in the mid-1930s when, as a recruiter for the Soviet intelligence, she had argued with Hiss, who then worked, she said, for Soviet military intelligence, about the branch of the Soviet spy network to which Noel Field, a US State Department employee, should report. Massing claimed to have ceased working for the Soviets in the late 1930s. Asked by the FBI agents about

Fischer, Massing recalled that when she was in Moscow between October 1937 and June 1938, "George Fischer was very pro-Soviet and vigorously defended the purge that was then in progress." She told the agents that Fischer had changed his pro-Soviet views in 1938 "but had never been very outspoken in his criticism of the Soviet regime because of the many friends and acquaintances of his who still live in Russia."

The FBI wondered whether Fischer had indeed abandoned his communist views or was simply hiding them so as not to betray clandestine work for the Soviets. FBI informers who had once been members of the Communist Party at the University of Wisconsin testified that he was actually anticommunist in his beliefs. His acquaintances at Harvard said the same. Dr. Demitri Shimkin, the associate director of the Russian Center at Harvard, believed that Fischer was a "left-of-center liberal." Shimkin's boss at the Center, Professor Kluckhohn, the one who had invited Fischer to join the Center's refugee project, stated that in his opinion Fischer constituted no security risk. Kluckhohn pointed out that two high-profile American diplomats, Averell Harriman and Chip Bohlen, knew Fischer and had a high opinion of him. According to FBI files, Fischer was also trusted by another key figure at the US embassy in Moscow during the war, George Kennan, who had taken a post at Princeton. Kennan had invited Fischer to serve as director of the Free Russia Fund, whose goal was to help involve émigré Soviet intellectuals in launching Soviet studies in the United States.[4]

Finding no evidence that Fischer had pro-Soviet sympathies, Special Agent Sullivan of the Boston FBI decided to close the investigation in April 1952. He stated in his memo that the investigation had "established no evidence of Communist party affiliation or sympathy on the part of the subject." Cleared for participation in the Harvard interview project, Fischer traveled to Europe. He played a significant role in carrying out the interviews with refugees on the Soviet political and social systems. That same year Fischer published his doctoral dissertation on the history of resistance to the Stalin regime as a monograph. His subject was General Andrei Vlasov's Russian Volunteer Army, a fighting unit created by the Germans during World War II. The army, recruited largely from Soviet POWs in Nazi concentration camps, was motivated to fight against the Soviets by Russian nationalist and anticommunist ideals. His graduate studies completed, Fischer went on to teach at Brandeis University, the affiliation given on the loose leaf from the Soviet embassy found by the FBI in January 1955.[5]

■

The 1955 FBI investigation into George Fischer began with a review of their recent files about the Soviet embassy. There the Bureau's agents noticed something they had previously overlooked. An FBI report, most probably based on an intercept of telephone conversations and filed on November 5, 1954, stated that a certain "George Yuri Fischer" had gotten in touch with the third secretary of the Soviet embassy, which happened to be the lowest diplomatic rank and equal to that of the assistant attaché, to inform him that he had arrived in Washington to attend the embassy reception scheduled for November 7, the anniversary of the Russian Revolution. According to the report, Fischer told the embassy official that he was ready to meet him on November 6. The official responded that he might give Fischer a call.[6]

The FBI did not know whether the meeting had actually taken place, but the Bureau's officers learned that Fischer had attended the reception on November 7. There was little doubt that his name on the August 7 calendar leaf from the Soviet embassy and his visit there three months later were connected, though the nature of that connection was anyone's guess. The plot seemed to thicken. Suspicion of Fischer increased when on March 18, 1955, FBI officers learned from "a highly confidential source, of known reliability, whose identity may not be disclosed," that Fischer intended to visit the Soviet embassy again on March 20. He got in touch with the same third secretary of the Soviet Embassy and arranged to meet him at his apartment in the early evening of the day of his forthcoming arrival in Washington.[7]

The confidential source told the FBI that Fischer had previously submitted two applications to the Soviet embassy, one for a travel visa to the USSR, the other for a change of citizenship. The FBI officers sounded the alarm, suspecting that Fischer was getting ready to defect, acquire Soviet citizenship, and disappear behind the Iron Curtain. "Fischer is U.S. citizen and there would be propaganda value to USSR in renunciation of U.S. by son of Louis Fischer, a prominent and prolific anti-Communist writer," read one of the FBI cables. Fischer seemed potentially valuable to the Soviets because he would be repudiating his father, who was no longer suspected of espionage against the United States or of continuing to hold procommunist views and indeed had become an anti-Soviet asset.[8]

The FBI Washington office got a surveillance team to follow Fischer's moves in the nation's capital once he arrived for his rendezvous with the Soviet official. At 6:41 on the evening of March 20, Fischer was spotted in northwestern Washington near the apartment building where his embassy contact resided. He stepped out of a green 1951 Ford convertible driven by a woman, whom the surveillance team described as "white, approximately 30 to 35 years old, brown hair, and wearing glasses." After dropping Fischer off, she drove away. Fischer entered the building, where he stayed until almost midnight. At 11:50 p.m. he left the building in the company of a man. The two got into a blue 1954 Ford sedan and, according to the surveillance report, "proceeded to drive a circuitous route through the N.W. area of Washington." The driver was probably checking for surveillance, and the FBI had to stop following the Ford at 12:21. At 12:55 they spotted Fischer and his companion at the building where Fischer was staying. The two stood talking on the sidewalk for about three minutes before parting. One of the FBI agents checked his watch. It was 12:58 a.m.[9]

The FBI now knew that Fischer's acquaintance with the Soviet official was more than casual. They wanted to know more but had nothing to go on except the surveillance report and an English translation of the letter that Fischer had sent to the embassy. It read: "Up to this time I have had absolutely no word from the embassy about my two applications—change of citizenship, and visa for this summer. I will be very grateful to you if, when I call you, you will be able to suggest to me who at the embassy I can see personally during my visit." Why Fischer wanted to change his citizenship—which, so far as the FBI knew, was American—before going to the Soviet Union remained a mystery.[10]

In late March, 1955, the FBI decided that the only way to figure out what was going on with George Fischer was to confront him. "The Bureau desires that an immediate effort be made to determine the present sympathies of Fischer, in view of the allegation that he may have applied for Soviet citizenship," read the FBI Boston office cable to FBI headquarters. According to the proposed plan of the interview, the agents were to tell Fischer that they were interested in him because of his visit to the Soviet embassy on November 7, 1954, and wanted to know whether he "expects to have a continuing reason for developing of acquaintance with Soviet personnel and whether he would be willing to assist us furnishing his evaluation of such personnel."

The ultimate goal of the interview was to find out whether Fischer had indeed applied for Soviet citizenship and the nature of his contacts with embassy officials. But the FBI officers were prohibited from asking those questions directly in order to avoid compromising FBI sources or reveal that Fischer had been under surveillance in Washington. "He should very tactfully be given an opportunity to volunteer information," read the FBI memo on the proposed interview. In April 1955 the Boston FBI was authorized to interview him, but it was easier said than done. They could not find Fischer at his home address, 39 Walker Street in Cambridge.[11]

Fischer was going through a divorce from his wife, Katherine Van Alan Hoag, a native of Pennsylvania and a daughter of the dean of Haverford College, Gilbert Thomas Hoag. They had married in September 1948. Fischer had moved to a different location, renting an apartment on Charles Street in Boston. He was probably under considerable stress. A post office official interviewed by the FBI reported that Fischer had got into trouble with not one but two postmen and was generally considered a troublemaker. Going through divorce, behaving erratically, visiting the Soviet embassy and meeting with a Soviet official at his apartment while applying for a travel visa to the USSR and possibly for Soviet citizenship: Fischer matched the profile of a man preparing to betray his country.[12]

FBI agents finally got to interview Fischer on May 18, 1955, four days after the newspapers announced the creation of the Warsaw Pact—the Soviet-led military alliance that was to serve as a counterweight to NATO in Central Europe. Fischer was open and direct in answering the agents' questions. As they wrote in their report, he furnished them with plenty of information about his visits to the Soviet embassy in November 1954 and March 1955. Yet he volunteered no information on the issue that was of greatest concern to the FBI but so sensitive that they had been instructed not to ask about it directly—the question of Soviet citizenship.

Fischer spoke in detail about his contact at the Soviet embassy, Third Secretary Anatolii Zorin, formerly of course the head of SMERSH at Poltava. The FBI already knew his name and address, 1451 Park Road, Washington, DC, where Fischer visited him in March 1955. However, they were surprised to learn about his connection with the Poltava air base, where Fischer had served during the war. Fischer told the FBI agents that Zorin had been an engineer before the war and served as a liaison with the Americans at the Poltava base. His role might have been equivalent to that of an officer of the American Counter Intelligence Corps.

Fischer told the FBI officers that he and Zorin had met by chance in October 1954, when Fischer was giving a lecture at the Counter Intelligence Corps (CIC) Center, headquartered at Fort Holabird, Maryland. After the lecture he went to Washington, and bumped into Zorin near the Statler Hotel on 16th Street, not far from the Soviet embassy. Decades later, in his memoir, Fischer wrote that the meeting had taken place after his visit to the Soviet embassy, after he had exited the building. It was Zorin who first recognized Fischer and shouted: "Yura! George!" Fischer apparently had difficulty in recognizing Zorin—he would later tell his wife that a few minutes passed before he actually remembered who Zorin was. In responding to the FBI agents' questions, Fischer said that he knew approximately ten Soviet officers from his time at Poltava but could not remember any of them well. Eventually he recognized Zorin, whom he addressed by the diminutive form of his first name, "Tolia."[13]

Since Fischer's name appeared on the calendar leaf from the Soviet embassy dated August 7, Zorin evidently had plenty of time to prepare for what seemed to Fischer to be a chance meeting. The former SMERSH officer told Fischer that after the war he had joined the diplomatic service and was now approaching the end of his term in Washington. In fact, the diplomatic post was a cover for Zorin. As late as October 1950, Zorin, then a lieutenant colonel assigned to the headquarters of the Kyiv military

district, was advising Poltava MGB officers on cases of Americans suspected of spying on the USSR. Fischer, naturally, was at the very top of that
list. US State Department records show Zorin and his wife residing in
Washington from 1952 to 1956; after that, references to the Zorins disappear from the diplomatic record. Zorin had not been lying when he told
Fischer that his posting in the United States was nearing its end.[14]

Upon their "chance" meeting in October 1954, Fischer and Zorin went
to a Greek restaurant for dinner. They recalled the good old days at Poltava.
"We chatted amiably, were happy to meet," remembered Fischer. Zorin
complained that the Soviet embassy had very little contact with the
Americans, as most people they approached would not even accept invitations to their receptions. "I hated the spy/loyalty craze. The witch hunt by
the U.S. government as well as McCarthy and Co.," wrote Fischer later.
"I told Tolia I'd love to do my bit against it." Fischer was promised an
invitation to the Russian Revolution reception on November 7, 1954,
which he subsequently attended.[15]

Recalling the reception, Fischer told the agents that while meeting with
Soviet officials, whose names he did not remember, as the encounters were
very short, he was not asked any suspicious questions, short of ones about
US public opinion, information that was available in the daily newspapers.
He did not plan to continue contacts with any of those officials—with the
possible exception of Zorin, given their history together. Also, he was not
sure whether he would actually go to the USSR, as his travel would have to
be funded by a US institution. Finally, he did not mind providing the FBI
with information on Soviet officials he might meet in the future but did not
want to be under an obligation to do so. He offered to contact the FBI if
anything of importance turned up at such meetings. That was the end of the
interview.[16]

The FBI now knew about Zorin and his background but still had no idea
about the validity of their suspicion that Fischer intended to acquire Soviet
citizenship. They decided to interview Fischer's estranged wife, Katherine
Hoag, in the hope that she might clarify the issue and contacted her in
September 1955. Hoag characterized her ex-husband as strongly anti-
Soviet. It turned out that he had been quite open with her about his Soviet

youth and his meeting with Zorin in Washington. She also knew that he had visited Zorin at his home in the American capital.

Most importantly, Hoag was able to shed light on the issue of Fischer's planned travel to the USSR and his citizenship. She told the agents that George was indeed planning to visit the Soviet Union for research purposes but was concerned that the Soviets would consider him one of their own—he had left the USSR in 1938 on a Soviet passport—and prevent him from leaving the country. "I wanted to apply for a Soviet visa right away," remembered Fischer later. "But father and mother worried about my old Soviet citizenship. It never lapsed, they said. Now it might be used by Moscow officials. They could give me grief, lock me up in the Old Country." That was the reason Fischer had gone to the Soviet embassy in the first place, explained Hoag. He had even written in that regard to his old acquaintance and now US ambassador to Moscow, Charles "Chip" Bohlen, requesting his help.

As far as the FBI officers were concerned, the issue was finally resolved. They recommended no further investigation into the question of citizenship. George Fischer wanted to remain a US citizen and have the right to leave the USSR whenever he pleased. The case seemed closed.[17]

■

If George Fischer was no longer suspected of spying for the Soviets, he had not yet succeeded in ridding himself of his Soviet citizenship and thus, as he correctly surmised, risked arrest if he paid another visit to the USSR. Besides, after the May 1955 visit by FBI officers, Fischer was clearly concerned about the possibility that his contacts with Zorin might have been interpreted as something more than an innocent meeting with an old friend, and that his correspondence with and visits to the Soviet embassy might be perceived as something other than an attempt to renounce his Soviet citizenship.

Fischer decided to "come clean" and get official approval for further contacts with the Soviets. Nonetheless he apparently did not trust the FBI. Instead, in late August 1955, a few weeks before FBI agents interviewed Katherine Hoag, he wrote to the Passport Office of the State

Department. "The double citizenship which arises out of my mother's former Soviet citizenship is of particular concern to me," wrote Fischer. He informed the State Department that he intended to contact the Soviet embassy again and asked "whether there are any objections on your part to me pursuing this matter further." On October 22, 1955, the Passport Office responded to Fischer, approving his contacts with the Soviet embassy.[18]

On November 7 Fischer was back in Washington, once again attending the Russian Revolution reception at the Soviet embassy. As before, he met with Zorin prior to the reception and continued socializing with him and his colleagues at the embassy. It was then that Zorin shared with him the difficulties he had encountered while working on his new assignment—the collection of data on violations of the Soviet-American Agreement signed as part of the establishment of diplomatic relations between the two countries back in 1933. Article 3 of the agreement prohibited the US government from sponsoring or supporting anti-Soviet activities. Zorin claimed that the US government was in fact funding private institutions engaged precisely in such activities, and he was working on a memorandum to the government asking it to stop them. Zorin was looking for people who could help him collect information on violations of the agreement, had a budget, and was prepared to pay for the information.

Fischer smelled a rat and did not react to Zorin's indirect proposal to cooperate. That seemed to be the end of the conversation, but later in the evening, Zorin raised the question again, suggesting that Fischer was well acquainted with the subject of Zorin's new inquiry. He then asked Fischer whether he could help with collecting the data. It all was very casual, and, given Fischer's opposition to McCarthyism, which he did not hide from Zorin, sounded quite natural. But Fischer, well aware that "cooperation" with the Soviets smacked of espionage, did not take the bait. He told Zorin that he was not interested.

Zorin would not take no for an answer and made his offer again. He mentioned that he had thought about getting help from someone whom Fischer knew quite well, except that this person was getting old. Fischer suspected that Zorin was referring to his mother, Markusha, about whom he had inquired earlier. Fischer did not react. Zorin made one more attempt to persuade Fischer to help him with his project. Again Fischer demurred, and they parted on their "customary amicable footing."[19]

Upon his return to Boston, Fischer decided to do something he could hardly have imagined himself ever doing—writing a letter to the FBI describing his recent visit to the Soviet embassy. It was dated November 8, 1955, the day of his return from Washington. The following day, November 9, he received a visit from the FBI and was interviewed about his conversations with Zorin. Fischer was clearly worried; the FBI officers commented in their report on his "nervous temperament." This was one of the reasons, along with his stated reluctance to report to the FBI on a regular basis, that they had advised against developing him as a double agent. This time around, however, Fischer was prepared to cooperate. He suggested that he would get in touch with his mother and let the FBI know whether she had been approached by the Soviets. In December 1955, at another meeting with FBI agents, he told them that Markusha had received no communication from the Soviet embassy. Fischer himself had no desire to continue contact with Zorin or Soviet officials in general. Still, he had good news from the Soviet embassy: his Soviet citizenship had finally been revoked, so he was free to visit.[20]

With Zorin leaving Washington in 1956, it seemed that the Poltava page of Fischer's biography had been turned. He would make numerous trips to the Soviet Union in the 1960s and meet many of his old Moscow friends there. Those trips bore no connection to his Poltava experiences, with the exception of one he took in the summer of 1963 to attend a meeting of the Dartmouth Conference of American and Soviet public figures that was held that year at Yalta. Not only was the place familiar to him from his days at the Yalta Conference of 1945, but also the head of the KGB department who oversaw the conference from his office in Kyiv was his old acquaintance, Major, not Colonel, of KGB, Anatoly Zorin. We do not know however whether the two happened upon one another on that occasion. Closer to the end of his life, Fischer gained possession of his FBI file and learned about the numerous investigations conducted into his allegedly pro-Soviet views.[1] He never saw his SMERSH files or learned about the fate of his Soviet acquaintances—who, like Zinaida Belukha, had been recruited by the KGB to spy on him. The Poltava KGB expected Fischer to return to Ukraine in the 1960s. He never did.

---

[1] See the list of the American participants of the Dartmouth Conference meeting in the Crimea in the summer of 1963 in the Central State Archives and Museum of Literature and Arts of Ukraine, fond 435, op. 1, no. 1544. For Zorin's report on a different matter from March 13, 1962, see SBU Archives, fond 16, op. 1, no. 944, fol. 197.

EPILOGUE

Two key figures in the Poltava story, George Fischer and Franklyn Holzman, renewed their acquaintance at Harvard, where in the 1950s they pursued doctoral degrees in Soviet studies. For both, although in different measure, the wartime experience in Poltava turned out to be an important stepping stone to their academic careers. Surprisingly, none of them decided to draw on those experiences for their research and teaching agendas.

Holzman remembered that when he asked Fischer during their encounters at Harvard whether he was going to write his thesis on wartime Poltava, Fischer, who as noted eventually wrote a doctoral dissertation and a book on Russian collaborators with the Nazis, answered in the negative. The reason he gave Holzman was that he was not sure exactly what had happened there. Holzman, who had told one of his fellow GIs at Myrhorod that he was going to write a book about Operation *Frantic*, was equally reluctant to commit his wartime experiences to paper and never produced the book he had wanted to write as a youth. These two accomplished scholars of the Soviet Union left it to others to write the history of the American experience at Poltava.[1]

The official histories of the different stages of the American shuttle-bombing operations in the Soviet Union written by James Parton, Albert Lepawsky, and William Kaluta bore all the hallmarks of military reports of the period, were often technical in nature, and remained sealed from the general public for decades to come. However, there was one military officer with full access to the official documents, who was eager to let the world know of what happened at the Poltava bases during the war years. This was John Deane. In 1947, by that time retired from the military service, he published his war memoirs under a title that summarized his view: *The Strange Alliance*. One of the nineteen chapters, "Shuttle Bombing," was concerned exclusively with setting up and then running the Ukrainian bases, while other chapters, notably "Repatriation of Prisoners of War," dealt directly or indirectly with aspects of the Poltava story.

Although Deane endured numerous setbacks and difficulties and bore many emotional scars as a result of Soviet handling of the Poltava-area bases, he believed that the whole effort had been worthwhile. Disappointed in his original high hopes for the future of the Grand Alliance, Deane nevertheless wrote that the Poltava-based air operations were "of immeasurable value to the United States," as they had made possible "eighteen strong attacks on important strategic targets in Germany, which would otherwise have been immune." "More important than that," he continued, "it must have had a shattering effect on the morale of the Germans.... To see Russia let down the bars and permit American operations on her soil must have destroyed the last hope the Germans may have had of dividing her enemies and concluding a separate peace with one or another."

About the deterioration of Soviet-American relations at the bases after the end of shuttle-bombing operations and the subsequent closure of the Poltava base, Deane remarked: "The truth was that the presence of the Americans in the Soviet Union, and particularly the Ukraine, which is an area of questionable loyalty, was no longer desired. The true attitude of the Communist party leaders toward foreigners could no longer be concealed, especially since there was no operational necessity for their presence." He was relieved to learn about the decision of USSTAF to close the base in April 1945. His hopes for the bright future of American-Russian relations were relegated to the past. Deane was, however, glad to discover the "vast difference in the attitude toward Americans that exists between the rank and file Russian people and their leaders." He probably had in mind the Soviets in general and, when it came to the civil population, the Ukrainians more than the Russians.[2]

Deane was convinced that the Bolshevik thinking about the capitalist West was among the main reasons for the problems experienced by the Grand Alliance. Stalin and his lieutenants never envisioned the Grand Alliance as anything more than a temporary agreement to facilitate military operations on separate fronts against a common enemy. Close cooperation on the ground, especially opening military bases on Soviet territory, was regarded as wholly undesirable—little more than a capitalist plot to undermine socialism and seize territory. Communist ideology was reinforced in this regard by Bolshevik phobia rooted not in Marxism but in the foreign interventions during the Russian Revolution, when American, British, and French expeditionary forces occupied Russian and Ukrainian ports from Murmansk to Odesa to Vladivostok and moved into the hinterland.

George Fischer got hold of Deane's book almost immediately and reviewed it for the July1947 issue of *Far Eastern Survey*, a journal that a few years later, in the McCarthy era, would be attacked as procommunist. Fischer was generally positive about the book, noting the thoughtfulness of the author's observations and the wealth of his "inside" information. He was not at ease, however, with Deane's readiness to explain the difficulties in American-Soviet relations as rooted in the Soviet leaders' ideological animosity toward the capitalist West. The book, wrote Fischer, was rich in "authoritative facts intermingled with controversial personal conclusions." Nor did he approve of Deane's occasional mockery of the Soviets and their behavior. Even so, Fischer preferred to defend Deane rather than condemn him and other disillusioned participants in the wartime encounter. "The often far from abstractly judicious bias and emotion of these Americans about the Russian experiences should not be hastily condemned or

disregarded," wrote Fischer, "but rather considered as an important preva-
lent byproduct of the ever problematic close contacts of our officials with
the Soviets."[3]

■

Fischer was right. The experiences of the Americans involved in the
Poltava story are of course essential to understanding their attitudes toward
the Soviets. The American rationale for opening the bases was primarily
strategic, but also involved high and largely unrealistic hopes of future
friendship with the Soviets. For the Americans, the military alliance meant
close cooperation on the ground and in the air, unencumbered by ideological, political, economic, or cultural insecurities. If anything, the opposite
was the case. Given their numbers, technological dominance, and economic power, the Americans felt themselves superior to their Soviet partners. Their expectations ran high, and their subsequent disappointment
was deep and long-lasting.

The American ambassador in Moscow, Averell Harriman, a prominent
figure in this book, was among the first to be disappointed. His initial optimism about relations with the Soviets gave way to distrust, leading him to
adopt a quid pro quo attitude in his dealings with them. A key factor in
Harriman's evolution was Stalin's refusal to allow the Americans to use the
Poltava-area bases to resupply the Warsaw insurgents in the summer of 1944.
He would become an early promoter of the Cold War. The same trajectory
was followed by another key player in the Poltava enterprise, General
Robert L. Walsh, who took active part in the postwar struggle for West Berlin.[4]

The attitude to the Soviet regime and its war effort for most American servicemen on the Poltava-area bases evolved from friendly to hostile. Beginning
with sincere admiration of the Soviet people and, to a lesser degree, of representatives of the Stalin regime for their resilience, sacrifice, and bravery in
fighting Nazi Germany, they became disillusioned. Soviet political culture
and everyday life repelled the Americans, irrespective of the policies implemented by the Soviet command. That was true of Colonel Thomas
Hampton, Major Michael Kowal, and First Lieutenant William Kaluta.

To more or less the same category belonged Private Palmer Myhra, who was probably inspired to write the story of his wartime experiences by the dream that Holzman shared with him in Ukraine. In his self-published memoir, *A Frantic Saga* (2008), Myhra wrote that his experience at Myrhorod had turned him into a lifelong adversary of the Soviet system. A believer in electoral democracy, he overcame numerous hurdles to vote in the US presidential election of 1944 while posted overseas; in the Soviet Union he saw complete disregard for democratic principles. "They voted alright," wrote Myhra with reference to Soviet citizens, "but had no choice of candidates." He continued, "After what I had seen in the Soviet Union I had no interest in socialist or liberal political tendencies. So all my life I have been a conservative Republican. I saw good reasons to be that."[5]

Those Americans who visited the bases for brief periods and were not affected by the Soviet espionage agencies there maintained their positive attitudes toward the Soviets long after their tours of duty at Poltava. The same was true of those in the permanent contingent at the bases who held leftist convictions that inspired sympathy toward the Soviet Union, its social experiment, and especially its war effort. Holzman certainly belonged to that category. "I always felt that my father had a sense of himself as part of the Soviet war effort," recalled Thomas Holzman, Franklyn's son.

> To him, the Soviet Union was where the actual war was being fought and won at great cost, and he was proud to play a small role in that effort. When he spoke to me about the war, it was mostly about the brave defenders of Stalingrad and Leningrad, the heroism of the Red Army, and how impressive the Soviets stationed with him were. He also spoke movingly of the terrible, almost unbelievable sacrifices of the Soviet people. I recall him testifying before Congress about Lend-Lease debts, urging that they be forgiven in light of the Soviet sacrifices in the War. He was probably less critical of the Soviets and more sympathetic in many ways than others on the Frantic bases. When the Russian Federation awarded him the Fiftieth Anniversary Commemorative Medal for Participation in the Great Patriotic War,

I think it meant an enormous amount to him because of the recognition it carried that he had been part of that effort.[6]

George Fischer shared Holzman's fascination with the Soviet war effort, though he went much further in distinguishing the regime from the people. In his memoirs, written in 2000, Fischer recalled his Poltava experiences in terms of a contest between an old love and an old hatred. The love was for the country he called Russia; the hatred was for Stalin and his policies. "In my work I did not doubt what side I was on. My hate of Kremlin evil would not let me waver," wrote Fischer. He died in 2005, loyal to his leftist beliefs and adamant in his opposition to Stalinism.[7]

Why did most of the Americans who spent considerable time at the bases or were of sufficiently high rank to have regular dealings with Soviet officials leave the Soviet Union in 1945 with a strong sense of resentment toward their hosts? In general, the factors contributing to their change of heart were not directly related to the ideological differences and opposing geostrategic agendas pursued by the two states. After all, the wartime geopolitical objectives—the defeat of Germany and Japan—were held in common by the two allies, and many Americans sympathized with socialism broadly defined. It was differences in political culture that proved decisive in alienating the two parties.

One example is the Soviet treatment of prisoners of war as traitors and criminals, and their refusal to allow American personnel in Eastern Europe to help American prisoners of war released from German camps to make their way home via the Poltava-area bases. Such treatment aroused, as we have seen, the ire of President Roosevelt himself. This was the most obvious manifestation of an attitude shared by Soviet officials, military officers, and rank-and-file soldiers that the American found appalling. For the Americans, there was no higher duty than saving their prisoners of war, who were regarded as heroes because of the hardships they had endured. As noted, the Soviet regime considered Red Army soldiers captured by the Germans as traitors at worst, and at best as second-rate citizens who did not deserve the same food and treatment as those serving in the ranks; indeed, they could be robbed with impunity.

Even more important was the issue of relationships. The Americans were incensed by the efforts of the Soviet secret police to curtail personal relations with their Soviet counterparts and by the campaign of harassment against women who dated Americans. The latter problem was hardly new to American officers and servicemen, who had already encountered it in Britain and liberated France, where locals resented relatively better-off American soldiers and the women who dated them. In the Poltava region, however, attacks on women who developed relationships with Americans were more brutal, encouraged by the regime but led by the secret police. It seemed to the Americans that the locals welcomed them, the authorities did not. It was as if they had landed in a country occupied by a foreign regime at odds with the general population.

Thus the Americans came to sympathize with local inhabitants, such as Ukrainians in Poltava and Poles in Lviv, and resent the Soviet authorities, whom they called "Russians." Most locals welcomed the arrival of the Americans and hoped that their presence would either free them from Soviet rule (an attitude widespread in Lviv) or liberalize the Soviet political system (as some in the Poltava region believed). Women who dated Americans were waging their own war against the regime: some of them came from families oppressed by the Soviets during the war, while others had had relationships with Germans and therefore found themselves on the secret police blacklists. Apart from romantic or material considerations, Ukrainian women who wanted to marry their American sweethearts dreamed of moving to the United States, which the Soviet authorities treated as the imperialist foe.

Soviet commanders, political commissars, and counterintelligence and secret-police officers regarded the Americans not as allies but as potential spies and agents of capitalist influence. Extremely insecure in economic and often in cultural terms, they took a fierce pride in the recent victories of the Red Army, contrasting them with the much more modest achievements of the Allies in Western Europe. The Soviet military and political authorities indoctrinated their subordinates and the local population accordingly, encouraging and often forcing them to spy on their American acquaintances. The Americans were aware of that and attributed most of the difficulties in dealing with the Soviets to the policies of individuals or of the regime in general, rarely blaming the population.

With very rare exceptions, the Americans rejected core elements of Soviet political culture: the cult of the leader; the party-run propaganda regime, which sought to inculcate officially approved views; and the police state, with its constant surveillance, intimidation, and restrictions on personal freedom. For most Americans, the Poltava experience with the Soviet authorities and their political culture led to the rejection of both.

▪

While intellectuals like Fischer and Holzman remained ambivalent about the broader meaning of their experiences at Poltava, Myhra, a lifelong farmer from Wisconsin, had no such doubts. *Frantic Saga* offers perhaps the most astute assessment of the long-term significance of the Poltava story published by any participant. "I truly believe that we who were at these Soviet air bases in the 1944 days of the hot war really did witness the very beginning of the coming Cold War." Myhra was gratified by the outcome of that conflict. "We were there and remember you as you remember us," he wrote, addressing his old acquaintances in Myrhorod. "The Cold War has come and gone.... I never thought I would see the day when there was no more Soviet Union, and Ukraine to become a nation unto itself."[8]

Myhra's words reflected the atmosphere that characterized the fiftieth anniversary celebrations of Operation Frantic in September 1994. That month the friendship forged by rank-and-file airmen and soldiers of the Grand Alliance at the Poltava-area bases was marked with public festivities organized by the Poltava civic authorities. Ukraine, which had recently become independent, was glad to welcome both American and Russian veterans of the shuttle-bombing operations. The Ukrainian authorities opened the Poltava air base to American visitors, though it had served during the Soviet period as home to elite strategic bombers, including the supersonic Tupolev 160, whose targets were in the United States. The guests arrived in B-1B Lancer bombers from Barksdale Air Force Base in

Louisiana and B-52N bombers from Dyess Air Force Base in Texas. President Bill Clinton used the occasion to "congratulate the Ukrainian, American and Russian airmen who participated in the difficult air campaign over Europe fifty years ago and landed their planes at Poltava."[9]

None of the major figures in this book was around or able to attend, but at least three American veterans of the shuttle-bombing operations took part. Among the three B-17 pilots who returned to Poltava in 1994 was Charlie Beecham of El Reno, Oklahoma. He came to Poltava and Myrhorod with pilots from the Barksdale base. "The celebration lasted three days," wrote Beecham to the editor of the local newspaper, "and a beautiful monument was dedicated at the entrance to Poltava Air Base. Each of us was presented a silver medallion, three inches in diameter. The inscription reads: "For Memory about the Meeting of Ukrainian and American Pilots on Poltava's Land."[10]

It was the last time that veterans of the three nations jointly marked the anniversary of "Frantic." Charlie Beecham died in 2012, soon after celebrating his ninetieth birthday. His obituary noted the five medals awarded him in the course of World War II as well as a sixth, one that he earned by delivering coal and other supplies during the Berlin Airlift of 1948–1949.

It was not only the passing of veterans that accounted for the lack of enthusiasm in Ukraine for future tripartite celebrations of "Frantic" anniversaries.[11] On the sixtieth anniversary in 2004, Ukraine was undergoing the turmoil of the Orange Revolution, having rejected the Russian-sponsored presidential candidate. On the seventieth anniversary in 2014, Ukraine was at war with Russia over its eastern territories in the Donbas.

Today, when part of the Poltava base has become a museum, one can visit the monument (mentioned by Charlie Beecham) to the American and Soviet airmen killed in the German attack on the base on June 22, 1944. But a visitor to the museum will also see photographs of the Ukrainian officers and soldiers who lost their lives in ongoing wars with Russia. Anyone approaching the monument will inevitably hear the roar of helicopters on the operational part of the base. It now serves as a training ground for Ukrainian helicopter pilots taking part in the Russo-Ukrainian war in eastern Ukraine. American planes and personnel are back in Ukraine, though not at Poltava. They are involved in training soldiers in western Ukraine for service in the east. The Soviet Union is long gone, and the United States now finds itself allied with one of its erstwhile partners against another. Even so, an essential continuity remains: as in World War II, the Americans are on the side of those who were wronged.

This is a continuation of the Poltava story that could hardly have been imagined in 1944, 1994, or even 2004. With the brief reconciliation between Cold War adversaries effectively over, and the winds of a new Cold War becoming chillier by the day, we need to look back at the American experience in Poltava in order to understand why the Grand Alliance disintegrated and to absorb the lessons for alliances yet to be formed. A fundamental lesson is that alliances can be sustained for some time by the need to fight a common enemy, but they can endure only on the basis of shared values. The Grand Alliance lacked that part.

ACKNOWLEDGMENTS

Funding provided by the Fulbright Program allowed me to research this book in Ukraine, where most of the events recounted here took place. I am grateful to the director of the Fulbright Program in Kyiv, Marta Kolomayets, and her staff, in particular Veronika Aleksanych, for their welcome and assistance. I also owe a debt of gratitude to my host institution in Ukraine, the Institute of History of the National Academy of Sciences, and its director, Valerii Smolii. At the Archives of the Security Service of Ukraine, which inherited the documents of Soviet military counterintelligence and secret police, my thanks go to the director, Andrii Kohut, and to one of the most efficient and helpful archivists I have ever worked with, Maria Panova.

The historians Hennadii Boriak and Roman Podkur in Ukraine, and Liudmila Novikova in Russia offered valuable advice. My colleagues at the Poltava Pedagogical University, Yurii Voloshyn and Ihor Serdiuk, arranged a tour of the Poltava air base used by American airmen in 1944–1945 and the museum that proudly exhibits unique artifacts and photos from that

period. In the United States, David Engerman and Hiroaki Kuromiya were
extremely generous in sharing with me their advice and copies of archival
documents in their possession. Natalia Laas offered her assistance in
making copies of some of the key documents available to me. As my research advanced beyond archival documents, I benefited enormously from
assistance provided by descendants and relatives of some of the key characters in my story: George Fischer's younger brother Vic Fischer, Franklyn
Holzman's sons Thomas and David, and, last but not least, Tony Reverditto,
a son of Igor Reverditto. I am grateful to them for the memories they shared
with me and the photographs and documents they provided.

At Harvard, I thank Alexandra Vacroux for helping to arrange access to
the Davis Center's archival collection and my colleagues at the Ukrainian
Research Institute, in particular its executive director, Tymish Holowinsky,
for their support and for keeping things going during my sabbatical and research trips to Ukraine. As always, Myroslav Yurkevich, formerly of the
University of Alberta, was of great help in editing and polishing my prose.
Jill Kneerim provided invaluable assistance in ensuring that the manuscript
would end up in the hands of the most enthusiastic and dedicated publish-
ers I could have hoped for, Tim Bent, Mariah White, and Melissa Yanuzzi at
Oxford University Press and Casiana Ionita at Penguin UK. Sarah Chalfant
took on the laborious task of promoting the book to non-English readers.
I am grateful to them for their help and advice. As ever, my special thanks
go to my wife, Olena, for her support.

NOTES

Front Matter

1. For the most recent accounts of the Poltava story, see Mark J. Conversino, *Fighting with the Soviets: The Failure of Operation FRANTIC, 1944–1945* (Lawrence, KS, 1997); Lee Trimble and Jeremy Dronfield, *Beyond the Call: The True Story of One World War II Pilot's Covert Mission to Rescue POWs on the Eastern Front* (New York, 2015).

Prologue

1. Lieutenant Colonel Pervushin to Lieutenant Colonel Akhov, "Svodka naruzhnogo nabliudeniia za ob'ektom "Turist," May 18, 1958, 11:40 a.m. to 16:25 p.m., 4 pp., Archives of the Security Service of Ukraine (Arkhiv Sluzhby bezpeky Ukraïny), Kyiv (hereafter SBU Archives), fond 13, no. 1207, "Proverka voennosluzhashchikh bazy VVS SShA v Poltave, t. 18," fols. 229–32.

2. Franklyn D. Holzman, *Soviet Taxation: The Fiscal and Monetary Problems of a Planned Economy* (Cambridge, MA, 1955); Colonel Akhov and Lieutenant Colonel Baruzdin to Lieutenant Colonel Zubkov, July 25, 1960, 4 pp., SBU Archives, fond 13, no. 1207, fols. 327–30.

3. Captain Khramov and Major Ovchinnikov, "Spravka na amerikanskogo voennosluzhashchego aviabazy VVS SShA v Poltave Fisher Iu. A.," May 1964, 8 pp., SBU Archives, fond 13, no. 1207, fols. 83–86ᵛ; Ken Gewertz, "From Russia with Thanks: Holzman Awarded Medal for World War II Service," *Harvard Gazette*, April 3, 1997; Franklyn Holzman, BBC interview on his experiences at Poltava, 1995 (courtesy of the Holzman Family and the Davis Center for Russian and Eurasian Studies at Harvard University).

Chapter 1

1. John R. Deane, *The Strange Alliance: The Story of Our Efforts at Wartime Cooperation with Russia* (New York, 1947), pp. 3-4; Geoffrey Roberts, *Molotov: Stalin's Cold Warrior* (Dulles, VA, 2012), pp. 21-90.

2. "Istoriia Khodynki," *Grand Park* <http://www.grandpark.info/index.php?go=Pages&in=view&id=4>; Roger Moorhouse, *The Devil's Alliance: Hitler's Pact with Stalin, 1939-1941* (New York, 2014), chap. 1, "The Devil's Potion."

3. Nikolai Gogol, "The Terrible Vengeance," in *The Collected Tales of Nikolai Gogol*, trans. Richard Pevear and Larissa Volokhonsky (New York, 1999), p. 90; David M. Glantz and Jonathan M. House, *When Titans Clashed: How the Red Army Stopped Hitler* (Lawrence, KS, 1995), pp. 168-78.

4. "Douglas C-54 Skymaster," *Warbird Alley* <http://www.warbirdalley.com/c54.htm>; Arthur Pearcy, *Douglas Propliners: DC-1-DC-7* (London, 1996).

5. Averell Harriman and Elie Abel, *Special Envoy to Churchill and Stalin, 1941-1946* (New York, 1975), p. 227;Frank Costigliola, *Roosevelt's Lost Alliances: How Personal Politics Helped Start the Cold War* (Princeton and Oxford, 2012), pp. 192-93.

6. Harriman and Abel, *Special Envoy*, pp. 228-29; Deane, *The Strange Alliance*, pp. 3, 9-11.

7. Deane, *The Strange Alliance*, p. 107; [Albert Lepawsky], "History of Eastern Command, U.S. Strategic Air Forces in Europe, 1941-1944," Headquarters USSTAF, 1944, National Archives and Records Administration (hereafter NARA), NA/RG 334, box 66, p. 7.

8. Kathleen Harriman to Mary, in Harriman and Abel, *Special Envoy*, p. 234.

9. Deane, *The Strange Alliance*, p. 3.

10. Cordell Hull, *The Memoirs*, 2 vols. (New York, 1948), 2: 1277; Deane, *The Strange Alliance*, p. 4.

11. Hamilton to Secretary of State, October 18, 1943, in *Foreign Relations of the United States* (hereafter FRUS), *Diplomatic Papers, 1943: General*, pp. 567-68; Minutes of Meeting Held at the Kremlin on October 18, 1943, ibid., pp. 563-65.

12. "The Moscow Conference: October 1943," *The Avalon Project* <http://avalon.law.yale.edu/wwii/moscow.asp>.

13. Frank Costigliola, "'I Had Come as a Friend': Emotion, Culture, and Ambiguity in the Formation of the Cold War, 1943-45," *Cold War History* 1, no. 1 (August 2000): 105-106.

14. Costigliola, "'I Had Come as a Friend,'" pp. 105-6; Kathleen Harriman to Mary, Moscow, November 5, 1943, p. 2, in Library of Congress, Harriman Papers, box 6, folder 9, Correspondence between Kathleen Mortimer and Mary Fisk.

Chapter 2

1. Deane, *The Strange Alliance*, p. 24; Harriman to Roosevelt, October 31, 1943, FRUS, *Diplomatic Papers, 1943: General*, p. 690.

2. Kathleen Harriman to Mary, Moscow, November 9, 1943, p. 3, in Library of Congress, Harriman Papers, box 6, folder 9, Correspondence between Kathleen Mortimer and Mary Fisk.

3. Deane, *The Strange Alliance*, pp. 24-25; Simon Sebag Montefiore, *Stalin: The Court of the Red Tsar* (New York, 2003), pp. 519-22; Hull, *Memoirs*, 2: 1308-10.

4. Mark J. Conversino, *Fighting with the Soviets: The Failure of Operation Frantic, 1944–1945* (Lawrence, KS, 1997), pp. 9–12.
5. Record of the Second meeting of the Three-partite Conference, October 20, 1943, *FRUS, Diplomatic Papers, 1943: General*, pp. 583–88, 778–81.
6. Ibid., p. 779; Hull, *Memoirs*, 2: 1310; Harriman and Abel, *Special Envoy*, p. 239; Deane, *The Strange Alliance*, p. 20.
7. *Molotov Remembers: Inside Kremlin Politics. Conversations with Felix Chuev*, ed. Albert Resis (Chicago, 1993), p. 45.
8. Conversino, *Fighting with the Soviets*, pp. 27–28; "Most Secret Protocol, Moscow," November 1, 1943, *FRUS, Diplomatic Papers, 1943: General*, p. 773.
9. Deane, *The Strange Alliance*, pp. 20–21; To Milattache, Embassy Moscow, no. 75, October 26, 1943, NARA, NA/RG 334, Box 63: US Military Mission to Moscow, Operation Frantic (October 26, 1943–March 31, 1944), 3 pp.; [Albert Lepawsky], "History of Eastern Command, U.S. Strategic Air Forces in Europe, 1941–1944," Headquarters USSTAF, 1944, NARA, NA/RG 334, box 66, p. 7.
10. To AGWAR Washington from Deane, no. 28, October 29, 1943, NARA, NA/RG 334, box 63, 2 pp.; Deane, *The Strange Alliance*, p. 16.
11. Conversino, *Fighting with the Soviets*, p. 29; Harriman to Washington, December 26, 1943, NARA, NA/RG 334, box 63, 3 pp.; Deane to Washington, December 27, 1943, ibid., 1 p.
12. Conversino, *Fighting with the Soviets*, p. 31; General Arnold to Deane, January 27, 1944, NARA, NA/RG 334, Box 63, 2 pp.
13. Harriman and Abel, *Special Envoy*, p. 296; Deanne to Slavin, January 31, 1944 (English text and Russian translation), NARA, NA/RG 334, Box 63, 2 pp.; Memorandum of Conversation, The American Ambassador, Marshal Stalin, Molotov, February 2, 1944, NARA, NA/RG 334, Box 63, 4 pp.
14. Deane, *The Strange Alliance*, p. 108; Deane to Washington, February 2, 1944, NARA, N/A RG 334, Box 63, 1 p.; Arnold to Deane, February 4, 1944, 1 p., NARA, N/A RG 334, Box 63.
15. Deane, *The Strange Alliance*, p. 108; Memorandum of Conversation, The American Ambassador, Marshal Stalin, Molotov, February 2, 1944, NARA, N/A RG 334, Box 63, 4 pp.

Chapter 3

1. Deane, *The Strange Alliance*, pp. 30, 108–109; Conversino, *Fighting with the Soviets*, pp. 23–25; Von Hardesty and Ilya Grinberg, *Red Phoenix Rising: The Soviet Air Force in World War II* (Lawrence, KS, 2012).
2. Deane, *The Strange Alliance*, pp. 108–109; Deane to AGWAR, Washington, February 5, 1944, 3 pp., NARA, N/A RG 334, Box 63.
3. Conversino, *Fighting with the Soviets*, p. 32.
4. Ibid., pp. 31–33; Deane to Slavin, February 25, 1944, NARA, N/A RG 334, Box 63, 1 p.; "Col. John S. Griffith," obituary, *New York Times*, October 16, 1974; From Milattache, London to US Milmission, Moscow, February 23, 1944, NARA, N/A RG 334, Box 63, 1 p.; Deane to Slavin, February 24, 1944, ibid., 1 p.; Deane,

"Procedure for First Meeting," February 27, 1944, ibid., 1 p.; "Shuttle Bombing," Minutes of Meeting, February 28, 1944, ibid., 5 pp.

5. Deane, *The Strange Alliance*, pp. 110–11; Meeting at Air Force Headquarters Building," March 16, 1944, NARA, N/A RG 334, Box 63, 4 pp., here 1.

6. Griffith to Milattaché Amembassy, London; AGWAR, Washington, April 2, 1944, NARA, N/A RG 334, Box 63, 3 pp.

7. Deane to Milattaché Amembassy, London; AGWAR, Washington, March 26, 1944, ibid., 2 pp.; "Meeting at Air Force Headquarters Building," April 5, 1944, ibid, 5 pp.

8. "Meeting at Air Force Headquarters Building," April 5, 1944, NARA, N/A RG 334, Box 63, 5 pp.; "Major General Alfred A. Kessler, Jr," US Air Force <http://www.af.mil/AboutUs/Biographies/Display/tabid/225/Article/106572/major-general-alfred-a-kessler-jr.aspx>; Conversino, *Fighting with the Soviets*, pp. 33, 40.

9. Deane to Nikitin, April 12, 1944, NARA, N/A RG 334, Box 63, 1 p.; Deane to Nikitin, April 12, 1944, ibid., 1 p.; Deane to General Evstegneeev, April 12, 1944, ibid., 1 p.; Deane to Nikitin, April 14, 1944, ibid., 1 p.; Nikitin to Deane, April 14, 1944, ibid., 1 p.; Deane to Milattaché Amembassy, London; AGWAR, Washington, April 15, 1944, ibid., 1 p.

10. Daily Diary, 4th Echelon of "Frantic" during trip from England to Russia, in James Parton, "The History of 'Frantic,' American Shuttle Bombing to and from Russian Bases, 26 October 1943–15 June 1944," Headquarters, Mediterranean Allied Air Force, 1944, in W. Averell Harriman Papers, Manuscript Division, Library of Congress, Washington, DC, Box 188, p. 1; Franklyn Holzman, BBC interview on his experiences at Poltava, 1995; Conversino, *Fighting with the Soviets*, pp. 37–38.

11. Stuart Nicol, *Macqueen's Legacy*, vol. 2, *Ships of the Royal Mail Line* (Brimscombe Port and Charleston, SC, 2001), pp. 130–49; Daily Diary, 4th Echelon of "Frantic" during trip from England to Russia, in Parton, "The History of 'Frantic,'" pp. 2–3; Palmer Myhra, *A Frantic Saga: A Personal Account of a United States' Secret Mission inside the Soviet Ukraine during World War II* (Iola, WI, 2008), pp. 17–18.

12. Daily Diary, 4th Echelon of "Frantic" during trip from England to Russia, in Parton, "The History of 'Frantic,'" pp. 4–9; Holzman, BBC interview; Ken Gewertz, "From Russia with Thanks: Holzman Awarded Medal for World War II Service," *Harvard Gazette*, April 3, 1997; Conversino, *Fighting with the Soviets*, pp. 53–54.

13. Agent Report, "Leninakanskii," May 29, 1944, 2 pp., SBU Archives, fond 13, no. 1168, fols. 39, 39ᵛ; Agent Report, "Shakhter," May 30, 1944, 2 pp., ibid., fols. 40, 40ᵛ; Agent Report, "Kravkov," June 2, 1944, 2 pp., ibid., fols. 41, 41ᵛ.

14. Daily Diary, 4th Echelon of "Frantic" during trip from England to Russia, in Parton, "The History of 'Frantic,'" pp. 8–9; Agent Report, "Pika," May 17, 1944, 3 pp., SBU Archives, fond 13, no. 1168, fols. 168–70.

Chapter 4

1. Chris Hansen, *Enfant Terrible: The Times and Schemes of General Elliott Roosevelt* (Tucson, 2012), pp. 357–59; Harriman to Deane, December 3, 1943, NARA, NA/ RG 334, box 63, 1 p.; Deane to Elliott Roosevelt, December 3, 1943, ibid., 1 p.

2. Harriman and Abel, *Special Envoy*, pp. 310–12.

3. Anderson to Spaatz, Report on Visit to Russia by Mission of USSTAF Officers, May 21, 1944, 9 pp., here 2, in Parton, "The History of 'Frantic,'" sections 42–50; To Colonel Weicker, Subject: Conference with General Grendall, May 13, 1944, 4 pp. in Parton, "The History of 'Frantic,'" sections 66–50; Hansen, *Enfant Terrible*, pp. 363–65; Conversino, *Fighting with the Soviets*, pp. 67–68; Anderson to Spaatz, Report on Visit to Russia by Mission of USSTAF Officers, May 21, 1944, 9 pp., here 3, in Parton, "The History of 'Frantic,'" sections 42–50.

4. Conversino, *Fighting with the Soviets*, pp. 45–46; Deane, *The Strange Alliance*, pp. 110, 115.

5. "Perminov, Aleksandr Romanovich," Tsentr genealogicheskikh issledovanii <http://rosgenea.ru/?a=16&r=4&s=%CF%E5%F0%EC%E8%ED%EE%E2>; Vladimir Savonchik, "14-ia smeshannia aviatsionnaia diviziia" <https://proza.ru/2014/10/01/804>; *Velikaia Otechestvennaia. Komdivy, Voennyi biograficheskii slovar'*, ed. V. P. Goremykin (Moscow, 2014), vol. 2, pp. 561–62.

6. Parton, "The History of 'Frantic,'" p. 10.

7. [Albert Lepawsky], "History of Eastern Command, U.S. Strategic Air Forces in Europe, 1941–1944," Headquarters, USSTAF, 1944, in NARA, N/A RG 334, Box 66, chap. 3, sections 22–23; Conversino, *Fighting with the Soviets*, pp. 44–45.

8. Lieutenant Colonel Sveshnikov to Commissar of State Security Viktor Abakumov, April 30, 1944, SBU Archives, fond 13, no. 1168, "Delo po agenturno-operativnomu obsluzhivaniiu aviabazy Amerikanskikh VVS, proizvodivshikh chelnochnye operatsii i bazirovavshikhsia na aerodromakh SSSR Poltava-Mirgorod-Piriatin," vol. 11, begun 1944, completed 1946, 3 pp.; Lavrentii Beria to Joseph Stalin, May 18, 1944, ibid., 2 pp.

9. [Albert Lepawsky], "History of Eastern Command, U.S. Strategic Air Force in Europe, 1941–1944" chap. 3, sections 15, 22–23, 33.

10. A. Nikitin, "Chelnochnye operatsii," *Voenno-istoricheskii zhurnal*, 1975, no. 11: 41–46, here 43.

11. Deane, *The Strange Alliance*, pp. 115–16; Conversino, *Fighting with the Soviets*, pp. 47–49; Sgt. Joe Lockard, "Yanks in Russia," *Yank, the Army Weekly* 3, no. 38 (March 9, 1945): 8–9.

12. Deane, *The Strange Alliance*, pp. 116–17.

13. Elliott Roosevelt, *As He Saw It* (New York, 1946), pp. 217–18.

14. Viktor Revehuk, *Poltavshchyna v roky Druhoï svitovoï viiny (1939–1945)* (Poltava, 2004), pp. 41–62.

15. G. A. Antipovich et al., *Poltava: kniga dlia turistov*, 2nd ed. (Kharkiv, 1989), pp. 51, 99–100; Revehuk, *Poltavshchyna v roky Druhoï svitovoï viiny*, pp. 242–67; V. S. Gribov, *1944. Aviabaza osobogo naznacheniia. Soiuznicheskaia aktsiia SSSR-SShA* (Moscow, 2003), p. 4.

16. Serhii Plokhy, *The Gates of Europe: A History of Ukraine* (New York, 2015), pp. 73–130; *Poltava 1709: The Battle and the Myth*, ed. Serhii Plokhy (Cambridge, MA, 2012).

17. "Pam'iatnyk slavy," *Poltava istorychna* <http://poltavahistory.inf.ua/hisp_u_9.html>.

18. See the following articles in the *Encyclopedia of Ukraine*, vol. 2 (Toronto, 1989): Pavlo Petrenko, "Kotliarevsky, Ivan"; Dmytro Chyzhevsky and Danylo Husar

Struk, "Gogol, Nikolai"; Roman Senkus, "Korolenko, Vladimir"; Sviatoslav Hordynsky and Vadym Pavlovsky, "Krychevsky, Vasyl H."

19. Plokhy, *The Gates of Europe*, pp. 245–90.

20. Daily Diary, Entry for May 14, 1944, 34 pp., here 10, in Parton, "The History of 'Frantic'"; Serhii Plokhy, "Mapping the Great Famine," in *The Future of the Past: New Perspectives on Ukrainian History* (Cambridge, MA, 2016), pp. 375–40; Revehuk, *Poltavshchyna v roky Druhoï svitovoï viiny*, pp. 41–62.

21. Lockard, "Yanks in Russia."

22. Agent Report, "Pika," May 17, 1944, 3 pp., SBU Archives, fond 13, no. 1168, fols. 168–70.

23. Anderson to Spaatz, Report on Visit to Russia by Mission of USSTAF Officers, May 21, 1944, 9 pp., here 8, in Parton, "The History of 'Frantic,'" sections 42–50; Deane, *The Strange Alliance*, pp. 116–17.

24. Roosevelt, *As He Saw It*, pp. 217–18.

Chapter 5

1. Deane, *The Strange Alliance*, p. 118.

2. Roosevelt, *As He Saw It*, p. 217.

3. Deane, *The Strange Alliance*, p. 118; Donald E. Davis and Eugene P. Trani, *The Reporter Who Knew Too Much: Harrison Salisbury and the New York Times* (Lanham, MD, 2012), chap. 2, "Foreign Correspondent"; Anderson to Spaatz, Report on Visit to Russia by Mission of USSTAF Officers, May 21, 1944, 9 pp., here 2, in Parton, "The History of 'Frantic,'" sections 42–50.

4. Kathleen Harriman to Mary, Moscow, June 4, 1944, 3 pp., here 1, in Library of Congress, Harriman Papers, box 6, folder 9, Correspondence between Kathleen Mortimer and Mary Fisk; Kathleen Harriman to Mary, Moscow, November 9, 1943, 3 pp., here 1.

5. Kathleen Harriman to Mary, Moscow, June 4, 1944, 3 pp., here 1, in Library of Congress, Harriman Papers, box 6, folder 9, Correspondence between Kathleen Mortimer and Mary Fisk.

6. "US Bombers at Soviet Airfields: Operation Titanic" (Operation Frantic) 1944 USAAF <https://www.youtube.com/watch?v=2A8HBB0_O-8>; "Skvoznoi udar. Aviabaza osobogo naznacheniia" (2004) <https://www.youtube.com/watch?v=PMtItXpVglU>.

7. Kathleen Harriman to Mary, Moscow, June 4, 1944, 3 pp., here 1, in Library of Congress, Harriman Papers, box 6, folder 9, Correspondence between Kathleen Mortimer and Mary Fisk; Deane, *The Strange Alliance*, pp. 116–17.

8. Kathleen Harriman to Mary, Moscow, June 4, 1944, 3 pp., here 2, in Library of Congress, Harriman Papers, box 6, folder 9, Correspondence between Kathleen Mortimer and Mary Fisk.

9. Deane, *The Strange Alliance*, p. 118; Kathleen Harriman to Mary, Moscow, June 4, 1944, pp. 2–3, in Library of Congress, Harriman Papers, box 6, folder 9, Correspondence between Kathleen Mortimer and Mary Fisk.

10. Deane, *The Strange Alliance*, pp. 119–20.

11. William N. Hess, *B-17 Flying Fortress: Combat and Development History of the Flying Fortress* (St. Paul, MN, 1994).

12. Raymond Arthur Davies, *Inside Russia Today* (Winnipeg, 1945), p. 55; Deane, *The Strange Alliance*, p. 120.

13. Kathleen Harriman to Mary, Moscow, June 4, 1944, pp. 2–3, in Library of Congress, Harriman Papers, box 6, folder 9, Correspondence between Kathleen Mortimer and Mary Fisk.

14. V. S. Gribov, *1944. Aviabaza osobogo naznacheniia*, p. 31; Petr Lidov, "Letaiushchie kreposti," *Pravda*, June 4, 1944, p. 3.

15. Conversino, *Fighting with the Soviets*, p. 61; Parton, "The History of 'Frantic,'" IV: Operations, Plans, sections 20, 21.

16. Conversino, *Fighting with the Soviets*, pp. 59–60.

17. Parton, "The History of 'Frantic,'" IV: Operations, Plans, sections, 18, 20–21; Conversino, *Fighting with the Soviets*, p. 60; Deane, *The Strange Alliance*, pp. 117–18.

18. Parton, "The History of 'Frantic,'" IV: Operations, Plans, sections 19, 21; Bill Gunston, *North American P-51 Mustang* (New York, 1990).

19. Parton, "The History of 'Frantic,'" IV: Operations, First Shuttle to Russia, section 22.

20. Parton, "The History of 'Frantic,'" IV: Operations, First Shuttle to Russia, sections 22, 23; Conversino, *Fighting with the Russians*, p. 62.

21. Davies, *Inside Russia Today*, p. 57; Deane, *The Strange Alliance*, p. 120; Kathleen Harriman to Mary, Moscow, June 4, 1944, 3 pp., here 3, in Library of Congress, Harriman Papers, box 6, folder 9, Correspondence between Kathleen Mortimer and Mary Fisk.

22. Deane, *The Strange Alliance*, p. 120.

23. Davies, *Inside Russia Today* pp. 56, 58–59.

24. Davies, *Inside Russia Today*, p. 56; Kathleen Harriman to Mary, Moscow, June 4, 1944, p. 3, in Library of Congress, Harriman Papers, box 6, folder 9, Correspondence between Kathleen Mortimer and Mary Fisk; Major Anatolii Zorin, Report on the arrival and departure of US senior officers and dignitaries, June 2, 1944, SBU Archives, fond 13, no. 1168, fol. 21.

25. Deane, *The Strange Alliance*, p. 121.

Chapter 6

1. Roosevelt, *As He Saw It*, p. 219.

2. Antony Beevor, *D-Day: The Battle for Normandy* (New York, 2009), p. 74; Graham Smith, *The Mighty Eighth in the Second World War* (Newbury, UK, 2001); Richard P. Hallion, "D-Day 1944: Air Power over the Normandy Beaches and Beyond," Air Force History and Museums Program 1994 <http://www.ibiblio.org/hyperwar/AAF/AAF-H-DDay/>; "D-Day: June 6th 1944 as it happened. Timeline of the D-Day landings of 6th June 1944 hour by hour as events unfolded on the day," <http://www.telegraph.co.uk/history/world-war-two/10878674/D-Day-6th-June-1944-as-it-happened-live.html>.

3. Deane, *The Strange Alliance*, pp. 150–51.

4. Winston Churchill, "The Invasion of France," June 6, 1944, House of Commons <https://www.winstonchurchill.org/resources/speeches/1941-1945-war-leader/the-invasion-of-france>; Davies, *Inside Russia Today*, p. 60.

5. Lieutenant Colonel Sveshnikov and Major Zorin to Commissar of State Security Abakumov, "Dokladnaia zapiska o reagirovanii amerikanskikh voennosluzh-ashchikh na otkrytie 2-go fronta," June 1944, 3 pp., SBU Archives, fond 13, no. 1168, fols. 42–44; Davies, *Inside Russia Today*, p. 60.

6. Myhra, *Frantic Saga*, p. 35; Davies, *Inside Russia Today*, p. 60.

7. Ibid., pp. 60–61.

8. Conversino, *Fighting with the Soviets*, p. 66; Harriman and Abel, *Special Envoy*, p. 314.

9. Parton, "The History of 'Frantic,'" "Publicity," sections 24–25; Memorandum of Conversation, Present: US Ambassador Averell Harriman, General Eaker, General Deane, Edward Page, V. M. Molotov, Mr. Berezhkov, June 5, 1944, 3 pp., here 2, ibid., sections 84–86; "Eastern Command Narrative of Operations. 2nd Operation (1st from the USSR bases—6 June 1944, 5th wing, 15th Air Force—Galatz, Rumania, Airdrome," 2 pp., ibid., sections 192–93.

10. Message from Spaatz to Walsh for Eaker, June 7, 1944, in Parton, "The History of 'Frantic,'" "Life at the Bases," section 168.

11. Deane, *The Strange Alliance*, p. 121.

12. Myhra, *Frantic Saga*, pp. 56

13. Myhra, *Frantic Saga*, pp. 29–31, 64–66.

14. Ibid., p. 65; Parton, "The History of 'Frantic,'" "Life at the Bases," section 25; Gribov, *Aviabaza osobogo naznacheniia*, pp. 56–60.

15. Daniel Altman, "Franklyn D. Holzman, 83, Economist, Critical of Moscow," *New York Times*, September 7, 2002; Franklyn Holzman to A. Holzman, Ukraine, June 29, 1944.

16. Gribov, *Aviabaza osobogo naznacheniia*, pp. 56, 59.

17. Ibid., pp. 59–60.

18. Ibid., pp. 58–59.

19. Ibid., pp. 52–53.

20. Ibid., pp. 54–55.

21. Memo from Lieutenant Colonel William M. Jackson to Colonel Kessler, Commanding Officer, Eastern Command, June 4, 1944, in Parton, "The History of 'Frantic,'" "Medical."

22. Gribov, *Aviabaza osobogo naznacheniia*, pp. 46–47, 56.

23. Parton, "The History of 'Frantic,'" "Medical," section 16; Captain Robert Newell, "Supplement to Original Sanitary Report," May 18, 1944, ibid.; Conversino, *Fighting with the Soviets*, pp. 72–73.

24. Parton, "The History of 'Frantic,'" "Medical," sections 16–17; Captain Robert H. Newell to Colonel Jackson, May 1, 1944, subject: Sanitary Report of temporary accommodations for some members of Detachment 5 at Poltava, May 1, 1944, ibid., Captain Robert H. Newell, "Initial Sanitary Report," April 28, 1944, 3 pp., ibid.; Conversino, *Fighting with the Soviets*, pp. 74–76.

25. Lockard, "Yanks in Russia."

26. Timothy Snyder, *Bloodlands: Europe between Hitler and Stalin* (New York, 2010), pp. 21–58; Anne Applebaum, *Red Famine: Stalin's War on Ukraine* (New York, 2017).

27. Snyder, *Bloodlands*, pp. 187–76; Timothy Snyder, *Black Earth: The Holocaust as History and Warning* (New York, 2015).

28. Conversino, *Fighting with the Soviets*, pp. 67–68; Lieutenant Colonel Chernetskii, head of the Poltava oblast Department of the Ministry of State Security to Sergei Savchenko, People's Commissar of State Security of the Ukrainian SSR, "Dokladnaia zapiska po anglo-amerikantsam," June 30, 1944, 10 pp., SBU Archives, fond 13, no. 1201, "K liternomu delu na Aviabazu VVS SShA s materialami po sviaziam amerikanskikh voennosluzhashchikh, nachato 25 aprelia 1944, okoncheno 30 avgusta 1952, na 293 listakh," fols. 52–57.

29. Parton, "The History of 'Frantic,'" "Return to Italy," sections 26–27; "Excerpt-MASAF Intops Summary no. 235, June 11. Focsani North Airdrome Installations—5 Wing," 4 pp., ibid., sections 201–204.

30. Message from Arnold to Deane for Harriman, June 14, 1944, in Parton, "The History of 'Frantic,'" section 220.

Chapter 7

1. Lieutenant Colonel Sveshnikov, "Kharakteristika voennosluzhashchikh amerikanskikh VVS v g. Poltava. Sostavlena na osnovanii agenturnykh materialov, poluchennykh s 1 maia po 10 iiunia 1944 g." June 14, 1944, 12 pp., here 6, SBU Archives, fond 13, no. 1168; Chernetskii to Savchenko, "Dokladnaia zapiska po anglo-amerikantsam," June 30, 1944, 10 pp., here 1–2, SBU Archives, fond 13, no. 1190, "Pervichnye agenturnye materialy na sviazi amerikantsev," vol. 7, begun January 20, 1945, completed December 30, 1951, fols. 52–53.

2. Gribov, *Aviabaza osobogo naznacheniia*, pp. 36, 52.

3. "Sveshnikov, Konstantin Alekseevich," in Nikita Petrov, *Kto rukovodil organami gosbezopasnosti: 1941–1954* (Moscow, 2010), p. 774.

4. Sveshnikov to Abakumov, April 30, 1944, SBU Archives, fond 13, no. 1168, fols. 28–30; Sveshnikov to Colonel Novikov, deputy head of the First Department of the Main Counterintelligence Directorate, People's Commissariat of Defense, SMERSH, May 8, 1944, ibid., fols. 36–37; "Zorin Anatolii Vladimirovich" <https://pamyat-naroda.ru/heroes/podvig-chelovek_nagrazhdenie46495496/>.

5. Lieutenant Colonel Sveshnikov and Major Zorin to Abakumov, "Dokladnaia zapiska ob agenturno-operativnom obsluzhivanii Amerikanskikh VVS v g. Poltava," May 25, 1944, 10 pp., SBU Archives, fond 13, no. 1168, fols. 1–10, here 7.

6. "Dokladnaia zapiska ob agenturno-operativnom obsluzhivanii Amerikanskikh VVS v g. Poltava," May 25, 1944, fols. 1–10, SBU Archives, fond 13, no. 1168; Major Zorin to Colonel Novikov, May 24, 1944, 1 p., ibid., fol. 19.

7. Sveshnikov and Zorin to Abakumov, "Dokladnaia zapiska ob agenturno-operativnom obsluzhivanii Amerikanskikh VVS v g. Poltava," May 25, 1944, fols. 1–2, SBU Archives, fond 13, no. 1168, fols. 1–10.

8. Major Derevenchuk, Agent Note, April 12, 1944, SBU Archives, fond 13, no. 1168, fol. 27; Head of the 1st department, Colonel Reshetnikov, and head of the 1st

division of the 1st department of the Poltava Ministry of Internal Affairs [MVD] Directorate, Lieutenant Colonel Meshcheriakov to Lieutenant Colonel Kovalkov, head of the Ministry of State Security [OKR MGB] department of Kazan garrison, January 29, 1953, SBU Archives, fond 13, no. 1179, "Perepiska po aviabaze serii K i OK po VVS SShA na 1953 god," fols. 12.

9. Lieutenant Colonel Sveshnikov to Colonel Novikov, June 1944, SBU Archives, fond 13, no. 1168, f. 70; Colonel Polkovnikov, head of the SMERSH department attached to Long-Range Aviation units, to Major General Gorgonov, Head, 1st department of the Main Directorate of SMERSH, People's Commissariat of Defense, July 18, 1944, 2 pp., ibid., fols. 76-77.

10. Lieutenant Colonel Sveshnikov, "Kharakteristika voennosluzhashchikh amerikan-skikh VVS v g. Poltava. Sostavlena na osnovanii agenturnykh materialov, poluchen-nykh s 1 maia po 10 iiunia 1944 g." June 14, 1944, 12 pp., SBU Archives, fond 13, no. 1168, fols. 58-69.

11. Lieutenant Colonel Sveshnikov to Lieutenant General Babich, Deputy Head of the Main Counterintelligence Directorate [SMERSH] of the People's Commissariat of Defense, May 25, 1944, SBU Archives, fond 13, no. 1168, fols. 23, 23ᵛ; Albert Lepawsky, Political Science: Berkeley, California Digital Library <http://texts.cdlib.org/view?docId=hb7c6007sj;NAAN=13030&doc.view=frames&chunk.id=div00034&toc.depth=1&toc.id=&brand=calisphere>.

12. Conversino, *Fighting with the Soviets*, p. 32.

13. Lieutenant Colonel Sveshnikov to Lieutenant General Babich, Deputy Head of the Main Counterintelligence Directorate [SMERSH] of the People's Commissariat of Defense, May 25, 1944, SBU Archives, fond 13, no. 1168, fol. 23; Major Samarin, head of a special group of the 9th department, 2nd directorate of the People's Commissariat of State Security of the USSR, "Agenturnaia zapiska po delu amerikanskogo poddan-nogo, Lipavskii, prozh. v tochke 'N' no. 114 za 14 aprelia 1944 g.," April 19, 1944, 1 p., SBU Archives, fond 13, no. 1171, fol.49; "Zvavich, Isaak Semenovich," *Sovetskaia is-toricheskaia èntsiklopediia*, 16 vols. (Moscow, 1973-1985), vol. 5, s.v.

14. Lieutenant Colonel Sveshnikov to Abakumov, September 25, 1944, 14 pp., SBU Archives, fond 13, no. 1168, fols. 260-73, here 271.

15. Lieutenant Colonel Sveshnikov to General Lieutenant Babich, May 25, 1944, SBU Archives, fond 13, no. 1168, fols. 23-23ᵛ; Lieutenant Colonel Sveshnikov to Colonel Novikov, Deputy Head of the First Department, Main Counterintelligence Directorate of the People's Commissariat of Defense, SMERSH, June 1944, SBU Archives, fond 13, no. 1168, fol. 67.

16 Agent Report, "Maia," March 1944, 1 p., SBU Archives, fond 13, no. 1171, fol. 72; Major Samarin, head, special group of the 9th department, 2nd directorate of the People's Commissariat of State Security of the USSR, "Agenturnaia zapiska po delu amerikanskikh poddannykh, prozhivaiushchikh v tochke "N," Dzhekson v 335, i Sigerd v no. 302," April 4, 1944, 1 p., ibid., fol. 73; Major Samarin, "Agenturnaia zapiska po delu amerikanskikh poddannykh, Dzhekson 335, Vagner i Tlik, no. 218, tochka "N,' " April 13, 1944, 1 p., ibid., fol. 71.

17. Agent Report, "Mikhailova," August 1, 1945, 2 pp., here 1, SBU Archives, fond 13, no. 1171, fols. 68-68ᵛ, here 68; Agent Report, "Soiuznik," July 1944, 1 p., ibid., fol. 59; Agent Report, "Roza," July 1944, 1 p., ibid., fol. 59.

18. Lieutenant Colonel Sveshnikov to Colonel Novikov, June 14, 1944, pp. 10–11, SBU Archives, fond 13, no. 1168, fols. 67–68; Colonel Chernetskii, head of the Poltava Directorate, People's Commissariat of State Security, to Sergei Savchenko, People's Commissar of State Security of Ukraine, "Dokladnaia zapiska po anglo-amerikantsam," June 30, 1944, 10 pp., here 6, SBU Archives, fond 13, no. 1190, fols. 52–57.

Chapter 8

1. Colonel Archie J. Old Jr., "Report on Shuttle Mission to Russia," July 6, 1944, 6 pp., here 3, Air Force Historical Research Agency, Maxwell Air Force Base (AFHRA), 5201–1, vol. II, pt. I, reel B5121.
2. "Major General Robert L. Walsh," *U.S. Air Force* <https://www.af.mil/About-Us/Biographies/Display/Article/105289/major-general-robert-l-walsh>; Conversino, *Fighting with the Soviets*, p. 51.
3. "Archie J. Old, Jr.," *Washington Post*, March 30, 1984, B–16; "Lieutenant General Archie J. Old, Jr.," US Air Force <https://www.af.mil/About-Us/Biographies/Display/Article/106026/lieutenant-general-archie-j-old-jr/>.
4. Old, "Report on Shuttle Mission to Russia," July 6, 1944, pp. 1–3; Conversino, *Fighting with the Soviets*, pp. 84–85; *Marvin S. Bowman*, "Stopping Over at Ivan's Airdrome," *Air Force Magazine*, April 1972, 51–55; Major Marvin S. Bowman Diary as compiled by Paul West, 100th Bomb Group Foundation, p. 6 <https://100thbg.com/index.php?option=com_content&view=article&layout=edit&id=140>; Deane, *The Strange Alliance*, p. 151; Philip K. Scheurer, "Anatole Litvak—A Movie Career on Two Continents," *Los Angeles Times*, February 19, 1967.
5. Old, "Report on Shuttle Mission to Russia," July 6, 1944, pp. 1–3 [50–52]; *Operatsiia "Frantik." Z istorii boiovoï spivdruzhnosti viis'kovo-povitrianykh syl SSSR i SShA, tsyvil'noho naselennia Ukraïny v roky Druhoï Svitovoï viiny. Zbirnyk dokumentiv i materialiv* (Kyiv, 1998), pp. 118–20, here 119.
6. Old, "Report on Shuttle Mission to Russia," July 6, 1944, p. 3 [52]; Interview, Brigadier General Alfred A. Kessler, July 5, 1944, 7 pp., here 3, AFHRA, 5201–1, vol. II, part I, reel B5121; *Bowman*, "Stopping Over at Ivan's Airdrome"; Glenn B. Infield, *The Poltava Affair: A Russian Warning: An American Tragedy: A Minute-by-Minute Account of the Secret World War II Operation That Foreshadowed the Cold War* (New York, 1973), pp. 143–44.
7. Conversino, *Fighting with the Soviets*, p. 88.
8. Infield, *The Poltava Affair*, pp. 113–14, 125.
9. Ibid., pp. 140–42; Vladimir Brovko, "Operatsiia 'Frentik,' ili amerikanskii Perl-Kharbor v Ukraine," pt. 4, in *Narodna pravda* <http://narodna.pravda.com.ua/history/4f1f1cad6ddb1/view_print/>.
10. Brovko, "Operatsiia 'Frentik,' " pt. 4; Infield, *The Poltava Affair*, pp. 142–43, 155.
11. Leonid Liubimskii, "Poltavskaia bitva protiv Gitlera," *Voenno-promyshlennyi kur'er*, no 17, May 3, 2006 <http://vpk-news.ru/articles/3172>.
12. Brovko, "Operatsiia 'Frentik,' " pt. 3.
13. Conversino, *Fighting with the Soviets*, pp. 86–87; General Kessler to Headquarters, Eastern Command USSTAF, June 25, 1944, 4 pp., here 1, in AFHRA, 5201–1, vol. II, pt. I, reel B5121.

14. Robert H. Hewell, "Analysis of Cases Requiring Treatment," July 17, 1944, 3 pp., here 2, in AFHRA, 5201-1, vol. II, pt. I, reel B5121; Joseph G. Lukacek <https://www.findagrave.com/cgi-bin/fg.cgi?page=gr&GSln=Lukacek&GSiman=1&GSob=c&GRid=2519832&>; Joseph G. Lukacek (119-1944) <https://www.ancientfaces.com/person/joseph-g-lukacek/123744280>; Lieut. Raymond C. "Ray" Estle <https://www.findagrave.com/cgi-bin/fg.cgi?page=gr&GRid=630544>.

15. Lieutenant Colonel William Jackson to The Surgeon, USSTAF, June 25, 1944, "Observation of Medical Services during Air Attack," 4 pp., here 2, in AFHRA, 5201-1, vol. II, pt. I, reel B5121; Lieutenant Colonel William Jackson, Case History of: 1st Lt. R. C. Estle, June 23, 1944, ibid., 1 p.

16. Lieutenant Colonel William Jackson, "Report of Activity of Two Russian Soldiers during Emergency of June 22," June 24, 1944, 1 p., in AFHRA, 5201-1, vol. II, pt. I, reel B5121.

17. P. A. Tupitsyn, Letter to the US Embassy in Ukraine [before June 1994], in Operatsiia "Frantik," pp. 260-66, here 265.

18. Colonel Archie J. Old Jr., "Report on Shuttle Mission to Russia," July 6, 1944, 6 pp., here 4, in AFHRA, 5201-1, vol. II, pt. I, reel B5121.

19. General Kessler to Headquarters, Eastern Command USSTAF, June 25, 1944, 4 pp., here 4, in AFHRA, 5201-1, vol. II, pt. I, reel B512; Colonel Novikov, "Spravka," June 22, 1944, SBU Archives, fond 13, no. 1168, fols. 104-5.

20. Petr Lidov, "Tania (pervyi ocherk o Zoe Kosmodemianskoi," Ot Sovetskogo informbiuro, 1941-1945 <http://bibliotekar.ru/informburo/27.htm>; "Zoia Kosmodemianskaia: chto bylo na samom dele?" Russkaia semerka <http://russian7.ru/post/zoya-kosmodemyanskaya-chto-bylo-na-samom/>.

21. S. S. Shkol'nikov, V ob"ektive—voina (Moscow, 1979), pp. 100-102; cf. Operatsiia "Frantik," pp. 244-45.

22. Captain Sherochenkov, Interrogation of Spassky Aleksei Mikhailovich, June 24, 1944, 3 pp., SBU Archives, fond 13, no. 1168, fols. 110-12; Valentin Kotov, "Petr Lidov. Sud'ba korrespondenta," Kommunisty stolitsy, January 27, 2012 <http://comstol.info/2012/01/obshhestvo/3085'>; Oleksandr Dunaievs'kyi, "Vin z namy nazavzhdy: do 70-richchia dnia narodzhennia P. O. Lidova," Prapor, 1976, no. 11: 82-85.

23. Lieutenant Colonel Baranov, "Spravka," June 22, 1944, SBU Archives, fond 13, no. 1168, fol. 103; cf. Operatsiia "Frantik," p. 124.

24. Colonel Novikov, "Spravka," June 22, 1944, SBU Archives, fond 13, no. 1168, fols. 104-5; Liubimskii, "Poltavskaia bitva protiv Gitlera"; Conversino, Fighting with the Soviets, pp. 85-86, 90.

25. Major Marvin S. Bowman Diary as compiled by Paul West, 100th Bomb Group Foundation, p. 6 <https://100thbg.com/index.php?option=com_content&view=article&layout=edit&id=140>.

26. Susan Heller Anderson, "Midred Gillars, 87, of Nazi Radio, Axis Sally to an Allied Audience," New York Times, July 2, 1988.

27. Myhra, Frantic Saga, pp. 39, 42-43, 49-50.

28. Colonel Sveshnikov to Abakumov, "Dokladnaia zapiska," July 16, 1944, 11 pp., SBU Archives, fond 13, no. 1168, fols. 171-82.

29. Ibid.; Conversino, *Fighting with the Soviets*, pp. 93–94.
30. Conversino, *Fighting with the Soviets*, p. 94; Report of Proceedings of Board of Officers, August 2, 1944, 5 pp., here 5, in AFHRA, 5201–1, vol. II, pt. I, reel B5121.
31. Deane, *The Strange Alliance*, pp. 121–22; Conversino, *Fighting with the Soviets*, p. 91.

Chapter 9
1. Howard Whitman, "Nude Welcome to Russia Shocks U.S. Bomber Pilots," *The Daily News*, July 19, 1944; "Howard Whitman of NBC-TV Series," *New York Times*, January 31, 1975.
2. Howard Whitman, "See Russia and Blush, Verdict of U.S. Flyers," *Chicago Daily Tribune*, July 19, 1944, p. 1.
3. Myhra, *Frantic Saga*, pp. 62–63; Franklyn Holzman to A. Holzman, June 29 and June 30, 1944; Igor' Kon, "Byl li seks na Sviatoi Rusi," *Russkii Globus*, no. 2 (February 2005) <https://www.russian-globe.com/N36/Kon.BulLiSexNaSvyatoyRusi.htm>.
4. Conversino, *Fighting with the Soviets*, p. 101.
5. Lieutenant Colonel Sveshnikov to Abakumov, September 25, 1944, 14 pp., here 12, SBU Archives, fond 13, no. 1168, fols. 260–73, here 271.
6. Albert Lepawsky to Commanding General, Eastern Command USSTAF (Through Deputy Commander for Administration), July 10, 1944, 3 pp., in AFHRA, 5201–1, vol. II, pt. I, reel B5121; Conversino, *Fighting with the Soviets*, pp. 96–97.
7. Colonel Chernetskii to Sergei Savchenko, "Dokladnaia zapiska po anglo-amerikantsam," June 30, 1944, 10 pp., here 6 [1187], SBU Archives, fond 13, no. 1190, fols. 52–57.
8. Albert Lepawsky to Commanding General, Eastern Command USSTAF (Through Deputy Commander for Administration), July 10, 1944, 3 pp., in AFHRA, 5201–1, vol. II, pt. I, reel B5121; Conversino, *Fighting with the Soviets*, p. 97.
9. [Albert Lepawsky], "History of Eastern Command, U.S. Strategic Airforce in Europe, 1941–1944," Headquarters USSTAF, 1944, chap. V, "Recreation and Conflict," subsection "Dates and Fights," pp. 132–34, in AFHRA, 5201–1, vol. II, pt. I, reel B5121.
10. Ibid., chap. V, p. 147.
11. Myhra, *Frantic Saga*, p. 47; [Albert Lepawsky], "History of Eastern Command, U.S. Strategic Airforce in Europe, 1941–1944," chap. V, pp. 132–33.
12. [Lepawsky], "History of Eastern Command, U.S. Strategic Airforce in Europe, 1941–1944," chap. V, p. 137.
13. Ibid., chap. V, p. 138.
14. Oleg Budnitskii, "Muzhchiny i zhenshchiny v Krasnoi Armii (1941–1945)," *Cahiers du monde russe* 52, nos. 2–3 (2011): 405–22; Anna Krylova, *Soviet Women in Combat: A History of Violence on the Eastern Front* (New York, 2011).
15. [Lepawsky], "History of Eastern Command, U.S. Strategic Airforce in Europe, 1941–1944," chap. V, p. 144; Conversino, *Fighting with the Soviets*, p. 98.
16. Niall Barr, *Yanks and Limeys: Alliance Warfare in the Second World War* (London, 2016), pp. 336–37.

17. Barr, *Yanks and Limeys*, pp. 337–38; Lynne Olson, *Citizens of London: The Americans Who Stood with Britain in Its Darkest, Finest Hour* (New York, 2010), pp. 239–47.

18. Mary Louise Roberts, *What Soldiers Do: Sex and the American GI in World War II France* (Chicago and London, 2013), p. 70; Duncan Barrett and Nuala Calvi, *GI Brides: The Wartime Girls Who Crossed the Atlantic for Love* (New York, 2014).

19. Roberts, *What Soldiers Do*, pp. 113–21, 131–32.

20. [Lepawsky], "History of Eastern Command, U.S. Strategic Airforce in Europe, 1941–1944," chap. V, p. 132.

21. Raymond Arthur Davies, *Inside Russia Today* (Winnipeg, 1945), p. 56.

22. Agent Report, "Iava," June 5, 1944, SBU Archives, fond 13, no. 1171, "Materialy byvshikh voennosluzhashchikh amerikanskoi aviabazy v g. Poltave, vol. 4. Nachato 6 iiunia 1944, zakoncheno 10 ianvaria 1952 g.," fols. 128–29, here 128; "Spravka na ofitsial'nogo sotrudnika amerikanskoi razvedki Zharova Al'berta M.," 2 pp., SBU Archives, fond 13, no. 1169; "Kontrol'no-nabliudatelnoe delo po Aviabaze Amerikanskikh VVS, proizvodivshikh chelnochnye operatsii i bazirovavshikhsia na aėrodromakh SSSR Poltava-Mirgorod-Piriatin," vol. 2, "Nachato: aprel' 1944, Okoncheno: sentiabr' 1950, v 3-kh tomakh," fols. 654–55, here 654.

23. "Spravka na ofitsial'nogo sotrudnika amerikanskoi razvedki Zharova Al'berta M.," SBU Archives, fond 13, no. 1169, fols. 654–55; Lieutenant Colonel Sveshnikov and Major Zorin to Abakumov, "Dokladnaia zapiska ob agenturno-operativnom obsluzhivanii Amerikanskikh VVS v g. Poltava," May 25, 1944, 10 pp., SBU Archives, fond 13, no. 1168, fols. 1–10, here 2–3.

24. Conversino, *Fighting with the Soviets*, p. 124; Lieutenant Colonel Sveshnikov to Abakumov, September 1944, 14 pp., here 4–6, SBU Archives, fond 13, no. 1168, fols. 263–65.

25. Colonel Gorbachev, Memo on Yekaterina Stankevich, August 8, 1949, 2 pp., SBU Archives, fond 13, no. 1169, fols. 693–693^v.

26. Lieutenant Colonel Sveshnikov, Memorandum, 4 pp., SBU Archives, fond 13, no. 1168, fols. 202–5.

27. General Perminov to General Shibanov, July 26, 1944, copy, 3 pp., SBU Archives, fond 13, no. 1168, fols. 200–201.

28. Lieutenant Colonel Sveshnikov, Memorandum, 4 pp., SBU Archives, fond 13, no. 1168, fols. 202–5; Colonel Chernetskii to the head of the 2nd directorate, People's Commissariat of State Security of the USSR Fedotov, February 7, 1945, SBU Archives, fond 13, no. 1201, fol. 145.

Chapter 10

1. Conversino, *Fighting with the Soviets*, pp. 113–16, 221–22.

2. Gerd Niepold, *Battle for White Russia: The Destruction of Army Group Centre June 1944* (London, 1987); Steven J. Zaloga, *Bagration 1944: The Destruction of Army Group Center* (Westport, CT, 2004).

3. Conversino, *Fighting with the Soviets*, pp. 117–19.

4. Ibid., pp. 111–12.

5. Ibid., pp. 121–23; [Lepawsky], "History of Eastern Command, U.S. Strategic Airforce in Europe, 1941–1944," Headquarters USSTAF, 1944, chap. V, section: "Recreation and Conflict," subsection: "Restaurants and Vodka," p. 125.

6. Agent Report, "Iava," June 5, 1944, 3 pp., SBU Archives, fond 13, no. 1171, fols. 128–29, here 128^v; [Lepawsky], "History of Eastern Command," chap. V, p. 124.

7. [Lepawsky], "History of Eastern Command," chap. V, p. 124.

8. Colonel Novikov, "Spravka," August 5, 1944, 2 pp., SBU Archives, fond 13, no. 1168, fols. 208–9.

9. Conversino, *Fighting with the Soviets*, pp. 106–8.

10. Franklyn Holzman BBC interview, 1995; Franklyn Holzman to A. Holzman, October 4, 1944.

11. Sveshnikov to Abakumov, "Otchet," July 31, 1944, 1 p., SBU Archives, fond 13, no. 1168, fol. 206; General Perminov, Order no. 45, July 26, 1944, 5 pp., SBU Archives, fond 13, no. 1168, fols. 233–35.

12. Captain Komkov, Captain Shirochenkov, Senior Lieutenant Abramov, Lieutenant Kuchinskii, "Akt," September 13, 1944, SBU Archives, fond 13, no. 1168, f. 274 [1103]; Kuchinskii, "Ob'iasnenie," September 14, 1944, ibid., fols. 275–76; Captain Shirochenkov, Interrogation of Lieutenant Kuchinskii, September 14, 1944, 4 pp., ibid., fols. 277–78^v; "Vypiska is protokola zasedaniia partiinogo biuro 42 BAO," September 14, 1944, 1 p., ibid., fol. 279; [Lepawsky], "History of Eastern Command," chap. V, p. 126.

13. Franklyn Holzman BBC interview, 1995; "Agenturnoe donesenie, Istochnik 'Mikhailova,' Prinial Markelov," August 1, 1945, 2 pp., SBU Archives, fond 13, no. 1171, fols. 68–68^v, here 68; Captain Kheisin to Colonel Tsurin, "Politdonesenie," September 5, 1944, 1 p., SBU Archives, fond 13, no. 1200, "K liternomu delu na aviabazu VVS SShA, chast' 2," f. 280.

14. Conversino, *Fighting with the Soviets*, p. 112.

15. Sveshnikov to Abakumov, September 18, 1944, 6 pp., here 2, SBU Archives, fond 13, no. 1168, fols. 302–3.

16. Ibid., fol. 302.

17. Sveshnikov, "Spravka," 1 p., SBU Archives, fond 13, no. 1171, fol. 126; Agent Report, "Konstantinov," 2 pp. ibid., fol. 133; Agent Report, "Avtomat," ibid., fol. 135; Lieutenant Kal'nitskii, "Spravka o byvshei aviabaze VVS SShA," January 23, 1954, 8 pp., SBU Archives, fond 13, no. 1169, fol. 702; Captain Ivanov, "Spravka," 2 pp., June 25, 1944, 2 pp., SBU Archives, fond 13, no. 1172, "Delo s materialalmi b[yvshikh] voennosluzhashchikh amerikanskoi aviabazy v g. Piriatin i Mirgorod. Nachato: 10 iiulia 1944, Zakoncheno: 30 ianvaria 1952, na 447 listakh," f. 349 G. S. Kurganov and P. M. Kurennov, *Tainy russkoi revoliutsii i budushchee Rossii* (Ingelwood, CA, 1950), chapter 22: "Vtoraia kniga posle Biblii."; L. A. Kutilova, I. V. Naum, M. I. Naumova, and V. A. Safonov, *Natsional'mye menshinstva Tomskoi gubernii. Khronika obshchestvennoi i kul'turnoi zhizni, 1885–1919* (Tomsk, 1999), p. 144.

18. Agent Report, "Avtomat," SBU Archives, fond 13, no. 1171, fol. 135; Agent Report, "Liliia," August 3, 1944, SBU Archives, fond 13, no. 1171, fols. 139–40; Agent Report, "Markov," ibid., fol. 143; Tony Reverditto's eulogy of Igor Reverditto, posted March 13, 2015, on the "Memory of Igor Reverditto" Facebook page, February 27, 2015, <https://www.facebook.com/groups/647340528728078/permalink/647348445393953/>.

19. Sveshnikov to Abakumov, September 18, 1944, 6 pp., here 2, SBU Archives, fond 13, no. 1168, fols. 301–302.

20. Conversino, *Fighting with the Soviets*, pp. 140–41.

21. Ibid., p. 141; [Lepawsky], "History of Eastern Command," chap. V, p. 125 [789]; Brigadier General Alfred Kessler, Letter of Recommendation for Igor Reverditto, September 15, 1944, posted by Trevor Reverditto on "Memory of Igor Reverditto" Facebook page, February 27, 2015, https://www.facebook.com/groups/64734 0528728078/permalink/647348445393953/.
22. Conversino, *Fighting with the Soviets*, pp. 139–40.

Chapter 11

1. Lockard, "Yanks in Russia," pp. 8–9.
2. Kathy Harriman to Mary, August 30, 1944, Library of Congress, Harriman Papers, box 6, folder 9, Correspondence between Kathleen Mortimer and Mary Fisk.
3. Norman Davies, *Rising '44: The Battle for Warsaw* (London, 2008).
4. Ibid., pp. 151–53; Plokhy, *Yalta: The Price of Peace* (New York, 2010), pp. 158–61, 172–73.
5. Harriman and Abel, *Special Envoy*, pp. 333–34; Stalin to Roosevelt, August 9, 1944, in *Correspondence between the Chairman of the Council of Ministers of the USSR and the Presidents of the USA and the Prime Ministers of Great Britain during the Great Patriotic War of 1941–1945. Correspondence with Franklin D. Roosevelt and Harry S. Truman (August 1941–December 1945)* (Moscow, 1957), pp. 151–55, nos. 214, 217–19.
6. *Correspondence between the Chairman of the Council of Ministers of the USSR and the Presidents of the USA and the Prime Ministers of Great Britain during the Great Patriotic War of 1941–1945. Correspondence with Winston S. Churchill and Clement R. Attlee, 1944* (Moscow, 1957), nos. 312, 313, 317.
7. Harriman to Molotov, August 14, 1944, Records of the U.S. Military Mission to Moscow 1943–45, NARA, RG 334, Subject Files, October 1943-October 1945, Box 22, file "Poland," 2 pp.; Harriman, Conversation, Subject: Dropping of Military Supplies on Warsaw, Moscow, August 15, 1944, Records of the U.S. Military Mission to Moscow 1943–45, NARA, RG 334, Subject Files, October 1943– October 1945, Box 22, file "Poland," 5 pp.
8. Harriman, Conversation, Subject: Dropping of Military Supplies on Warsaw, Moscow, August 15, 1944, Records of the U.S. Military Mission to Moscow 1943–45, NARA, RG 334, Subject Files, October 1943-October 1945, Box 22, file "Poland," 5 pp.
9. Deane to Walsh and Spaatz, August 15, 1944, Records of the U.S. Military Mission to Moscow 1943–45, NARA, RG 334, Subject Files, October 1943–October 1945, Box 22, file "Poland," 1 p.; Harriman to Vyshinsky, August 16, 1944, ibid., 1 p.; Harriman, Conversation. Subject: Dropping of Military Supplies on Warsaw, August 16, 1944, ibid., 2 pp.; Vyshinsky to Harriman, August 17, 1944, ibid., 1 p.
10. *Correspondence between the Chairman of the Council of Ministers of the USSR and the Presidents of the USA and the Prime Ministers of Great Britain during the Great Patriotic War of 1941–1945. Correspondence with Winston S. Churchill and Clement R. Attlee, 1944*, no. 321; Harriman, Conversation. Subject: "Frantic" bases and "Exploration," August 17, 1944, Records of the U.S. Military Mission to Moscow 1943–45, NARA, RG 334, Subject Files, October 1943–October 1945, Box 22, file "Poland," 2 pp.

11. Conversino, *Fighting with the Soviets*, pp. 119–20; Davies, *Rising'44*, pp. 301, 719; Harriman and Abel, *Special Envoy*, p. 342; Roosevelt and Churchill to Stalin, August 20, 1944, in *Correspondence between the Chairman of the Council of Ministers of the USSR and the Presidents of the USA and the Prime Ministers of Great Britain during the Great Patriotic War of 1941–1945. Correspondence with Franklin D. Roosevelt and Harry S. Truman (August 1941–December 1945)*, p. 156, no. 220; Stalin to Roosevelt and Churchill, ibid., p. 157, no. 223; Allied Support for Warsaw: Roosevelt-Churchill-Stalin Communications. Selected Documents <http://www.warsawuprising.com/doc/Roosevelt_Churchill_Stalin.htm>; Churchill, *The Second World War*, vol. 6, *Triumph and Tragedy* (Boston, 1953), pp. 1233–34.

12. Conversino, *Fighting with the Soviets*, pp. 119–20; Davies, *Rising'44*, pp. 301, 719; Harriman to Hull, August 22, 1944, *FRUS, Diplomatic Papers: Europe*, vol. 4, pp. 901–902; Harriman and Abel, *Special Envoy*, p. 344.

13. Davies, *Rising'44*, pp. 350–58; Conversino, *Fighting with the Soviets*, pp. 146–47.

14. Conversino, *Fighting with the Soviets*, p. 144.

15. Ibid., pp. 143–45.

16. Ibid., pp. 137, 247.

17. "Message of the Soviet Government in Reply to the Message of the British Government of 5th September 1944," Moscow, September 9, 1944, 2 pp., in Records of the U.S. Military Mission to Moscow 1943–45, NARA, RG 334, Subject Files, October 1943–October 1945, Box 22, file "Poland," p. 1; General Marshall to Deane, Subject: Polish patriots in Warsaw, September 12, 1944, ibid., p. 1; Deane and Lieutenant General Montague Brocas Burrows, Head of the British Military Mission, to Army General Antonov, September 14, 1944, 1 p., ibid., p. 1.

18. General Eisenhower to Chiefs of Staff, September 12, 1944, 1 p., in Records of the U.S. Military Mission to Moscow 1943–45, NARA, RG 334, Subject Files, October 1943–October 1945, Box 22, file "Poland" ; General Walsh to General Deane, September 13, 1944, ibid., p.1; Memorandum of Conversation, Present: Harriman, Deane, Archibald Clark-Kerr, Molotov, Pavlov, evening of September 12–13, 1944, ibid., p. 1; General Deane to Rear Admiral Archer, Acting Head, British Military Mission, September 13, 1944, ibid., 2 pp.

19. Conversino, *Fighting with the Soviets*, p. 146.

20. Ibid., pp. 148–51, 156; General Spaatz to General Arnold, info for Deane, Subject: Supplies to Insurgents, September 22, 1944, p. 1, in Records of the U.S. Military Mission to Moscow 1943–45, NARA, RG 334, Subject Files, October 1943–October 1945, Box 22, file "Poland"; Deane to Colonel Makarov, Red Army General Staff, September 21, 1944, ibid., p. 1.

21. Conversino, *Fighting with the Soviets*, p. 157; General Spaatz for General Doolittle, Subject: Partisan Situation in Warsaw, September 30, 1944, Records of the U.S. Military Mission to Moscow 1943–45, p. 1, NARA, RG 334, Subject Files, October 1943–October 1945, Box 22, file "Poland" ; Deane to Colonel Makarov, October 2, 1944, ibid., p. 1.

22. Harriman and Abel, *Special Envoy*, pp. 348–49; Warsaw Uprising 1944, Project in-Posterum <http://www.warsawuprising.com/faq.htm>.

Chapter 12

1. Myhra, *Frantic Saga*, pp. 82–85.
2. Lieutenant Colonel Sveshnikov and Captain Belykh to Abakumov, "Dokladnaia zapiska o vyezde voennosluzhashchikh amerikanskikh VVS iz SSSR," October 28, 1944, 4 pp., SBU Archives, fond 13, no. 1168, fols. 319–22; William Kaluta, "History of Eastern Command, US Strategic Air Forces in Europe, October 1, 1944–March 31, 1945," chap. 1: Background, p. 4, in NARA, RG 334; United States Military Mission to Moscow, Operation "Frantic," October 1943–October 1945, Box 66: Engineer to Intelligence.
3. Kaluta, "History of Eastern Command, US Strategic Air Forces in Europe, October 1, 1944–March 31, 1945," chap. I, p. 3.
4. Conversino, *Fighting with the Soviets*, p. 120.
5. Kaluta, "History of Eastern Command, US Strategic Air Forces in Europe, October 1, 1944–March 31, 1945," chap. I, p. 4; Conversino, *Fighting with the Soviets*, p. 161.
6. Lieutenant Colonel Sveshnikov to Abakumov, "Dokladnaia zapiska o sokrashchenii amerikanskikh voenno-vozdushnykh baz na territorii SSSR," December 2, 1944, 11 pp., SBU Archives, fond 13, no. 1168, fols. 328–38; Kaluta, "History of Eastern Command, US Strategic Air Forces in Europe, October 1, 1944–March 31, 1945," chap. IV: Personnel Administration and Organization, p. 2.
7. General Major Novikov, Deputy head, 1st department, SMERSH main directorate, "Spravka po 169-i aviatsionnoi baze osobogo naznacheniia voenno-vozdushnykh sil Krasnoi Armii," 2 pp., SBU Archives, fond 13, no. 1168, fols. 310–11; Lieutenant Colonel Sveshnikov to Abakumov, "Dokladnaia zapiska o sokrashchenii amerikanskikh voenno-vozdushnykh baz na territorii SSSR," December 2, 1944, 11 pp., SBU Archives, fond 13, no. 1168, fols. 328–38, here 329–30.
8. Kaluta, "History of Eastern Command, US Strategic Air Forces in Europe, October 1, 1944–March 31, 1945," chap. I, p. 5; Conversino, *Fighting with the Soviets*, p. 162.
9. "Colonel Thomas Hampton," Wings of War Webseum <https://militariawingswwii.wordpress.com/2012/03/29/new-lot-just-in-1930s-through-wwii-beyond-col-thomas-k-hampton/>; Lieutenant Colonel Sveshnikov to Abakumov, "Dokladnaia zapiska o sokrashchenii amerikanskikh voenno-vozdushnykh baz na territorii SSSR," December 2, 1944, 11 pp., SBU Archives, fond 13, no. 1168, fols. 328–38; Kaluta, "History of Eastern Command, US Strategic Air Forces in Europe, October 1, 1944–March 31, 1945," chap. V: Personnel Relations, p. 1; chap. IV, p. 1.
10. George Uri Fischer, *Insatiable: A Story of My Nine Lives* (Philadelphia, 2000), p. 104.
11. Ibid., p. 106.
12. Conversino, *Fighting with the Soviets*, p. 126; Fischer, *Insatiable*, p. 109; Major Zorin to Abakumov, "Dokladnaia zapiska ob operativno-agenturnom obsluzhivanii amerikanskoi aviabazy 'chelnochnykh pereletov,'" June 23, 1945, 30 pp., SBU Archives, fond 13, no. 1169, fols. 559–88.
13. "Michael Kowal," in American Air Museum in Britain <http://www.americanair-museum.com/person/240532>; Lieutenant Colonel Sveshnikov to Abakumov, "Dokladnaia zapiska o sokrashchenii amerikanskikh voenno-vozdushnykh baz na

territorii SSSR," September, 1944, 11 pp., here 3, SBU Archives, fond 13, no. 1168, fols. 301–6.

14. Conversino, *Fighting with the Soviets*, p. 127.
15. Kaluta, "History of Eastern Command, US Strategic Air Forces in Europe, October 1, 1944–March 31, 1945," chap. V, Personnel Relations, p. 33.
16. Ibid., chap. V, pp. 18, 35.
17. Ibid., chap. V, p. 17.
18. Ibid., chap. V, p. 33.
19. Ibid., chap. II, pt. I, Operations, p. 15.
20. Ibid., chap. V, Personnel Relations, pp. 11, 35.
21. Ibid., chap. IV, Personnel Administration and Organization, pp. 4–5; Ibid., chap. V, Personnel Relations, pp. 3–4; Lieutenant Colonel Sveshnikov to Abakumov, "Dokladnaia zapiska o sokrashchenii amerikanskikh voenno-vozdushnykh baz na territorii SSSR," December 2, 1944, 11 pp., here 11, SBU Archives, fond 13, no. 1168, fols. 328–38.
22. Kaluta, "History of Eastern Command, US Strategic Air Forces in Europe, October 1, 1944–March 31, 1945," chap. I, p. 5.

Chapter 13

1. Deane, *The Strange Alliance*, p. 246
2. Ibid., p. 247; Harriman and Abel, *Special Envoy*, pp. 363–64.
3. Ibid., p. 363.
4. Ibid., pp. 355–56, 358–61; Plokhy, *Yalta*, pp. 158–61.
5. "William A. Fitchen," *The Orange County Register*, October 17, 2007, <https://obits.ocregister.com/obituaries/orangecounty/obituary.aspx?n=william-a-fitchen&pid=96327178>.
6. Kaluta, "History of Eastern Command, US Strategic Air Forces in Europe, October 1, 1944–March 31, 1945," chap. I, Background, p. 41.
7. Brigadier General Edmund W. Hill, Chief USA Air Force Division, United States Military Mission, Moscow, to Ambassador Harriman, December 28, 1944, in NARA, RG 334, United States Military Mission to Moscow, Operation "Frantic," October 1943–October 1945, Box 67: Interrogation Reports to Photo Reconnaissance.
8. Reports of Observations in Poland: Report by Lt. Col. Thomas K. Hampton, NARA, RG 334, box 67, p. 1.
9. Ibid.
10. W. H. Lawrence, "Nazi Mass Killing Laid Bare in Camp; Victims Put at 1,500,000 in Huge Death Factory of Gas Chambers and Crematories," *New York Times*, August 30, 1944.
11. Kathy Harriman to Mary, August 30, 1944, Library of Congress, Harriman Papers, box 6, folder 9, Correspondence between Kathleen Mortimer and Mary Fisk; Barbie Zelizer, *Remembering to Forget: Holocaust Memories through the Camera's Eye* (Chicago, 2000), pp. 51–52.
12. Reports of Observations in Poland: Report by Sgt. Samuel Chavkin, NARA, RG 334, box 67, p. 10; Report by Capt. Joe R. Johnson, ibid., p. 3.

13. "Lvov," *Holocaust Encyclopedia*, <https://encyclopedia.ushmm.org/content/en/article/lvov>.

14. Reports of Observations in Poland: Report by Lt. Col. Thomas K. Hampton, NARA, RG 334, box 67, p. 1; Report by Capt. Joe R. Johnson, ibid., p. 2; Report by Capt. Michael H. Kowal, ibid., p. 5; Report by Sgt. Samuel Chavkin, ibid., p. 8.

15. Letter to British Ambassador in Moscow, September 16, 1944, in Reports of Observations in Poland, NARA, RG 334, box 67, p. 6; Mieczysław Karol Borodej, *Niebieska Eskadra* <http://niebieskaeskadra.pl/?control=8&id=2540>.

16. Reports of Observations in Poland: Report of Major Robert H. Wiseheart, NARA, RG 334, box 67, pp. 1–2.

17. Captain William Fitchen, Interrogation Form: [First] Pilot Lt. R. E. Beam, December 10, 1944; Sgt. John R. Dmytryshyn, Frantic: Interrogation Reports. Eastern Command, NARA, RG 334, box 67, pp. 7–8.

18. Captain William Fitchen, Interrogation of T/Sgt E. G. Kelly and S/Sgt A. G. Stubaus, December 18, 1944, 6 pp., here 3–6, Frantic: Interrogation Reports. Eastern Command, NARA, RG 334, box 67.

19. Plokhy, *Yalta*, pp. 166–75.

20. Lieutenant Colonel Sveshnikov to Abakumov, "Dokladnaia zapiska o sokrashchenii amerikanskikh voenno-vozdushnykh baz na territorii SSSR," December 2, 1944, 11 pp., here 7–8, SBU Archives, fond 13, no. 1168, fols. 328–38.

21. Ibid., fol. 8; Major Zorin to Major General Novikov, "Dokladnaia zapiska o povedenii amerikanskikh voennosluzhashchikh pri vylete na vynuzhdennye posadki samoletov," December 1944, 5 pp., SBU Archives, fond 13, no. 1171.

22. Kaluta, "History of Eastern Command, US Strategic Air Forces in Europe, October 1, 1944–March 31, 1945," chap. IV, Personnel Administration and Organization, p. 16; Agent Report, "Markov," SBU Archives, fond 13, no. 1172; no. 1168, fol. 125.

Chapter 14

1. "V novyi 1945 god sovetskie liudi zhelali drug drugu skoroi pobedy nad fashistskoi Germaniei," TASS, January 1, 2015 <http://tass.ru/70-letie-pobedy/1682585>.

2. *My Dear Mr. Stalin: The Complete Correspondence of Franklin D. Roosevelt and Joseph V. Stalin*, ed. Susan Butler (New Haven and London, 2005), p. 184; Plokhy, *Yalta*, p. 28; Martin Gilbert, *Churchill and America* (New York, 2005), p. 325.

3. Franklyn Holzman to A. Holzman, January 1, 1945; Franklyn Holzman, BBC interview, 1995.

4. Colonel Akhov and Lietenant Colonel Baruzdin to Lieutenant Colonel Zubkov, July 25, 1960, 4 pp., SBU Archives, fond 13, no. 1207, fols. 327–30.

5. Kaluta, "History of Eastern Command, US Strategic Air Forces in Europe, October 1, 1944–March 31, 1945," chap. V, Personnel Relations, p. 34.

6. Ibid.

7. "LTC William Roman Kaluta," *Find a Grave* <https://www.findagrave.com/cgi-bin/fg.cgi?page=gr&GRid=48767213>; Roman M. Kaluta, *US 1940 Census* <http://www.archives.com/1940-census/roman-kaluta-ny-55936655>; Tatiana Shugailo, "Istoriia gazety 'Russkii golos' i ee obshchestvenno-politicheskie pozitsii,"

Katalog pressy russkogo zarubezh'ia (Vladivostok, 2017). Lieutenant Colonel Sveshnikov to Abakumov, "Dokladnaia zapiska o sokrashchenii amerikanskikh voenno-vozdushnykh baz na territorii SSSR," December 2, 1944, 11 pp., here 4, SBU Archives, fond 13, no. 1168, fols. 328-38.

8. Major Zorin to Major General Gorgonov, "Dokladnaia zapiska ob izuchenii razvedyvatel'noi deiatel'nosti amerikanskikh voennosluzhashchikh Poltavskoi aviabazy," February 12, 1945, 11 pp., here 5-7, SBU Archives, fond 13, no. 1169, fols. 415-25; Captain Zakharov, "Vypiska iz dokladnoi zapiski gvardii kapitana Zakharova," July 10, 1944, 1 p., SBU Archives, fond 13, no. 1172, fol. 106.

9. Kaluta, "History of Eastern Command, US Strategic Air Forces in Europe, October 1, 1944-March 31, 1945," chap. V, Personnel Relations, pp. 30-31.

10. Colonel Chernetsky, Captain Mikhaliuk, Senior Lieutenant Nevedov to the head of the 2d directorate, People's Commissariat of State Security of the USSR, Commissar of State Security Third Class Fedotov, "Dokladnaia zapiska o rezul'tatakh operativno-agenturnogo obsluzhivaniia amerikanskoi aviabazy v Poltave za period: dekabr' 1944-ianvar' 1945," February 7, 1945, 18 pp., here 16-18, SBU Archives, fond 13, no. 1201, fols. 146-63.

11. Kaluta, "History of Eastern Command, US Strategic Air Forces in Europe, October 1, 1944-March 31, 1945," chap. V, Personnel Relations, pp. 28-29.

12. Ibid., p. 29; Major Zorin to Lieutenant Colonel Guliaev, SBU Archives, fond 13, no. 1171, fol. 93; Major Zorin to Major General Gorgonov, "Dokladnaia zapiska ob izuchenii razvedyvatel'noi deiatel'nosti amerikanskikh voennosluzhashchikh Poltavskoi aviabazy," February 12, 1945, 11 pp., here 5, SBU Archives, fond 13, no. 1169, fol. 417; Colonel Reshetnikov and Lieutenant Colonel Meshcheriakov to Lieutenant Colonel Kovalkov, January 29, 1953, SBU Archives, fond 13, no. 1179, fol. 12; Captain Mikhaliuk and Senior Lieutenant Nefedov to Colonel Sliuger, "Dokladnaia zapiska o razrabotke sviazei amerikantsev v UNKGB po Poltavskoi oblasti za fevral' mesiats 1945 goda," March 7, 1945, 8 pp., here 6, SBU Archives, fond 13, no. 1201, fols. 181-88.

13. Captain Shpagin, "Spravka," March 27, 1945, 5 pp., SBU Archives, fond 13, no. 1169, fols. 466-70.

14. Major Zorin to Major General Novikov, "Dokladnaia zapiska ob izmenenii otnoshenii mezhdu lichnym sostavom amerikanskoi bazy i voennosluzhashchimi 169 ABON," February 7, 1945, 5 pp., SBU Archives, fond 13, no. 1169, fols. 410-14.

Chapter 15

1. Harriman to Roosevelt, December 6, 1944, Franklin D. Roosevelt Library, Map Room, Presidential Trips, Crimean Conference, box 21, Argonaut 1, section 1; Plokhy, *Yalta*, pp. 27-28.

2. "The President's Special Assistant (Hopkins) to the President," FRUS, *Diplomatic Papers: Conferences at Malta and Yalta, 1945*, p. 39; Plokhy, *Yalta*, pp. 37-38.

3. Harriman to Roosevelt, December 6, 1944, Franklin D. Roosevelt Library, Map Room, Presidential Trips, Crimean Conference, box 21, Argonaut 1, section 1.

4. Harriman and Abel, *Special Envoy*, p. 392.

5. Kaluta, "History of Eastern Command, US Strategic Air Forces in Europe, October 1, 1944–March 31, 1945," chap. I, Background, p. 21, NARA, RG 334 (Underservice Agencies), United States Military Mission to Moscow, Operation "Frantic," October 1943–October 1945, Box 66: Engineer to Intelligence.

6. Major Zorin, "Spravka," January 1945, SBU Archives, fond 13, no. 1171, fol. 119; Major Zorin to Major General Novikov, "Dokladnaia zapiska o sluchae s portfelem gl. Marshala angliiskoi aviatsii Teder A. V.," January 26, 1945, 3 pp., SBU Archives, fond 13, no. 1169, fols. 390–93; Kaluta, "History of Eastern Command, US Strategic Air Forces in Europe, October 1, 1944–March 31, 1945," chap. I, Background, pp. 22–23; Conversino, *Fighting with the Soviets*, pp. 173–74.

7. Kaluta, "History of Eastern Command, US Strategic Air Forces in Europe, October 1, 1944–March 31, 1945," chap. I, Background, pp. 21–22.

8. Ibid., p. 23.

9. Major General Slavin to Admiral Alafuzov and Komissar gosbezopasnosti Abakumov, February 8, 1945, SBU Archives, fond 13, no. 1169, fol. 457.

10. Meeting of the Joint Chiefs of Staff, February 5, 1945, in *FRUS: Conferences at Malta and Yalta*, p. 594; Plokhy, *Yalta*, pp. 216–22.

11. "Roosevelt-Stalin Meeting, February 8, 1945," in *FRUS: Conferences at Malta and Yalta*, pp. 766–71; *My Dear Mr. Stalin*, pp. 292–93.

12. Plokhy, *Yalta*, pp. 166–70.

13. Harriman and Abel, *Special Envoy*, pp. 406–14; Plokhy, *Yalta*, pp. 241–51; "Third Plenary meeting, February 6, 'The Polish Question,'" *FRUS: Conferences at Malta and Yalta*, pp. 667–71.

14. Deane, *The Strange Alliance*, pp. 182–90; "Bilateral Document, Agreement between the United States and the Soviet Union Concerning the Liberated Prisoners of War and Civilians," *FRUS: Conferences at Malta and Yalta*, pp. 985–87.

15. Deane, *The Strange Alliance*, pp. 186–90; Harriman and Abel, *Special Envoy*, p. 416; Plokhy, *Yalta*, pp. 298–305.

16. Deane, *The Strange Alliance*, p. 184.

17. Churchill, *Triumph and Tragedy*, pp. 362–63.

18. Robert E. Sherwood, *Roosevelt and Hopkins: An Intimate History* (New York, 1948), p. 879; Plokhy, *Yalta*, pp. 328–29.

19. Fischer, *Insatiable*, pp. 116–17.

20. Conversino, *Fighting with the Soviets*, p. 177.

Chapter 16

1. *My Dear Mr. Stalin*, pp. 297–99.

2. Deane, *The Strange Alliance*, pp. 190–96; Harriman and Abel, *Special Envoy*, pp. 419–20.

3. *My Dear Mr. Stalin*, pp. 298–99.

4. Lt. Col. James D. Wilmeth et al., "Report on a Visit to Lublin, Poland, February 27–March 28, 1945," section "Russian Reactions," p. 13, NARA, RG 334, Box 22, Prisoners of War; Kaluta, "History of Eastern Command, US Strategic Air Forces in Europe, October 1, 1944–March 31, 1945," chap. I, p. 70; Deane, *The Strange Alliance*, p. 191; Conversino, *Fighting with the Soviets*, pp. 188–90.

5. Kaluta, "History of Eastern Command, US Strategic Air Forces in Europe, October 1, 1944–March 31, 1945," chap. I, p. 71; Deane, *The Strange Alliance*, pp. 195–96; Conversino, *Fighting with the Soviets*, p. 193.

6. Wilmeth et al., "Report on a Visit to Lublin, Poland, February 27–March 28, 1945," p. 12.

7. Deane, *The Strange Alliance*, pp. 191–94; Kaluta, "History of Eastern Command, US Strategic Air Forces in Europe, October 1, 1944–March 31, 1945," chap. I, p. 73; Wilmeth et al., "Report on a Visit to Lublin, Poland, February 27–March 28, 1945," p. 15.

8. Kaluta, "History of Eastern Command, US Strategic Air Forces in Europe, October 1, 1944–March 31, 1945," chap. I, pp. 73–74.

9. Wilmeth et al., "Report on a Visit to Lublin, Poland, February 27–March 28, 1945," pp. 1–3; *Communiqué of the Polish-Soviet Extraordinary Commission for Investigating the Crimes Committed by the Germans in the Majdanek Extermination Camp in Lublin*, ed. A. Witos et al. (Moscow, 1944); Tomasz Kranz, "Ewidencja zgonów i śmiertelność więźniów KL Lublin," *Zeszyty Majdanka* 23 ([Lublin], 2005): 7–53.

10. Wilmeth et al., "Report on a Visit to Lublin, Poland, February 27–March 28, 1945," pp. 4–5; Conversino, *Fighting with the Soviets*, p. 196.

11. *My Dear Mr. Stalin*, pp. 299–300.

12. Captain William Fitchen, Interrogation Form: [First] Pilot Lt. Peede, March 17, 1945, Frantic: Interrogation Reports. Eastern Command, "Report on Former Prisoners of War," 4 pp., here 3, NARA, RG 334, box 67; Kaluta, "History of Eastern Command, US Strategic Air Forces in Europe, October 1, 1944–March 31, 1945," chap. I, pp. 50, 73; Conversino, *Fighting with the Soviets*, p. 190.

13. Captain William Fitchen, "Report of an interview with three former prisoners of war, First Lieutenant Cory, Second Lieutenant Murphy, and Second Lieutenant Gaich," February 21, 1945, 4 pp., Frantic: Interrogation Reports. Eastern Command, NARA, RG 334, box 67; "Beliaev, Vladimir Pavlovich," *Bol'shaia Sovetskaia Ėntsiklopediia* (Moscow, 1969), s.v.; Iurii Nagibin, *Dnevnik* (Moscow, 2009), pp. 124–28.

14. Captain William Fitchen, "Report of an interview with three former prisoners of war, Capt. Slanina, Second Lieutenant Young, and First Lieutenant Englander," February 22, 1945, p. 1, Frantic: Interrogation Reports. Eastern Command, NARA, RG 334, box 67; Kaluta, "History of Eastern Command, US Strategic Air Forces in Europe, October 1, 1944–March 31, 1945," chap. I, pp. 73–77.

15. Kaluta, "History of Eastern Command, US Strategic Air Forces in Europe, October 1, 1944–March 31, 1945," chap. I, p. 78; Captain Robert M. Trimble et al., "Report on Flight to Rzeszow, Staszow, Lwow, Poland, March 17, 1945," 5 pp., here 1–3, Frantic: Interrogation Reports. Eastern Command, NARA, RG 334, box 67; Trimble and Dronfield, *Beyond the Call*, pp. 117–42.

16. Trimble et al., "Report on Flight to Rzeszow, Staszow, Lwow, Poland, March 17, 1945," 5 pp., here 3–4.

17. Ibid., p. 4; "Report by Sgt. Richard J. Beadle," 2 pp., Frantic: Interrogation Reports. Eastern Command, NARA, RG 334, box 67.

18. Trimble et al., "Report on Flight to Rzeszow, Staszow, Lwow, Poland, March 17, 1945," 5 pp., here 4; Trimble and Dronfield, *Beyond the Call*, pp. 168–74, 180–82.

19. *My Dear Mr. Stalin*, p. 300.
20. Harriman to Roosevelt, March 12, 1945, in *FRUS: Diplomatic Papers, 1945, Europe*, vol. 5; Deane, *The Strange Alliance*, p. 198; Harriman and Abel, *Special Envoy*, pp. 420–21.
21. *My Dear Mr. Stalin*, p. 300.
22. Ibid., pp. 301–302.
23. Harriman and Abel. *Special Envoy*, pp. 421–22.
24. Lt. Col. James D. Wilmeth, Memorandum to General Deane, Reference: Lublin Trip, Poltava, USSR, April 13, 1945, 9 pp. in NARA, RG 334, Box 22; Kaluta, "History of Eastern Command, US Strategic Air Forces in Europe, October 1, 1944–March 31, 1945," chap. I, p. 78.
25. Kaluta, "History of Eastern Command, US Strategic Air Forces in Europe, October 1, 1944–March 31, 1945," chap. I, pp. 78–79; Conversino, *Fighting with the Soviets*, p. 196.

Chapter 17

1. Major Zorin to Abakumov, April 2, 1945, pp. 1–2, SBU Archives, fond 13, no. 1169, fols. 471–72.
2. William Kaluta, "Eascom History, 1 April 1945 to 23 June 1945," chap. 1, Operations, p. 7, in NARA, RG 334; United States Military Mission to Moscow, Operation "Frantic," October 1943–October 1945, Box 66: Engineer to Intelligence.
3. Major Zorin to Major General Novikov, April 10, 1945, "Informatsionnaia dokladnaia zapiska," 4 pp., SBU Archives, fond 13, no. 1169, fol. 499.
4. Plokhy, *Yalta*, pp. 358–64.
5. Harriman and Abel, *Special Envoy*, pp. 432–39.
6. *My Dear Mr. Stalin*, pp. 303–17.
7. Fred L. Borch, "Two Americans and the Angry Russian Bear: Army Air Force Pilots Court-Martialed for Offending the Soviet Union during World War II," *Prologue Magazine* 43, no. 1 (Spring 2011) <https://www.archives.gov/publications/prologue/2011/spring/court-martials.html>.
8. Conversino, *Fighting with the Soviets*, pp. 201–202.
9. Borch, "Two Americans and the Angry Russian Bear."
10. Lieutenant Colonel Sveshnikov, "Spravka," April 30, 1944, 2 pp., here 2, SBU Archives, fond 13, no. 1168, fol. 32; Trimble and Dronfield, *Beyond the Call*, pp. 230–31.
11. Borch, "Two Americans and the Angry Russian Bear"; Conversino, *Fighting with the Soviets*, pp. 203–204.
12. Kaluta, "Eascom History, 1 April 1945 to 23 June 1945," chap. 1, Operations, pp. 1–2; Conversino, *Fighting with the Soviets*, p. 203.
13. Major Zorin to Major General Novikov, April 10, 1945, "Informatsionnaia dokladnaia zapiska," 4 pp., here 3, SBU Archives, fond 13, no. 1169, fol. 499.
14. Ibid.; Kaluta, "Eascom History, 1 April 1945 to 23 June 1945," chap. 1, Operations, pp. 1–2.
15. Kaluta, "Eascom History, 1 April 1945 to 23 June 1945," chap. 1, Operations, p. 1.

16. Agent Report, "Kozlov," April 1, 1945, SBU Archives, fond 13, no. 1169, f. 491; Agent Report, "Moskvichka," April 2, 1945, ibid., fol. 490.
17. Fischer, *Insatiable*, p. 122.
18. Ibid.; "Soviet Denunciation of the Pact with Japan, April 5, 1945," *The Department of State Bulletin* 12, no. 305 (April 29, 1945) <http://avalon.law.yale.edu/wwii/s3.asp>.
19. Dmitrii Volkogonov, *Triumf i tragediia: Politicheskii portret I. V. Stalina* (Moscow, 1989), bk. 2, pt. 1, p. 373; Zorin to Abakumov, April 2, 1945, p. 2, SBU Archives, fond 13, no. 1169, fol. 471; Major Zorin, "Spravka," April 3, 1945, 2 pp., SBU Archives, fond 13, no. 1169, fols. 485–86; *Arkhiv rozstrilianoho vidrodzhennia: materialy arkhivno-slidchykh sprav ukraïns'kykh pys'mennykiv 1920–1930-kh rokiv*, comp. Oleksandr and Leonid Ushkalov (Kyiv, 2010), p. 376.
20. Kaluta, "Eascom History, 1 April 1945 to 23 June 1945," chap. 1, Operations, p. 6; Major Zorin to Major General Novikov, April 10, 1945, "Informatsionnaia dokladnaia zapiska," 4 pp., here 3, SBU Archives, fond 13, no. 1169, fol. 499 .
21. Kaluta, "Eascom History, 1 April 1945 to 23 June 1945," chap. 1, Operations, p. 6.
22. Ibid., chap. 1, Operations, pp. 3–4, 8; Trimble and Dronfield, *Beyond the Call*, pp. 233–40, 243.
23. *My Dear Mr. Stalin*, p. 322.

Chapter 18
1. On Melby, see Robert P. Newman, *The Cold War Romance of Lillian Hellman and John Melby* (Chapel Hill, NC, 1989).
2. Harriman and Abel, *Special Envoy*, pp. 440–41.
3. Ibid., pp. 441–43; Sherwood, *Roosevelt and Hopkins*, pp. 883–84.
4. Harriman and Abel, *Special Envoy*, pp. 445–46; Conversino, *Fighting with the Soviets*, p. 205; Costigliola, *Roosevelt's Lost Alliances*, pp. 319–20.
5. Kaluta, "Eascom History, 1 April 1945 to 23 June 1945," chap. 2, Activities, p. 1.
6. Ibid., chap. 2, Activities, pp. 1–2.
7. Franklyn Holzman to A. Holzman, April 14, 1945; Franklyn Holzman, BBC interview, 1995.
8. Kaluta, "Eascom History, 1 April 1945 to 23 June 1945," chap. 1, Operations, pp. 6–7; chap. 2, Activities, p. 1.
9. Conversino, *Fighting with the Soviets*, pp. 206–207.
10. Plokhy, *Yalta*, pp. 382–83.
11. Harriman and Abel, *Special Envoy*, pp. 447–53; Costigliola, *Roosevelt's Lost Alliances*, pp. 320–27.
12. Samuel Chavkin, "Russia-based Yanks parade with Red Army," Franklyn Holzman collection; Kaluta, "Eascom History, 1 April 1945 to 23 June 1945," chap. 1, Operations, pp. 6–7; chap. 2, Activities, p. 2.
13. Kaluta, "Eascom History, 1 April 1945 to 23 June 1945," chap. 2, Activities, p. 3; Conversino, *Fighting with the Soviets*, p. 208.
14. Fischer, *Insatiable*, p. 120; Bertha Markoosha Fischer, *My Lives in Russia* (New York, 1944).
15. Fischer, *Insatiable*, pp. 121–22.

16. Major Zorin to General Major Gorgonov, "Dokladnaia zapiska ob izuchenii razvedyvatel'noi deiatel'nosti amerikanskikh voennosluzhashchikh Poltavskoi bazy," February 12, 1945, 11 pp., here 6, SBU Archives, fond 13, no. 1169, fols. 415-25; Major Zorin to Major General Novikov, "Dokladnaia zapiska ob izmenenii otnoshenii mezhdu lichnym sostavom amerikanskoi bazy i voennosluzhashchimi 169 ABON," February 7, 1945, 5 pp., here 5, SBU Archives, fond 13, no. 1169, fols. 410-14; Agent Report, "Kozlov," June 1945, 1 p, SBU Archives, fond 13, no. 1172, fol. 98; Captain Zakharov, "Vypiska iz dokladnoi zapiski gvardii kapitana Zakharova," July 10, 1944, 1 p., SBU Archives, fond 13, no. 1172, fol. 106.

17. Major Zorin to Abakumov, "Dokladnaia zapiska ob operativno-agenturnom obsluzhivanii amerikanskoi aviabazy 'chelnochnykh pereletov,'" June 23, 1945, 30 pp., here 10, 17, 24, 25, 28, SBU Archives, fond 13, no. 1169, fols. 559-88; Colonel Chernetskii, Captain Mikhaliuk and Senior Lieutenant Nefedov to Fedotov (Moscow), "Dokladnaia zapiska o rezul'tatakh agenturno-operativnogo obsluzhivaniia amerikanskoi aviabazy v Poltave za period dekabr' 1944—ianvar' 1945," February 7, 1945, 18 pp., here 1, SBU Archives, fond 13, no. 1201, fols. 146-48.

18. Colonel Reshetnikov and Lieutenant Colonel Meshcheriakov, "Spravka na voennosluzhashchego byvshei Poltavskoi bazy VVS SShA—Chavkina Samuila," January 1952, 3 pp., SBU Archives, fond 13, no. 1171, fols. 60-62; Major Zorin and Captain Mikhaliuk, "Spravka: Chavkin, Samuil," 3 pp., SBU Archives, fond 13, no. 1171, fols. 157-58; Agent Report, "Valik," November 15, 1944, 1 p., SBU Archives, fond 13, no. 1171, fol. 65; Agent Report, "Markov," January 1945, 1 p., SBU Archives, fond 13, no. 1171, fol. 90; Lieutenant Colonel Sveshnikov to Abakumov, "O sokrashchenii amerikanskikh voenno-vozdushnykh baz na territorii SSSR," December 2, 1944, 11 pp., here 6, SBU Archives, fond 13, no. 1168, fol. 333.

19. Franklyn Holzman to A. Holzman, February 21, May 1, and May 10, 1945.

20. For SMERSH reports on Philip Mishchenko and Yelena Semizhenova, see SBU Archives, fond 13, no. 1171, fols. 3-36.

21. Kaluta, "Eascom History, 1 October 1944 to 1 April 1945," chap. 5, Personnel Relations, pp. 31-32.

22. Ibid.

23. Agent Report, "Markov." May 1945, 1 p., SBU Archives, fond 13, no. 1172, fol. 125.

24. Trimble and Dronfield, *Beyond the Call*, pp. 256-58.

Chapter 19

1. "Spravka na byvshego komandira 169 aviabazy osobogo naznacheniia VVS VS SSSR general-maiora aviatsii Kovaleva Stepana Korneevicha," SBU Archives, fol. 13, no. 1169, fols. 673-76.

2. Plokhy, *Yalta*, pp. 102-16; Norman M. Naimark, *The Russians in Germany: A History of the Soviet Zone of Occupation, 1945-1949* (Cambridge, 1997).

3. "Perminov, Aleksandr Romanovich," The Generals of World War II <http://www.generals.dk/general/Perminov/Aleksandr_Romanovich/Soviet_Union.html>.

4. "Minutes of the Eighteenth Meeting of the Air Directorate, Held at Berlin, December 18, 1945, 10:30 a.m.," *FRUS: Diplomatic Papers, 1945: European Advisory Commission,*

Austria, Germany, vol. 3; "U.S. Note Documents Western Position on Unrestricted Air Access to Berlin," *Department of State Bulletin*, vol. 45 (July–September, 1961) <http://www.ebooksread.com/authors-eng/united-states-dept-of-state-office-of-public-co/department-of-state-bulletin-volume-v-45-jul--sep-1961-tin/page-99-department-of-state-bulletin-volume-v-45-jul--sep-1961-tin.shtml>.

5. *Sovetskaia administratsiia v Germanii, 1945–1949. Deiatel'nost' upravleniia SVAG po izucheniiu dostizhenii nemetskoi nauki i tekhniki v Sovetskoi zone okkupatsii*, ed. V. V. Zakharov (Moscow, 2007), pp. 398–40; Georgii Litvin, *Na razvalinakh tret'ego Reikha, ili maiatnik voiny* (Moscow, 1998), chap. 1; *Sovetskaia voennaia administratsiia v Germanii, 1945–1949: Spravochnik* (Moscow, 2009), p. 840.

6. John Gaddis, *George F. Kennan: An American Life* (New York, 2012), pp. 215–22; Joseph Stalin, "Rech' na predvybornom sobranii izbiratelei Stalinskogo izbiratel'nogo okruga g. Moskvy, February 9, 1946," *Propagandist*, nos. 1–4 (February 1946): 11.

7. Montefiore, *Stalin*, pp. 532–37.

8. Marshal of Aviation Aleksandr Golovanov in Feliks Chuev, *Soldaty imperii: besedy, vospominaniia, dokumenty* (Moscow, 1998), p. 267; A. M. Khorobrykh, *Glavnyi marshal aviatsii A. A. Novikov* (Moscow, 1989), p. 268.

9. Vladimir Zhukhrai, *Stalin: pravda i lozh'* (Moscow, 1996), p. 235.

10. Aleksandr Melenberg, "Trofei marshala Zhukova," *Novaia gazeta*, June 9, 2003.

11. "Postanovlenie Politbiuro TsK KPSS 'O t. Zhukove G. K., Marshale Sovetskogo Soiuza,'" January 20, 1948, Fond Aleksandra Iakovleva, Arkhiv <http://www.alex-anderyakovlev.org/fond/issues-doc/1002762>.

12. "Kutsevalov, Timofei Fedorovich," *Generals of World War II* <http://www.generals.dk/general/Kutsevalov/Timofei_Fedorovich/Soviet_Union.html>.

13. "Kriukov, Grigorii Viktorovich," Geroi strany <http://www.warheroes.ru/hero/hero.asp?Hero_id=1841>; "Doch' Lidii Ruslanovoi i generala Kriukova rasskazala o frontovykh budniakh," *Moskovskii komsomolets*, May 7, 2015.

14. "Spravka na byvshego komandira 169 aviabazy osobogo naznacheniia VVS VS SSSR general-maiora aviatsii Kovaleva Stepana Korneevicha," SBU Archives, fond 13, no. 1169, fols. 673–76.

15. See the list of awards and Shchepankov's report at *Pamiat' naroda* <https://pamyat-naroda.ru/heroes/podvig-chelovek_nagrazhdenie43320375/>.

16. "Spravka na byvshego komandira 169 aviabazy osobogo naznacheniia VVS VS SSSR general-maiora aviatsii Kovaleva Stepana Korneevicha."

17. Major Zorin, "Spravka," January 9, 1945, SBU Archives, fond 13, no. 1171, fols. 116–18; "Ivan Ivanovich Moskalenko," in *Kto rukovodil organami Gosbezopasnosti, 1941–1954: Spravochnik*, ed. N. V. Petrov (Moscow, 2010); "Kovalev, Stepan Korneevich," *Bessmertnyi polk, Moskva* <http://www.polkmoskva.ru/people/1061143/>.

Chapter 20

1. "Major General Robert L. Walsh," *U.S. Air Force* <https://www.af.mil/About-Us/Biographies/Display/Article/105289/major-general-robert-l-wals>.

2. Michael J. Hogan, *The Marshall Plan: America, Britain, and the Reconstruction of Western Europe, 1947–1952* (Cambridge, 1987); John Lewis Gaddis, "Reconsiderations: Was the Truman Doctrine a Real Turning Point?" *Foreign Affairs*

52, no. 2 (1974): 386–402; Dennis Merrill, "The Truman Doctrine: Containing Communism and Modernity," *Presidential Studies Quarterly* 36, no. 1 (2006): 27–37; Michael Holm, *The Marshall Plan: A New Deal for Europe* (Abingdon, UK, 2016).

3. Vladislav Zubok and Constantine Pleshakov, *Inside the Kremlin's Cold War: From Stalin to Khrushchev* (Cambridge, MA, 1996), pp. 50–51.

4. William R. Harris, "The March Crisis of 1948, Act I," *Studies in Intelligence* 10, no. 4 (1966): 3–5.

5. Ibid., pp. 5–8.

6. Jean Edward Smith, *Lucius D. Clay: An American Life* (New York, 1990), p. 488.

7. Roger Gene Miller, *To Save a City: The Berlin Airlift, 1948–1949* (College Station, TX, 2000); "Major General Robert L. Walsh," *U.S. Air Force* <http://www.af.mil/AboutUs/Biographies/Display/tabid/225/Article/105289/major-general-robert-l-walsh.aspx>.

8. Jean Edward Smith, *Lucius D. Clay: An American Life*, 2nd ed. (New York, 2014), pp. 335–38; "William Whipple Jr, 36," *Princeton Alumni Weekly*, April 2, 2008; Fischer, *Insatiable*, p. 125.

9. Fischer, *Insatiable*, pp. 126–28; Markus Wolf, *Die Troika: Geschichte eines Nichtgedrehten Films* (Berlin, 1989), Russian translation: *Troe iz tridtsatykh* (Moscow, 1990), p. 109.

10. Fischer, *Insatiable*, pp. 129–32; Wolf, *Troe iz tridtsatykh*, pp. 306–11; George Fischer, Letters to family dated March 9 and 11, 1946, Berlin; Victor Fischer with Charles Wohlforth, *To Russia with Love: An Alaskan Journey* (Fairbanks, 2012), pp. 81–84; Vladimir Gall, "Instruktor-literator, perevodchik, parlamenter . . . ," in Vladislava Zhdanova, *Nashim oruzhiem bylo slovo: Perevodchiki na voine* (Frankfurt am Main, 2009), pp. 122–59.

11. "Spravka na amerikanskogo voennosluzhashchego byv. bazy VVS SSha—Fisher, Georg," SBU Archives, fond 13, no. 1172, fols. 143–44; Fischer, *Insatiable*, pp. 132–33; Markus Wolf and Anne McElvoy, *Man without a Face: The Autobiography of Communism's Greatest Spymaster* (New York, 1997), pp. 27–29, 287, 316–17.

12. "Spravka na amerikanskogo voennosluzhashchego byv. bazy VVS SSha—Fisher, Georg," SBU Archives, fond 13, no. 1172, fols. 143–44; Fischer, *Insatiable*, pp. 132–33; Wolf and McElvoy, *Man without a Face*, pp. 27–29, 287, 316–17.

13. Lieutenant Colonel Solopov to head of MGB in Poltava region, May 13, 1953, SBU Archives, fond 13, no. 1179, fols. 20–21; Major General Budarev and Major General Novikov to Lieutenant General Raikhman, February 15, 1947, p. 1, SBU Archives, fond 13, no. 1169, fols. 656–60.

14. Lieutenant Colonel Solopov to head of MGB in Poltava region, May 13, 1953, SBU Archives, fond 13, no. 1179, fols. 20–21; Vladimir Talmi, "Polnyi krug: N'iu-Iork–Moskva i obratno. Istoriia moei zhizni," *Zametki po evreiskoi istorii*, no. 184 <http://berkovich-zametki.com/2015/Zametki/Nomer10/Talmi1.php>.

15. Major General Budarev and Major General Novikov to Lieutenant General Raikhman, February 15, 1947, SBU Archives, fond 13, no. 1169, fols. 656–60.

16. Major Zorin, head of counterintelligence division SMERSH, 68th region of aviation bases, to Abakumov, "Dokladnaia zapiska ob agenturno-operativnom obsluzhivanii

amerikanskoi aviabazy 'chelnochnykh' pereletov," June 23, 1945, 30 pp., here 17, SBU Archives, fond 13, no. 1169, fol. 575.

17. Deputy commander, counterintelligence department, 4th Air Force Army Lieutenant Colonel Sagalov and head of 1st division of the same department, Major Panov, to head, counterintelligence directorate, Kyiv military district, June 12, 1947, SBU Archives, fond 13, no. 1184, "Raznaia perepiska po delu 'Soiuzniki,'" f. 9.

18. Head, first counterintelligence directorate, Kyiv military district, Lieutenant General Osetrov and head, first department of the same directorate, Lieutenant Colonel Bulantsev to deputy head, MGB department, 4th Air Force Army Sagalov, June 26, 1947, SBU Archives, fond 13, no. 1184, "Raznaia perepiska po delu 'Soiuzniki,'" f. 10.

19. Colonel Shabalin, head, 4th department, counterintelligence directorate, Kyiv military district, "Spravka na lits, prokhodiashchikh po materialam dannogo memoranduma," p. 4, SBU Archives, fond 13, no. 1185, "Raznaia perepiska po delu 'Soiuzniki,'" fols. 323–27; Lieutenant Colonel Kovalkov to head of MGB, Poltava region, January 13, 1953, SBU Archives, fond 13, no. 1179, fol. 12.

20. Georgii Litvin, *Na razvalinakh tret'ego Reikha, ili maiatnik voiny* (Moscow, 1998), chap. 1.

21. Lieutenant Colonel Kovalkov to head of MGB, Poltava region, January 13, 1953, SBU Archives, fond 13, no. 1179, fol. 12; Colonel Reshetnikov and Lieutenant Colonel Meshcheriakov to Lieutenant Colonel Kovalkov, January 29, 1953, SBU Archives, fond 13, no. 1179, fol. 12; "Maksimov, Viktor Ivanovich," biography and photo on website of Kazan Institute of Architecture and Construction <http://old.kgasu.ru/sved/vov/maksimov_viktor_ivanovich/>.

22. Colonel Surkov, head of MGB counterintelligence department, 12th Air Force Army, to head, counterintelligence department, MGB, Kyiv military district, October 1948, SBU Archives, fond 13, no. 1185, fol. 137.

23. Colonel Shabalin, head, 4th department, MGB counterintelligence directorate, Kyiv military district, "Spravka na lits, prokhodiashchikh po materialam dannogo memoranduma," November 1950, SBU Archives, fond 13, no. 1185, fols. 323–27; Lieutenant Colonel Prikazchikov to head, MGB counterintelligence directorate, Kyiv military district, November 22, 1950, SBU Archives, fond 13, no. 1186, fols. 36–36ᵛ; "Prakhin, Efim Danilovich," *Geroi strany* <http://www.warheroes.ru/hero/hero.asp?Hero_id=6652>.

Chapter 21

1. Introduction, Osobyi arkhiv Litvy, Fond K-1: Komitet gosudarstvennoi bezopasnosti Litovskoi SSR (KGB), Opis' no. 2 (former fond no. 2: Kontrarazvedovatel'nyi otdel NKVD-MGB-MVD-KGB SSSR), <http://media.hoover.org/sites/default/files/documents/lithuanian_kgb_opis02_register.pdf>.

2. "Belukha, Andrei Iakovlevich," *Kadrovyi sostav organov gosudarstvennoi bezopasnosti SSSR* <http://nkvd.memo.ru>; Agent Report "Avtomat," in SBU Archives, fond 13, no. 1171, fol.135.

3. Agent Report, "Liliia," August 3, 1944, in SBU Archives, fond 13, no. 1171, fols. 139–40; Agent Report, "Markov," ibid., fol. 143.

4. Spravka po arkhivnym delam no. 15078 i 216 na Belukhu Z. A.," December 9, 1968, in SBU Archives, fond 13, no. 1207, fols. 99–100.

5. Agent Report, "Tishchenko," December 28, 1950, SBU Archives, fond 13, no. 1192, fols. 310–310ᵛ.

6. Ivan Nalyvaiko, *Hirkyi spomyn zhakhlyvoho teroru: istoryko-publitsystychni narysy* (Poltava, 2004). "Agent Report, "Dmitrieva," April 28, 1949, in SBU Archives, fond 13, no. 1192, f. 304; Agent Report, "Tishchenko," December 28, 1950, ibid., fol. 310.

7. Agent Report, "Dmitrieva," April 28, 1949; Agent Report, "Kuznetsova," January 9, 1951, in SBU Archives, fond 13, no. 1192, fol. 311; Agent Report, "Bocharova," January 12, 1951, in SBU Archives, fond 13, no. 1192, fol. 312.

8. Agent Report, "Tishchenko," December 28, 1950, SBU Archives, fond 13, no. 1192, fols. 310–310ᵛ.

9. Agent Report, "Kuznetsova," January 23, 1951, in SBU Archives, fond 13, no. 1192, f. 313; Agent Report, "Bocharova," March 20, 1951, ibid., fol. 318–318ᵛ.

10. Major Rogovtsev and Lieutenant Colonel Meshcheriakov to Colonel Reshetnikov, September 6, 1951, in SBU Archives, fond 13, no. 1192, fols. 301–2.

11. "Kudy podivsia unikal'nyi arkhiv z mini-muzeiu na chest' Klary Luchko?" *Ltava*, July 1, 2015.

12. Spravka po arkhivnym delam no. 15078 i 216 na Belukhu Z. A.," December 9, 1968, in SBU Archives, fond 13, no. 1207, fols. 99–100.

13. Colonel Khoroshun and Colonel Akhov (Poltava) to Colonel Perfiliev (Moscow), November 11, 1958, in SBU Archives, fond 13, no. 1207, ff. 45–47; Colonel Dubas to Colonel Akhov, November 25, 1958, ibid., fol. 48.

14. "Spravka po materialam perepiski Chuchko E. V." May 30, 1964, in SBU Archives, fond 13, no. 1207, fols. 80–80v.

15. "Spravka," May 29, 196, in SBU Archives, fond 13, no. 1207, fols. 75–77v; "Spravka," June 11, 1964, ibid., fols. 78–79; Colonel Brazhko (Kyiv) to Lieutenant Colonel Mishchenko (Poltava), June 4, 1964, ibid., fol. 82.

16. "Igor Constantine Reverditto," <https://www.legacy.com/obituaries/name/by/reverditto/igor>; Jan Herman, Stage Review: 'Psycho Beach Party' Has a Screw Loose: The show has energy and brass, but it lacks the one subversive ingredient that might have justified all the silliness," *Los Angeles Times*, August 24, 1990 <http://articles.latimes.com/1990-08-24/entertainment/ca-1360_1_psycho-beach-party>; Tony Reverditto's eulogy of Igor Reverditto, posted March 13, 2015, on the "Memory of Igor Reverditto" Facebook page, February 27, 2015, <https://www.facebook.com/groups/647340528728078/permalink/647348445393953/>.

17. "Nachalniku KGB Poltavskoi oblasti. Zaiavlenie," December 10, 1968, in SBU Archives, fond 13, no. 1207, fols. 96–96v.

Chapter 22

1. Office memorandum to: Director, FBI, from: SAC, Boston, subject: George Fischer, George Yuri Fischer, March 10, 1955, 2 pp., George Fischer FBI File.

2. Major Zorin, head of SMERSH counterintelligenece division, 68th region of aviation bases, to Abakumov, head of SMERSH, "Dokladnaia zapiska ob

agenturno-operativnom obsluzhivanii amerikanskoi avizbazy 'chelnochnykh' pereletov," June 23, 1945, 30 pp., here 8, SBU Archives, fond 13, no. 1169, fol. 566.

3. Office Memorandum from SAC, Denver to Director, FBI, Subject: George Yuri Fischer, March 14, 1955; To: SAC, Boston from Director, FBI, April 18, 1951, Subject: George (NMI) Fischer, Security matter–c, April 18, 1951; Memorandum to: Mr. A. H. Belmont, Purpose: To advise you on results of name checks, April 18, 1951, 7 pp., here 6, in George Fischer FBI File.

4. Thomas F. Sullivan, Boston FBI, Report on George (NMI) Fischer, aka Yuri Fischer, Character of case: Security matter–C, February 12–August 21, 1951, 8 pp., here 4–6, in George Fischer FBI File; Milwaukee, Wisconsin FBI, Report on George Fischer, Security Matter–C, November 6–December 13, 1951, 4 pp., here 2–3, ibid.; George Kennan to J. Edgar Hoover, March 29, 1951, 2 pp., ibid.

5. Report, New York FBI, Subject: George (NMI) Fischer, aka Yuri Fischer, February 1–March 7, 1952, 3 pp., in George Fischer FBI File; Report, Philadelphia FBI, Subject: George (NMI) Fischer, aka Yuri Fischer, December 7–14, 1951, 3pp., ibid.; Memorandum from: SAC, Boston to Director, FBI, April 12, 1952, ibid.; Fischer, *Insatiable*, p. 134ff.; George Fischer, *Soviet Opposition to Stalin: A Case Study in World War II* (Cambridge, MA, 1952); David Engerman, *Know Your Enemy: The Rise and Fall of America's Soviet Experts* (New York, 2009), pp. 52–53, 61.

6. Memorandum to: Director, FBI, From SAC WFO, January 17, 1955, Subject: Anatoli V. Zorin, George Yuri Fischer, in George Fischer FBI File.

7. AirTel, FBI Washington Field to Director, FBI and SAC, Boston, March 22, 1955, in George Fischer FBI File.

8. A. H. Belmont to L. V. Boardman, April 5, 1955, in George Fischer FBI File.

9. AirTel, FBI Washington Field to Director, FBI and SAC, Boston, March 22, 1955, in George Fischer FBI File.

10. SAC, WPO to Director, FBI, March 29, 1955, in George Fischer FBI File.

11. SAC, Boston to Director, FBI, April 16, 1955, 2 pp., in George Fischer FBI File.

12. Fischer, *Insatiable*, p. 134ff.; A. H. Belmont to L. V. Boardman, April 5, 1955; Boston FBI to Director, FBI, September 5, 1955, in George Fischer FBI File.

13. Boston FBI report, May 31, 1955, 6 pp., in George Fischer FBI File; Fischer, *Insatiable*, p. 193.

14. "Polkovniku Shabalinu," October 20, 1950, marginalia from October 30, 1950, SBU Archives, fond 13, no. 1186, "Raznaia perepiska po delu 'Soiuzniki,'" f. 11; Department of State, *Diplomatic List*, December 1952 (Washington, DC, 1952), p. 169; Department of State, *Diplomatic List*, February 1956 (Washington, DC, 1956), p. 43.

15. Fischer, *Insatiable*, p. 193.

16. Boston FBI report, May 31, 1955, 6 pp., in George Fischer FBI File.

17. SAC, Boston to Director, FBI, July 13, 1955; Boston FBI Report, September 16, 1955, 4 pp., in George Fischer FBI File; Fischer, *Insatiable*, p. 193.

18. Office memorandum, From SAC, WFO to Director, FBI, December 6, 1955, in George Fischer FBI File.

19. SAC Boston to Director, FBI, November 9, 1955; John Edgar Hoover, Director, FBI to Dennis A. Flinn, Director, Office of Security, Department of State,

November 10, 1955; SAC Boston to Director, FBI, December 14, 1955, "George Fischer, WA. IS-R," in George Fischer FBI File.

20. FBI Teletype, Boston to Director, November 21, 1955; "Letter to the Director, FBI Boston Office," November 8, 1955; "Interview of Subject December 13, 1955," in Boston FBI Office Report on George Fischer, WA. Character of Case: Internal Security-R, February 28, 1956, in George Fischer FBI File.

Epilogue

1. Franklyn Holzman, BBC interview on his experiences at Poltava, 1995; Fischer, *Soviet Opposition to Stalin*; Myhra, *A Frantic Saga*, p. 80.

2. Deane, *The Strange Alliance*, pp. 123–24.

3. George Fischer, review of John Deane, *The Strange Alliance*, in *Far Eastern Survey* 16, no. 11 (June 4, 1947): 131–32.

4. Costigliola, *Roosevelt's Lost Alliances*, pp. 291–311.

5. Myhra, *Frantic Saga*, p. 80; Sarah Bredesen, "Iola Man Writes about Rural 'Characters,'" *The Country Today*, September 26, 2007, p. 6.

6. Thomas Holzman's e-mail to the author, January 5, 2019; Ken Gewertz, "From Russia with Thanks: Holzman awarded Medal for World War II Service," *Harvard Gazette*, April 3, 1997.

7. Engerman, *Know Your Enemy*, pp. 199–200; Fischer, *Insatiable*, pp. 122, 196.

8. Myhra, *Frantic Saga*, pp. 6, 107–108.

9. Bill Clinton, "Greeting on the Occasion of the 50th Anniversary of Operation 'Frantic,'" in *Operatsiia "Frentik,"* p. 7, cf. pp. 267–73.

10. Charlie Beecham, "To the Editor: Operation Frantic," *The Daily Oklahoman*, January 15, 1997.

11. "Charles N. Beecham," *Mail Tribune*, March 13, 2012.

INDEX

Strippy, Clarence, 181
Strunnikov (reporter), 98–99
Stubaus, R. G., 173
suicide, 195, 214
Sukhov, Georgii, 95–97
Sullivan, Thomas F., 272–274
supplies
    abundance and waste of US goods and
        supplies, 65–67, 71–72, 97, 128
    bartering, 162
    left behind in Soviet Union, 239
    stealing. *See* theft of US goods and
        supplies, *See also* lend-lease program
surveillance. *See* espionage and
    intelligence gathering
Susloparov, Ivan, 230
suspension of operations, 151–163
Sveshnikov, Konstantin, 77–85, 118,
    120–121, 127, 131–133, 157–159,
    174, 215, 258

"Taiga" (code-name), 267–268
Taiwan, 271
Tandet, Philip, 119–120, 256
tank production in Germany, 143–144
target choices, 52–53
    advance of Soviet army, decreased
        number of targets, 123
    Luftwaffe targets, 62–63
    oil refinery targets, 23, 52–53, 88–89
Tarnów, Poland, 167
technology
    aviation technology knowledge, 4–5,
        36, 65–66, 241–242, 286
    continuing supply of newest aircraft,
        4–5
    German technological secrets, 249
    shift in balance of power, viii
    types of planes, 5
Tedder, Arthur, 189, 230
Teheran Conference, 58–60
tension in relationship. *See* deterioration
    of Soviet-US relations
territorial acquisitions by Soviet Union
    1939 Poland, 6–7, 137

post-war. *See* Eastern Europe
theater company, 131–132
theft of US goods and supplies, 124,
    128–129, 151, 160–162, 242,
    245–247
theft/plunder of German property,
    239–249
"third front" in Eastern Europe, 46–47
"Tishchenko" (code-name), 265
Tommy (American sergeant), 66–67, 115
trade, illicit. *See* black-marketeering
Trans-Siberian railway, 164–165
Trimble, Robert, 206–208, 221–222, 227,
    231, 235
"trophy case", 244–245, 247–249
Trotskyites, 157–158, 256
Truman, Harry, 225–226, 228–229, 251,
    253
Truman Doctrine, 251
trust between Soviets and Americans,
    133–134, 189–190, 250–251, 255
    distrust, x, 133–134
    shared humanity, 11
    See also deterioration of
        Soviet-US relations
Tupitsyn, P. A., 95–97
Turkey, 16–17, 251

Ukraine
    anti-Soviet ideology, 70–73
    Cold War espionage suspicion, 260
    folk art, 128
    genocide, 70
    Orange Revolution, 291–292
    "population exchange" between Poland
        and Ukraine, 173–174
    Revolution of Dignity, ix–x
    starvation of Ukrainians, 39–40, 70
    Third Reich invasion, 71
    US takeover of, 71–72
Ukrainian Insurgent Army, 173
Ukrainian nationalist organization,
    219–220
unexploded mines, 95–97
uniforms, 67–68, 227